Jesus and the Village Scribes

The Sea of Galilee

"If you have faith like a mustard seed, you might say to this mulberry tree: Be uprooted and planted in the sea! And it would obey you." (Q 17:6)

JESUS AND THE VILLAGE SCRIBES

Galilean Conflicts and the Setting of Q

William E. Arnal

FORTRESS PRESS
MINNEAPOLIS

JESUS AND THE VILLAGE SCRIBES
GALILEAN CONFLICTS AND THE SETTING OF Q

Translations of biblical and other ancient texts are by the author unless otherwise noted.

Cover image: First-century wooden tablet. John Bowker, *The Complete Bible Handbook: An Illustrated Companion*. London: Dorling Kindersley, copyright © 1998.
Cover design: Marti Naughton
Book design: Peregrine Graphics Services
Interior photographs: John S. Kloppenborg Verbin. Used by permission.

Library of Congress Cataloging-in-Publication Data
Arnal, William E. (William Edward)
  Jesus and the village scribes : Galilean conflicts and the setting of Q
/ William E. Arnal.
    p. cm.
Includes bibliographical references and index.
  ISBN 0-8006-3260-5 (alk. paper)
    1. Q hypothesis (Synoptics criticism) 2. Sociology, Christian—History—Early church, ca. 30–600. 3. Galilee (Israel)—History I. Title.

BS2555.52 A76 2001
226'.066—dc21   2001018183

Manufactured in the U.S.A.   AF 1-3260
05   04   03   02   01   1   2   3   4   5   6   7   8   9   10

Contents

Illustrations

ABBREVIATIONS

AASF	Annales Academiae Scientiarum Fennicae
AJT	*American Journal of Theology*
Ant.	Josephus, *Antiquities*
Apoc. Zeph.	*Apocalypse of Zephaniah*
BA	*Biblical Archaeologist*
BAGD	W. Bauer, W. F. Arndt, F. W. Gingrich, and F. W. Danker, *A Greek-English Lexicon of the New Testament*
BASOR	*Bulletin of the American Schools of Oriental Research*
b.	Babylonian Talmud tractates
b. B. Meṣiʿa	*b. Baba Meṣiʿa*
b. Ketub.	*b. Ketubah*
BBB	Bonner biblische Beiträge
BETL	Bibliotheca ephemeridium theologicarium Lovaniensium
BTB	*Biblical Theology Bulletin*
CBQ	*Catholic Biblical Quarterly*
CRBS	*Currents in Research: Biblical Studies*
CSHJ	Chicago Studies in the History of Judaism
DJD	Discoveries in the Judaean Desert
ET	English translation
GBS	Guides to Biblical Scholarship
GNS	Good News Studies
HTR	*Harvard Theological Review*
IDB	*Interpreter's Dictionary of the Bible*
IDBSup	*IDB Supplementary Volume*
IEJ	*Israel Exploration Journal*
Illyr.	Appianus, *The Illyrian War*
IQP	International Q Project
IRT	Issues in Religion and Theology
JAAR	*Journal of the American Academy of Religion*
JBL	*Journal of Biblical Literature*
JFSR	*Journal of Feminist Studies in Religion*
JJS	*Journal of Jewish Studies*
JR	*Journal of Religion*
JRS	*Journal of Roman Studies*
JSNT	*Journal for the Study of the New Testament*
JSNTSup	JSNT Supplement Series
JTS	*Journal of Theological Studies*
KBANT	Kommentare und Beiträge zum Alten und Neuen Testament
LCL	Loeb Classical Library
Life	Josephus, *The Life*
m.	Mishnah tractates
m. ʿArak.	*m. ʿArakin*
m. B. Bat.	*m. Baba Batra*

m. B. Meṣiʿa	*m. Baba Meṣiʿa*
m. Bek.	*m. Bekorot*
m. Giṭ.	*m. Giṭṭin*
m. Ketub.	*m. Ketubot*
m. Kil.	*m. Kilʾayim*
m. Maʾaś. Š.	*m. Maʾaśer Šeni*
m. Mid.	*m. Middot*
m. ʾOhol.	*m. ʾOholot*
m. Peʾah	*m. Peʾah*
m. Šabb.	*m. Šabbat*
m. Sanh.	*m. Sanhedrin*
m. Šeb.	*m. Šebiʾit*
m. Šeqal.	*m. Šeqalim*
m. Taʿan.	*m. Taʿanit*
m. Ṭehar.	*m. Ṭeharot*
MTSR	*Method and Theory in the Study of Religion*
Mur	Murabbaʾat documents, DJD 2
n.F.	neue Folge
n.s.	new series
Neot	*Neotestamentica*
NovT	*Novum Testamentum*
NovTSup	Novum Testamentum Supplements
NTAbh	Neutestamentliche Abhandlungen
NTS	*New Testament Studies*
OGIS	*Orientis graeci inscriptiones selectae*
PEQ	Palestine Exploration Quarterly
P. Ness.	*Papyrus Nessana*
P. Oxy.	*Papyrus Oxyrhynchus*
par(s).	parallel(s)
Praep. Ev.	Eusebius, *Praeparatio Evangelica*
Q¹	the formative stratum of Q: hortatory instructions
Q²	the main redaction of Q: editing and insertion of Deuteronomistic materials
Q³	final glosses on Q
Q^Lk	version of Q used by Luke
Q^Mt	version of Q used by Matthew
1QS	Rule of the Community (Manual of Discipline)
SAC	Studies in Antiquity and Christianity
SBLSP	*Society of Biblical Literature Seminar Papers*
SBEC	Studies in the Bible and Early Christianity
SBS	Stuttgarter Bibelstudien
SecCent	*Second Century*
SEG	*Supplementum epigraphicum graecum*
SESJ	Suomen Eksegeettisen Seuran julkaisuja
SJCA	Studies in Judaism and Christianity in Antiquity

SJLA	Studies in Judaism in Late Antiquity
SNTSMS	Society for New Testament Studies Monograph Series
TDNT	*Theological Dictionary of the New Testament*
THKNT	Theologischer Handkommentar zum Neuen Testament
TJT	*Toronto Journal of Theology*
t.	Tosefta tractates
t. Pe'ah	*t. Pe'ah*
t. Qidd.	*t. Qiddušin*
VCSup	Vigilae Christianae Supplements
War	Josephus, *The Jewish War*
WMANT	Wissenschaftliche Monographien zum Alten und Neuen Testament
WUNT	Wissenschaftliche Untersuchungen zum Neuen Testament
y.	Jerusalem Talmud tractates
y. Ma'aś.	*y. Ma'aśerot*
y. Pe'ah	*y. Pe'ah*
y. Soṭah	*y. Soṭah*
ZNW	*Zeitschrift für die neutestamentliche Wissenschaft*
ZTK	*Zeitschrift für Theologie und Kirche*

PREFACE

MANY MORE PEOPLE HAVE contributed to this project than can be mentioned. Among instructors and other senior scholars who have had an important impact on what follows should be included: Ron Cameron, Stevan Davies, Michel Desjardins, Heinz Guenther, Burton Mack, Neil McMullen, Stephen Patterson, Peter Richardson, James Robinson, Leif Vaage, Donald Wiebe, and Johannes Wolfart. The students in the various courses I have taught at the University of Toronto, Wilfrid Laurier University, and New York University have also been my teachers: they have sharpened my perspective and stimulated new ideas.

Among colleagues, friends, and other partners in crime who made noteworthy contributions—either to my sanity or to the substance of this book, or both—the following stand out: Herb Berg, Willi Braun, Ken Derry, Stephan Dobson, Keith Haartman, Ernest Janzen, Amy and Justin Juschka, Philip Klaassen, Russell McCutcheon, Tom MacKay, Ken MacKendrick, Tony Michael, Kristen Sweder, Rachel Urowitz, and Francesca Ventola. Timothy Hegedus, in addition to contributing to the general efforts on behalf of my sanity, also, at some cost to his own, was the first person to read drafts of several of the following chapters, which his comments helped significantly to improve. Several of my colleagues and graduate students at New York University—particularly Gail Armstrong, Jamie Marcu, Nathaniel Morehouse, Frank Peters, Vincent Renzi, Robert Sagerman, Larry Schiffman, Alexej Sivertsev, Elliot Wolfson, and Angela Zito—have contributed substantially to the provision of an agreeable working environment. The same is true of the highly professional and congenial administrative staff I have had the pleasure to work with at both University of Toronto (especially Cynthia Gauthier and Lesley Lewis) and New York University (especially Eileen Bowman and Janine Paolucci).

My former wife, Michele Arnal, and my immediate relations—Brad Arnal, Marian Arnal-Cook, and Oscar Cole Arnal—have assisted me in a variety of ways, the full extent of which is known only to them and to me. The Social Sciences and Humanities Research Council of Canada funded a good portion of the research that went into this text, in the form of a doctoral fellowship from 1990 to 1994. Thanks are also due to K. C. Hanson, my editor at Fortress Press, whose input has made this a much better book than it might otherwise have been.

In addition to these individuals, institutions, and others unnamed, three persons have made indispensable and unique contributions to the following work. First, my doctoral supervisor, John Kloppenborg, in addition to being an outstanding course instructor, provided exemplary guidance through all stages of the doctoral process and subsequently as well. He has offered only the most useful suggestions and critiques, while simultaneously permitting me to pursue my own ends, independently if need be, and tolerating divergences of opinion. Perhaps even more significantly, it was Professor Kloppenborg's scholarly writing, particularly *The Formation of Q*—which I read before coming under his supervision—that impelled and inspired me to pursue scholarly work in the area of Christian origins, and specifically on Q, in the first place. That influence has by no means ceased: his further and subsequent published work on Q has remained, for me, the best source of additional new direction and insight into the problems raised by the Synoptic Sayings Source and early Christian history in general. His prominence in my bibliography speaks for itself.

Second, my colleague, friend, and partner, Professor Darlene Juschka, has contributed to this work (and others) to such an extent that it is no longer clear to me which aspects of it are mine and which are hers. Every idea, every direction pursued or not pursued, has been tempered in the crucible of her sagacious and erudite commentary, and reflects long-standing and continual discussion with her about Q, religion, and life in general.

Third and finally, Michael Geoffrey Smith, my son, has been a central part of my education, formal and otherwise, from the very beginning. He has been present—uncomplaining, helpful, and wonderful company—every step of the way, and more consistently so than any other individual. There is no way for me adequately to express the extent of my gratitude for his involvement in my life.

INTRODUCTION

THE FOLLOWING STUDY—focusing on Q's language of reversal—was generated by the suspicion that the standard and conventional view of the social practice of the earliest Jesus movement was fundamentally flawed. That standard and conventional view, of course, at least among more recent and innovative scholarship, is that the first followers of Jesus were wandering radicals: itinerant preachers whose proclamation of the reign of God referred to their own itinerant lifestyle. The Jesus movement fostered by these individuals focused on an ascetic practice of renunciation, and, in consequence, the very peculiar rhetoric of some of the sayings ascribed to Jesus—sayings that appear to exhort poverty and homelessness as positive values, sayings that promise happiness to the poor and hungry, sayings that criticize the acquisition of worldly goods—is explained as the by-product and direct ideological reflection of (voluntarily) wandering beggars.

This hypothesis, while attractive in a variety of ways, not least because of its sociological cast, immediately presents the student of Christian origins with a series of problems. The motivation for this purported behavior remains vague, if it is described at all. The circumstances—the concrete material context—of such radical itinerancy are also left rather cryptic and obscure. The hypothesis is also undermined by textual deficiencies: the reading of the sayings tradition that supports the itinerancy thesis tends to an inconsistent literalism and a failure to explore the contextual force and rhetorical use of individual sayings. This study thus began as an effort to consider the deficiencies of the itinerancy hypothesis as they pertained to a single documentary source containing material critical for the theory, namely, the Sayings Gospel Q.

Q is not the only location for material employed by the itinerancy hypothesis, but it is one of the documents that is most broadly illuminated and explained by this hypothesis. Social description of the forces behind Q has depended to a tremendous extent on the assumption that wandering radicals are at least partly responsible for some stages in the development of the material preserved in Q. Not only does Q have, like the Gospel of Mark, apparent direct references to homelessness and travel, it additionally seems to exhort radical behavior as a central part of its platform. Itinerancy is the practice that is generally assumed to undergird this exhortation—it is thus assumed to be a major interest and theme of the Sayings Source. Oddly, however, while itinerancy is rather frequently used to describe Q, Q is not so often used to describe itinerancy. That is, of a piece with the persistent textual failings of the itinerancy hypothesis, Q as a coherent document is rarely given careful consideration as evidence for wandering radicalism; but the itinerancy hypothesis, assumed to apply to Q, is used as a basis for a social description of the people responsible for the document. Such a procedure is of course methodologically dubious. The itinerancy hypothesis must be verified rather than simply posited; and more than this, even if the existence of wandering radicals be granted, they must be shown to be linked to Q and the traditions behind Q before they can be deemed relevant to the document's social history. Early Christian itinerancy there may (or may not) have been; such behavior's relationship to the composition of Q is another question altogether.

It is Q's language of reversal that marks the document as a fertile application for the itinerancy thesis. Q not only refers to homelessness and to travel but also encourages what appears to be a radical countercultural stance, in which love of enemy, giving without restraint, turning one's back on material gain, and similar behaviors are enjoined. A variety of other Q sayings appear to imagine a world in which conventional values are inverted and turned on their heads, prompting the suspicion that perhaps Q imagines that the world itself is about to be turned on its head in some (unspecified) way. This study, therefore, focuses on the question of such rhetoric as an entry point into the question of itinerancy and the larger issue of the social description of the persons responsible for Q and its traditions.

Such a focus on Q, and on its rhetoric of uprooting, raises several preliminary problems, however. Most of these problems are associated with Q itself, as an hypothesized and certainly no-longer-extant document. Q as a single, written, ancient document does not exist. Rather, Q is an hypothesized source undergirding much of the sayings material found in the Gospels of Matthew and Luke. As such, the study of Q is, and continues to be, vulnerable to accusations of frivolity. The persistent refrain that Q is only a hypothesis is used to indict any of the more productive or interesting work on Q, as if it were somehow legitimate to posit the document, perhaps as a solution to source-critical problems, but were not legitimate to explore the document for its redactional, historical, or social-historical significance. Thus scholarship on Q, which is assuredly at the present time one of the most fecund areas of research into the gospel traditions, is at least viewed with suspicion (and at most dismissed outright) even by those who subscribe to the two-document hypothesis as the best solution to the problem of synoptic relationships (namely, the assertion that Matthew and Luke drew independently from the Gospel of Mark and a now-lost source designated "Q").

Here is not the place to defend the two-document hypothesis, the postulation of Q, or the specifics of the reconstruction of Q's original wording. It will be sufficient here to point out that, although there is a contingent within New Testament scholarship that does cast doubt on the validity of the two-source theory, and to which we owe many insightful and unquestionably correct insights about the ideological tendentiousness of that theory's initial formulation, such scholarship has something of the character of creationism in the context of academic biology: it attempts to use the tools and language of the discipline, but remains a marginalized position, one that represents an effort to turn back the clock on scholarly progress. Books on biological issues do not need to provide initial justifications for their assumption of evolutionary theory.

Nor are such studies required to acknowledge the hypothetical character of the theories they rely on by conscientiously refraining from building upon them. The history of human intellectual endeavors—in the sciences or in the humanities—is a story of hypothesizing on hypotheses. The biologist assumes both evolutionary theory and the particular classifications within that theory when considering any given species. Hypothesis is piled on hypothesis, although few would claim that efforts to classify a particular species are irresponsible or frivolous. Likewise, in New Testament scholarship, an exegesis of any given passage in, say, the Gospel of Mark, is laboring under a whole series of assumptions and hypotheses, most of them, like the evolutionary hypotheses of the biologist, well founded: that Mark is the earliest Gospel, that our understanding of Koine Greek is accurate, that what we call Mark represents a single text, and most of all, that the textual reconstruction of Mark in the exegete's Greek Bible is not simply a synthetic backproduct but corresponds more or less to the autograph (the manuscript as originally written by its author). Work on Q is not much different. Q may not exist; but then again, neither does Mark—both are reconstructions; both are hypotheses. Hypothesis piled on hypothesis is really just knowledge growing from knowledge. The process should continue until better alternative hypotheses are formulated or until the hypotheses in use can be proven false. The following pages will therefore take for granted the erstwhile existence of Q as a single document roughly coextensive with the synoptic double tradition and (originally) written in the Greek language (see Kloppenborg 1987:41–88).

New Testament scholars should be far more sanguine than they are about making use of the recent advances in research on Q that are coming to prove so productive. Comprehensive efforts to take Q scholarship

seriously in historical reconstructions of Christian origins can be counted on one hand.[1] The arguments against using recent Q scholarship,
moreover, often do not even engage that scholarship, and indeed, could
be formulated without having read any of it. Meier is typical in this
regard:

> Nevertheless, some educated guesses can be made on the order,
> extent, and even wording of Q—though they must all remain in the
> realm of the hypothetical. It is at this point that my ability to
> believe is exhausted—which just happens to be the point at which
> most speculation about Q begins to "rev up." Contemporary schol-
> ars have attempted to pinpoint the community that produced the Q
> document, the geographical area from which it originated, the stages
> of tradition and redaction it went through (some scholars assigning
> almost every verse of Q to a particular stratum of tradition or redac-
> tion), and its different theological stances. It is here that I fear that
> exegetes are trying to know the unknowable. To adapt a famous dic-
> tum of Ludwig Wittgenstein: whereof one does not know thereof
> one must be silent. (1994:179)

Attempting to know the unknown, of course, is simply to pursue
knowledge. And, as Kloppenborg has noted,

> Such a view is convenient to Meier's purpose; it allows him to
> ignore compositional features in Q in a way he would not dare to in
> the case of Mark or Matthew. If he thought that the compositional
> history of Q was unknowable, the appropriate posture would be to
> use all Q sayings with extreme caution; instead, he assumes that
> unknowable means nonexistent so that he can short-circuit schol-
> arship. This is an (unargued) attempt to turn the clock back to the
> time of von Harnack, who regarded Q as an unedited deposit of
> dominical sayings. (1996a:326, n. 85)

One might add that the reluctance to approach scholarship on Q seriously has much less to do with its hypothetical character than with its
novel implications. The problem with Q is not that it does not exist but
that it tends to call into question some of the cherished historical conclusions of the last four or five decades of New Testament scholarship. Scholars having strong commitments to those conclusions can handily avoid
having to defend them in any strenuous or rigorous way by dismissing as
hypothetical the document that is causing most of the trouble.[2]

Such an approach will not be taken here. The results of the last
decade (or so) of Q scholarship will be taken seriously, and an effort will
be made to build upon those results and to supplement them. Two of
those results in particular should be noted here, as they constitute critical assumptions behind the arguments of the final chapter. The first of

these assumptions is the now-dominant thesis that Q is a *literarily stratified* document, that is, that it evolved into the final form in which Matthew and Luke used it in a series of literary stages. The most thorough and accepted form of this hypothesis is that of John Kloppenborg, as enunciated in *The Formation of Q*. Up to the present, Kloppenborg's carefully argued conclusions have been employed fruitfully in a handful of detailed studies of Q and the sayings tradition, and have not been effectively refuted by anyone. Efforts at refutation simply have not addressed the detailed arguments in favor of stratification, either dismissing it out of hand as "hypothetical" (as a way to avoid engaging the arguments) or attacking the presupposition that "wisdom" and "apocalyptic" forms are not incompatible, a point that Kloppenborg never assumes or invokes (see Arnal 1997b:315–16; Kloppenborg 2000:113, n. 7; 141–42, n. 61; 146–47, n. 71).

Dale Allison's recent attempt to provide an alternative model of Q's literary development is a case in point. It begins with the observation that Kloppenborg's "distinction between sapiential and prophetic layers is worrisome."[3] What is more worrisome, of course, is that this "distinction" is not used as a criterion for separating the literary layers of Q in Kloppenborg's analysis, and Kloppenborg himself notes that among the standard motifs of the secondary ("prophetic," that is, polemical) redaction of Q is the characterization of those preaching repentance as envoys of divine Sophia.[4] Allison continues with a variety of other critical observations, none of which really gets to the heart of the literary and redaction-critical methodology employed by Kloppenborg to stratify Q, or, for that matter, to the heart of Q's own compositional features (see Kloppenborg 2000:113, n. 7). Signs of continuity or resemblance between the two strata are taken to be evidence of the falsity of the stratification, such as the observation that both Q 6:20-23 (Q[1], that is, the first literary stratum of Q) and Q 7:18-23 (Q[2], that is, the second literary stratum of Q) seem to allude to Isa 61:1-2 (Allison 1997:6–7),[5] or that motifs in the primary stratum have an "affinity" to prophetic language or are not experientially grounded. Again, however, the heart of Kloppenborg's hypothesis is not the incompatibility of these two strata, nor any supposed gulf that separates them, but the pattern of redactional interests displayed in the amendment and organization of the units that comprise Q.

Allison's own alternative stratification of Q, moreover, is based upon the methodologically indefensible equation of compositional structures with compositional layers. Thus, for instance, the degree to which Q 3:7—7:35 hangs together as a unified composition is taken as evidence that it was compiled at one time, and its thematic affinities with Q 11:14-52 as evidence that these two blocks were composed simultaneously (see Allison 1997:8–11, 16–21, 33–34). There is in fact no reason to assume that a compositional structure may not contain materials from an earlier redaction or collection—one would rather assume that subsequent redactions would precisely tend to enclose such earlier materials (see Kloppenborg 1987:98), and we are left wondering how to distinguish the various thematic interests present in this earlier material from the perspective of the redactor who brought them together. What is needed, therefore, is a method that will "allow us to distinguish the redaction of smaller clusters which eventually found their way into Q, or earlier, formative recensions of Q, from the theological and literary perspective of the final edition" (Kloppenborg 1987:96); and it is precisely this task that neither thematic analysis nor the simple identification of overarching literary structures can accomplish. So Allison's efforts to establish the literary coherence of, for example, Q 3:7—7:35 has little direct bearing on the issue of Q's literary development. Moreover, Allison's relative dating of his various strata of Q, strangely, is based upon the assumption that itinerant preachers are responsible for the "kernel" of the Q material, which was subsequently expanded by settled communities. Not only is this assumption the very question being considered here, but its use to sequence the various layers of Q is a confusion of literary history with tradition history (and a questionable tradition history at that!) and hence a methodological step backward from Kloppenborg's work. In short, Allison, along with most other critics of Kloppenborg's reconstruction of Q's literary history, is unequipped, both methodologically and in terms of his familiarity with Kloppenborg's actual arguments, to offer substantive alternatives or even serious objections.

To repeat, the phenomenon behind Kloppenborg's stratification of Q is not some supposed essential incompatibility between things "sapiential" and things "prophetic"; rather, it is the peculiar character of Q's literary features and organization. In particular,

> The tracing of a compositional history of Q is not a matter of placing its sayings into two or more "piles," sorted by form or by supposed theological orientation. Still less is it accomplished by smuggling a social or theological history into the analysis. Nor is there any assumption that hortatory materials are necessarily early, or authentic, or that the Jesus movement was originally "sapiential" or "apocalyptic" or "prophetic." . . . The sole reason for positing two strata in Q is the particular configuration of literary data encountered in Q: the contents divide roughly into two types of material, each with a distinctive literary organization and rhetorical posture. Where the two are juxtaposed (e.g., in Q 10), the results are

> rather jarring *from a literary point of view*. (Kloppenborg 2000:147, emphasis original; cf. 124–26, 131, 140)

Indeed, the criticisms so far leveled at Kloppenborg's stratification are so consistently beside the point, and yet so "tediously repeated" (Kloppenborg 2000:141–42, n. 61, citing Allison 1997; Collins 1993; Horsley 1994c; and Witherington 1994), that it is difficult to avoid seeing a Freudian "return of the repressed" in the accusations of prejudgment. It is difficult to avoid surmising that the prime difficulty critics have with this stratification hypothesis is neither its methodology nor even its substantive results with regard to Q, but rather its implications for the historical Jesus and the earliest development of Christianity. In particular, critics who are wedded to the congenial image of Jesus as an apocalyptic preacher (on the attractiveness of which see Arnal 1997b:313–16) must minimize the significance of an ancient Christian document that apparently only adopted apocalypticism secondarily. One way to do so is to deny the validity of these results. It would appear, then, that it is the critics of the stratification of Q—at least some of them—who are "smuggling a social or theological history into the analysis."

Kloppenborg's stratification will be presumed and used in what follows. This stratification argues that Q developed in three discrete written stages:

> *Q¹ (formative stratum):*
> 6:20b-23b, 27-49; 9:57-62; 10:2-11, 16; 11:2-4, 9-13; 12:2-7, 11-12, 21b-31, 33-34; 13:24; 14:26-27, 34-35; 17:33
>
> *Q² (redactional stratum):*
> 3:7-9, 16-17; 6:23c; 7:1-10, 18-23, 24-28, 31-35; 10:12-15, 21-24; 11:14-26, 29-36, 39-52; 12:8-10, 39-40, 42-46, 49, 51-53, 54-56, 57-59; 13:25-30, 34-35; 14:16-24; 17:23, 24, 26-30, 34-35, 37b; 19:12-17; 22:28-30
>
> *Q³ (late addition and glosses):*
> 4:1-13; 11:42c; 16:17

The rhetoric of uprootedness in Q is located primarily in the first, formative stratum (Q¹). Both of the original (apparent) Q references to travel or homelessness derive from this stratum as well. While some of the secondary, redactional material also implies or predicts significant social reversals and inversions, these sayings do not especially support the itinerancy hypothesis, nor are they especially mysterious in terms of their point of reference or their implications for the social location of those who transmitted them. These sayings conceptualize reversal in terms of apocalyptic judgment, fictively (as a literary motif) or otherwise, and presuppose some kind of sectarian formation that is marginalized with regard to its larger context because of its sectarian identity. Thus they fall largely outside the parameters of the present inquiry.

A further presupposition of the present study involves the conclusions of Ronald Piper, who has demonstrated the existence in Q of a series of compact and formally stereotypical argumentative clusters (Piper 1982, 1989). These clusters, composed at least in part of originally loose and independent material, share the following form: (1) a general opening saying; (2) sayings producing arguments directly in support of the initial instruction; (3) rhetorical questions and new illustrations; (4) final argument and application (Piper 1982:416). Piper has identified at least six such clusters in Q deriving from Q^1, and these clusters will play a major role in the final chapter of this study.

Another matter usually pertaining to studies of Q is the issue of reconstruction of the text. Because this erstwhile document is in fact no longer extant, it must be reconstructed from the Matthean and Lukan double tradition (those passages represented in both Gospels). Where Matthew and Luke disagree in their wording or ordering of the double tradition, individual judgments must be made as to which, if either, evangelist preserves the original Q form. This process can, as many have observed, be a highly subjective one. In order to avoid this critique, as well as to avoid producing pages and pages on issues of detailed reconstruction that have already been addressed by perhaps hundreds of different scholars, I have attempted, for the most part, to rely on the text of Q carefully reconstructed by the Society of Biblical Literature's International Q Project (IQP), under the direction of James M. Robinson: *The Critical Edition of Q* (Hermeneia Supplement). Over the course of the last several years, this group has attempted to reconstruct the wording of the entirety of Q, taking into account the various arguments proffered for discussion by group members, and compiling as comprehensive a list as possible of published arguments on each variation between Matthew and Luke. I have thus tried to follow the finished text of Q produced by the collective efforts of the IQP, even where I have not entirely agreed with it, simply for the sake of consistency and standardization. Where I have departed from the IQP's rendition of the original text, I have noted the divergence; in the few instances where the deviation is critical to the argument, I have attempted briefly to justify the reconstruction I prefer.

Methodologically, the study presupposes the value and validity of sociohistorical approaches to biblical texts, and it is oriented to historical reconstruction rather than hermeneutical conclusions. The critical study of the New Testament is here understood not as a technique for determining the truth or meaning or even original sense of the texts in question, but rather as a historical approach to the inaugural period of what eventually became one of the great religious traditions of the world. As such, the study of the New Testament may shed light both on Western history in general and on religion as an academic problem and area of interest. I have, moreover, taken a fairly materialist stance throughout, attempting to link the development of ideas to the social conditions in which they arose and assuming that some sort of causality exists along this nexus, with the material pole serving as the primary causal force.

The following study of Q's rhetoric of uprootedness takes a rather convoluted route to its destination. The history of the itinerancy hypothesis is treated in chapters 1 and 2, if not exhaustively, then at least thoroughly. Chapter 1 describes the first scholarly appearance of the modern itinerancy hypothesis in Adolf von Harnack's work on the *Didache* very shortly after the document's discovery. Some effort is made to relate Harnack's conclusions to his own *Sitz im Leben,* not necessarily as a directly causative factor but as a predispositional undercurrent, as a kind of cultural subtext undergirding and lending resonance to his conclusions. The same process is then followed in chapter 2 for the modern reappearance of the itinerancy hypothesis and its close relative and most important rival, the Cynic hypothesis, in scholarship from about 1960 on. The efforts to describe earliest Christianity as a movement of itinerants and to relate that description to the Synoptic Sayings Source reach their culmination, of course, in the work of Gerd Theissen. Scholarship on Q subsequent to Theissen has tended to presuppose his insights. Even the most current and innovative approach to the synoptic tradition, the effort to draw connections between the early Jesus movement and Greco-Roman Cynic philosophers, is ultimately dependent on Theissen's suggestions regarding the itinerancy hypothesis. A rather different setting from that of Harnack, obviously, has actuated this revivification of his hypothesis and its application to Q.

Chapter 3 addresses what I regard to be the weaknesses and failings of these recent arguments for the wandering radicalism of the Jesus movement. Sociologically, the hypothesis is theoretically vacuous, and textually it is unfounded, or at least insufficiently supported to serve as the basic assumption behind sociohistorical reconstructions of Christian origins. Not only is it extraordinarily difficult to connect Q to purported itinerants, it is even difficult to find evidence that such itinerants once existed anywhere within the Jesus movement at all. The solution to these shortcomings is simple: the Jesus movement needs to be situated rather more firmly within its economic and social context. Myriad studies have focused on the cultural background of the various New Testament writings, working from the idealist presumption that ideas form the background to, and are generative of, ideas. To whatever degree this may be partially true, its truth is nevertheless partial: people react to social and to economic forces, and use cultural artifacts or techniques to communicate those reactions.

Thus chapter 4 attempts to reconstruct the context out of which Q (probably) emerged: Galilee in the early first century C.E. The focus of this chapter is on the material situation rather than the cultural trappings of that situation (especially the red herring of the Hellenistic versus Judaic context of Q): it focuses especially on economic considerations and on the social ramifications of economic forces. Moreover, on the assumption that new cultural forces (and Q does appear to represent a fairly novel cultural irruption) are the result of social and material changes and ruptures, this description in large measure focuses on the changes that the first-century Galilean system of production suffered during the early Roman period, specifically during the tetrarchy of Antipas. Chapter 5 analyzes Q's rhetoric of uprootedness in order to uncover the program it advances. That program revolves around an effort to reaffirm local reciprocity and communal values; if anything, it is sedentary and even a little conservative, rather than radical and itinerant. Such a program, in its turn, can be understood as a reaction to the economic changes brought about by Antipas and to reflect the social uprootedness of the Q tradents that those changes caused.

Ultimately, the following conclusions are suggested by these chapters. First, the itinerancy thesis, even where it is innocent of specifically theological motivations, is culturally tendentious and has gained its enormous scholarly popularity more from its resonance with contemporary sociocultural trends than from its superior treatment of the evidence. Second, the actual textual evidence for the itinerancy hypothesis is very tenuous indeed, requiring for the most part a prior assumption of itinerancy in order for the texts in question actually to evince itinerancy. The entire thesis probably needs to be reconsidered, and should certainly be called into question as regards Q. Third, the immediate material context for the rise of the Jesus movement, Q included, is one of socioeconomic crisis. This crisis was caused by a deliberate effort to restructure the northern Galilean local economy along lines more conducive to a monetized Roman imperial economy oriented to both trade and booty. Galilean isolation from the coast had allowed the region a measure of autonomy both social and economic, and thus had, to a degree, allowed geography and the technological limits of ancient transport to put a natural brake on the extent to which the region could be exploited by whatever political power happened to control it. Antipas's foundation of new cities within the Galilee, however, most especially Tiberias, put an end to this autonomy and caused significant social and economic changes. It was the foundation of cities and the consequent loss of local autonomy, rather than widespread poverty, Roman military oppression, or rampant Hellenization, that most marked the period and region with which we are concerned. Fourth and finally, the reaction of the Q tradents was a reaction of local village scribes to these changes, which deleteriously affected their social standing. Their rhetoric of uprootedness is a symbolic reflection of their loss of independent local standing and power. But more than this, it is also a careful argumentative strategy to enlist local support for a program intended to reaffirm village autonomy, to promote a return to the days of yore, in which (or so the Q tradents imagined) local relations were marked by a kind of idealized reciprocity and justice: the communal and ancestral values of the good old days. As such, this imagined state of affairs could be designated the reign of God.

Threshing floor

"His pitchfork is in his hand, and he will clear his threshing floor . . ."
(Q 3:17a)

1.
ITINERANT PREACHERS AND THE *DIDACHE*

IN 1873 A GREEK MANUSCRIPT of the *Didache,* or *Teaching of the Twelve Apostles,* was discovered in the Patriarchal Library of the Holy Sepulchre in Constantinople and was published ten years later, bringing to light for the first time in centuries this ancient, apocryphal "church order."[1] In this document provisions are laid out for the treatment of certain "travelers" (παρόδιος) who "come" (ἐρχόμενος) to the more settled Christians to whom the *Didache* is addressed (12:2). Chapters 11–15, in fact, seem to be preoccupied with issues of the authenticity of such figures and the support they may expect, and so the author offers specific precepts for the reception of particular types of preachers, discussed under the rubric of "apostles," "prophets," and "teachers." Apparently, the two former categories, at the very least, refer to peripatetic figures: "Now concerning the apostles and prophets, according to the doctrine of the gospel behave as follows. Every apostle who comes to you, let him be received as the Lord. But he is to stay no longer than one day, or, if necessary, another day as well. But if he stays a third day, he is a false prophet. When an apostle leaves, let him receive nothing except bread, sufficient to pass the night; and if he asks for money, he is a false prophet."[2]

The Gospels make reference to missionary journeys on the part of Jesus' disciples, and of course to the wandering of Jesus himself, and Acts and Paul's letters make it clear that Paul's missionary work was also characterized by journeys. But it was the discovery of the *Didache,* with its comments on itinerant apostles, prophets, and teachers, that gave modern New Testament scholarship its first indication of the possible existence of a class of professionally homeless preachers of the Christian message long after what had been thought of as the apostolic period. The assumption—initially brought to scholarly attention by the *Didache*—that such figures existed serves as the sine qua non of the itinerancy hypothesis as it has been articulated in modern New Testament scholarship, and particularly as it has evolved into the dominant interpretive filter for Q's rhetoric of uprootedness. Adolf von Harnack was the first to articulate explicitly the historical implications of the discovery of the *Didache* and to spell out in detail just what this writing revealed about early Christian itinerants (see Patterson 1993:172–73).

Harnack's Thesis

In 1884, barely one year after the publication of the newly recovered manuscript, Harnack published a commentary on the *Didache* in the Texte und Untersuchungen series.[3] In this commentary he devoted an entire chapter to the *Didache*'s presentation of those apostles, prophets, and teachers whose behavior is the primary concern of *Didache* 11–15. It was Harnack's detailed study that first articulated explicitly what was implicit in the newly discovered manuscript: that *Didache* 11–15 appears quite clearly to give evidence of the existence of peripatetic preachers who relied upon the churches they visited for material provision. Harnack devoted his discussion of these chapters to detailing the precise characteristics and history of these itinerants.

For Harnack, four essential characteristics define them. First and foremost, the entire discussion of the apostles, prophets, and teachers in chapters 11–15 is to be understood, he claims, in terms of their designation, earlier in the document (*Did.* 4:1), as "speakers of the Word of God." That is, the primary activity described for these figures is, precisely, their teaching or preaching activity. Second, Harnack imagines those to whom the *Didache* refers as prophets and apostles (at least) to be unaffiliated with any particular local church community. These texts, Harnack argues, not only provide an indication of actual homelessness but also imply that such itinerants did not derive their authority from election by any local congregation: neither their mission nor their authority was in any way locally based. Third, such wanderers were impoverished; they were employed exclusively and full-time in their missionary activity, and had no other trade or means of support. Rather, they depended upon the generosity of the local congregations they visited to supply them with food (*Did.* 11:6: bread; 11:9: a meal; 13:1-2: food; 13:3-7 actually specifies that the first part of any offerings is to be given to prophets), lodging (11:5-6 and 12:2-3 refer to the lengths of time for which an itinerant may stay with the community), and possibly money and other types of material goods (11:6, 12 warn against apostles and prophets who ask for money; 13:7, conversely, exhorts the reader to provide prophets with money, clothing, and "all your possessions"). Fourth, and as a corollary to their homelessness, these figures are charismatic. For the itinerants themselves, as well as in the perception of those who receive them, their mission and authority have been granted to them directly by God, rather than by any office conferred on them by local churches, in spite of the authority they exercise over such congregations in their teaching capacity.

Harnack also regards the *Didache*'s delineation of the teaching office in the church under the threefold rubric of apostles, prophets, and teachers as significant, having implications for reconstructing the specific roles of these preachers, as well as for drawing inferences about their place within the history of the church. This tripartite classification occurs in other sources, most strikingly in the Pauline and deutero-Pauline letters. In 1 Cor 12:28, particularly, Paul repeats these titles, in precisely the same order as they are given in the *Didache,* and even indicates that these "offices" are derived from God: "God established in the church first apostles, second prophets, third teachers." Similar occurrences appear in Eph 4:11 and Acts 13 (see also Rom 12:6-7). The fact that exactly the same distinctions—expressed in exactly the same terms and in exactly the same order—occur relatively frequently and in very early sources leads Harnack to surmise that these words are in fact titles, and designate fairly specific roles or "offices," with their own specific standards of behavior (Harnack 1884:96–97). Thus the apostles are traveling founders of churches, who rely for their livelihood upon the generosity of the communities they have founded, while the prophets and teachers offer guidance to communities already established. As for the distinction between prophets and teachers, according to Harnack the designation "teacher" (διδάσκαλος) did not in fact refer to itinerant teachers (as do the other two classifications) but to a settled and remunerative teaching capacity within the community. All three of these "offices" are held in very high esteem, and those who fill them exercise a strong position of leadership and authority.

In addition, and perhaps more significantly, the early and common repetition of this threefold designation leads Harnack to the conclusion that these "offices" significantly predate the *Didache* and that they were common to the early Jesus movement as a whole, rather than being restricted to a particular set of congregations. The great antiquity of this classification, however, does not lead Harnack to retroject this form of ministry into the lifetime of Jesus. Instead, he concludes, the rise of this threefold grouping, and the esteem in which its membership was held, is to be attributed to the "Spirit" that possessed the earliest followers of Jesus in Jerusalem.

Finally, Harnack believes that this particular type of church organization was coming to be phased out around the time the *Didache* was composed. In the early period, presumably when the "Spirit" was more active than during the postapostolic period, it was appropriate and beneficial to organize the church as a whole on the basis of charismatic itinerants who served a churchwide teaching function, and who thus ensured a measure of church unity. However, as time went on, local forms of hierarchical institutional authority developed and ultimately supplanted the itinerants (as well as the nonitinerant teachers). The *Didache,* which Harnack dates to the second century (Harnack 1884:158–59), stands at the juncture of this transition, and gives evidence for it. Particularly in *Did.*15:1-2, there is evidence that the author is seeking to promote bishops and deacons as authorities of the same stature as the itinerants: "Therefore elect for yourselves bishops and deacons worthy of the Lord, men who are even-tempered and not lovers of money, and truthful, and who have been tested. For they perform for you also the duties of the prophets and teachers. Therefore do not disregard them. For they are your honored ones together with the prophets and teachers."[4]

In chapters 11–12 the itinerants are the object of various restrictions (the length of time they are permitted to remain with the local community, and the amount and form of remuneration they may seek), while in chapter 13 they are the recipients of considerable material bounty. At last, in the text quoted above, the reader is asked not to despise or neglect (ὑπεριδεῖν) bishops and deacons, and the ministry of the itinerant teachers is used as a positive model for these local offices. The ambivalence of the text reflects a power struggle, or at least a transition from one kind of authority and organization to another. Harnack argues, therefore, that we see in the *Didache* not only the church's most ancient form of office and organization (itinerant preachers of the word and local teachers) but additionally the decisive historical movement of the church away from these charismatics and toward a "monarchical episcopate."

Not only is Harnack's sketch of the itinerants themselves paradigmatic for more recent reconstructions, but indeed (and surprisingly) it foreshadows, albeit imperfectly, the fashion in which the more recent itinerancy hypotheses have been applied to early synoptic tradition. For although Harnack does not regard the apostles, prophets, and teachers of the *Didache* to have originated with Jesus, neither does he regard the Gospel stories in which Jesus is presented as commissioning his disciples (notably, the Mission Charge [Mark 6:6-13 and parallels; also Luke 10:1-16//Matt 9:37-38; 10:7-16]) as irrelevant to the issue of itinerancy. The connection is to be found in the *Didache*'s "ordinance of the Gospel" (τὸ δόγμα τοῦ εὐαγγελίου *Did.* 11:3), according to which the author of the *Didache* says one is to treat apostles and prophets. This "ordinance" must refer—says Harnack—to the Mission Charge of the Synoptic Gospels, a conclusion confirmed to Harnack's satisfaction by the presence in Matthew 10 (in which the Mission Charge appears) of further instructions explicitly concerned with the reception of itinerant prophets: "Whoever welcomes a prophet in the name of a prophet will receive a prophet's reward; and whoever welcomes a righteous person in the name of a righteous person will receive the reward of the righteous" (10:41). Thus the Mission Charge is drawn into the discussion of itinerancy, although not necessarily as itself evincing itinerants but rather as the foundational prescription of their behavior and role.

A second surprising facet of Harnack's discussion is that it is implicitly sociological. Again, Harnack does not take the crucial step made by later scholars and argue that synoptic texts (especially the "Mission Charge"), and the ideology therein, are the products of a specific social setting, best defined in terms of the itinerancy of those who transmitted the material. He does, however, employ an incipiently structural-functionalist model for explaining and describing the relevance of the itinerant "preachers of the word." In Harnack's understanding of history in general, he reveals a strong concern with the *function* (conceived almost teleologically) of historical phenomena. In *What Is Christianity?* he says as much:

> we must call to mind a piece of advice which no historian ought ever to neglect. Anyone who wants to determine the real value and significance of any great phenomenon or mighty product of history must first and foremost inquire into the work which it accomplished, or, as the case may be, into the problem which it solved. . . . the great edifices of history, the States and the Churches, must be estimated first and foremost, we may perhaps say, exclusively, by what they have achieved. It is the *work done* that forms the decisive test. (Harnack 1957, 193–94, emphasis original)

Moreover, a strong concern with the social background of Christianity in general is also evident in Harnack's writings. When these two emphases are combined and applied to the discussion of itinerant preachers, Harnack comes very close to the kind of sociological conclusions typical of Gerd Theissen's work, in which certain historical forms appear to arise (and persist) precisely because they serve certain functions. In the case of the itinerants, the function they serve—a function replaced subsequently by the institutionalized episcopate—is the provision of unity and homogeneity within a far-flung, socially and culturally diverse church. Harnack also approximates the sociological tendencies of recent scholarly approaches to itinerancy in his comparison of the description offered of these itinerants in the *Didache* with similar phenomena in non-Christian sources, notably *Peregrinus* in Lucian.

Harnack's World and Its Subtexts

In retrospect, the itinerancy hypothesis as proposed by Harnack probably owes as much to the *Sitz im Leben* in which the *Didache* was rediscovered as it does to the *Didache* itself. It is impossible, in my view, to appreciate the significance of Harnack's ideas about the *Didache* without contextualizing those ideas within the framework of the dominant concerns and issues of the late nineteenth and early twentieth centuries: the Age of Progress, emergent German nationalism, and Protestant liberalism.

The itinerancy hypothesis as articulated by Harnack reflects the concerns of the Age of Progress insofar as it offers a reconstruction of the Jesus movement in which process and culture are the key variables. Harnack's hypothesis moves the center of historical interest from the event to the structure, from nature (especially the miraculous) to culture (behavior, belief, conviction, charisma), from stasis to development. The Jesus movement becomes the story of the quest of roving geniuses to spread culture to the ends of the earth. All of these shifts in interest can be linked to the sense of progress that characterized the age. The itinerancy hypothesis may not be a direct product of this interest in progress, but it certainly allows for a view of earliest Christianity in which such an interest may find a place.

Not only is the emphasis on culture and process in the Age of Progress is reflected in Harnack's thesis. In addition, contemporary missionary spirit is obviously reflected in the content of that thesis. Harnack's belief that culture requires militaristic defense is structurally paralleled by his view that the "pure" Christian message had to make compromises in order to survive in the world. And finally, liberalism, of course relishing the notion of so individualistic and moralistic a phenomenon as "wandering radicalism" (*Wanderradikalismus*), was sufficiently sanguine about the process of embodiment as to tolerate decidedly nonliberal phenomena such as nationalism in its name. This last, however, was only acceptable provided that some kind of institutional separation could be made to protect the raw necessities of life from intruding upon the pure and ethereal beauty of reified culture at the same time as temporal realities protect that beauty. The itinerancy thesis allows for a pure foundation followed by an historically distinct period of compromise, thus replicating, along temporal lines, such an institutional separation.

Yet none of these basic notions requires wandering charismatics. One cannot say, apparently, that the specific lineaments of the itinerancy thesis itself—wanderers, their radicalism, even their alleged charisma—were conjured out of the cultural moods of Harnack's era. Merely, it would appear, Harnack describes these elements in such a way as to accommodate the most important preconceptions of his day. The essential pith of the hypothesis seems to remain unsullied. In fact, however, the very contents of the hypothesis appear to have resonated with the cultural context of late-nineteenth-century imperialism and nationalism to a greater degree of precision than the loose connections described above might suggest. Two examples—more could doubtless be found—illustrate the degree to which the idea of wandering was linked in Harnack's era to: (1) imperial expansion, (2) culture, and (3) "authentic" living. The first example is obvious: the thesis of wandering Indo-Europeans who invaded India as well as central Europe, bringing with them a distinctive language family but also a powerful race and virile culture.[5] The sharp contrasts drawn between the "Aryan sensibility" and the "Jewish sensibility" were not unique to Nietzsche; many saw the linguistic spread of Indo-European languages as evidence of the vibrant, strong, and expansionary (and hence evolutionarily superior) character of the Aryan race. Travel is mission, and mission is its own authorization, a kind of responsibility to subdue the world. Harnack's traveling charismatics are simply the religious equivalent of this racial schema: travel is the vehicle by which culture is spread, and the spread of culture is the way in which conquest is rationalized. Christianity's conquest of the Roman Empire forms a structural parallel to German expansionism, rationalizing that expansionism in much the same way that the Indo-Aryan wanderings were used.

A second, even more striking example of this contemporary fascination with wandering is the development of a German youth organization in the period before World War I known as the "migratory birds" (*Wandervögeln;* see Holborn 1969:411–13). An essentially apolitical group, they were primarily interested in reviving their own cultural purity by escaping from the cities into the woodland and walking about in the countryside. They were not migrating to any particular location but rather pursued these rural excursions as devices for putting themselves in touch with their own roots: the din of the town drowned out their inner voices. The parallel to itinerancy as conceived by Harnack is plain. Not only does this practice assume the same idealist dichotomy between cultural essence and its institutionalization, but it also, as a corollary, seeks the unconnected life (or a few moments of it) as the best way to access that cultural essence. Thus the idea of wandering and travel emerges—as it does with the Indo-European hypothesis—as this era's most succinct symbolization of cultural purity, essence, authenticity, virility, and creativity. In placing a great wandering at the foot of ecclesiastical history, Harnack is merely replicating what his own culture thinks about history: that it is the playing out of the process by which a fiery and vibrant genius comes to temporal incarnation.

While the tendentious character of any hypothesis can never serve logically to falsify it, in Harnack's case the sociocultural context of his historical inquiries are so resonant with the hypothesis itself that it is impossible to avoid the speculation that the itinerancy hypothesis, among other historical conclusions, serves as a kind of working-out of a contemporary political subtext. This working-out need not, in fact, take place in the mind or according to the intentions of the author. My point here is not to seek some originary point outside of Harnack for Harnack's own ideas, an originary point that will explain them and reveal them in their purity and essence. Harnack, at an unconscious level, may or may not have intended some of the ramifications I have spelled out above (I doubt that, at a conscious level, very many at all are intentional); nor is it likely that Harnack's social context in some way symbolically intruded its own grand currents into Harnack apart from his intention. Rather, my point is to draw out the meaning of these hypotheses as—metaphorically—contemporary judicial decisions about a text of law, a meaning that can only be mediated socially and therefore will only transmit current along the webs of conduction already socially provided. To put it another way: I am investigating the conditions of possibility of Harnack's communicating through the vehicle of the history of the Jesus movement, the networks of shared assumption that allow his work to be interpretable at all to his contemporaries. In the case of the itinerancy hypothesis, its hermeneutical circuit board—and hence the limits and foundations of its reception and transmission of meaning—revolves primarily around the pressing contemporary questions of imperialism, nationalism, and individualism, and their ideological corollaries of universalism, romanticism, idealism, and so forth. To a certain degree, then, the itinerancy hypothesis is the product of this historical constellation and derives its meaning, potency, and especially cogency from this constellation (see also Draper 1999).

Pot, basket, and utensils

"So do not be anxious, saying: What are we to eat? What are we to drink? What are we to wear?" (Q 12:29)

2.
THE SAYINGS TRADITION AND ITINERANT PREACHERS

THE IMPORTANCE OF THE *Didache* for sociohistorical reconstructions of the Jesus movement is underscored by the extent to which Harnack's reading of the text has remained the standard one for more than one hundred years. Since the 1960s and up to the present, in spite of changing circumstances, this conception of radical itinerants has been progressively retrojected further and further back into the dim recesses of the originary moments of the Christian movement. Notable contributions to the contemporary version of the itinerancy hypothesis were made throughout the 1960s, most notably by Heinz Schürmann (1968 <1960>), Georg Kretschmar (1964; see 1974), and Ernst Käsemann (1969a <1960>; 1969b <1962>). And in 1972 Paul Hoffmann identified the people responsible for Q as itinerants (3d ed. 1982). This trend in scholarship culminated in the work of Gerd Theissen during the 1970s, a corpus that in its turn has served as a bedrock for the development of further itinerancy hypotheses. We now turn to a scrutiny of some of the more recent defenders of Harnack's ideas.

Gerd Theissen

In his 1973 essay (ET 1992), expanded in book form in 1977 (ET 1978), Gerd Theissen developed his enormously influential articulation of the itinerancy hypothesis. He approached the question in a consistent and synthetic fashion, bringing together most of the insights (and sources!) of previous work to bear on a theory relevant to the synoptic tradition as a whole, and indeed, something like a grand unified theory of the Jesus movement. In his discussion, he treats the whole of the earlier ("Palestinian" as opposed to "Hellenistic") synoptic tradition as an amorphous unity: issues of literary sources and form-critical and tradition-historical distinctions tend to be ignored.

Theissen contended that the ethical radicalism of much of the sayings tradition argued against the traditional form-critical postulation of a "congregational" setting in life. He proposed instead to determine what kinds of people and situations lie behind these traditions by employing a clearly articulated threefold methodology (1978:2–3). He claims that appropriate sociological conclusions about the setting of sayings material can be arrived at by deductions of its character: *analytical,* from the form and content of the sayings; *constructive,* from direct statements about the situation presupposed by the sayings; and *analogous,* from contemporary parallels (see also 1982). The critique of wealth embedded in many of the sayings, for instance, would fall into the first category; much of the Mission Charge, which speaks directly of travel, would fall into the second; and the analogy of other peripatetic contemporaries of the Jesus movement into the last.

Working with this basic approach, Theissen claimed in his 1973 article that all three types of evidence support an hypothesis that makes itinerant charismatics formative for the synoptic tradition. Particularly on the basis of his analysis of the "radical ethics" of the tradition, Theissen concludes that

> the ethical radicalism of the sayings transmitted to us is the radical-
> ism of itinerants. It can be practised and passed on only under
> extreme living conditions. It is only the person who has severed his
> everyday ties with the world . . . who can consistently preach renun-
> ciation of a settled home, a family, possessions, the protection of
> law, and his own defence. It is only in this context that the ethical
> precepts which match this way of life can be passed on without
> being unconvincing. This ethic only has a chance on the fringes of
> society; this is the only real-life situation it can have. (1992:40)

His book takes the same thesis and expounds it in considerably more detail, filling in holes, expanding on suggestions, and generally present-ing his views more fully and more convincingly than had been the case in the 1973 article (also 1982:27–28).

Theissen identifies itinerants as the formative factor behind the earli-est Jesus movement. Jesus himself, Theissen claims, did not intend to found communities but to call into being a movement of wandering charismatics: "travelling apostles, prophets and disciples who moved from place to place and could rely on small groups of sympathizers in these places" (1978:8). The charismatic property of these figures is emphasized: "Use of the term 'charismatic' keeps in view the fact that their role was not an institutionalized form of life, a position which someone could adopt as a result of his own decision. The role of the charismatic is grounded in a call over which he had no control" (1978:8). It is these figures who are responsible for shaping the earliest synoptic tradition, especially the sayings of Jesus; the peculiarity of much of this radical material becomes much more explicable when one considers the formative role such homeless radicals had (1978:10).[1] These peculiar say-ings are largely constituted by material that promotes removal from ordi-nary settled life, including an endorsement of homelessness, rejection of family, disdain for possessions, and defenselessness (1978:1–14).[2] It is only itinerants themselves, those who had in their own lives really rejected these things, who could convincingly advance such an ethos; and such views would only have been adopted in the first place by marginal types, by "outsiders." Their charisma and itinerant lifestyle were supported, says Theissen, by intense eschatological expectation (1978:15–16). In addition to the indirect evidence afforded by these ethical precepts, such itinerants are more directly attested in the instructions of the Mission Speech and Jesus' call to individual disciples. In addition, there are references to Christian itinerants in Lucian's *Peregrinus* (16), and in the Pseudo-Clementine *Epistulae ad virgines*, as well as in the *Didache* (1978:9–10). Theissen is also able to cite "comparative" evidence. In a move that is only peripheral—even opportunistic—in regard to his own argument, Theissen makes an offhand suggestion that has proven to be of considerable importance to subsequent scholarship: that the itinerants he proposes have an analogy in the contemporary Cynic philosophers of the Hellenistic world (1978:14–15). It also should be mentioned that although Theissen does regard Paul's behavior as comparable to that of the Cynics, he draws a sharp distinction between Palestinian itinerant charismatics and Hellenistic "community organizers," with Paul of course falling into the latter category (1978:115; 1982:27–28, 35–40). The charismatics exist for the sake of their lifestyle, while the community organizers are itinerant only for the sake of founding settled Christian communities.

One of the more significant additions of the book is its greater emphasis on the activity and role of "sedentary sympathizers," figures whom Theissen considers a necessary complement to the itinerants, providing their central condition of possibility and at the same time evolving a form of Christian practice in their own right. Although the majority of the materials of the synoptic tradition have itinerancy as their original setting, a handful of traditions either directly attests to local groups (and hence constitutes "constructive" evidence; 1978:17)[3] or reflects, in its distinctive norms, the existence and setting of such figures (and hence constitutes "analytical" evidence; 1978:18–21).[4] These norms are distinctive precisely by virtue of being watered down; that is, they stand apart from the rest of the synoptic tradition by being less radical or by pertaining to the ordinary requirements of settled living (leadership, community hierarchy, membership standards, and so on). Finally, hunting for "comparative" data, Theissen adduces the Essenes as a contemporary example of a religious community with gradational norms. According to Josephus and the Dead Sea Scrolls, while full members adhere rigidly to an arduous and comprehensive code of conduct, initiates and other peripheral members live out only an attenuated version of these values

(1978:21–22). Thus there arises, according to this more developed formulation, a symbiotic—but not serene—relationship between these two
groups. The itinerants, on the one hand, embody and transmit the gift
of the Spirit and the teachings of Jesus; they provide continuity with
the "perfection" of a lived radicalism, as well as speaking with the
authority of Jesus' own voice and that of the Spirit. At the same time,
the sedentary supporters, while failing to take up the itinerant lifestyle
that would give them direct access to the charismatic authority of the
Holy Spirit and the lived words of Jesus, provide the economic support
without which these figures would have been unable to practice their
extremist and marginal lifestyle. Theissen summarizes the situation
thus: "The radical attitude of the wandering charismatics was possibly
[*sic*] only on the basis of the material support offered to them by the
local communities. To some degree the local communities relieved them
of worries about their day-to-day existence. In turn, the local communities could allow themselves to compromise with the world about
them because the wandering charismatics maintained such a clear distinction" (1978:22–23).

    While Theissen argues here that all three types of sociologically rele-
vant evidence—constructive, analytical, and comparative—underpin the
existence and basic characterization of such sedentary supporters, the
argument is more tautological than this might suggest. As his preponderant focus on the itinerants themselves suggests, the real basis for
adducing these sedentary supporters is their logical necessity to the
itinerancy hypothesis: both as provision for the economic needs of the
itinerants and as a pipeline to the written, organized, and obviously
settled brand of Christianity that represents the immediate setting of all
of our surviving records. Once Theissen has adduced the existence of
these figures, he can show how, given their existence, the more conservative or worldly elements of the synoptic tradition must be attributed
to them. But the presence of these elements in no way, in its own right,
demonstrates this initial assumption.

    Theissen also attempts to place this entire historical reconstruction
within an explicit and comprehensive sociological theory that could, to
some degree, account for both the genesis and the subsequent development of the radical experiment that Christianity was in its inception.
The model he uses is a structural-functionalist one, in which religious
renewal movements (and other social phenomena) serve—or aim to
serve—a useful social function with respect to the organic totality of the
culture or society of which they are a part. Theissen is careful not to
make the relationship overly mechanical or consistent. He points out,
for instance, that the effects of religious (and other social) phenomena

cannot be derived from their origins: "If religious phenomena have at least relative, functional and oppositional autonomy, an analysis of the effects of religious phenomena cannot be identical with an analysis of the factors which condition them, since as a result of these religious phenomena new elements come into play which cannot be derived from the conditioning factors" (1978:98).[5] Nor does Theissen believe that the precise character of a response to social crisis is dictated by that crisis: renewal movements arise as responses to social crises and can be explained that way, but the choice of which type of response to adopt is not susceptible to reductionistic explanation, at least not on a sociological level (1978:97; see 32). Oddly, Theissen claims that his basic approach tends toward a conflict model of society rather than an integration model (1978:2, 94; see also 1983:29–30, 234–35). It focuses on crises and views these crises, rather than stable circumstances, as the motivating impulse behind the formation of religious groupings and agenda. On this issue, it must be noted, Theissen is simply wrong: the functionalist model necessarily prioritizes integration as the primary and explanatory social goal. Conflict is ubiquitous simply because it serves as that which integrating impulses resolve. In the way he actually treats his material (as opposed to the way he claims to treat it), Theissen is no exception to this overall orientation toward integration within structural functionalism.

Thus a functional explanation or characterization of a religious renewal movement will explore the factors that lead up to and define the crisis to which the movement is a response. And it will examine the fashion in which and the extent to which the movement creates useful rejoinders to this crisis, what compensatory efforts the movement represents in response to these factors, that is, what social functions it ends up serving (1978:1). Theissen's book accomplishes both of these objectives. He discusses at some length the "socio-economic," "-ecological," "-political," and "-cultural" factors that would have generated a sufficient crisis in first-century Palestine to account for the emergence of new religious movements (1978:31; 1983:28–29, 231–64). The book concludes with an "analysis of function" (1978:97–119). The overall effect of these additions to the discussion is to lend the book an even more explicitly sociological ambience than is alone provided by the effort to derive social information from religious texts using a consistent methodology. It also, of course, serves to contextualize the Jesus movement as he describes it within a global theoretical framework, as an effect of certain definite historical processes and phenomena, conceived in a very particular way. As a result of this approach, I do not think it would be much of an exaggeration to say that, within the field of Christian origins (an important caveat), Theissen is the eminent sociological theorist of our time.

Socioeconomic factors, in this instance, relate to the social rootlessness of the itinerant prophets as Theissen has reconstructed them (1978:33–34).[6] Alongside direct evidence of economic crisis in the form of concentration of landholdings (1978:41–42),[7] Theissen finds contemporary analogies that confirm that social rootlessness was related to the then-prevalent factor of economic crisis: emigrants, new settlers, robbers, beggars, vagabonds, resistance fighters, prophetic movements, and movements of withdrawal such as the Qumranites (1978:34–37; see 1982:28–29). In these cases, a strong link can be drawn between the rootlessness and economic forces by noting that these movements tended fairly consistently to criticize riches or the wealthy (1978:39).[8] In particular, the problematic phenomenon of double taxation lacked religious legitimation and hence was a factor in the generation of either outright rebelliousness or ethnocentricity and xenophobia in some religious movements of the time (for example, the Zealots and more aristocratic religious movements, respectively); thus a part of the economic crisis was the question of the legitimacy of state taxes (1978:44–45). The Jesus movement rejected both of these responses, undermining aristocratic privileges and legitimacy by questioning the necessity of accepted religious duties, and at the same time repudiating the Zealot stance that paying Roman taxes was incompatible with God's rule (1978:44–45). It can thus be viewed as one response among many to the longing for renewal brought about by the shattering of traditional values in the contemporary economic fluctuations (1978:45).

The other three factors also exercised considerable force on the development of the Jesus movement. "Socio ecological" factors concern primarily the tension between city and countryside (1978:47–58). Economic pressure was greater in the countryside, while the cities, and especially Jerusalem, which benefited economically from its religious centrality, tended as a result to greater conservatism (1978:52). Like analogous movements (Essenes, resistance fighters, John the Baptist's movement), the Jesus movement operated in the countryside and had an ambivalent—if not downright hostile—attitude toward urban centers. From a socioecological perspective, it is probably quite significant—certainly no accident—that Jesus was finally executed not in Galilee, and not in the countryside, but in Jerusalem (1978:57). A constant state of political crisis, military action, and jurisdictional fragmentation also ensured that "socio-political factors" would heighten apocalyptic enthusiasm and give birth to a variety of "radical theocratic movements," movements that hoped in some way or another for an act of God that would replace a discredited (and hence illegitimate) aristocracy and restore the genuine rule of God over God's people (see 1978:59, 76; see

1982:29). Finally, a threat of cultural assimilation was behind the "socio-cultural" crisis: "Our hypothesis is that the tendencies to intensify norms within Jewish renewal movements are a reaction to the drift towards assimilation produced by superior alien cultures. The first evidence for this connection was produced by the observation that tendencies to intensify norms are often caused by concern for inter-cultural segregation" (1978:87). This intensification of norms, especially those centering around aggression, is also matched by the Jesus movement in the social sphere but is repudiated in the religious sphere in order to prevent the fragmentation that typically ensued from such efforts (1978:78–79, 93; 1982:32–33).

In the context of these various factors, we learn that the teaching of the itinerants served the function of containing the aggression fostered by the various forces of social disruption:

> the best description of the functional outline of the Jesus movement for overcoming social tensions is an interpretation of it as a contribution toward containing and overcoming aggression. In this connection, four forms of containing aggression emerge: aggression was: (1) compensated for by counter-impulses; (2) transferred to other objects and ascribed to other subjects; (3) internalized and reversed so as to fall on the subject of the aggression; (4) depicted in christological symbols and transformed. (1978:99)

While these various crises created, as their overwhelming threat to social integration, an impulse toward aggression, the Jesus movement aimed to contain that impulse through its radical ethics, through its transfer of violent impulses to an eschatological consummation, through condemnation of proponents of aggressive behavior, and through its projection of the scapegoat role onto—and simultaneous identification with—the figure of the Son of Man (1978:109–10). The hope that the movement could permeate society to the extent to which any real transformation would be possible was predicated on the expectation of an eschatological miracle; apocalypticism was intrinsically tied to the social function of the Jesus movement (1978:111).

The Fate of Theissen's Hypothesis

Like Harnack's more limited proposal of itinerancy, Theissen's work has been formative for nearly all subsequent research and has set the agenda for social inquiry into earliest Christianity even among those who disagree with his conclusions. Since its first appearance in published form, Theissen's itinerancy hypothesis has had an undeniable influence on the shape of synoptic scholarship. The ends to which it has

been harnessed and the passages to which it has been applied are manifold. In spite of various modifications and criticisms, scholars continue
to use, expand upon, and debate the itinerancy model. Much mainstream
New Testament scholarship simply assumes its applicability. Itinerants
are usually assumed to have existed and to have played some significant
role in the shaping of the traditions about Jesus and the actual historical
development of movements of Jesus' followers. In particular, the role of
prophets and prophecy, frequently conceived in terms of Theissen's itinerants, has been emphasized as important for earliest Christian history
since the appearance of Theissen's 1978 work. Moreover, several New
Testament passages have been interpreted in light of a setting in life
much like the one that Theissen proposes. This has affected, of course,
how these texts are understood and how their data are marshaled to
reconstruct earliest Christian history. It is impossible to describe the
manifold ways in which Theissen has influenced the field of New Testament studies and Christian origins or even Q scholarship specifically—
to do so would require a survey of practically everything written about
the synoptic tradition since the mid-1970s. It will suffice, instead, to note
here a few of the more significant applications of Theissen's itinerants,
which have changed the shape of Q scholarship and of synoptic scholarship as a whole.

   First, the general application of Theissen's theory to synoptic scholarship has meant that prophecy and apocalypticism have played an
increasingly central and persistent role as the assumed ideological framework of the earliest Jesus tradition. *Mission,* also, is perceived as a fundamental historical and sociological factor in the development of earliest
Christianity. It has meant, as well, that sociological description of the
earliest Jesus people—those who passed along the pregospel traditions—
has tended to avoid descriptions that locate the Jesus people within a
broader social milieu, focusing instead on the wandering activity of these
figures and its social causes or ramifications. Descriptions of group
dynamics are passed over in the absence of any real group, and instead,
when internal questions of authority and structure are raised, the focal
point is on the interrelations between the charismatics and their sedentary auxiliaries. The impact of these tendencies is felt very strongly in Q
scholarship.[9]

   At the most general level, the association between charismatic
prophecy and Christian mission—as well as the view that this mission
was somehow historically determinative, or essential to the complexion
of what the Jesus movement ultimately became—has exercised a strong
influence since Käsemann's work and has been perhaps the primary
focus of scholarship on the social history of "Palestinian Christianity"

since Theissen's work in the 1970s.[10] Eugene Boring's 1982 study of Christian prophecy, for instance, stands as both an influential critique and an outgrowth of Theissen's work.

Boring assays both to revise and refine traditional form-critical investigations into the genesis of the Jesus traditions, and simultaneously provides a description of the mechanism whereby Theissen's itinerants might have had a formative effect on the sayings material (Boring 1982). Citing Harnack's characterization of charismatic itinerancy in the *Didache* as his starting point,[11] Boring argues for the existence of itinerant prophets in the first-century Syro-Palestinian Christian movement, invoking the *Didache* not only as evidence for the existence of these prophets, but also as evidence for what they were like (1982:47–48). Criticizing Harnack's assumption that the prophets discussed in the *Didache* are exclusively wandering, however, and indicating his doubts about Theissen's "questionable analogies" to Cynicism and other ancient wandering (1982:58–59), Boring conceptualizes his prophets as subsisting in an ecclesiastical setting and as being distinguished as a class less by itinerancy than by "inspiration" or "enthusiasm"; they are, says Boring, "spiritual ones" (1982:81). He associates these prophets with miracle-working charismatic authority independent of formal institutions, viewing them as necessary to the life of the early churches for certain special functions, as delivering prophetic speech in the name of Jesus and by the authority of their charisma or inspiration, as not engaging in normal occupations but requiring the economic support of their congregations, and as distinguished from the ordinary members of their congregations by their ascetic poverty and rejection of family life (1982:87–92). They are, moreover, imbued with and motivated by an intense expectation of the apocalyptic end (1982:136). His basic thesis is not too far removed from that of Theissen: "There is some significant evidence, then, that early Christian prophets typically were committed to poverty and sexual abstinence, and we may expect to find that sayings originating from, or shaped by, such prophets may sometimes manifest this commitment" (1982:94). Boring, in a nutshell, is distancing himself from Theissen's (and Harnack's) characterizations without really offering anything much different: he does not deny that such figures traveled, but he does relativize the importance of this activity and argues that it was not omnipresent. In common, both Boring's prophets and Theissen's itinerants are marked by a (relatively mild) ascetic discipline.

This overall acceptance of Theissen's charismatic radicals is in evidence when Boring is discussing Q, where he makes little effort to preclude wandering as a significant factor in the history of Q's tradents. Finding in Q abundant instances of what he considers to be the literary or formal characteristics of early Christian prophetic speech—speaking for the risen Lord in the first person ("I-sayings"), eschatological correlatives, sentences of holy law, blessings and curses, and initial introductory phrase ("Amen, I say to you")—he concludes that a large number of sayings in Q either originated as oracles of Christian prophets or at least show the marks of prophetic reformulation.[12] Boring uses these conclusions to argue for the nonsapiential character of Q and of the impetus behind it, and believes that the radical position of the document would have been impossible without an appeal to the revelation to which the prophet—not the wise man—has access. For instance, in defining the "prophetic" character of the persecution beatitude in Q 6:22-23, he looks askance at James Robinson's characterization of Q as a wisdom collection:[13]

> The saying [6:22-23] is typical of Q in general, which is not to be seen as a collection of proverb-like catechetical materials for the moral instruction of the early church but as a setting-forth of a radical understanding of life that can only be understood as *revelatory.* Such forms of speech are at home in Jesus' own mouth, and in the mouths of his inspired post-Easter spokesmen, but are not particularly appropriate to teachers and non-charismatic transmitters of tradition.[14]

The Syro-Palestinian Christians that Q represents drew their collection of Jesus' sayings from charismatic prophets who spoke the original words of Jesus, as well as their own charismatic utterances, indistinguishably as "words of the risen Lord." These sayings, and the early Jesus people influenced by them, are infused with a spirit of eschatological imminence.

Boring's study dovetails with that of Theissen most provocatively in the case of the so-called Mission Instruction (Q 10:2-16). Boring claims that the speech as it now stands in Q is evidently composite and searches its constituent pieces for evidence of prophetic construction, which he finds in abundance. In particular, he associates the intense eschatological expectation of some of the material—notably Q 10:4, which he believes argues against the adequate provisioning of missionaries because the dawning of the new age is expected immediately—with charismatic prophecy, a feature in marked contrast, he assumes, to "Cynic-Stoic preachers" (Boring 1982:144–45; so also Aune 1983:213). The collection of this material into an organized and coherent speech infuses the cluster as a whole with the prophetic and eschatological tenor missing in a handful of the original constituent units, and hence the formulation of the speech itself probably represents the continuing influence of the charismatic prophets within the Q group (Boring 1982:149). We thus have, as with Theissen, a Q whose composition is strongly marked by the influence of charismatics, whose eschatological expectations lead to an ascetic or otherwise "radical" ethos. But where Boring departs from Theissen is in his image of the relationship between prophet and community. Boring notes that the Mission Speech, although spoken by a prophet and in prophetic mode, does not necessarily address prophets. He concludes that while some of the missionaries envisioned in this speech may have been prophets, we have no basis for concluding that all of them were, nor any reason to imagine that all prophets were wanderers.[15] Thus we return to the original thesis, that prophecy is an ecclesiastical function of settled communities. Q's Mission Speech presupposes such a settled and structured community from which missionaries are sent out and to which they return, and so, in associating prophecy with such a community, we do not necessarily assert, à la Theissen, that such charismatics must have been genuine itinerants (Boring 1982:149).

Nonetheless, the thesis here clearly owes something to Theissen: it is partly articulated in opposition to or as corrective of his thesis and is partly a further elaboration of it. David Aune has shown how Boring's conclusions, or any direct focus on Christian prophecy, will lead to conclusions much like those of Theissen. While Aune follows many of Boring's deductions (although thinking that his case is somewhat "overblown"), he states that it is impossible to sustain any arguments that at least some of the prophets could not have been itinerants (Aune 1983:211, 213). What we see here is a reconciliation of Boring's and Theissen's views, so that Theissen's entire thesis—including the postulation of itinerants; the gradual development of their roles; and their being supplanted by internal, regular, and less charismatic community mechanisms—is allowed to stand side by side with Boring's view that charismatic prophets were responsible for much of the shaping of the Jesus tradition. Such prophecy, among itinerants, served the function of uniting scattered Christian communities and providing leadership roles in the earliest period, functions that were then supplanted by a more stable internally based leadership structure at a later period. The prophetic behavior of some of the itinerants not only provided the driving force behind their peripatetic activities but also motivated their reformulation of the Jesus traditions to reflect their radical ethos. We see, in fact, that most of the characterizations of the Jesus movement (or the people behind Q) as prophetic rely on the conception of their behavior as it is articulated by Theissen: apart from an occasional tinkering with details, as, for example, in Boring, "prophetic" is just a specification of the charismatic impulse behind this itinerancy. We are left with a complex of descriptions characterizing all (relevant) aspects of Q's history:

prophetic (traditionally and formally), eschatological or apocalyptic (ideologically), and itinerant (socially).

Even more interesting have been the attempts to build a grand unified theory of Christian origins on the foundation of Theissen's early itinerants. According to such schemata, the historical Jesus was itinerant or at least encouraged itinerancy; his immediate followers were itinerant; and the theological and historical development of the subsequent Christian movement can be attributed to and understood in terms of the behavior and activities of these itinerants, including the eventual usurpation of their roles by other, noncharismatic figures.

Stephen Patterson and the *Gospel of Thomas*

Stephen Patterson, for instance, has argued recently that Theissen's itinerants also underlie the traditions of the *Gospel of Thomas*, a text that he believes witnesses not only to their existence and "radical" perspective on the world but additionally to the conflict that developed between these charismatic preachers and their "sedentary sympathizers" in the last third of the first century (Patterson 1993a:126–70). Such texts as *Thomas* sayings 14, 42, 73, and 86 attest fairly directly to itinerant activity and homeless wandering among the *Thomas* tradents.[16] The overall pattern of ethics, congruent with these basic indications of itinerancy, revolves around cutting family ties (8, 31, 55, 76, 99, 101, 105), intentional poverty (36, 54, 63-65, 69, 95, 100, 107, 109, 110),[17] and a relativization of purity requirements and political norms (6, 14, 27, 52, 53, 71, 78, 89). There is also evidence of an only minimal internal organizational structure (12, 30, 49), consistent with a charismatically inspired network of itinerants.[18]

Where this reconstruction most notably departs from—but supports!—Theissen's readings of the synoptic tradition is in its conclusion that *Thomas* (almost) uniquely offers us the unadulterated perspective of the itinerants themselves, rather than those who were forced to deal with these figures. *Thomas*, says Patterson, shows no indications of the perspective of the settled Christians who, according to Theissen's theory, are responsible for recording and transmitting—albeit in an attenuated, sanitized, or segregated way—the tradition of Jesus' sayings originally passed down by the itinerants. Patterson, in other words, has found evidence of an earlier stage, has found a "missing link" critical to the itinerancy hypothesis in *Thomas*. This is not to say that *Thomas* is actually earlier than the Synoptic Gospels or directly reflects a presynoptic setting.[19] Rather, it attests to the strand of development that ran counter to the synoptic position in the period in which itinerants and an emerging local householder leadership were struggling for power over the nascent Christian communities. The synoptic position, of course, was that of the householders rather than the itinerants.[20] *Thomas* may be thus be seen, especially in its final stages, as a testimony to the itinerants' stand in the course of this conflict, in which a gnosticizing theological vision is marshaled to support an embattled itinerant social radicalism in the face of the local communities' increasing marginalization of the itinerants (see Patterson 1993a:196–214).

Not only does Patterson's inclusion of *Thomas* widen the scope of Theissen's sociohistorical reconstruction, as well as provide us with the hitherto lacking voice of the itinerants themselves, it additionally extends the historical sketch of itinerancy and its consequences both forward and backward in time. The concluding chapter of Patterson's book on *Thomas* offers a preliminary sketch of the way that the gospel might be used to investigate the historical Jesus. He argues that, given the independence of *Thomas* from the synoptic tradition, those aspects that they have in common will most likely constitute the best places from which to launch suppositions about Jesus himself (1993a:217–31; see 1991:1–4, 32). The common ground that in fact emerges from such a comparison is, unsurprisingly, constituted by a collection of wisdom sayings and parables. The content of this material, however, is interesting for its fairly consistent drift toward an ethos of "social radicalism" (1993a:233–41; 1991:25, 33; 1993b:205–20). Although Patterson does not say outright that the source for the radical character of the preaching of the historical Jesus was an advocacy of itinerancy, he does include itinerancy as an aspect of the "common ground" and as a feature of the radical ethos, which, he asserts, goes back to Jesus in a general way:

> Thomas and Q share in their advocacy of the lifestyle of the wandering beggar. The tradition preserved in Thom 14:4 (par. Luke 10:8-9, Q) perhaps best reflects its practical dimensions. . . . Utterly destitute, the wise sage is called upon to dispose of his or her money (Thom 95, par. Matt 5:42//Luke 6:34-35a, Q), and to take no care for such necessities as clothing (Thom 36 [Coptic], par. Matt 6:25-33//Luke 12:22-30, Q) or food (Thom 69:2, par. Matt 5:6//Luke 6:21a, Q). Their poverty is to be a sign of blessing (Thom 54, par. Matt 5:3//Luke 6:20b, Q). (1993a:234)

In the other temporal direction, Patterson pursues evidence of itinerancy in a range of Christian writings that attest to conflict or competition between local authorities and charismatic wanderers. Looking to the *Didache* (chaps. 11–13), the Epistle of James, and the Johannine letters (2 and 3), he finds evidence to support both the claim that there were itinerants among the Christian groups during the late first and early second centuries and that there was a power struggle between these figures and local, sedentary community leadership (1993a:171–95). We have already seen that Harnack used the *Didache* as his point of departure in describing a charismatic ministry of itinerants in the Jesus movement. The evidence from the *Didache* cited by Patterson is not much different from that deduced by Harnack.[21] What makes Patterson's analysis so interesting is that it brings *Thomas* into the discussion as a representative of the stance of those figures whom the author of the *Didache* aimed to suppress or control. Patterson says, "Whether one should properly call the wandering teachers, apostles and prophets known to the didachist 'Thomas Christians' is probably an unanswerable question" (1993a:177). But the fact that the question can even be posed is an indication of the potential such an analysis of *Thomas* has to unify in a comprehensible way a series of disparate strands or sources of early Christian history.

In addition to the predictable citation of the *Didache,* Patterson also turns to some of the New Testament epistolary literature as evidence for this same phase of power struggle. In 2 and 3 John, for instance, we see an analogous controversy centering on issues of hospitality (1993a:188–95). Third John apparently is defending the authority and right to hospitality of itinerants who impose on the generosity of the churches they visit: "You do faithfully whatever you do for the friends, even though they are strangers to you; they have testified to your love before the church. You will do well to send them on in a manner worthy of God; for they began their journey for the sake of Christ, accepting no support from non-believers. Therefore we ought to support such people, so that we may become co-workers with the truth" (3 John 5-8). Second John, which Patterson thinks was written by another hand in imitation of the "presbyter" responsible for 3 John, intends to defuse this argument, by marshaling the presbyter's voice, this time, against itinerancy: "Many deceivers have gone out into the world, those who do not confess that Jesus Christ has come in the flesh; any such person is the deceiver and the anti-christ! . . . Do not receive into the house or welcome anyone who comes to you and does not bring this teaching; for to welcome is to participate in the evil deeds of such a person" (2 John 7, 10-11). Here, as with the *Didache,* we see a conflict between itinerants and householders, and can trace, at least a little, the development and some main events of this process. Also, as in the case of the *Didache,* we could speculate, without really being sure, that the itinerants in question, including those whose voices we hear in 3 John, are or are akin to Patterson's "Thomas Christians."[22]

The Letter of James is also adduced in support of the itinerancy hypothesis and drawn into the hypothesis as a result (Patterson 1993a:178–88). Patterson argues that James's tripartite disquisition on rich and poor (2:1-26) actually conceals a struggle between wealthy local patrons, to whom this church appears to be turning, and "the poor," which does not denote simply the economically deprived but rather serves as a (technical) designation for a body of people within the church who feel that they ought to be in control and be honored (the wording of James 2:5, "the poor in the world" supports the notion that *the poor* is a technical term). This interpretation of "poverty" in James, coupled with the fact that Abraham, cited as an instance of "justifi[cation] by works" (2:21-24), was a proverbial example of hospitality in Jewish sources of the time, and the letter's citation of the prostitute Rahab (2:25), indicate that the author of James, also, is defending the status of the itinerants against the encroachments of local patrons. Patterson concludes by linking James not only to the phenomenon of itinerancy but, speculatively, to *Thomas* and its environs as well:

> what we have found in the three central treatises is a defense of three areas in the life of the wandering radical—poverty and the right of the "poor" to be heard; itinerancy and the right of itinerants to receive hospitality; and teaching and the reservation of this right for those who would fulfill some form of ascetic requirement and become "perfect." In addition, the author describes him or herself as one such teacher. We can only offer an hypothesis, but it seems quite likely that the same sort of transition from wandering radical leadership to local authorities that we have already observed in the Didache is part of the picture also in James. . . . Whether there was any historical connection between the author of James and Thomas Christianity would be impossible to know. But the possibility should not be excluded. Both James and the Gospel of Thomas draw upon the authority of James. The epistle of James . . . stands very close to the sayings tradition. (1993a:186–87)

In brief, although this is not his primary aim, Patterson has in fact used the interpretive filter of Theissen's itinerancy thesis to construct a network of connections and developments that link and explain Jesus' activity (at least somewhat); the early sayings tradition; its manifestations in the Synoptics and Q, on one hand, and *Thomas*, on the other; a collection of epistolary literature; and the *Didache*. What emerges is a Jesus movement initially driven by a kind of radical asceticism that takes the specific form of wandering homelessness (Patterson 1999). The ethos of the sayings tradition is molded by these people, who in their turn transmit it to, and rely for support upon, local sympathizers who do not adopt this ethos of radical homelessness in its entirety but are supportive of the basic message. Eventually, a considerable amount of early Christian literature came to address the conflict between itinerants and their former supporters. At issue were questions of support, prestige, and authority. Sedentary communities, as they developed their own local forms of administration, progressively undercut the role or status of the itinerants. The writings that reflect this process can be placed on a continuum, depending upon the historical period they evince and the stance they take. One can find traces of successive stages of the conflict from one perspective (for example, in the *Didache,* that of the settled householders) or find the opposing voices of the two protagonists (as in the synoptic tradition, or the shift from 3 John to 2 John).

John Dominic Crossan and Itinerancy

John Dominic Crossan also has come up with a broad sketch of the history of the Jesus movement in which itinerants and the relationships devolving from them form a central aspect. By his reading, the historical Jesus shows a primary interest in a radical egalitarianism marked by what Crossan calls "open commensality," which extinguishes concepts of ranking from the social process (1991:261–64). In particular, the conjunction of this open commensality around eating with his healing activity serves as an indication for Crossan that Jesus did in fact intentionally inaugurate a social movement (1996:114). The first traces of this movement are to be found among itinerants, whom Crossan sees reflected in the earliest layer of Q posited by John Kloppenborg. Crossan explicitly indicates that the continuity he sees running between the early itinerants reflected in Q^1 and the historical Jesus is not necessarily one involving the verbatim transmission of speech materials. Rather,

> the continuity is not in mnemonics but in mimetics, not in remembrance but in imitation, not in word but in deed. They were living, dressing, and preaching as physically similar to Jesus as was possible. More simply: most of them were originally as poor and destitute as he was. . . . it is the continuity of lifestyle between Jesus and itinerants that gives the oral tradition its validity even if one were ready to accept every single aphorism or parable we now have as reconstructed summary or redacted expansion. (1996: 117; see 1998:278–82)

Crossan considers especially revealing the Q^1 cluster of instructions found in Q 6:20-23, 27-49, which, he notes, would have immediately preceded the Mission Speech (Q 9:57-62; 10:2-11, 16) in the earliest edition of Q (1996:114). The radical injunctions of the first segment of this speech (6:20-23, 27-36) are oddly juxtaposed with a concluding set of warning injunctions (6:37-49). While this basic structure—a set of admonitions followed by a description of the consequences of following, or failing to follow, such advice—is rather typical of wisdom writings, the opposition usually articulated is between accepting or rejecting the wisdom, not between acceptance with, or acceptance without, doing what the wisdom requires (1996:115; 1998:358).

Crossan concludes that the first segment of the speech is simply a straightforward advocacy of the itinerants' way of life. The second segment, however, with its peculiar opposition between acceptance with practice and acceptance without practice—an opposition that would necessarily be secondary to any between simple acceptance and rejection—suggests a group of people who, on the one hand, were willing to accept the message of the itinerants and see themselves in alliance with them but, on the other hand, were unable to live out such an ethic in its entirety. Reasonably enough, Crossan can thus conclude that "we hear in that specific warning the reproach of itinerant to householder, the reproach of one who has given up everything against the one who has not given up enough" (1996:116). We thus have access, in the Q^1 warnings of Q 6:37-49, to the itinerants' perception of the householders.

The *Didache,* by contrast, serves, according to Crossan, to provide us with the voice of the householders themselves. Crossan is less interested than Patterson in stratifying the *Didache,* instead arguing that its constituent material stems from different times but was drawn together in a single constitutive moment. The *Didache,* especially the material in chapters 11–13 (discussing the hospitality to be accorded to itinerants) and 15:1-2 (discussing the appointment of local leaders), "is redolent with transitional social formation. It bespeaks the moment when itinerant authorities are being combined [with] but not yet confronted let alone replaced by resident ones (bishops and deacons). Finally, then, it is those itinerant authorities that I focus on here but as seen not from their own point of view, as in the Q *Gospel,* but from that of the householders" (1996:119; see 1998:373–82). Crossan sees the controls and restraints being put on hospitality to itinerants to be phrased and implemented in a very delicate way, reflecting the gradual process by which the local authorities came to supplant itinerant leadership. One controls the itinerants by limiting their stays, by compelling them to work in the instance of permanent settlement, and by requiring their teaching to conform to the community's norms. The *Didache* reproduces lists of (radical) sayings that in some cases even conform in superfluous details to those found in Q; Crossan speculates that its author has access to summaries of the itinerant lifestyle akin to the sayings complexes found in Q.[23] But this tradition is qualified in a number of ways, such as the addition of warnings against rapacious demands (see *Did.*1:5-7) and the stipulation that one need not attain perfection (*Did.* 6:2).

Crossan's conclusions are worth quoting at length because of the way they draw together the various threads I noted above into an overarching map of the earliest, originary moment of the Jesus movement:

> During his life Jesus was the centre of a network of companions, itinerants empowered to perform the kingdom's presence by the social and ethical . . . radicalism of their lives and by the reciprocity and mutuality of their interaction with householders to whom they brought healing and with whom they shared an open commensality. I emphasize strongly that Jesus held no monopoly on the kingdom and that those companions . . . were not sent to tell others about Jesus or to bring others back to Jesus. But there is, as far back as I can see, a paradoxical tension built into the kingdom program in that necessary interaction of itinerants who move on and householders who stay put. *Is the kingdom with the itinerants or is it in that dialectic between itinerants and householders? If the itinerants believe the former option, is that why they start to quote Jesus rather than perform the kingdom, they start to beat the householders over the head with Jesus, that is, they begin to change the kingdom movement into the Jesus movement?* (1996:124) (emphasis original)

Women and Itinerancy

A related point that deserves to be raised in its own right is the way in which the activity of women has been worked into the hypothesis. Patterson has suggested that there are some indications in the *Gospel of Thomas* that women may be full members of the group responsible for *Thomas*. Citing *Thomas* saying 114, paradoxically but convincingly, as evidence that there *are* women within the group, Patterson hints that "becoming male" as it is here exhorted may be an allusion to the dangers faced by itinerant "*Thomas* virgins" (see 79), who are forced to adopt male guises as protection.[24] Crossan likewise posits female itinerants but suggests a different subterfuge: "The only way the earliest kingdom movement could have had women as itinerant prophets in that cultural situation was they traveled with a male as his 'wife'" (1996:120). Crossan finds evidence for this practice in a variety of places: the *Didache*'s reference to the enactment of a "worldly mystery of the church" (*Did.* 11:11), Paul's reference to a "sister wife" in 1 Cor 9:5, the companions implied by various synoptic texts (Mark 6:7; Luke 10:1; 24:13, 18), and the apparent Pseudo-Clementine references to female itinerants in the epistles to virgins.[25]

Luise Schottroff, however, is to be credited with drawing out the fullest description of the itinerant mission's implications for women. In a paper discussing the role of women in the itinerant mission of the people responsible for Q, she notes that the basic message of these Q itinerants was one that created conflict within and problems for the patriarchal household, breaking up families as a result of homeless wandering and intrafamilial conflict (see Q 9:58; 12:51-53; 14:26; Schottroff 1995:354). These indications of an antipatriarchal stance behind Q make her question the applicability of Theissen's model of a symbiosis between radical itinerants and patriarchal households, in which, she believes, the itinerants come to be regarded as "moral freaks" and in which the household model is normative (1995:354). A Q that leads to the breakdown of families and that effectively proclaims the end of the patriarchal order—albeit from an androcentric perspective—is not very likely, says Schottroff, to exist in any easy harmony with patriarchally structured sedentary household-based groups. In addition, Schottroff believes, the signs of intrafamily conflict among women (Q 12:53) and the prohibition against divorce (Q 16:18) should be taken as an indication that women were also to be numbered among the itinerants (1995:354–55). She concludes:

> Even though the sayings source's androcentric language conceals the presence of women among the messengers of Jesus (especially in the mission speech Q 10:2-12), they are nevertheless to be counted among those who considered their labour to be for the kingdom of God, and not for the patriarchal household: these were women labourers for God's harvest (Q 10:2). Whether sedentary or itinerant, they lived as messengers of God in a new community. Traces of this community are present in the portrayal of solidarity among the male and female disciples, who together lived as sheep among wolves (Q 10:3). (1995:355; see 360)

The observation that Q is critical or corrosive of family structures is not unique to Schottroff, nor is the assumption that the alternative to these patriarchal structures tends to be itinerancy.[26] Elisabeth Schüssler Fiorenza, for instance, in her groundbreaking feminist analysis of Christian origins, argues that Theissen's description of the itinerants reveals an androcentric bias—in this instance, a tacit assumption that the itinerants are men and that any women in view for the early traditions are to be located among the not very radical sedentary householders.[27] Instead, says Schüssler Fiorenza, the Galilean "house churches" responsible for the earliest transmission of the sayings of Jesus espoused a radical break from the patriarchal household at every level, not a restricted religious virtuosity among a select group that allowed most Jesus people to continue living as though nothing had changed (1983:147–48).

Arland Jacobson is, like Schüssler Fiorenza, critical of Theissen's approach to itinerancy but still views Q as destructive of ordinary family relationships. He imagines a very limited itinerancy (noting that Q

10:4 seems to prohibit provisions for travel), with the majority of the Q people, by contrast, persisting in small common "households" based on fictive family identity.[28] These households, much more than any itinerant wandering, are responsible for the plethora of indications in Q of family-related conflict and rejection of home (Q 9:58; 12:22-31, 51-52; 16:13).[29] Q probably does, says Jacobson, reflect a limited practice of itinerancy, but its rhetoric of uprootedness is more a reflection of the separation from family generated by the Q people's program of creating fictive-kinship household units that were in competition with the household units from which its members originally came.

Applications of the Itinerancy Thesis to Q

The application of these various theories of itinerancy to Q has been straightforward and widespread. Very few scholars have explicitly denied the applicability of the itinerancy thesis to Q.[30] Very few, in fact, have managed to resist using the itinerancy hypothesis as a basis for articulating some kind of social description of the Q people.[31] A few examples of the latter are in order, if only to demonstrate a tendency to assume itinerancy as a starting point in the social description of the Q people, and then to move on to fill in the details of their behavior. It is notable that normally this social description is inhibited by the itinerancy hypothesis, not facilitated by it: the social description of the Q people tends in fact to be simply an historical elaboration of the specific behavior of itinerants as reflected in Q. An actual social description of the shared circumstances that generated, fostered, or even allowed such peculiar behavior is thus avoided. In this respect, at any rate, Theissen's work remains superior to and more useful than that of most of his protégés.

Anthony Blasi's work is a good example of both the ordinary application of the itinerancy thesis to social description of the Q people and the limitations of this application. Blasi actually begins his study by acknowledging and justifying these limitations. Like Theissen, Blasi argues that Q's references to social roles (Theissen's "constructive evidence" [1978:3]) provide useful social information, but he departs from Theissen's approach by marginalizing "analytic" evidence, arguing that "nontheological inessentials" were more likely to be modified in sociologically telling ways than the theological core of the material (Blasi 1986:229). The "laborer" itinerants described in the Q Mission Speech are, for Blasi, full-time articulators of a subcultural ethos, who operate within a larger pool of the population that is likewise somewhat resistant to the dominant culture, albeit in a less ostentatious way. It is this intended audience—disgruntled but still sedentary and caught up in ordinary social intercourse—to which the Q prophets address their words for "babes" (Q 10:21). The social composition of this audience was mixed: it included the destitute but also embraced secure householders, as the material's optimism (for example, the "God will provide" sense of Q 11:9-13) and its more specific addresses to those who have financial resources (for example, 6:30, 34) indicate (Blasi 1986:242–45). Conflict was generated between these itinerants and the households on which they were dependent for support not only because of differing values but also as a result of recruiting new itinerants from within these sedentary households, a practice that would have created serious economic difficulties for its "victims" (1986:246). As a result, it is no mystery that, when settled Christian groups became large and financially independent enough to support a local resident clergy, they availed themselves of the opportunity.[32]

Another, rather more sophisticated, example is the work of Werner Kelber on orality and textuality (Kelber 1983). In his introductory chapter, which explores the models biblical scholarship has used in its analysis of oral traditions, Kelber approvingly cites Theissen's work as an example of the principle of social identification—that oral tradition will persist when and to the extent that there is a fit or match between its content and the circumstances of the people who pass it on (1983:24). By virtue of this insight, Theissen is able to deduce an antisocial lifestyle from antisocial sayings: one in which wandering charismatic prophets pass on the words of Jesus while emulating the lifestyle those very words endorse (1983:24–25). It is thus on the basis of its making sense of the character of the Jesus movement's oral tradition that Kelber endorses Theissen's work: "Theissen's study is impressive because it combines characteristic sayings of the synoptic tradition, a model of oral transmission, and a plausible social milieu into a grand thesis which accounts for oral transmission according to the rule of social identification" (1983:25). Kelber qualifies his praise for Theissen's accomplishment, however, by noting that the relationship between forms of speech and settings in life is certainly not isomorphic. Settled individuals could—and do!—assent to such sayings in principle, without actually living out their implications literally. A saying or type of saying can function in more than one social setting (1983:25–26).

In the book's concluding chapter, Kelber asserts that Q is an example of an "oral hermeneutic" (1983:199–203). As a sayings collection, Q in fact stands generically at a tremendous remove from the narrative Gospels, as much so as the Gospels stand from the New Testament epistles. The sayings collection was not the first step on the road to narrative Gospels as we find them in the canon but represented a tendency all its own, a tendency, as Robinson has correctly identified, toward a contemporizing view of Jesus' words as a living authority in the present (Kelber

1983:200, 203, citing Robinson 1971). While the gnostic revelation discourses may continue the generic trajectory of the Sayings Gospel, narratives of Jesus' earthly life, by contrast, serve to locate the sayings firmly in the unalterable past (Kelber 1983:203). The content of Q conforms with its "prophetic" oral hermeneutic, casting those who communicate Q's message as speaking for Jesus himself.

> The hermeneutical principle of prophetic speech is unequivocally stated in Matt. 10:40//Luke 10:16: "He who hears you hears me, and he who rejects you me, and he who rejects me rejects him who sent me." This formula of legitimation authorizes the prophetic representatives of Q to speak in accordance with the hermeneutical purpose of the genre. Endowed with prophetic authority, they speak the sayings not as mere human words, but as words of Jesus, and not the Jesus of the past, but in his present authority. (1983:202)

It is obvious that this conclusion is supported by Theissen's hypothesis. Charismatic prophets stand behind—and take the weight of—Kelber's use of Q as example to illustrate his hypotheses about the contrast between orality and textuality. At the same time, the apparent success of Kelber's approach to orality has doubtless contributed to the popularity of the itinerancy/prophecy hypothesis, especially as it pertains to Q.

Others—including most Q specialists—continue to maintain similar sketches of Q's social circumstances. Jacobson, while backing away from a literal interpretation of the Mission Speech à la Theissen, nevertheless argues its fundamental importance for any efforts to reconstruct the "self-understanding and actual behavior" of the people responsible for Q (Jacobson 1992:144). Hoffmann continues to accept the validity of his general characterization from decades earlier (Hoffmann 1995: 190, 196). While arguing against Theissen's characterization of the Q prophets' destitution as voluntary, Luise Schottroff accepts Theissen's basic description of Q's background. So also, with attendant variations, do Wendy Cotter (1992:43–47), Helmut Koester (1982:147–48, 156), Migaku Sato (1988:8–9; 1995:156), Risto Uro (1987:124–32), and Dieter Zeller (1994). Among these scholars—variations notwithstanding—there seems to be a developing consensus that Q, while offering additional confirmation to Theissen's hypothesis insofar as it possesses a radical substratum of which itinerants were probably the original tradents, is itself the product of a more settled group, rather than such itinerants themselves.[33] This conclusion is, of course, perfectly consistent with Theissen's general thesis but involves something of a tendency to reject a literal interpretation of Q's ethics, while maintaining, like Theissen, a relatively literal reading of the Mission Instructions.

One of the advantages of the grand unified approaches surveyed above is that they allow us to hear the voices of the itinerants themselves in various documents of the Jesus movement, rather than to hear their voices *behind* writings that were written by local supporters, often with the intention of limiting the itinerants' significance, as Theissen and these more specialized studies of Q would have it. On the other hand, a difficulty with adducing documents directly representative of the itinerants' perspective is that it raises the question why on earth itinerant radicals are running around composing documents. An advantage of Theissen's original hypothesis and its manifestations in most Q scholarship is that the forms or media we encounter in the transmission of the synoptic (and especially sayings) tradition show a perfect and predictable fit with their tradents at the various stages through which the tradition has (supposedly) passed. That is, the itinerants are associated with oral traditions, while the incorporation of these traditions into larger—and mitigating—written works is undertaken as part of the domestication of the tradition by supportive, but less radical, householders. Texts such as the *Gospel of Thomas* (and Q to a much lesser degree) show sufficient primitivity of form and lack of organization (isolated sayings not organized into thematic or argumentative clusters) that one might at least deny that such texts represent conscious efforts to domesticate the tradition. But this qualification still leaves unanswered the conundrum of why and how such texts might have been composed *by itinerants* in the first place.[34] Are itinerants literate? If so, what does this tell us about their original social location? Do itinerants, who claim to have given up all wealth and social connections, carry around just enough money in their nonexistent purses (so Q 10:4) to buy paper and hire scribes? The hypothesizing of so many written sources supposedly produced by the itinerants suggests that the grand unified itinerancy theory, at least in its more recent and comprehensive manifestations, is not as well thought through as it might be. In addition, it is worth speculating that this attribution of certain documents to itinerants themselves might actually be an indication that the itinerancy thesis is in fact wrong. That documents like the *Gospel of Thomas*, which as a written work is hard to attribute to itinerants, express almost perfectly the purported perspective of these itinerants may in fact suggest that the radical ethics of the synoptic tradition (and elsewhere) require a different explanation. Hence the broader work of scholars such as Patterson (on *Thomas*) and Crossan (on Q[1]) may stand as oblique testimony to failures even within the more usual and more conservative application of theories of itinerancy to Q.

Significant Criticisms, Tangents, and Alterations

The broad acceptance of Theissen's work as a standard or starting point in the study of the social history of Q and of the synoptic tradition as a whole should not be taken to imply that his views have entirely escaped the scrutiny of scholarly critique. Even in the more positive treatments listed above, certain nuances of Theissen's work have fared poorly, and certain deficiencies have been rectified. And, predictably, a number of important outright rejections and global critiques of Theissen's ideas have appeared. Three significant departures from the original thesis are notable. First, several scholars have addressed deficiencies in Theissen's actual reading of the texts in question, with respect to a variety of different issues. Second, Theissen's sociological framework has been questioned from a theoretical perspective. And finally, a number of scholars have pursued in considerable detail and with considerable vigor the analogy Theissen has suggested between the roving preachers of the Jesus traditions and Hellenistic Cynic philosophers.

The desultory critiques of the substance of Theissen's readings of the texts in question all allege, to various degrees, that something is amiss in the particulars of what he deduces from the relevant synoptic texts. The earliest critique of this sort focuses on the issue of the willfulness with which the itinerants embraced their radical lifestyle. Theissen locates a number of factors that might have called forth the itinerant response or encouraged it but regards this behavior as essentially voluntary. Itinerancy is a chosen response and it is limited to a minority stratum within the broader society. Thus one major critique of his view is to be found in the claim that vagabond radicalism was in fact not voluntary but was thrust upon the wandering prophets. Schottroff, for instance, largely adopts Theissen's reconstruction and pursues it in productive and novel directions. But both she and Wolfgang Stegemann fault Theissen for seriously misrepresenting the earliest itinerant Jesus movement insofar as he made its radical behavior the product of an ethical or ideal choice to embrace poverty and homelessness.[35] In fact, says Schottroff, the sayings tradition and Q in particular reflect the very real anxieties and deprivations of the genuinely and literally impoverished, in sharpest contrast to the rather self-indulgent and romanticized detachment of the philosophically inclined leisure class. Such passages as Q 7:24-26 reflect this setting of poverty and concomitant contempt for the affluent.[36] Sayings such as the first beatitude (Q 6:20b) understand poverty as an actual given condition and not as a voluntarily chosen lifestyle or an ethical outlook (Schottroff 1986:124, n. 58, citing a considerable secondary literature). Likewise, Q's exhortations to avoid anxiety (Q 12:22-31; see

11:9-13; 12:4-7) are to be taken as seriously and concretely as other hortatory synoptic passages: rather than being reinterpreted in line with philosophical exhortations to stoic indifference, they are to be understood as genuine expressions of the economic anxieties—which include anxieties about the very persistence of life itself—of the ordinary people (Schottroff 1986:39–43). Ultimately Q's response to these anxieties is not a practical one but rather, trusting an absolutely unique vision of economically grounded eschatological reversal, involves renouncing the anxiety itself and placing one's trust in God's care. The Mission Charge operates within this framework of the renunciation of anxiety in the face of involuntary deprivations. The only additional provision is the exhortation to renounce anxiety about homelessness as well, a special predicament of the itinerants. The itinerant lifestyle, therefore, is by no means a spectacular voluntary renunciation but is rather an extreme application of the remedy Q proposes for involuntary poverty: trust in the beneficence and providence of God (1986:44–46). She thus deconstructs Theissen's distinction between the social setting of the itinerants and that of their "sedentary supporters":

> Matthew 6:25-33, Q [Q 12:22-31] is not describing the special existence of the wandering messengers of Jesus as contrasted with that of sedentary Christians; nor was anxiety about the minimum for survival a special problem of Christians. The renunciation of preparedness [in the "Mission Charge," Q 10.2-12] is an implementation of Mt. 6:25-33, Q: it was no less possible for (still) sedentary Christians to obey the exhortation in that passage and to set aside their anxiety. (1986:47)

Schottroff's overall presentation is marred by several weaknesses. She is clearly motivated by a theological concern with the material, for instance, and thinks about it in terms of its present relevance (1986:21). This orientation has serious consequences for the substance of her exegesis: at times her analysis is simply overtheologized, apologetic, or confessional—it seeks to explain why Q's vision is valid, important, and profound (1986:31–32, 51–57). An additional problem lies in the incompatibility of her critique with a continued acceptance of the outline of Theissen's thesis. If the characterization of the lifestyle of the Q people is to be understood as involuntary, how are we ever to deduce actual itinerancy from the text? Presumably, the "radical ethics" that carry much of the weight of Theissen's deduction of the itinerants' existence would now attest only to the attitude of all Jesus people to a poverty already held in common. If no social distinctions are to be drawn between the itinerants and their sedentary supporters, almost all of the evidence that the itinerants were there in the first place simply evaporates. True,

Schottroff makes the specific injunctions of the Mission Charge the exclusive province of itinerants; but if the kind of renunciation envisioned here is common to all early Jesus people, why should we take homelessness as a preeminent index of their social behavior? Or, to put the matter differently, why assume that the itinerancy supposedly attested in Q 10:2-12 is any more voluntary than any of the other renunciations mentioned in Q?

Despite these problems, Schottroff's analysis of Q's rhetoric of uprootedness has identified a significant weakness in Theissen's reconstruction. This problem is, of course, his ethical or "principled" understanding of poverty and deprivation. The first three Q beatitudes, as Schottroff rightly notes, are indeed focused on economic poverty and genuine deprivation: this cluster of sayings is not exhortation to adopt the characteristics of those who are blessed (in which direction Matthew redacts the material) but is rather a pronouncement about the status of those who already may be described in this way.[37] The tendency to make the poverty of the synoptic sayings tradition a voluntary and principled act does indeed, as Schottroff argues, reflect the affluence of the exegetes who find it in the text. It is a danger of our modern position of privilege, as well as our reification of matters "moral" and "religious," to identify any deprivation we encounter behind our "canonical" texts as having a significance with which we can identify—say, a principled asceticism, of the very sort that was so attractive for the contemplation of wealthy ancients[38]—rather than to see in them situations for which we have little point of reference, that is, concrete poverty. Or, as Stegemann puts it, Theissen's hypothesis

> becomes a promise of mercy when we come to be judged. And perhaps it is our very prosperity that makes it impossible for us to conceive of the poverty of the first followers of Jesus as other than a form of social renunciation. It is not that we are unwilling but rather are unable to imagine the followers of Jesus, and Jesus himself, as belonging to the poorest of the poor, to the lowly of Palestine. On the other hand, the simple, carefree life that even we sometimes dream of manifests to a dangerous degree the traits peculiar to the daydreams of the rich. (Stegemann 1984:166)

This is not to say that Schottroff is correct in understanding as involuntary the deprivation supposed to reside behind the synoptic tradition. She has, however, in making this claim, identified a major (liberal and affluent) assumption behind Theissen's work, one unsupported by the evidence, and in the process has thereby disclosed one of the chief but misleading attractions of his hypothesis.

In addition, Stegemann has criticized both Theissen and by implication many of those who follow his work with failing sufficiently to differentiate discrete sources, and their various histories and settings, from the use of sayings in particular literary contexts. He accuses Theissen, correctly enough, of failing to practice ordinary critical awareness of the complexity and tendentiousness of the texts.[39] In spite of the impression of solidity behind Theissen's reconstruction of itinerants—a solidity especially fostered by Theissen's invocation of various other, comparable types of social uprooting in this period—there are very few texts on which to hang such a rich description: we actually have but meager information about what following Jesus entailed. Moreover, this information, when it appears for instance in Mark 1:18-20; 10:28-30,[40] seems to have been mediated through secondary stages of the history of the Christian movement. Theissen wishes to reconstruct the behavior of the Jesus movement in Palestine prior to 70 c.e. and thus seeks to isolate the "earliest traditions" from synoptic redaction, but in fact he fails to do so. For instance, Mark 10:28-30's apparent reference to itinerancy derives not from Jesus' saying itself but from its redactional context, that is, Peter's assertion in v. 28 that they have given up everything and followed Jesus. The saying itself, when denuded of this secondary and redactional interpretation, does not refer to itinerancy but to the social rewards—"houses and brothers, and mothers, and children"—that devolve upon those who have had to cut other social ties as a result of associating themselves with a Christian community (Stegemann 1984:157–58, 160). Similarly, in failing to examine the literary and redactional interests of a discrete Q, from which several of the itinerancy "proof texts" derive, and instead identifying Q sayings with an unmediated access to the setting of Jesus' earliest followers, Theissen avoids the question whether Q has altered or reinterpreted earlier material, perhaps material reflecting a very different situation (Stegemann 1984:156, 161). This methodological failure creates serious problems:

> The Q texts that Theissen uses are the ones most likely still to reflect the *social* situation that he has analysed as being the historical and sociological context for the Jesus movement. But the representatives of this Jesus tradition in Q are not identical with the earliest Jesus movement, nor does a "Cynical" interpretation square with their way of life. For, although the texts . . . reflect (also) the homeless existence of wandering prophets in Syria and Palestine before a.d. 70, they do not advocate a pattern or ethos of homelessness. These individuals do indeed live the desperately poor life of the starving, but not as a result of an ethical principle that calls for a lack of possessions. (1984:160–61)

Stegemann further notes that the one certain example we have of a traveling preacher of the Jesus movement, Paul, shows no interest whatsoever in the "radical ethics" of the synoptic tradition (1984:154). Theissen's proof texts do not reflect a setting of wandering itinerants but are in fact literary fictions on the part of the synoptic evangelists, especially Luke; they are the products, ironically enough, of a settled community setting, one in which the wealthy members of an established group (that of Luke) are to be shamed into more generous behavior (1984:155, 164–65). There were traveling missionaries and preachers, says Stegemann, but these figures neither served as decisive community authorities, nor did they consciously emulate and promote a lifestyle established by Jesus and his immediate disciples (1984:154–55).

More focused studies of itinerancy lying behind Q largely avoid this uncritical appropriation of texts noted by Stegemann but in turn raise new problems. For instance, some students of Q have noted that many of the categories Theissen seems to take for granted depend on older form-critical descriptions of early Christian settings—mission, church, a sharp distinction between Palestinian and Hellenistic environments, and the like—that must be abandoned as anachronistic or at the very least largely inapplicable to Q's specific setting (Kloppenborg and Vaage 1991:11–12). John Kloppenborg has argued as well that the geography and demography of Galilee, the most probable locale of the tradents of Q, does not lend itself to long journeys or extended campaigns (Kloppenborg 1991:89). Kloppenborg also suggests that the language of the Mission Charge (Q 10:2-12) is not suggestive of local leaders: the socially demeaning image of laborers (Q 10:7: "For the worker is worthy of his food/wages"), the exhortations not to deprive such people of their subsistence, and the absence of any titles of leadership surely indicate that these individuals were at best marginal to the groups they visited (Kloppenborg 1991:89–90). Thus, if the Mission Charge is evidence for itinerant radicals, it is equally evidence that such radicals were not founders of communities or leaders of the settled sympathizers they addressed.

Burton Mack, likewise, addresses pointed questions to Theissen's characterization of the itinerants, especially the use of a "prophetic" paradigm to understand them (Mack 1988a:620–23; 1988b:84–87 and n. 7; 1993:42–43). Much like Kloppenborg, Mack at least appears to accept the notion that there were wandering preachers but imagines these figures to have been few and far between, and to have devoted more of their time and effort simply to survival than to actual preaching. Eventually, "mission work" seems to have been entirely eschewed (1988b:84–85). The weakness of the indications of itinerancy in Q, alongside all of these necessary qualifications, has caused some to question whether any practice of itinerancy lies behind Q at all (Arnal 1995b:481–82; Mack 1988a:622–23, 634).

In addition to these textually based critiques of Theissen's hypothesis, his work has also been questioned on methodological grounds, particularly by Richard Horsley. His comments chiefly center around Theissen's adoption of a "structural-functionalist" perspective, which Horsley believes is both abstracting and conservative. He finds it abstracting because the approach focuses on the teleological, systemic, and schematic apprehension of an ill-defined social totality (that is, society). A more concrete approach, he believes, would also address the subjective aims of the people behind various institutions, particular historical societies and the data about those societies, and economic problems, exploitation, technological changes, and irreducible conflicts within a given "society" (1989:35, 148–49). He finds it conservative because the approach assumes that equilibrium, rather than change and conflict, is the relevant sociological datum; and because it inquires into the "needs" of societies as they are given rather than into the needs of the people who make up those societies (Horsley 1989:35–37).

Horsley also demolishes the evidence Theissen adduces for itinerancy and erects his own hypothesis about the social situation particularly behind Q, in which itinerants do not figure at all. Horsley asserts that the gospel traditions—in line with a long Israelite history of radical theocratic criticism of the social status quo—deliberately challenge the ruling classes and deliberately criticize and threaten the institutions by which they maintain their power (1989:35, 39; 1991b:175). In lieu of the itinerancy hypothesis, Horsley proposes that the radical injunctions of the sayings tradition and Q in particular reflect a project of "renewal" on the part of settled individuals in "local communities" who wish to address disturbing and exploitative social changes, especially pertaining to increasing levels of debt among the peasantry.

The counterhypothesis Horsley proposes, however, is even more vague and unconvincing than Theissen's reconstruction. One gets very little actual textual analysis of Q (or any other specific early Christian writing) from his work; instead, some general views on the social history of the early Jesus movement are projected wholesale onto the text. A basic insight governs textual readings or, more accurately, disguises their omission. Although Horsley is quite correct to criticize the sociological vagueness of Theissen's views, his own reconstruction is just as vague and almost as insensitive to textual details. This lack of convincing alternatives must necessarily suggest to many readers that, for all of Theissen's failures, his study still represents the (only) viable sociological scenario. Horsley represents, more or less by default, the only strong voice raised against the itinerancy hypothesis as a whole; few others have taken this position or offered such a sharp critique of Theissen's views. His alternative hypothesis, however, is articulated in a very undisciplined way and with too little reference to the actual text of Q.

The Cynic Tangent

Finally, one of the more popular, controversial, and resonant applications of Theissen's views involves a considerable shift of focus, while remaining true to and inspired by Theissen's original work. Theissen's analytic and constructive conclusions are the ones most focused on by both his adherents and the critics surveyed so far. A wholly distinct tangent, however, has evolved from Theissen's comparative conclusion that Greco-Roman Cynic philosophers provide a contemporary analogy to the itinerants' behavior. The Cynic hypothesis, itself a source of "renewal" and rather savage controversy in recent scholarship, might thus be seen as a variant of the itinerancy hypothesis, as well as representing a stab in its own right at a viable alternative social description of the Jesus movement.

Proponents of the Cynic hypothesis argue that Greco-Roman Cynic philosophers provide the best analogy not only to the peripatetic behavior of the Jesus people but additionally to their socially critical ideology. Cynicism is the one instance in the world of earliest Christianity in which one might find a wandering lifestyle in connection with a radical and self-consciously contentious ethos. The comparison, according to the proponents of the hypothesis, allows fundamental insights into the impetus and intentions behind the Jesus movement. Interestingly, these observations about earliest Christianity or Q have occasionally been extended to the historical Jesus, so that according to some scholars, Jesus himself is best understood by analogy to Cynicism (see Mack 1988b:65–69; Crossan 1991:340, 421–22).

The Cynic hypothesis proceeds from the marked similarity between the style, content, and in some cases specific form or details of the material in the sayings tradition (or Q) and the literary remains of Cynicism. F. Gerald Downing, for instance, argues that, in terms of genre, Q was modeled after or finds its closest analogy to the "Lives" of Cynic philosophers such as Diogenes Laertius's life of Diogenes of Sinope (Downing 1988b). Downing additionally notes the extensive similarities of substance between Q and the message of Cynic philosophers such as Diogenes and Antisthenes. Likewise, the synoptic Mission Charge appears to reflect the same traits that for Epictetus embody the ideal Cynic (Downing 1987b:445; 1987a:51–52). On the basis, then, of these generic and thematic similarities, Downing concludes that Theissen's analogy is more than merely an analogy. The people responsible for Q were aware of and directly influenced by Cynicism—they deliberately adopted its favorite literary genre to communicate the teachings of Jesus, and those teachings themselves were infused with Cynic ideas (1987b:447–49; 1988b:219–21). This is not to say that Christians, including those responsible for Q, might not have insisted on subtle differences, might not have aimed to distinguish themselves as not really Cynics; the point is influence and perception, not absolute identity (Downing 1987a:126–49; 1988b:222).

Others have argued for a Cynic (or Cynic-like) substratum behind Q; it is among such proposals that one can see something like a revival of Theissen's description of the social characteristics of the Q people. Typically, these scholars take Kloppenborg's literary stratification of Q, by the same token,[41] as a starting point, and argue for a Cynic or Cynic-like derivation of the first and earliest literary stratum of Q. Later strata, it is assumed or argued, depart from this Cynic(-like) orientation. This scheme provides a way of understanding the inversionary rhetoric in Q's earlier material as reflecting an itinerant and deliberately ascetic behavior of a group of Galilean Cynics, who sought, via their peculiarly antisocial dramatizations, to repudiate the cultural assumptions of their day and age. The Cynic comparison thus provides not only an analogy but also a rationale for Q's many eccentric locutions.

> Like the Cynics, the "Galilean upstarts" whom Q's formative stratum represents conducted in word and deed a form of "popular" resistance to the official truths and virtues of their day. Registered in their unorthodox ethos, ethics, ideology, and ad hoc social critique as well as the sparse but vivid memory they maintained of certain "anti-heroes" of the recent past (John and Jesus) was both a decisive "no" to the typical habits and aspirations of their immediate cultural context, as well as a curious confidence in their own peculiar ability to achieve here and now, in the body and despite considerable adversity, a higher form of happiness. (Vaage 1994:106)

Such an interpretation of the aims or results of Cynic-like behavior among the early Jesus people is common to most Cynical readings of Q, regardless of the minor differences between them. These differences tend to revolve around what aspects of Q or the early sayings tradition are best described as Cynic-like, and what kind of continuity or discontinuity there is between this material and material that appears to be less Cynic-like. Most proponents of the Cynic hypothesis view the Cynic component of the tradition as earlier (or earliest), and non-Cynic ideologies as later.[42] In practice this rigid insistence on the equation of

"Cynic" with "early" leads to a stratigraphical free-for-all, as any elements of the sayings tradition felt to be amenable to a Cynic comparison are, after the fact, determined to be early, and those elements felt to be incompatible with Cynic ideology are assigned to later strata.[43] Such a procedure of course begs the essential question, as well as generating a host of only marginally different but competing reconstructions. Since the question of a Cynic Q and the issue of Q's stratification are matters that are different and not necessarily related, there is little justification for such a conflation of issues: it represents a methodological step backward (confusing literary history with tradition history) and makes its own hypothesis (that Cynic-like material forms the basis of the Jesus tradition) the basis for arriving at specific textual conclusions. This critique is not to imply that Kloppenborg's stratification, and the specific substantial details of it, are immune from all criticism or modification. But the minutiae of Q's stratification will not be settled this way, and in fact the procedure not only makes the Cynic hypothesis appear that much more shaky but must also generate doubt about the stratification of Q itself.

There is really no good reason at all, especially prior to considering the evidence, that one or another stratum exclusively must be comparable to Cynicism. If the issue is really comparison rather than identity (see further below), Q is comparable to Cynicism at every level of its development, and in fact its comparability will be that much more illuminating if plotted over the course of its developmental changes and shifts. The comparison would, easily, still be worthwhile, even if Q^1 were less Cynic-like than Q^2, or Cynic-like in different ways than Q^2. If there is indeed some kind of social continuity between Q's layers, we need to imagine, at least at first glance, that later developments will illuminate the directions in which Cynic-like ideology could modulate under various social pressures; thus secondary developments are not irrelevant and should not simply be dismissed as later, and less interesting, corruptions of the original impulse. These difficulties imply that, disclaimers to the contrary, proponents of the Cynic comparison are no more historiographically sophisticated than the theologically minded commentators they seek to discredit: there is at issue here a conception of origins as normative, pristine, enviable—and of later developments as rigidifying an initially supple "experiment."[44]

Common to all advocates of the Cynic hypothesis is an insistence—with greater or lesser clarity and force—that what is being proposed is by no means identity so much as comparability. The Q people, it is insisted, were not card-carrying Cynics, for the simple reason that Cynics did not carry membership cards. On theoretical grounds deriving from the

arguments of Jonathan Z. Smith (1990), Vaage maintains that there is little point in conceiving comparison as the establishment of genetic links;
rather it is a "disciplined exaggeration" of some compatible aspect(s) of
two phenomena that may shed light on some hitherto unrecognized
aspect of one or both items (Vaage 1994:10–11; 1995b:199–200, 205–6).
Mack likewise is usually careful to describe the early Jesus movement as
"Cynic-like," as operating with an ideology and set of intentions "analogous" to those of the Cynics (Mack 1997). Both Downing and Seeley go
slightly farther than the modest claim of mere comparability, arguing for
some kind of influence emanating from Cynic philosophical circles
being disseminated at a popular level and appropriated by the early Jesus
movement in its self-understanding.

> It might be said that the Greco-Roman texts referred to above rep-
> resent upper-class, elite philosophizing which has nothing to do
> with the more popular style of a group like the Jesus movement.
> But Downing has demonstrated that boundaries separating the cul-
> ture of the "elite" from that of the "popular" must be considered
> rather porous. The impression he gains is of "a very pervasive oral
> culture sharing much common content with the refined literature of
> the aristocracy." Dio Chrysostom, for example, presupposes a situ-
> ation "where very similar material can be used for audiences from
> the whole range of places and social contexts; and one in which
> what is said to a fairly select group is almost certain to be dissemi-
> nated much more widely." It appears, then, that class distinctions
> could be and were crossed by popular philosophical traditions.
> (Seeley 1992:234)

Criticism of the Cynic hypothesis, New Testament scholarship's
most prolific—and vacuous—new growth industry, seems to have badly
misunderstood this point about comparison. The claim is constantly
made by such critics that Jesus, or the earliest Christians, or the Q people cannot have been Cynics, for a variety of reasons. For instance, "to
claim that Jesus' use of aphoristic wisdom and biting wit is best understood within the context of Hellenistic Cynicism is to miss the most
plausible context: Jewish wisdom" (Eddy 1996:460). Leaving aside the
question of why such a putative context is more plausible, this criticism
utterly misses the point: the sayings tradition *is* "Jewish wisdom" (Hellenistic, for that matter) and as such reasonably can be understood by
comparison to Cynicism or other contemporary ideologies. Likewise,
critiques that point to the greater variety within Cynicism than is con-
ceded by advocates of the Cynic hypothesis (Betz 1994:472–73; Eddy
1996:459; Tuckett 1989:351–56, 365; 1996:375–78) may quite possibly be
correct but irrelevantly so: the real issue is not so much a label as it is the

comparability of the sayings tradition with a broad spectrum of behavior that we think we understand (what is normally called Cynic philosophy), thus shedding light on what is at issue behind the sayings tradition. That the synoptic material may correspond identically to no particular discrete strand within Cynicism but rather to an artificial amalgam of loosely related and temporally distant Cynic-like figures is a difficulty only if one seeks to identify the synoptic tradition with some particular brand of Cynicism, which in fact no one is trying to do. Substantive historically based critiques, such as, for instance, the claim that there is no evidence for a Cynic presence in Jewish or Galilean society, that Cynicism is an urban or upper-class phenomenon, or that the injunctions of the Mission Charge to eschew Cynic-like equipment are intended to demarcate the Q people from Cynics are all likewise open to the charge of missing the point, if less egregiously so. Each one of these critiques refutes the position that Jesus or his early followers were self-conscious and identifiable Cynics, a thesis that is not on the table at all, at least explicitly.

As Smith has argued at length in *Drudgery Divine* (1990), and as advocates of the Cynic thesis have tirelessly asserted, comparison is simply not about showing that one thing is identical to some other thing; it is about setting two things side by side in order to highlight the ways certain definable aspects of them are similar, in contrast to other potentially comparable things, and the ways in which they differ, in spite of such similarity. I may wish to compare a cat with a dog: my comparison might then proceed on the basis of rough similarities in size, the fact that they are popular domestic pets, and the fact that both are mammals; or it might focus on the ways they differ in terms of stamina, agility, superficial appearance, sociality, trainability. Who would think of objecting to my comparison by assuring me that cats and dogs are distinct species? So, by the same token, are the early followers of Jesus comparable to Cynics? Of course they are, in spite of so much spilled ink asserting otherwise, for the simple reason that they are comparable to anything: striking textile workers, wallpaper, automobiles, umbrellas, pine trees, or anything one might think of. Critics would do better, and would be addressing the argument as it is framed, to focus instead on showing why legitimate comparison with Cynicism yields intellectually uninteresting results. For it is only on such grounds that the procedure will be legitimately discredited.

Yet this methodological strength is also the nub of the debilitating problem with the Cynic hypothesis. If, for instance, we accept Seeley's argument that social class distinctions do not relate in any fixed way to the philosophical tradition, what gains are made for social description by the comparison of the Jesus people with such a tradition? Or, to frame the issue as broadly as possible: if comparison is indeed a disciplined exaggeration for our own (ideally, stated) theoretical and practical purposes, what are these purposes? What are the set grounds, the fixed questions that the comparison is imagined to address? The fact that such questions are rarely, if ever, recognized suggests the reason for critics' failure to understand the case: the case is being made inconsistently. Proponents of a Cynic-like Jesus movement, Vaage in particular, seem to use Smith rather opportunistically, sliding over into a sloppy equation of the Jesus movement with Cynicism from time to time, and really failing to understand or appreciate the nuances of Smith's view of comparison. Smith makes it very clear that any comparison for non-genetic purposes implies two usually unstated qualifications or terms to the comparative pair· "x is like y" really means "x resembles y more than z with respect to . . ." or "x resembles y more than w resembles z with respect to . . ." (1990:191). Yet the details of the repressed terms of this equation are sketchy at the best of times: Vaage, for instance, can conclude that "it would have been extremely difficult to distinguish the persons whom Q represents from *other* Cynics elsewhere in the ancient world" (1994:30, emphasis added) and elsewhere refer to a "strong degree of similarity," framed absolutely (1994:11), but without ever telling us what theoretical factors are elucidated by the comparison, or on what specific bases it is offered.[45] Since Vaage never tells us what questions he aims to answer, we are in no position to assess the success of his venture. This sloppiness in framing the comparison is by no means restricted to Vaage's work.[46] In addition, the various efforts that have been made to reply to critics of the Cynic hypothesis by showing a Cynic presence in the environs of Galilee or among the social classes to which the Jesus movement is imagined to have belonged likewise (mis)direct attention away from this constructive aspect of comparison and reveal the inconsistency with which Smith's methodological rigor is applied. We are thus left either with an identity equation (the Q people were Cynics) with all its attendant problems, as well as its methodological naïveté, or with the assertion that the people behind Q were merely, in some unspecified way, comparable to the Cynics, which raises the questions, So what? What have we learned?

On the other hand, if the point of the comparison, in spite of various methodological sleights of hand, is positing cultural influence, the analysis is downright retrograde. Not because it is necessarily incorrect but because it aims to stand in for detailed social description or sociological explanations for the peculiar behavior or literary expressions of the Q people. To attempt to explain this behavior by saying that they adopted

Cynic modes of expression is simply a refusal to acknowledge the more important questions. This is especially so if we accept Seeley's and Downing's claims that such rhetoric was not restricted to upper-class circles, since such a conclusion utterly detaches the behavior from sociologically recognizable settings. In other words, the Cynic hypothesis is simply not a social description at all; it is rather an indication of the cultural model or precedent that would have been drawn upon, suggested, or implied by the behavior and ideology of either Jesus or the earliest Jesus movement. Insofar as such a conclusion is imagined to be a social description or to be an alternative to Theissen's views, it represents a methodological step backward: to the extent that we adopt the Cynic hypothesis as it now stands, we know less about the earliest Jesus movement than we were taught by Theissen.

As a result, I think, the Cynic comparison, if comparison it be, is not a useful extension of or alternative to the social description of the earliest followers of Jesus as it is provided by Theissen. But this is not to say that these views have not in any way potentially advanced our knowledge. There are a number of things to be learned, or at least (re)considered as a result of the work of scholars like Mack, Vaage, Downing, and Seeley. One advantage of the Cynic hypothesis is that it provides a much more plausible context for voluntary homelessness and self-reliance than other advocates of itinerancy are able to provide: it establishes a prior model through which people behaving in such a way could conceptualize their activities. Specifically, the comparison highlights the extent to which Q^1 at any rate is very interested in the theme of avoiding cultural artifice and allows us better to see such a critique as constituting an ideological program in its own right. And this in turn suggests that whatever is at issue for Q or Q^1 may be somewhat less serious, momentous, and original than we are used to thinking. The burden of Vaage's analysis of the Q woes against the Pharisees (Q 11:39-52), for instance, is simply to demonstrate that the standard Christian view of Pharisees as hidebound hypocritical traditionalists committed to conflict with Jesus (or with the early Christians) is not what is at issue in Q (Vaage 1994:66–86). Likewise, his analysis of Q's "love your enemies" speech (Q 6:27-35), instead of viewing the speech as the pinnacle of an ethical revolution, rather normalizes it and sees it as a set of practical guidelines for coping with hostility (Vaage 1994:40–54). The Mission Charge (Q 10:2-16) can likewise be seen as a set of practical guidelines (guidelines for what, exactly, remains unclear), in contrast to the more established assumption that it represents the initiation of some kind of unique sacred commitment to evangelize (Vaage 1994:17–39). In sum, the Cynic hypothesis allows Christian origins to be thought out without invoking an anachronistic modernist notion of "religion," which assumes, for instance, the primacy of the "Sacred," the effective priority of myth over ritual, a focus on religious experience as awe at the Sacred's epiphany, an individualistic anthropology, and a concomitant emphasis on charismatic or founder figures (Mack 1991:36). The Cynic hypothesis—whether right or wrong—is intellectually progressive simply because it forces us to reimagine, creatively, what these people were really thinking and doing; it makes us question very deeply ingrained presuppositions. This is also presumably why it has generated such a negative response, all out of proportion to its actual claims or influence.

Context and Cultural Significance

As the lengthy review above must imply, the impact of the itinerancy hypothesis and of Theissen's work as a whole has been nothing short of astonishing. Theissen's single article and his slim booklet (1978) have had an impact on synoptic scholarship far out of proportion to what one might expect. From the 1960s onward, almost no serious social analysis has been done on the early sayings tradition from a perspective radically at odds with that of Theissen (Horsley is the main exception). Although some very recent work holds out the promise of fresh social analysis of the specifically local (Galilean, village, and so on) derivation and orientation of Q,[47] the majority of studies still take the itinerancy hypothesis as a starting point, something for further research to work out in detail. And the Cynic hypothesis, likewise, although not nearly as acceptable (in part because it rigorously eschews mystification), continues to generate a massive amount of interest and controversy. This popularity and broad exposure—especially in the face of the various theoretical and evidentiary failings of the itinerancy hypothesis in any form—is interesting in its own right. Why should the itinerancy thesis experience a resurgence in recent times, after its fall to obscurity along with the nineteenth-century liberal theology out of which it was constructed? That itinerancy and its liberal corollary, "charisma," should be touted by Harnack in the 1890s as an originary impetus behind the development of ecclesiastical institutions is unsurprising. That the hypothesis, or some variant thereof, should be picked up from the mid-1960s of our own rather antiliberal era is of far more interest. I would suggest, in fact, that the main intellectual impulse behind the resurgence of the itinerancy hypothesis is its contemporary resonance (and, indeed, relevance). This contention is worth exploring because of the light it casts on the itinerancy hypothesis itself as well as on the discipline of biblical studies as a whole.[48]

The itinerancy hypothesis is attractive to our own era for very different reasons than those that might have made it attractive to nineteenth-century liberals. The world has moved on, but some of the past's relics, apparently, have found new and interesting applications.[49] In classic ideological fashion, the itinerancy and Cynic hypotheses reflect contemporary conditions, respond to them, and, albeit inadvertently, retrench them. The continued desire to see religion as a unique entity marked by its own distinctive differentia—which will necessarily be different from ordinary life, exceptional, and serious—is doubtless the most obvious impulse behind the postulation of itinerancy, at least in the form offered by Theissen.[50] Itinerancy is a vibrant and explicit living out of charisma and as such preserves the distinctive innovation behind the rise of Christianity.

A concern with travel and a fixation with culture also mark the current era, albeit in a different way than they did in the late nineteenth century. The increased requirement of mobility over the last several decades and the consequent erosion of "located" professional sensibilities and self-imagination has meant that the image of itinerant tinker is resonant and sympathetic for many professionals. It is difficult to avoid the conclusion that the image of wandering teachers as a creative stimulus behind the Jesus movement is at least in part the product of a desire to find in the past—especially in formative moments of the past—analogues for our own experiences, deeply ingrained and taken for granted. This reflective tendency is probably not to be understood as a conscious need to see the Q people, specifically, as being like us so much as it is a largely imperceptible tendency to frame the past in terminology and concepts that resonate with our own experiential knowledge. Likewise, both standard itinerancy views and the Cynic hypothesis focus on the cultural aspects of earliest Christianity: this focus represents in part the same idealism that influenced Harnack but also reflects a more modern focus on defiance of convention as the truly revolutionary stance, an attitude inherited from the 1960s and with us still.[51] Striking retrojections of contemporary cultural concerns also appear frequently in Mack's work. From *The Lost Gospel* (Mack 1993):

> This stance of social critique was a call for individuals to live against the stream, not a program offered for the reform of society's ills. (46)

> Either way, the Cynic's purpose was to point out disparities sustained by the social system and refuse to let the system put him in his place. (116)

> In our time there is no single social role with which to compare the ancient Cynics. But . . . there is precedent for taking up an alternative life-style as social protest, from the utopian movement of the

nineteenth century, to the counterculture movement of the 1960s, to the environmentalist protest of the 1980s and 1990s. (117)

What counted most, they said, was a sense of personal worth and integrity. One should not allow others to determine one's worth on the scale of social position. (119)

Vaage's comments in *Galilean Upstarts* are similarly focused (1994):

In modern terms, the Cynics might called "contracultural" dissidents. They were "popular" philosophers, unremittingly opposed to the dominant social values of the ancient Mediterranean world, explicitly rejecting the usual aristocratic "educated" means of achieving and enhancing human well-being (*eudaimonia*). The Cynics made clear their basic disagreement with contemporary "commonsense" ideals of the "good" life by living, speaking, and acting in such a way that, however diverse in detail, their general comportment consistently cut against the grain of prevailing cultural assumptions regarding both prosperity and propriety. (13)

[The Cynics are characterized by] an indefatigably ineffable "knee-jerk" resistance to conformity with the customary categories of ancient social placement. (14)

It is probably this culturally focused (and hence superficial) aspect of the Cynic hypothesis that irritates James Robinson so much that he has felt compelled in recent years to write a multitude of different articles devoted principally to a fervent criticism of these views (Robinson 1994a, 1994b, 1996a, 1996b). His comments are often revealing, pointing to the superficiality of the critique Jesus is imagined to have engaged in,[52] a superficiality resulting directly, it would appear, from the understanding of the early Christian movement as being anticonventional for the sake of being anticonventional. Ultimately this reduces to mere rudeness, rudeness as an alternative lifestyle, which addresses nothing, understands nothing, and is simply an expression of nebulous dissatisfaction faced with the cynical assumption that no solutions really exist.

Another factor contributing to the culture fixation of our scholarship—reflected in the limitation of most versions of the itinerancy hypothesis to issues of lifestyle—is the gradual death of the political as an important factor in Western social life. Whatever the causes (they are doubtless multiple and complex), very poor voter turnout, lack of distinct agenda among different candidates for office, image-driven politics, and most significantly, popular cynicism seem to characterize mainstream political practice. The most effective grassroots movements, on the other hand, are defined by identity blocks that tend to refer less to shared sociopolitical interests and more to prior visible belonging in some (real or fictive) category based on gender, ethnicity, or physical characteristics. Thus, while labor union membership, for instance, as well as voter participation, is going through the floor, extraordinarily resonant and successful "political" activity is being undertaken by feminism based on the identity "woman," by the Nation of Islam based on the identity "African American," or even by white supremacist movements based on the identity "Aryan," or some such thing. Or again, consider the subnational separatist movements currently in vogue everywhere. From Quebec to Ireland, Rwanda, the Czech Republic, Slovakia, Yugoslavia, the former Russian Central Asian republics, and Tibet, strong—if synthetic—national states are being replaced by fragmented collocations of historic, ethnic, religious, or cultural jurisdictions. The point is that all of these movements, gathering momentum and on the rise, tend to be culture-driven, while political (in the modernist sense) associations and purposes are clearly on the wane.

In a sense such cultural movements are autochthonous: they make themselves, and hence their interests, in the very act of fabricating themselves as an identity. This procedure also parallels what is posited for the Christians, in the general reluctance to conceive of the early Christian settings as anything but Christian (or religious) settings. Rather than entertaining the very sensible possibility that Christians became Christians because of common interests and agenda they shared prior to their adopting of the movement, many scholars assume the very contemporary position that Christians created their agenda by becoming Christians. There is little about *potential* Cynics—at least as far as one can determine from the work of Mack, Vaage, Downing, and most others—that would distinguish them from their contemporaries. It is only once they *are* Cynics that one can locate them, describe them, even explain them. Likewise, with non-Cynic or prophetic itinerants, although Theissen isolates various factors that account for social malaise in the period in question (that is, the anomie that was the function of the Jesus movement, and any other social movement, to address), these factors serve only as a backdrop against which the activities of the Jesus people take place.

One might further note that the itinerancy hypothesis thrives in a postmodern environment because it both manifests and posits the characteristics of postmodernity: as such it is a resonant and comprehensible (and self-referential) historical proposition. First, like the general worldview of postmodernity, the itinerancy hypothesis is not historical in the strong sense; that is, it avoids concrete attribution of events to the past, and the past workings-out of those events, tending instead toward broad characterization of types of behavior.[53] Second, as already noted, the itinerancy hypothesis understands and emphasizes particularity, typically in terms of group identity. Third, it shows a strong interest in the activity of opting out: such an interest is reflective and reinforcing of postmodernism's critique and suspicion of "totalizing discourses." Fourth, the itinerancy hypothesis offers a reading of canonical texts that is itself disjunctive, deconstructive, corrosive of the emplacement of the texts in our cultural canon and that reveals the texts in question to be equally disjunctive in their original conception. Finally, at least as far as the Cynic hypothesis is concerned (and, more arguably, the standard form of the itinerancy hypothesis as well), the very same denaturalizing critique of fixed and shared social structures that characterizes postmodern theory (and experience) is retrojected into the very originary moment of the Christian religion.[54]

This postmodern emphasis on disjunction, atemporality, denaturalizing criticisms, and so forth is at least in part an almost inevitable anomic response to sociocultural changes that are rendering both the human and the natural world increasingly opaque. Hence, for instance, the emphasis on—even obsession with—disjunction presents itself as an effort to make meaningful the very absence of coherence. The absence of coherence in our own social practice thus is subjected, rather ironically, to ideological naturalization at the very hands of the intellectual and cultural movement that claims entirely to eschew the naturalization of the social in all its forms. This inability to conceptualize our own world finds its most important conceptual analogue in a refusal to totalize, or indeed even posit, social causality. Hence discrete behaviors are subjected to minute narration, while the historical narrative in which such behaviors might be embedded remains as invisible as the mysterious mechanisms, processes, and intelligibility of the too-large world in which we currently find ourselves aimlessly whirling.

In the roving of Theissen's itinerant preachers we thus have not only an instance of a fantasy of alternative or escape, a utopian rebuilding of the social world from scratch, a desperate effort to retroject onto a specific historical locale our fondest fantasies of a real state of nature from which to rebuild a simpler world more susceptible to the willful choices of coherent human agents.[55] Nor merely do we have, in the itinerants' liminal and ambivalent relationship to their own supposed social context, a fictive recapitulation of the disjunctive world as it stands, an historical painting lacking any obvious frame, any clear angles, any obvious demarcation between inside and out, lacking, as in our own natural world, any clear difference between wilderness and park. In addition, we also have a steadfast and almost willful refusal to conceptualize the local (which in itself is but part and parcel of the global village, the media explosion, the commodification of culture), and the consequent inability to make sense of social totality.[56]

Theissen's approach to the earliest Christian texts, and to a degree the Cynic hypothesis, are also self-referential in their reflection—in a variety of ways—of the loss of prestige suffered by most academics in recent times, especially in the humanities. The very fact that such a reading is against the grain of the ordinary canonical treatment of these texts would itself probably be impossible were academics still the predominant ideological mainstays and favored retainers of the (genuinely) powerful classes. In addition, the conceptualization of the originary impulse behind the formation of the Jesus movement as one devolving from the transmission of ideas, or as a consequence of the practice of teachers, is much more obviously self-referential. The presentation of these wandering teachers as marginal, as antisocial, as running against the grain both reflects the increasing marginality of today's academic institutions and attempts to reaffirm their significance in the face of that marginality.[57]

This increasingly negative (and appropriately so, I might add) apprehension of modern, scholarly work and of the world we live in is projected, like that of the ancient apocalyptists, working in similar circumstances, onto a fictive or ideal field. In this case, it is not the heavens but rather Roman antiquity that serves as the receptacle for our own impressions of what the world is like, brought about, with various distortions, by what the world really is like for us. Hence in first-century Galilee we encounter the following as among the circumstances to which the itinerants or Cynics are reacting. First, there is imperialism and a concomitant threat of erasure of indigenous cultures, alongside increasing concentration of wealth in the face of a population explosion.[58] There is militarism, lack of care for other people, and the concentration of wealth in the hands of the few, to their own exclusive benefit.[59] There is a rigidity and limitation of cultural options.[60] There is a society characterized by hierarchy and patronage; characterized, in other words, by mediation of the very marrow of social life and social good (Crossan 1991:421–22). There is an economic crisis generated by the lack of general circulation of finance capital (Crossan 1991:221–24; Goodman 1982). There is a world scarred by the tensions created in a pluralistic and multicultural society.[61] And, best of all, there is an empire held together by "a soulless superimposition of law and order, a network of military surveillance and economic exploitation that was incapable of commanding the loyalty of the peoples they governed" (Mack 1993:65).

Identity- and minority-based criticisms and readings of the biblical texts are normally assigned to the abyss of tendentious hypotheses, in part because we can read their ideological subtext with all too much ease. A Jesus who cares, anachronistically, about nature is most obviously the product of environmentalist concerns; Jesus as an emancipatory teacher about the roles of women in his society is clearly motivated by feminist concerns; Jesus as dark-skinned is motivated by African American or black concerns; and so forth. But the ideological subtext of the dominant culture or of the broader social totality, which encompasses even marginal groups, is normally much harder for us to read, simply by virtue of its proximity, of our own embeddedness in it.[62] We have memorized the texture and foliage of the individual trees without even an inkling that we could also map out the parameters of the forest in which they stand. In the case of the itinerancy and Cynic hypotheses, the ideological subtext is as present as in more obviously tendentious efforts but remains rather more obscured (and hence respectable): "It is spread out upon the earth, and people do not see it" (*GThom.* 113). The ideological force of the hypothesis in this case is very similar to that of feminist or environmentalist or black rewritings of history: it signifies both an effort to escape a certain bondage and as such offers a legible signature of the present times; it simultaneously occludes its own insights, encoding in its very solutions the structural characteristics it aims to erase. In this case, the projection of postmodern or, differently, hippie assumptions onto the world of the present or the past will alike promote insularity, nostalgia, passivity; it will exacerbate, in the end, the very sociopolitical helplessness that these approaches aspire to address.

Lest this characterization appear unremittingly negative, I should note that I think the projection of contemporary concerns onto the past is both inevitable and in many ways positive. On the one hand, the task of the historian is probably less to present the past as it was and more to present the past to the present in terms that will be meaningful *for* the present: thus it is an act of ideological translation. The very popularity of the itinerancy hypothesis attests to its success in investing the past with meaningful or comprehensible terms of reference. The identification of this subtext does not in any way refute the hypothesis. One can hope, however, that such a reading will render the hypothesis a little more transparent, a little more understandable, and, ultimately, will help divest it of its magic and allow it to be considered more temperately, on its own merits.

Olive press

"For John came neither eating bread nor drinking wine, and you say: He has a demon." (Luke 7:33)

3.
THE PROBLEM WITH
ITINERANT PREACHERS

SOME CRITICS OF Theissen's view of itinerancy, especially in regard either to details or to its theoretical backbone, have provided more or less compelling criticisms of some features of his work. I have discussed the ideological subtexts of the itinerancy hypothesis, both in its original manifestation in the work of Harnack and in its more contemporary forms. Yet, so far, no concerted effort has been made here to demonstrate the actual inadequacy of the hypothesis. Tendentious though it may be, substantial direct consideration needs to be given to the way in which the itinerancy thesis treats its (ostensible) data. This attention necessarily includes both the treatment of general historical data by the sociological methods employed in such scholarship, as well as its treatment of the direct evidence for itinerancy: the Gospel and *Didache* texts themselves and the sayings tradition on which these texts appear to be based. It could very well be that, tendentious or ill theorized as the hypothesis is, it is nevertheless securely attested in the evidentiary record. In fact, however, this is not the case.

Methodological Shortcomings

Since the early 1990s Theissen's hypothesis has received substantial criticism or modification. His work pays scant attention to source-critical distinctions and to the relative age of the traditions under examination. The itinerancy hypothesis has also been criticized on the grounds that the poverty and homelessness enjoined by Q and the synoptic tradition as a whole probably reflect a rationalization of involuntary destitution rather than an exhortation to adopt it deliberately. Many (too many!) scholars have criticized Theissen's Cynic analogy and the thesis of peripatetic Cynic preachers responsible for the radical ethos of the tradents of Q. In some respects, the Cynic thesis represents a regressive move away from the properly sociological aspects of the earlier investigations of itinerancy, as it shows a tendency to regard ideological influences or parallels per se as a sufficient illumination of developments in ethos; concrete and material context is not sufficiently stressed.[1] Nevertheless, the comparison with the Cynic movement at least offers a strongly analogous model from the contemporary culture, free of the numinous associations that scholars are often liable to attribute to Judaism (and of course free from the scholarly tendency to protect Christianity's pedigree by emphasizing Jewish roots at the expense of other influences), from which one may make inferences about the functions and motives behind ancient countercultural movements. Finally, Richard Horsley has argued that Theissen's structural functionalism is an inappropriate sociological vehicle with which to examine a society characterized to its core by conflict, and he advocates in its place a "conflict model" (Horsley 1989).

The inability of these critiques to provide plausible alternatives should not blind us to their ultimate accuracy. Theissen's initial postulation of itinerants uses the evidentiary texts in a fashion largely innocent of sophisticated distinctions between early and secondary or redactional materials. Although this criticism does not apply to later itinerancy-oriented analyses of Q, the fact that the classic form of the thesis was formulated devoid of such considerations in the first place is highly problematic: an uncritical reading of the texts serves as the basis for a postulate that is then applied as a given to more critical readings of the texts in question. As it happens, Q's literary history has been pushed back considerably by recent studies, and its tradents have at least in some scholarship been associated with a sector of the population assumed to be reasonably literate (see Kloppenborg 2000). We are no longer able to assume that Q specifically, or the sayings tradition in general, represents a deposit of mixed oral lore, communicated by largely illiterate yokels or by a bucolic, if disaffected, peasantry. Nor can we assume, in the face of such evidence of rhetorical deliberation, that the material preserved in Q is an unselfconscious and transparent reflection of the behavior of the people who did the preserving. This incertitude might in fact suggest, at least on its face, that Q's rhetoric of uprootedness is precisely that: rhetoric.

At the least, the question implies that more sophisticated literary studies of Q will stand at odds with the assumptions of Theissen, rather than as a supplement to them; that the recognition of the literary and even intellectual character of the document, possibly right from its inception, will militate against the assumption that rural beggars formed the original nucleus of the Q community. The argument that occupies this chapter, therefore, is that the itinerancy hypothesis is fundamentally flawed and inadequate in a number of critical respects, both sociological and evidentiary.

Horsley's claim that Theissen's version of the itinerancy hypothesis suffers from serious methodological and theoretical defects I would generally affirm. Little or no methodological framework is established for working with any kind of precision from the itinerancy hypothesis to the texts in which it purportedly is manifested. That is, Theissen never bothers to articulate a firm theory of the relationship between literary texts and their social contexts, between the production of the written word and the concrete social realities in which it is produced.[2] Theissen's distinction between, and discussion of, "analytic," "constructive," and "comparative" types of evidence might suggest otherwise, but in fact these categories in no way depend upon any particular broad understanding of text-context relationships, designating instead particular categories of evidence that tend to be read by Theissen in much the same way,[3] that is, as more or less literal and transparent descriptions of what people are actually doing (White 1986:253 and n. 12). Moreover, the argument from the texts is somewhat circular. An initial insight, itinerancy, determines the fashion in which radical-sounding synoptic material of various types will be read. Such a reading, of course, then provides the evidence for the postulated itinerants in the first place. The texts, in other words, whether those drawn upon for analytic, constructive, or comparative conclusions, do not evince itinerancy until one has assumed itinerancy. Where does the assumption stem from? In some measure, obviously, the material associated with the Mission Charge in Q (esp. Q 9:57—10:16) suggests some practice of travel, associated with some ethos of mission. But the precise character of this travel and its association with a particular lifestyle is not clearly or obviously elaborated in these texts; I would suggest that the details of this lifestyle stem in fact from Theissen's imagination. This kind of tautology is in many cases inevitable when our primary sources for reconstructing a social world are literary. Still, by starting with some kind of conceptual clarity about the relation of ideology to social location and indicating from evidence extraneous to the texts at issue what the salient details of that social location might have been, we can reduce this circularity considerably.

In this connection, Horsley is entirely correct to note that nearly all of the discussion of itinerancy, although sociological in essence, seems to eschew developed sociological theorizing. Theissen assumes the appropriateness of his structural functionalism; he does not demonstrate it, as Horsley indicates at some length. Those who have adopted and adapted his thesis have failed in this regard even more profoundly, barely even recognizing the theoretical groundwork on which Theissen's sociology of the Jesus movement is based.[4] Part of this theoretical innocence stems from the quite admirable desire to let the facts speak for themselves. Admirable indeed but quite naive: the facts are not properly sociological in nature but literary, and require interpretation if they are to generate sociological or even historical conclusions. Such an interpretation can be neither coherent nor convincing without a sufficient theoretical basis by way of justification. That structural functionalism cannot serve as such a basis is by no means evident, although Horsley goes some way toward showing its broad weaknesses; what *is* evident is that structural functionalism cannot be assumed to constitute such a basis.

Horsley's work, nonetheless, cannot stand as an adequate alternative to Theissen's hypothesis. Horsley does offer considerable justification for the model he adopts. But although his work at least gives sociological theorizing its proper place and stresses the conflict involved in the production of Q rather than its function in terms of the orderly working of an oppressive society, Horsley fails to apply this basic theoretical framework to any concrete social context. As a result, his social reconstruction of the people behind Q and of the aspirations reflected in their countercultural language is unconvincing. Horsley places too much stock in the continued applicability and explanatory value of a "prophetic" conception of the Q people. He argues that they represent a Jewish "renewal movement." The prophets depicted in the Hebrew Bible, however, are a type that had passed into oblivion many centuries before Q was composed and can have little relevance (I would go so far as to say no relevance) for understanding either the conditions that generated Q's radical ethos or even for understanding the content of that ethos. This objection is valid even if the Q people actually did think of themselves in terms of the Israelite prophets, for this imagination can only have been of the character of an analogy. But because Horsley invokes a theological category of unquestionable pedigree—prophet—he is able to slough off the hard work involved in finding a specific and concrete context for Q and its project.[5] As with Theissen's invocation of charisma, a vague and theologically resonant category is offered in lieu of a genuinely convincing social history. At issue is what the Q people were doing and saying in first-century Galilee, not several-centuries-old behavior that they happened to valorize.[6] Horsley's more atemporal conceptualization of the behavior of the Jesus movement as an effort at renewal explains nothing. Nevertheless, his concern to preface his work with a theoretical and methodological justification is obviously a step in the right direction, as is his preference for an emphasis on conflict rather than on adaptation.

A Realistic Context?

The absence of an appropriate theoretical basis for the itinerancy hypothesis (and most other social reconstructions of the Q people) manifests itself most clearly and damningly in the numerous defects of the itinerancy hypothesis as it now stands, inadequacies in its concrete conceptualization. The overall picture is romantic without being realistic. We are told of wandering charismatic radicals, cast in the Old Testament prophetic mold. Little is said, however, by way of plausible accountings for their behavior. Other than the rather vaguely applied Cynic analogy, we are not really told how such itinerancy could be possible in the context of first-century Palestine (or particularly first-century Galilee, where Q is usually imagined to have been composed). Again, what are the concrete features of the behavior of these specific itinerants, and how do these features relate to the specific characteristics of the text(s) they are alleged to have authored? The Cynic analogy does not tell us; it only informs us that (vaguely) analogous behavior was taking place in different social contexts.

This general failure to conceive of context realistically involves two main problems. First, what kinds of circumstances would have made itinerancy possible or impossible, plausible or implausible for the itinerants in the concrete context of first-century Galilee? Does the geography and demography of the area imply the possibility or likelihood of extended travels? Would these travels have involved longer or shorter distances? What kinds of technology would have been necessary for such travels? Would the itinerants have required and used sandals, and walked by foot, or would they have traveled with pack animals? Did such travelers attach themselves to other parties on the road? Or would the distances involved have been so negligible as to make all of these considerations superfluous? If the itinerants carried no provisions with them, what did they eat while on the road? Were they dependent for hospitality in transit as well as when they arrived at a given destination? Would the authorities, local, Herodian, or Roman, have permitted the behavior that Theissen describes? Would Cynic-like figures have been tolerated in such an environment? Where and how did these characters propagate their message: houses, village squares, marketplaces?

And what about the alleged sympathizers who would possibly have had to support these missionaries financially and at the very least would have had to be willing to hear their message? Anthropologically or sociologically, what evidence can we marshal to suggest how, precisely, first-century Palestinian villagers would have received destitute strangers? Would the pervasive patron/client and honor/shame value system make villagers unlikely to give a hearing to people who clearly had nothing to offer by way of recompense? What could possibly motivate people to listen never mind actually fall in with, these fanatics? Finally, if, as so many claim, Galilean villagers lived at near-subsistence levels, even frequently falling below, from where did they get the money, food, or whatever they had to support these preachers?

This brings me to the second, quite related, problem: the setting. While some effort is made by the advocates of early Jesus movement itinerancy to link the radical sayings of Q to a setting in life, the setting proposed is really a setting in the church: life beyond the Christian community is often neglected. Yes, Theissen talks of various "environmental" and "ecological" factors contributing to the role of the itinerants, but in fact the setting to which all of their literary activity is related is a setting exclusive to the tradents' lives as members of "the church." Only infrequently do scholars relate the sayings of Q, or, indeed, the peripatetic behavior of the early Jesus movement, to the conditions of the larger secular world of which even the churches were a part so that they become truly explanatory. This list of questions and objections is offered solely to make the point that the itinerancy hypothesis is not normally grounded in a careful investigation of the social realia of the period and place in which the itinerants are alleged to have existed. The hypothesis has not been sketched in enough detail to demonstrate even the possibility of such wandering preachers in the real social world of their day. Whether there is or is not a genuine textual warrant for positing radical itinerants in the earliest Jesus movement, the thesis remains inadequate at the conceptual level.

Textual and Evidentiary Weaknesses

As it turns out, the conceptual failings of the itinerancy hypothesis are only reinforced, rather than mitigated, by a consideration of its evidentiary basis. The one sure instance of repeated travel we have in the early textual record, Paul, cannot be cited by itinerancy proponents as evidence for their hypothesis. Paul quite clearly is associated with an urban environment, is interested in "community organization" rather than itinerancy as a lifestyle, and does not appear to share the "radical ethics" of the synoptic tradition (see Theissen 1982a:36–37, 40). Even such late-first-century texts as the *Didache*, the text that raised the likelihood of itinerants in the first place, fail to provide any strong evidence of itinerant radicals in the sense promoted by Theissen. Much earlier writings, for which such a postulate is even more unlikely given the lack of time for the Jesus movement to have established an international or translocal basis, show even fewer indices of actual itinerancy. An analysis of the texts on which the itinerancy hypothesis has been founded—the direct literary evidence of the Jesus movement—reveals that in addition to its ruinous methodological shortcomings, the itinerancy hypothesis is postulating something that the texts do not attest and that we therefore have no reason to assume ever existed.

The Evidence of the Didache

It was in Harnack's work on the *Didache* that the basics of the itinerancy hypothesis were first drawn out, and it is here in particular that one finds the most important clear evidence that there were such things as itinerants in the churches. Harnack's sketch is paradigmatic for the character of the itinerancy hypothesis as it developed over the course of the twentieth century: nearly all of its fundamental features recur in subsequent reconstructions. And in fact more recent advocates of itinerancy return again and again to the *Didache* as the text that best expresses the basic characteristics of ancient itinerancy and that best establishes the existence of itinerants. It is the (apparently) obvious and explicit appearance of itinerants in the *Didache* that allows us to be so confident that they may also lurk behind Q. As it turns out, however, the text of the *Didache* provides very little support for Harnack's—or Theissen's—overly tidy and romantic reconstruction of the situation.

Harnack's typology of "apostles, prophets, and teachers," which he considers to be an ancient classification of charismatic "office," and on the basis of which he sketches out greater and lesser degrees of peregrination and authority, is inconsistent with what the text actually says. Audet notes, for instance, that the threefold classification is nowhere connected in the *Didache* with any concept of hierarchy (Audet 1958:439); Paul's delineation of a hierarchy of "office" in 1 Cor 12:28 is situational and ad hoc, specifically designed to counter the Corinthians' claims to spiritual superiority in view of their proficiency at speaking in tongues.[7] Audet adds that the alleged "charisma" of the offices in the *Didache* is only attested for "prophets": it is only in connection with them—not with apostles and teachers—that we hear of speech "in the spirit" (*Did.* 11:7-9, 12; Audet 1958:439). In fact, one might go further than Audet: nowhere in the *Didache* is any threefold typology, as such, attested at all: in one place we hear only of teachers (*Did.* 11:1-2); elsewhere apostles and prophets (11:3); "those who come in the name of the Lord" (12:1); prophets and teachers (13:1-2); and prophets, teachers, bishops, and deacons (15:1-2; see Draper 1995:299). Nor are these offices rigorously distinguished from one another; the three terms in question appear to be interchangeable, at least in part. In the crucial chapter 11, for instance, we find that an apostle can be accused of being a pseudoprophet (11:5-6), while a prophet is characterized by his teaching activity (11:10).

The same kinds of objections might be made with respect to the supposed traveling activity of such figures. The text speaks repeatedly of
"coming" (ἐρχόμενος πρὸς ὑμᾶς) as a central activity under consideration in chapters 11–13. Yet this "coming" is connected explicitly with
teachers in 11:1-2, people whom Harnack considers to be sedentary, and
nowhere with prophets (but see 13:1), whom Harnack thinks are itinerant (also Niederwimmer 1977:156–57). It is clear, moreover, that the
author of the *Didache* did not view "coming" as synonymous with or
denotative of actual travel, for in 12:2 he feels the need to specify: "If the
one who comes is a traveler." Certainly, travel is sometimes at issue here:
the text's considerable discussion of how long "apostles" might stay and
how they are to be sent on their way (11:4-6), as well as comments about
the absorption and reception of other travelers (12:2-4), precludes any
contrary supposition. But the "coming" associated with these figures is
not itself intrinsically linked to itinerancy, and it is debatable whether
travel is the defining feature of their activity. Given these discrepancies,
it is far more likely that the author of the *Didache* used the verb *to come*
to denote appearance or manifestation, rather than actual geographical
travel.[8] The verb itself cannot, in any consistent way, specify or depict
itinerancy.

Much of the more sophisticated scholarship on the *Didache* since
Harnack has come up against the text's failure to speak explicitly of an
order of itinerants and local leaders, and has dealt with this, appropriately, by punishing the refractory text itself. Discrepancies between what
the text actually says and the image of a tripartite order of charismatics
are attributed to redactional layering of the text, which then is held to
reflect either changing estimations of the itinerants, differing descriptions of them, or shifts in the overall situation of the author. For
instance, in *Did.* 11:3 a discussion of "apostles and prophets" is opened,
but in chapter 13 (and see 15:1-2), the discussion has moved, without
comment, to "prophets and teachers." Working from the assumption
that these designations represent stable and relatively fixed offices, it
becomes necessary to posit a redactional shift between chapters 11 and
13, alongside concomitant changes in settings. The latter, supposedly
more sedentary, figures represent the focal interest of the later material
(for example, Niederwimmer 1977:161). The situation is similar for the
distinction between the passing hospitality to be accorded to "apostles"
(*Did.* 11:3-6; see 12:2) and the acceptance to be accorded those who seek
a permanent home (12:3-5; 13:1-2). Stephen Patterson regards this change
in topic as due to a shift in situation: while earlier material dealt with
itinerants, this material deals with refugees, perhaps from the (first)
Judean Revolt or from the later Bar Kochba rebellion (Patterson

1993a:176–77). That such a shift has taken place is also indicated, according to Patterson, by the differences in tone between chapters 11 and 13. The latter seems to accord a great deal of status to the itinerants and enunciates their worthiness to benefit from this status, while the former aims to restrict the legitimacy of their claims, whether these be claims to authority or claims to material benefit.

John Kloppenborg refers to the *Didache* as a "manifestly stratified composition" (1996b:24, n. 93). Jonathan Draper, similarly, accuses even advocates of itinerancy, such as Kretschmar and Theissen, of "confusion" generated by a failure to take redactional stages into account in their reading of the text (1991:348–49 and n. 7). Yet Draper describes the redactional history of the *Didache* in a fashion almost entirely opposite that of Patterson. He argues that the instructions on apostles (11:3-6) represent the earliest segment of the text, while those regarding prophets are the latest redaction.[9] His argument rests on the observation that the instructions concerning apostles have a marked formal similarity to the remainder of the document, introduced with the stock phrase "now about/concerning . . . do this:" (see 7:1; 9:1) and exhibiting "brevity" and "casuistic development," while the instructions regarding prophets are detailed, vivid, and self-contradictory. The injunctions about correct teaching in 11:1-2 he considers a later gloss on 11:3-6, made, however, before the instructions on prophets were added (1991:353).

It is worth questioning, however, how necessary such an hypothesis of the literarily stratified character of this section of the text really is: the material on travelers in chapters 11–13 (and 15:1-2) is fairly coherent thematically and formally, and its jumpiness probably stems more from the amassing and incorporation of earlier tradition to buttress or nuance the author's views rather than from a multiplicity of textual redactions. Such a literary procedure can also be seen in the text's various allusions to the Old Testament and to older sayings tradition regardless of whether this material is drawn from independent tradition or from the texts of the Synoptic Gospels: in either case, it still represents the usage of materials predating the composition of the text and the issues addressed by it. The resulting pastiche style is relatively predictable in a document of this sort. Jonathan Draper asserts: "a community rule evolves by trial and error, by erasing words and phrases, by inserting new words or phrases above the line or in the margin, which are later incorporated into the text. This process is graphically displayed in the manuscript of the *Community Rule* [Manual of Discipline] from Qumran. Certainly whole new sections may have been added from time to time, but one should not hypothesize a wholesale, consistent composition for every change."[10]

This is not to say that the *Didache* is not an obviously composite document: its incorporation of an earlier integral writing—the Two Ways document—is practically incontestable.[11] But at issue is not whether earlier materials of various sorts (including both complete written documents and fragmentary oral traditions) have been incorporated into the *Didache* but whether there has been overarching and tendentious redactional modification of the materials in chapters 11–13 (and 15:1-2) from divergent perspectives at some point after these instructions had been committed in writing to the text of the *Didache*.[12] This issue really boils down to two important questions: Are these instructions self-contradictory? And, if so, does that contradiction reveal stages of development in the significance of the figures they describe? The evidence of the text, in my view, suggests a negative answer to both. Indeed, the instance where we can be most sure of the *Didache*'s use of earlier traditions—the Two Ways section—actually supports a view of the document as a compilation of earlier materials. It is certain that this Two Ways schema significantly predates the composition of the *Didache:* something like a prototype of it exists in the Qumran Manual of Discipline (1QS), which may have been composed as early as 100 B.C.E. (Vermes 1990:61) and under completely different circumstances than the *Didache.* We therefore cannot regard the incorporation of the Two Ways material in the *Didache* as anything like a "*Didache*[1]." In general, we need not regard aporias (seams) in the text (which may indicate the use of traditional materials), therefore, as necessarily due to redactional levels—that is, stratification—within the *Didache* itself. Rather, as in the Synoptic Gospels, a whole shifting and variegated mass of perpetually modified traditions has been worked together into a single document: aporias in the *Didache* need not be treated in and of themselves any differently than analogous aporias are treated when they appear in, say, the Gospel of Mark.[13]

Nor do Draper's claims about the way community rules develop entirely support his reconstruction of the temporal sequence behind this material. Although we can assume that he is correct to regard community rules as especially susceptible to revisions, it is not necessary that these revisions take the form of later glosses to or corrections of a basic completed text. On the contrary, we can also regard such rules as developing by incorporating materials already formulated in the life of the community into a larger fixed document that exhibits a certain amount of internal coherence. Hence, material that formally matched the compositional characteristics of the document as a whole might be regarded as later than slightly idiosyncratic sections (especially if these idiosyncratic sections do not exhibit the consistent coherence among themselves that would be the necessary and sufficient basis for a stratification hypothesis). Such a process matches the *Didache*'s pastiche style. And it avoids the postulation of glosses or redactions that serve only to contradict material already in place and subsequently left intact, which would be an unusual and counterintuitive redactional process. As a general rule, we should prefer reconstructions of stages in a document's compositional history that postulate a lesser, rather than a greater, degree of self-contradiction in the resultant text. This is something of a truism: additions add to the meaning of themes already contained in the document, normally, rather than deliberately contradicting them. If contradiction of traditional concepts were required—and it does seems to have been required in ancient Christian writing often enough—the most expeditious thing to do would be to omit the offending material and replace it with something else.

These considerations do not entirely address Draper's specific claim that *Did.* 11:7-12 (apparently) was added after 11:3-6 was already in place in the text. Two further considerations militate against this particular conclusion. First, the very fact that 11:3 begins with the stock phrase used to introduce advice elsewhere in the *Didache* ("Now concerning the . . . do thus") is an indication that the material in 11:3-6 is a function of the redaction that embraces the whole document. Unless all of 11:7-12, and likely chapters 12 and 13 as well, represent extensive glosses, 11:3-6 would appear to be a redactional composition opening this general topic, which is then fleshed out by older, traditional materials. It is notable that 11:3 does in fact refer to prophets, thus anticipating the material in 11:7-12 (and chaps. 12 and 13); Draper's effort to explain this reference away as a gloss begs the question. Second, the argument that 11:3-6 is something of a redactional clasp is supported by the fact that 11:7 is linked to a foregoing assertion about baptism (10:7), both verbally and thematically. In 10:7 the prophets are to be allowed to hold the Eucharist however they see fit, even if their procedure is at odds with the formal instructions laid down in 9:1—10:6. *Didache* 11:7 then reiterates the caution and latitude to be extended to these "prophets" in a slightly broader context: do not examine any prophet who is speaking in the Spirit. Indeed, 11:9, which specifies that a prophet who orders a meal in the spirit is a false prophet, may reflect an original connection with the material on the Lord's Supper, although in the form in which we now have this proposition, its significance has been generalized. In any case, 11:7-12 seems to be linked to and flow out of the specific eucharistic injunction at 10:7. This may serve as an indication that the *Didache*'s redaction has here modified and reorganized—has intruded itself upon—already extant material, which included specific guidelines on the Eucharist and related injunctions about testing prophets generally.

Hence it is unlikely that 11:3-6 predates, as Draper suggests, the instructions in 11:7-12 (and chaps. 12 and 13). Moreover, the redactional opening formulation of this intrusion serves as an indication that neither did this intrusion occur as a later reinterpretation of an earlier draft of the *Didache* but rather arose at the point at which the document was compiled.[14]

And finally, it does not appear plausible to claim, as Patterson does, that the temporal or redactional rift in this material occurs between 11:3—12:2a, on the one hand, and 12:2b—13:7, on the other, with the former section being the earlier.[15] Such a view, in Patterson's formulation, assumes that older instructions dealing with itinerant charismatics have been retained after such charismatics ceased to be an issue at all— hence the possibility of such positive exhortations to generosity in chapter 13. These instructions have been modified by the inclusion of rules governing the acceptance of refugees from the Judean Revolt of either 66–70 c.e. or 132–135 c.e. Not only does this claim presume the peculiar process of textual stratification criticized above, in which later materials are postlaminated onto an original composition, it also assumes a tendency in the *Didache* to include material that no longer has any point of reference, and indeed claims that a reversal of the sense of that older material by a redactional addition (that is, chap. 13's apparent high estimation of the no-longer-extant itinerants) was made precisely because it no longer had any real referent! If in fact a consideration of wanderers had become outdated or was not imagined to refer to any meaningful current process, we would imagine that such matters would simply be eliminated from the text or left intact without modification. And indeed, the manuscript tradition Patterson cites to support the view of a supposedly original text ending at 12:2—the Coptic manuscript— actually suggests that at a later stage of the document's transmission history, this is precisely what happened: specific injunctions dealing with support of travelers had lost their relevance and so were not copied out. But what is especially notable in regard to Patterson's thesis is that the complexes in 11:3-6 and in chapter 12 are thematically, formally, and stylistically almost identical, for instance, in their use of participles, use of ἐστιν ("is" or "to be") as a copula, frequent use of present and future tenses, profuse use of second-position conjunctions, abundant use of negatives (οὐκ or μή), copious use of "if" (εἰ), and the frequent use of ἐάν ("if") plus subjunctive. Note the strong parallels in the Table 1.

This parallelism at least suggests that the two texts derive from the same hand. Of course, it is quite possible that one of the segments was modeled on the other by a later hand. It seems, however, extraordinarily unlikely that a secondary author would be able to replicate the style of

Didache
11:3-6 and 12:1-5

3 In the matter of apostles and prophets, act this way, according to the ordinance of the gospel.

4 Let every apostle who comes to you be received as the Lord.	1a Let everyone who comes in the name of the Lord be received,
7 Do not test any prophet who speaks in the Spirit, and do not judge him, for all sins will be forgiven, but this sin will not be forgiven.	1b and then, when you have taken stock of him, you will know—for you will have insight—what is right and false.
5 He shall stay <only> one day, or, if need be, another [day] too. If he stays three days, he is a false prophet.	2 If the person who comes is just passing through, help him as much as you can, but he shall not stay with you more than two or three days—if that is necessary.
	3 If he wants to settle in with you, though, and he is a craftsman, let him work and eat.
6a When the apostle leaves, let him receive nothing but [enough] bread [to see him through] until he finds lodging.	4 If he has no craft, take care in your insight that no Christian live with you in idleness.
6b If he asks for money, he is a false prophet.	5 If he is unwilling to do what that way calls for, he is using Christ to make a living. Be on your guard against people like this.

Table 1: A comparison of two segments of the *Didache* often regarded to have been produced by different hands.

his source so well and even more unlikely that he would want to, especially if he is addressing, as Patterson claims, an entirely different issue (refugees rather than itinerants). This problem is compounded by the fact that, according to Patterson's hypothesis, when the secondary author wishes, unaccountably, to return to the outdated matter of itinerancy, he opts to do so in a fashion that does not parallel the foregoing material and that is not juxtaposed with it. Instead, he erects a strong parallelism and a juxtaposition with the very different matter of refugees (12:2b-5) and then returns to the issue of itinerants at a later point

(13:1-7) without invoking that parallelism or imitation. Patterson's reconstruction of the textual history of this section of the *Didache* as well, then, is probably inaccurate.

If on the basis of these considerations, we assume, with Niederwimmer, that a single hand has amassed the material in chapters 11–13 but has in this process used already extant traditions, a plausible compilation history of the *Didache* can be attempted. If the material in chapter 13, which advocates strong generosity to be extended to "prophets" (or the poor), had been written later than the material that restricts such generosity (especially chapter 11), its very generality would contradict the earlier material. The addition of these chapters would be a statement that, in essence, the original strictures in 11:3-6 (and 11:7-12) were wrong: one should, instead of being cautious with such figures, shower them with goods. If so, one wonders why such preredactional, supposedly older advice was not simply omitted altogether: there would be no reason to include such traditions in the document if one wanted to argue precisely the opposite. On the other hand, if chapter 13 either predates or is contemporary with the strictures in chapter 11, these latter instructions can be viewed as a supplement to, a detailed and more conservative elaboration of, the advice already given, rather than an outright contradiction. Yes, this newer material is saying, do show generosity to those to whom it is due, but make sure you're not being duped: test their authenticity on the basis of their behavior, and limit the extent of your generosity within reasonable bounds. Note also that at least some of the contents of chapter 11 include, in spite of reservations about being swindled, a major assumption shared by the other material (that is, esp. 10:7; 13:1-7): the sanctity of expressions of the Spirit. Hence 11:7, in spite of what appears to be a pressing concern with establishing the credentials of prophets, forbids people to test them while they are "speaking in Spirit." This segment of the document (chaps. 11–13; and 15:1-2) probably evolved as follows.

Stage 1

Earlier and traditional (or preredactional) community standards are reflected in 11:7-12; 13:1-7; and 15:1-2. All of this material concerns the respect to be accorded to particular distinguished roles within the community: prophets (11:7; 13:1; 15:1-2), teachers (13:2; 15:1-2), the poor (13:4; 13:5?), and bishops and deacons (15:1-2). As Draper points out, charismatic gifts in the kind of "strong group–low grid" community implied by the *Didache* are treated with respectful reservation: "Societies with strongly defined group boundaries tend to view spirit-possession as dangerous, if potentially beneficial, and to limit it to a specialist class"

(Draper 1995:296–97; see 1995:287–91). Respect is also urged for teachers, who are, in the language of this material, at times indistinguishable from prophets (see, for instance, 11:10; also 15:1-2). All of this material tends to conflate teaching with prophecy; these two roles are also specifically singled out as compatible with bishops and deacons: apostles are not mentioned. *Didache* 15:1-2 is also linked to the discussion of prophets in chapters 11 and 13 in terms of wording, as well as explicit cross-references. The motive clause used to urge respect for both sets of offices is identical: "for they are" . . . "your high priests" (13:3) or "your honored ones" (15:2). And as the bishops and deacons are like the prophets and teachers, so the prophets and teachers are like high priests. In all of these texts, a positive estimation, translatable into both respect and generosity, is urged for figures who, we must assume, while exercising a special role in the community, have not consolidated their authority. An effort at concretizing and formalizing intracommunity structures is in progress.[16]

Stage 2

The redactional prehistory of these segments is not important for our purposes. Nevertheless, it should be noted that even here, prior to the compositional redaction of the *Didache,* some tendentious intervention has already taken place, which serves to unify even older fragments into a relatively coherent argument. Candidates for redactional creation at the hand of an earlier collector include 13:2, 3c ("for they are your high priests"), 4;[17] and 15:1-2. An original association of 10:7 and 11:7, even if only at an oral level, may antedate these interventions, as may an association of the material in 9:5—10:6 with that in chapter 14.

Stage 3

The redactional level, that of the collector who put together the various traditions into what is now the *Didache,* is comprised, in our section, not only by the actual incorporation of the material but also by the addition of the two parallel sets of instructions charted in Table 1, 11:3-6 and 12:1-5 (against Niederwimmer 1977:149). These additions serve to bracket, in chiastic fashion, the older set of traditional rules at 12:7-12 that actually pertain to how to recognize charisma and how to respect and reward those who possess it. This new, redactional material, however, shifts the emphasis to the issue of hospitality and the disbursement of "church funds." The new material is linked to the earlier traditions by its formal concern with "apostles," identifiable functionaries, and also by the issue of giving. In the earlier material dealing with giving (chap. 13), however, the question is what to do with surplus resources, not how to conserve them. All of this material, at any rate, has been brought together under the rubric of a broad concern with internal organization and, specifically, links the matter of hospitality and support both to the treatment of an emergent class of official functionaries and to the reception of "foreign" Christians in general (chap. 12). The differentia of specific offices, and even the "prophets" themselves, are not in fact at issue here. Instead they come under consideration as a factor within a larger discussion of "giving."

Stage 4

It is unclear where in this sequence 11:1-2 belongs. It may have been added by the same hand that combined the instructions on prophecy to the eucharistic material, that is, the immediately preredactional compilation of church instructions. It shares with that stage a focus on teachers and on testing gifts. And since it precedes the typical περὶ δέ ("in the matter of") redactional introduction in 11:3, verses 1-2 would be an uncharacteristic—but hardly impossible!—departure for the redactor. Its reference back to "whoever comes and teaches you all these things" need not refer to the Two Ways (which would certainly make the material redactional): it could equally refer to the foregoing instructions on liturgical matters. But, at the same time, this short section also displays the terminology of "reception," which is echoed in the redactional 11:4 and 12:1.[18]

To reiterate, this reconstruction is not intended to be a stratification proposal so much as an articulation of the sources behind this section of the *Didache*, which is to be regarded as a unitary composition making use of disparate materials. It yields, then, the following chronological sequence (see Niederwimmer 1977:151–52; 1989:67 and n. 19):

1. *9:5—10:6; 14:1-3 (and 7:1b—8:3).* These rules for the Eucharist, in tandem with the instructions on baptism and fasting (7:1b—8:3), exist independently but alongside such material as the Two Ways source and perhaps the apocalyptic speech in chapter 16.
2. *11:7-12; 13:1, 3ab, 5-7.* Loose instructions on the treatment of prophets are also in use among this group.[19]
3. *13:2, 3c, 4; 15:1-2 (11:1-2?).* The community rules for the Eucharist, baptism, and fasting (no. 1 in this list) are combined with the instructions about prophets (no. 2 in this list), perhaps on the basis of catchword association ("prophets") or perhaps because both represent community-sanctioned sets of rules. This combination breaks up the unity of the instructions on baptism, into which the instructions on prophets are interpolated in two large chunks. The traditional material on prophecy is further embellished by this hand by the addition of 13:2, 3c, 4 and 15:1-2, as a conclusion.[20] Possibly 11:1-2 belongs to this stage as well.

4. *11:3-6; 12:1-5 (and 7:1a; 9:1-4).* Using a similar technique, the Didachist himself, in addition to combining the set of community rules (no. 3 in this list) with a traditional moral exhortation (the Two Ways) and perhaps concluding the whole package—appropriately enough—with a short apocalyptic speech (chap. 16), adds his two cents' worth to this set of rules by interjecting comments on the provision of hospitality into the discussion: 11:3-6 and 12:1-5. He also adds a more detailed—and slightly redundant—description of the proper way to carry out the Eucharist at 9:1-4, introduced here by the characteristic περὶ δέ (now, concerning) formula, and uses the same formula in 7:1a to form a redactional clasp between the Two Ways material and the more specific community rules.[21]

The literary stratification of the *Didache*—its composition, as a document, in layers—is to be rejected in favor of a model involving the incorporation into one literary redaction of various, and various types of, preexisting traditions. Propositions that it is stratified may in fact depend on the itinerancy hypothesis, in that they see contradictions between segments of chapters 11–13 only because of the assumption that apostles, prophets, and teachers are in fact distinct offices, an assumption not actually borne out by the text. At the very least, such stratifications support the assumptions of the itinerancy hypothesis by obscuring the degree to which these roles are interchangeable in this text and by focusing attention on the roles allegedly being described here. If we assume, conversely, that this text is unified by a coherent redactional intention, however, it may turn out that the material does not actually provide any evidence for the practice of itinerancy in earliest Christianity.

So what is this coherent redactional intention that supposedly unifies this material? And how are the apparent aporias and topical shifts in the text, caused by the incorporation of earlier materials, to be understood as contributing to a common viewpoint? In fact, there is considerable continuity in the description of the figures and the main issues associated with them in chapters 11–13 (and 15:1-2). Both the traditional material and the redactional additions to it deal with—and are thus linked by—the same broad issue: the formal organization of church groupings, that is, rules not so much simply for the conduct of Christians (already provided by various moral exhortations and even liturgical rules), but for the management of institutions (or incipient institutions) that are in the process of growing out of organizations of Christians and that have been made problematic precisely by their relative novelty.

The main issue in the traditional material (everything prior to the intervention of the Didachist) is that of the treatment and definition of an emergent clergy, or, more precisely, of a developing distinction between clergy and laity. The issue is neither the strict definition of official roles from one another nor a conflict between one set of offices and another (that is, itinerant offices such as prophets and perhaps teachers, and sedentary offices such as bishops and deacons). This is apparent in the text's failure to distinguish sharply between prophets and teachers, its imputation to prophets of a teaching role, and especially its chain of association between priesthood, prophets and teachers, and bishops and deacons. The same focus is also evident in the text's consideration (15:1-2) of bishops and deacons as well as prophets and teachers (apostles, the best candidate for an actual office implying travel, are not dealt with at all in this preredactional material): it is not merely charismatics or figures allegedly external to the group who are under consideration here.[22]

If we turn to the Pauline letters and the (pseudo-Pauline) Pastorals, a trajectory in which this set of issues can be located immediately presents itself. Paul's letters make use of all of the descriptors of behavior referred to in this material: teachers (Rom 2:20-21; 1 Cor 12:28-29), prophets (Rom 12:6; 1 Cor 12:10, 28-29; 13:2, 8; 14:6, 22, 29, 32, 37-39; 1 Thess 5:20), bishops (Phil 1:1), and deacons (Rom 16:1; 2 Cor 11:23; Phil 1:1). All of these functions, and even the titles applied to them, must therefore have existed from a very early date. But it is clear that such figures, in the authentic Pauline letters, do not in any way represent fixed offices or anything like a distinct clergy (see Meeks 1983:134–36). The impression we derive from 1 Cor 14:29-32, for instance, is that, while special claims may be being made on the basis of such gifts, prophecy in particular is an open prerogative of all of the members of the group and pertains in no way to the overall structure or organization of the group but rather to its behavior in the context of liturgy: "If there is no one to interpret [prophetic utterance], let them be silent *in church* and speak to themselves and to God. Let *two or three* prophets speak, and let the others weigh what is said. . . . For *you can all prophesy* one by one, so that all may learn and all be encouraged" (1 Cor 14:28-29, 31, emphasis added).[23] The same is certainly true of "deacons," and more arguably, of "bishops" as well (see Meeks 1983:79). Meeks notes, against Harnack, that a rigid classification of the roles here is not supported by the text: in particular, no sharp lines are drawn by Paul between local and translocal authority, or between charismatic and noncharismatic authority (1983:60, 136).

But a very different situation emerges once we get to the Pastorals. By this time, church offices are sufficiently fixed and formal that the author feels the need to list, at some length, the qualifications for those who desire the jobs of bishop (1 Tim 3:1-7; Titus 1:7-9) and deacon (1 Tim 3:8-13). The letter to Titus goes so far as to subsume the bishopric under the more general category of "elders," whom Titus (fictively) is told to "appoint" (καθίστημι; Titus 1:5). "The church order which the [Pastoral] letters advance is designed to strengthen the church in its battle with heresy. The church is described as 'the household of God' (1 Tim. 3:15; cf. 2 Tim. 2:20) in which the bishop serves 'as God's household manager' (Tit. 1:7)" (Malherbe 1983:98). Thus the church order being described here is not being generated or implemented ad hoc from the imagination of the author. The Pastoral letters in no way fix ecclesiastical roles, nor do they feel any need to encourage respect for or recognition of such roles. Rather, the offices in question are taken for granted in the author's effort to fix *who* should fill such established roles. He discusses, in other words, what qualifications are most suitable for offices whose functions are already taken for granted: "if someone does not know how to manage his own household, how can he take care of God's church?" (1 Tim 3:5). The author is probably involved in some kind of power struggle (see esp. 1 Tim 6:3-5, 20-21; 2 Tim 3:1-9; Titus 1:9; 3:9-10), but that power struggle is being fought on the battlefield of ecclesiastical offices already in place: the victorious group will be the one that manages successfully to control the established government of the church.

The preredactional material in *Didache* 11:7-12; 13:1-7; 15:1-2 provides us a fascinating glimpse of a stage almost perfectly equidistant between the relatively unorganized structuration of the Pauline churches during the apostle's own lifetime and the fixity of the institutional apparatus that had evolved by the time of the Pastoral letters. In the (preredactional) *Didache*, the broadest and most central type of the behaviors described appears to be prophecy: this term serves as the overall rubric guiding the discussion. The term, as Audet's observations suggest, is intrinsically linked to being "in the spirit," that is, being possessed by the word of God (so also Niederwimmer 1977:156). *Prophet* is a general designation, and what it designates is not an office or even a lifestyle but a charismatic authority and ability to speak in the spirit, to state the will of God. This understanding has already surfaced in Paul's use of the term, and while there is no particular reason to suppose that Paul's designation is synonymous with that of the *Didache*, the text itself bears out such an identification, especially *Did.* 11:9, 12, which assume ecstatic utterance but indicate that the contents of such utterances are not themselves predetermined. What prophets do, then, is teach the word of God; as such they are teachers, although in their (self-)designation, they are making special claims to charisma. What this suggests is that church offices are growing out of the specialization of charisma: as Draper suggests, charismatic activity is viewed with suspicion and associated—in apparent contrast to Paul's practice—with a specialist class. That a group might not have a prophet (*Did.* 13:4) would be inconceivable for Paul, simply because for Paul "prophecy" is a type of behavior (albeit associated with a "gift") rather than a type of person.

The thrust of the advice given in this preredactional material is to normalize the role of such a distinct class. Hence, since they do represent an identifiable group and additionally since they are defined by charisma —rather than decisions made by the church in the church's own interests— some care must be taken to distinguish "true" prophets from "false" ones (11:8b).[24] There is still, however, sufficient respect for the charismatic gift in its own right that "testing" of prophets is forbidden (11:7). If we assume that originally 13:1 followed immediately upon 11:12,[25] 13:1 provides a fitting conclusion to this segment and a transition into 13:2-7: having established who a true prophet is, it implies, this is how we should treat such a figure. Even if the phrasing "wishing to stay with you," echoed in 12:3, does not represent a redactional gloss to this segment, it is very unlikely, given its immediate argumentative context, that the phrase suggests itinerancy on the part of these prophets. Since the question is their truth or falsity, the assumption at issue in 13:1 is almost certainly the establishment of someone *as* a prophet in the group, rather than someone's settling down with the group after a period of travel.[26] Having offered rules to establish the parameters of the specialist group (11:7-12), chapter 13 offers marks of distinction that accord the group special respect. They are to be given the "firstfruits." In spite of the reference to money in 13:7, we should probably take these injunctions as intended to be signs of respect rather than an institutionalization of actual support: the point is that the best of the group's produce should be reserved for the prophets, not that prophets must be paid any fixed amount.[27] Even more significant is the explanation or rationalization offered here for the respect and distinction to be accorded charismatics. A traditional (see Q 10:7; 1 Cor 9:13-14; 1 Tim 5:17-18) justification for feeding teachers—that the worker deserves his food (*Did.* 13:1-2)—is overshadowed by a new consideration: "for they [the prophets] are your *high priests.*" This specialized and liturgical role for prophets might also lurk behind the enigmatic reference in *Did.* 11:11 to enacting a "worldly mystery of the church," as well as behind the link between prophets and the Eucharist assumed in 10:7.

The other church roles in the process of hardening at this point are those of bishops and deacons, roles that existed as early as the time of Paul but with little fixity or broad authority. In 15:1-2 the compiler of the preredactional material exhorts the reader: "do not despise" bishops and deacons. As is the case with prophets, some concern is expressed here about the quality of those who fill such roles, but the advice given is general and stereotypical: it has none of the specificity of that given in the Pastorals. Instead, the issue here is the need to appoint such figures, that is, to maintain these functions in a consistent way, to ensure against their falling into desuetude, and to respect the individuals who fill them. It is surely notable that the rationale given for ensuring such respect and stability to the bishopric and deaconate is that "they also minister to you the ministry of the prophets and teachers" (15:1). It is by association with prophecy that an institutional role can be justified for bishops and deacons. Thus as charisma comes to be seen to pertain to a special class, this class then becomes the basis for the erection of a fixed institutional apparatus. As this process developed, the materials that laid out rules or practices for each particular role were drawn together by a preredactional compiler under the main theme of regularizing a developing clergy and administrative machinery.

The interests of the Didachist, both in his collection and incorporation of this material and in his additions to it, are relatively distinct from the concerns of the traditional material he uses. The main issue at this stage of the document's development is the use and disbursement of communally held church resources (as opposed to the resources of individual members of the group). The question revolves around money. It is the matter of finances, not of office, that unifies this final version of the text of chapters 11–13. *Didache* 11:3-6 concerns itself with hospitality; 11:7-12 with false charismatic demands for food or money; 12:1-5 returns to hospitality, with no office or distinct function in sight; and 13:1-7 specifies how prophets and teachers are to be rewarded. Thus it is under this thematic rubric that the Didachist incorporates the traditional material of 11:7-12; 13:1-7; and even 15:1-2. The discussion of how to distinguish true from false prophets in 11:7-12 is understood now in terms of prohibitions against demanding church resources, even if those demands are in the name of the Spirit (or under the authority of an official position). That the redactor sees the restrictions of 11:3-6 and those of 11:7-12 as representing similar problems emerges from his introduction to the cluster: "Now concerning the apostles *and prophets*" (11:3, emphasis added). Chapter 13 establishes the principle that clergy deserve church support, even if real prophets are no longer in view for the Didachist. The clergy in question—bishops and deacons—are then linked to this principle by the association of bishops and deacons with prophets and teachers in 15:1-2 (see 1 Pet 5:1-2). This material also serves to reinforce the church's defenses against its members being defrauded by specifying that bishops and deacons cannot be "lovers of money." At issue in the redactor's incorporation of the preredactional material, then, is the financial question of support of or recompense for the arising class of professional religious, an embryonic priesthood. The redactor fails to distinguish between the offices in question largely because most of them are defunct. If the Pastorals are any indication, only bishops and deacons remain.

New problems, however, have also arisen for the redactor in connection with the theme of church finances, and it is these problems that he addresses in the material he adds to the text (11:3-6; 12:1-5; possibly 13:1). In both 11:3-6 and 12:1-5, some kind of travel is absolutely required by the texts: both speak explicitly of people who "come" (11:4; 12:1-2) and the acceptable duration of their stays (11:5; 12:2). If this late stage of redaction, however, is approximately contemporary with the Pastoral letters (very late first century or early second century), there would be serious ramifications for the itinerancy hypothesis. Even if this stage presupposes genuine itinerants, the phenomenon could easily be a function of the increasingly developed character of the translocal links between individual groups—churches—in the late first or early second century. We see hints of this phenomenon already in the letters of Ignatius. Under such circumstances, there is at least the social and practical possibility of wandering Christians—including noncharismatic travelers (see 12:2-5)—moving from city to city in search of passing hospitality from the Christian groups based there (contrast Crossan 1998:373). This possibility is attractive to Jonathan Draper, who then uses it to recast the Harnackian understanding of the historical processes at work behind the *Didache:*

> It is usually assumed that the instructions with respect to bishops and deacons in *Did* 15.1-2 represent a response to the gradual decline and disappearance of the charismatic ministry and a step in the *Katholisierungsprozess* (process of community institutionalization). The instructions may more properly be seen as a response to the new situation which is caused by the intrusion of wandering charismatic prophets into an existing structure of resident bishops and deacons. (1995:291)

If this is so, the details of Draper's reconstruction and argumentation notwithstanding,[28] the fact that the *Didache* may thus evince itinerancy has no probative value whatsoever for earlier periods, simply because the conditions that actuate and enable the phenomenon were not in place at that earlier time. Itinerants would not have constructed and fostered an organized, community-based, and translocal set of churches but rather the converse: such a set of organized and settled churches was what made itinerancy possible and brought it into being, this occurring, of course, at a much later date than Theissen suggests.

I would argue, however, that itinerancy is not even indicated under the redactor's later conditions. Theissen's brand of itinerancy is not required by the references to travel in this redactional material. Draper, for instance, regards the references to apostles as references to Paul and Pauline missionaries: what is at work behind the *Didache*'s advice is the necessity to dampen the impact of an outsider who is advocating abolition of Torah to a moderately Torah-obedient community (see Draper 1991:360–72). The strong parallelism, however, between the advice given on apostles (11:3-6) and that concerning ordinary travelers (12:1-5) militates against Draper's suggestion. If the regulations against apostles really concern dogmatic issues rather than questions of hospitality, we would expect both that the advice on apostles would be more clearly distinguished from that of ordinary Christian travelers and that it would tend to be conflated with 11:7-12, in which dogmatic considerations are at least somewhat at issue for defining prophets.

What the stylistic and substantial parallelism between 11:3-6 and 12:1-5 indicates, rather, is that in "apostles" (11:3) and "those who come in the name of the Lord" (12:1) we are dealing with very similar figures, at least insofar as the redactor's purposes are concerned. There is little in the actual descriptions offered of these two groups to distinguish them from each other, and so it can probably be affirmed that the most important feature separating the two figures is implied by the terms used to describe them: "apostles" are *sent* to the community, while those dealt with in chapter 12 "come"; some of those who "come" apparently wish to settle (12:3-4), while no such provision is offered for apostles. Both figures are travelers, and both raise the prickly issue of hospitality. "Apostles," which 11:3 (see vv. 5-6) treats as largely undifferentiated from (its redactional understanding of) prophets, appear to be traveling visitors from other communities and locales[29]—the hospitable treatment of whom, as Harnack correctly implies, serves symbolically to unify the Christian movement. It is unclear to what extent these figures can claim special status in the groups from which they come: we simply do not know whether they are official delegates, charismatic authority figures, prophets (that is, part of the special class of charismatics) from other groups, or something else altogether. In any case, no provision whatsoever is offered for long-term contact: they are not imagined to settle among those whom they visit (11:4: "but if he stays for three days, he is a false prophet"), and the advice given about them precludes any legitimate request for funds or provisions (11:6: "when an apostle leaves, let him receive nothing except bread, sufficient to pass the night"). The assumption is made that such travelers are legitimately there in order to visit the church and are to be shown hospitality during such a visit (see

Niederwimmer 1977:155–56). Thus the text suggests the reverse of what is assumed by most commentators, that is, that among the purposes of an apostolic visit to a church is the necessity for support.

The persons dealt with in 11:3-6 and 12:1-5 are distinguished from each other not by shifts in settings but by a slight shift in the circumstances of the recipients of the hospitality. "Those who come in the name of the Lord" in 12:1 appear to be ordinary disciples who, in their travels, request the hospitality of other disciples they encounter in the towns through which they pass. Such people are distinguished on the basis of whether they are travelers who are just passing through or are coming to settle down. In the first case, a limit is placed on the time during which the traveler may be shown hospitality, after which he (or she?) has worn out his welcome (12:2). In the second case, the extent of hospitality is restricted by demanding that new arrivals work for their food (12:3). If the newcomers are unable to support themselves, the issue shifts from the question of hospitality to the question—exhibited in the redactor's use of earlier material—of the internal distribution of church monies: along the pattern established by 13:4, newcomers may be recipients of church charity (12:4a). What marks these figures—apostles and those who come—apart is nothing more than the claims they might make for support. And it is for *this* reason that the author of the *Didache* feels they have to be regulated. Impostors and opportunists must not be allowed to feed on the natural hospitality of the church for those who speak in the Lord's name on behalf of other congregations, or anyone claiming to be a Christian and seeking welcome on those grounds.

This practice of Christians making use of their identity as Christians to claim hospitality is reflected in other New Testament documents dating from approximately the same time (see later, *Peregrinus*). This synchronicity cannot be a coincidence: for such a practice to arise, a sense of translocal institutional solidarity is required, as well as a sufficiently large, far-flung, and populous church to encourage reliance on such a practice. Thus the question of hospitality becomes a pressing issue right around the time that the Pastoral letters and the General Epistles were composed. The Epistle of James implies that hospitality is also something of an issue in liturgical contexts: "If a person with gold rings and in fine clothes comes into your assembly, and if a poor person in dirty clothes also comes in, and if you take notice of the one wearing the fine clothes and say, 'Have a seat here please,' while to the one who is poor you say, 'Stand there,' or 'Sit under my footstool,' have you not made distinctions among yourselves?" (James 2:2-4).[30] The Johannine letters, as well, focus on the matter of denying hospitality to those deemed to be doctrinally unsound.[31] And 3 John appears to be a letter of recommendation in support of travelers' claims to hospitality: "The Christian practice of hospitality was open to abuses, as not only they but also pagans were aware. As one way to regulate the practice to some degree, at least, letters . . . were written to introduce travelling missionaries to the churches along the way" (Malherbe 1983:101–2).

Such an overall reading of *Didache* 11–13, 15 would allow us to dispense with any assumption of general conflict behind this text, an assumption not borne out either by the overall tenor or the substance of the *Didache*. What we witness here at the level of redaction, predictably enough in light of the evidence of Paul's letters, is an attempt to regulate the internal disbursement of resources,[32] and particularly the flow of money as it is influenced by the church as church: "no man shall live among you in idleness because he is a Christian" (*Did.* 12:4). This framing of the issue reflects a situation roughly comparable with that of the perhaps slightly later Pastoral epistles; the provision for charity and hospitality to fellow Christians and the establishment of a fixed chain of authority go side by side with the efforts at doctrinal self-definition we see in the later New Testament writings. Such a reading of the *Didache* also dispenses with the rather artificial layering of the text (so Patterson, Niederwimmer, Draper, and so on) or the tendency to read it as a very delicate treatment of such figures (so Crossan). The supposed inconsistencies and equivocations of the text—which generate such speculations—are imposed on the text from without. The real inconsistency is the fact that the text itself does not support the depiction of a threefold office of charismatics.

Itinerancy in Q?

Here is not the place to determine in any positive way either what is at issue in Q's rhetoric of uprootedness or what is specifically in mind in Q's apparent references to mission. Part of the critique of the itinerancy hypothesis already offered is that it is insufficiently concrete about the context in which itinerancy is supposed to have taken place. Since a social description of Q's context has not yet been offered here, to try to solve the problem of Q's rhetoric at this point would be to repeat—and compound—the weaknesses of Theissen's effort. It is necessary, however, to linger over Q briefly at this point, if only to establish that it offers no unanswerable indications of Theissen's postulated itinerancy.

Apart from Q's rhetoric of uprootedness itself—the basis of Theissen's "analytic" (1978:3) conclusions—the direct and prominent indication of itinerancy in Q is held to be the large chunk of material on discipleship

(Q 9:57—10:24), especially the so-called Mission Charge (Q 10:2-12). This speech has routinely been taken in Q scholarship to refer to—and, more importantly, to provide evidence for—itinerancy as a social factor underlying and informing Q.[33] Risto Uro describes the Q Mission Speech as providing the best general evidence for early "wandering charismatics":

> Charismatic authority and itinerancy are, indeed, significant clues to the social situation presupposed in the early mission instructions. The extreme poverty of the equipment rule becomes conceivable, if one views it against the background that Theissen has pictured to us: the ascetic wandering was practicable to those who had forsaken the normal life and felt themselves to be appointed by God to a special task (hence the word "charismatic"). The ethos of the early mission instructions is not that of a normal society, and the behaviour demanded in them is not that of an ordinary man. (Uro 1987:129)

That the mission instructions do communicate a broad ethos, a set of instructions for how to live, is reinforced by their juxtaposition in Q with 9:57-62, particularly 9:58. Here Jesus warns a prospective follower that allegiance to him will mean adopting a mode of living—one presumes permanently—even less sedentary than that accorded to animals: "Foxes have holes and the birds of the sky have nests, but the Son of man has nowhere to lay his head." The Markan version of the Mission Charge (Mark 6:8-13) does not quite foster the same impression, for in the context of Mark, the instructions are offered as rules governing travel only over the course of a specific trip (see the description of the disciples' return in Mark 6:30): they are not broadly applicable and do not reflect a lifestyle or ethos. Obviously, Mark's narrative framing of the speech is redactional and does not tell us much about its original import. Nonetheless, the contrast between the way the material is framed by Mark and the way it is framed by Q indicates the extent to which the speech's specific point of reference is unclear. On internal grounds alone, there is no necessity to take the speech as a broad characterization of its tradents' ethos.

The juxtaposition of the Mission Speech with the saying in 9:58, however, may serve to indicate that, at least to some degree, an ethos and lifestyle are genuinely at stake for Q's version of the speech. This saying, which originally circulated independently (see *GThom.* 86), may by itself refer only to Jesus and his purported itinerant lifestyle,[34] but more likely it is a proverb commenting on the vulnerability of humankind ("the Son of Man" in the generic sense).[35] The saying, however, has been secondarily associated in Q with two other chreiai, Q 9:59-60, and Q 9:61-62.[36] This cluster employs hyperbole to suggest the strong degree of commitment required of followers of Jesus (see

Kloppenborg 1987:192). The point behind Q 9:59-60 is that one ought not let a sense of filial responsibility (and, by extension, other social obligations) divert one's focus from the duties entailed by following Jesus; it is not an exhortation literally to leave one's parents unburied. Likewise, 9:61-62 encourages the reader not to allow a longing for one's past attachments or lifestyle to impede commitment to the kingdom; it does not intend to prohibit actual backward glances. Thus, also 9:58 is simply an indication to prospective followers that the duties and consequences of following Jesus involve loss and discomfort; it is hardly to be read in its Q context as a literal indication that Jesus has nowhere to spend the night. Thus, although 9:57-62 does seem to be endorsing a type of general ethos, the point being advanced does not seem to have to do with itinerancy at all but with the issue of commitment to discipleship, even when it involves arduous duties or disagreeable consequences. As a thematic introduction to the Mission Speech, which charges the followers of Jesus with specific duties, gives rules for dealing with rejection, and sends them out "as sheep among wolves" (10:3), such a cluster of chreiai cannot serve as evidence of itinerancy but only as an indication that the people behind Q wished to underscore the importance of commitment before laying out the injunctions of 10:2-12 (see Kloppenborg 1987:202).

The injunctions of the Mission Speech proper (10:2-12) certainly do concern themselves with travel (10:4), the proper reception of hospitality (10:7), and the possibility of rejection (10:10-11), so it is understandable that they would be read as offering evidence of itinerancy. Regardless of the compositional history of the core Q^1 cluster,[37] if the individual injunctions do clearly and unequivocally evince itinerancy, one will be forced to conclude that itinerancy was either practiced by the Q people or was an aspect of the lifestyle of the pre-Q tradents of these sayings. However, any such unequivocal indications of itinerancy are lacking:

> There is little in Q 10 to suggest that the "workers" were expected to stay for a long duration in any village, or that they intended to "found" a community there. There is indeed no indication that the "workers" were leaders at all, either in the communities from which they were sent forth or in the villages that accepted them. . . . It is important in this regard to note that these workers are not invested with the titles "apostle" (1 Cor 9:1; *Did.* 11.3-6), "prophet" (*Did.* 11.3-11; 13.1), or "teacher" (*Did.* 13:2), any of which would have made their role as (potential) leaders clear. (Kloppenborg 1991:89–90)

These remarkable absences are reinforced somewhat by a consideration of Q's environment. The area in which the Q people operated—

Galilee—was very small and very compact, with the result that travel between two points would normally have involved a journey of no more than several hours. Itinerancy "would have looked more like morning walks" (Kloppenborg 1993:22). The probable social dynamics—conservative and tightly knit—of the rural villages and small towns in question in Galilee also militate against any assumption that traveling strangers could have expected acceptance of a publicly proclaimed "radical" or "countercultural" message (Kloppenborg 1993:22). Basic hospitality may have been extended to travelers, but the formal reception of someone with a program is an altogether different proposition. Moreover, Q offers several indications that it takes for granted the continuation of a sedentary, village-based life, with family connections and ordinary life proceeding largely as usual.[38] Realities of settled village life, such as lending and borrowing (6:34-35; 12:57-59), lawsuits (12:57-59), and continuing family relations (11:11-13; see also 9:59-62; 14:26, which function rhetorically on the supposition that family relations continue to be meaningful), persist. One is left to wonder, who is itinerant in the face of all these persisting relationships, typical of sedentary life?

It remains to be seen what one is to make either of this speech or of Q's rhetoric of uprooting if itinerancy is not at issue (or at least in the absence of any solid evidence that itinerants were at work behind Q). It would be unsatisfying, however, simply to leave matters at this unhappy impasse without suggesting some way that the Mission Speech, or more specifically, its Q¹ core, might be understood in the absence of actual itinerants. Recent social studies of Q have suggested the possibility—a possibility that needs to be explored in light of the extant evidence of Galilean social life—that the people responsible for Q, especially its first layer, were village- or town-based scribes (Kloppenborg 1991:81–86). Kloppenborg has pointed out that, given the restricted density of such figures, any network comprised of them would have to span several villages (1991:86). If so, it is quite conceivable that the instructions given in 10:2-12 (and 10:16) do indeed pertain to mission but not as it is ordinarily conceived. They may refer, specifically, to a class of scribal figures with a distinct ideological agenda (embodied, largely, in Q¹), attempting to disseminate that agenda as fully as possible among their fellow administrators in neighboring villages. This is not itinerancy but rather a constructive local agenda involving short trips. The prohibitions against carrying purse, knapsack, sandals, and staff not only reflect the very short distances involved but may also be intended to eliminate the appearance of travel and to normalize the activity being undertaken.[39] Such figures, then, as they enter a village to approach a fellow village scribe (κωμογραμματεύς) or village administrator (κωμαρχής), do not take on the appearance of a traveling stranger but rather an acceptable local functionary. That is, the decision not to don Cynic equipment is made to avoid the appearance of beggary that might attach to a stranger, not to radicalize that appearance (and practice) even further. The conflation of acceptance at the level of house (10:5-7) with acceptance at the level of village (10:8-11) may simply reflect the techniques used by these figures and the implications of the social environment in which they operated: to be rejected in the house of the village scribe or the village administrator is equivalent to being rejected by the entire town. Rejection there precludes any further chances at acceptance by that town and eliminates from use the instrument by which the kingdom agenda was to be promoted there. The sheep saying (10:3) reflects these scribes' trepidation at the prospect of rejection; the harvest saying (10:2), on the other hand, their hopes in undertaking the "mission" in the first place: the desire to draw in "workers" (fellow scribes) for the "master's" (God's) "harvest" (the kingdom as it is conceived at the Q^1 stage, as a condition of resolution and bounty). Such views are offered here only to demonstrate the possibility of an alternative reading of Q's rhetoric; they will be taken up more fully in the final chapter after an effort has been made to describe the social situation such figures may have encountered in the Galilee of Herod Antipas.

Conclusion

This review of some of the primary texts pertinent to the question of the erstwhile existence of ancient Christian itinerants has indicated, I hope, that both the reconstruction of the history of the earliest synoptic sayings tradition and the interpretation of Q's inversionary rhetoric require a better explanation than itinerancy is able to offer. The texts at issue—not only Q itself but such mainstays of itinerancy as the *Didache*—provide no firm evidence of Theissen's version of itinerancy at all. If such figures did not exist in the first place, they do not offer much of an explanation for why Q is so fond of inversionary rhetoric. A study of this rhetoric in Q, therefore, that does not assume itinerancy as its starting point and that invokes significant social description of the context in which Q was composed is required. Such a study has the potential to generate a sophisticated social description of the people responsible for Q, since it is precisely this inversionary language that is Q's most sociologically significant feature.

Basalt grinding stones
"Two women will be grinding at the mill; one is taken and one is left."
(Q 17:35)

4.
The Socioeconomics
of Roman Galilee

A Socioeconomic Description

THE SPECIFIC SOCIAL CIRCUMSTANCES in which Q was composed primarily involve a set of political-economic and societal shifts brought about directly or indirectly by Roman domination and imperial policy. A description of these changes provides the concrete context in which Q arose and to which it was addressed. Q can thus be described and rendered more transparent and intelligible in terms of the set of circumstances that its compilers would have taken for granted and that would have formed the universe that Q addresses, directly or not. Documents grow in worlds and are part of those worlds; they do not materialize out of the ether. The significance and function of the document—at least as conceived by those initially responsible for it—is as a piece of, a functional contribution to the world of which it is a part. And that world, while partially constituted by the document itself, cannot simply be extracted from Q by inference: Q, like most argumentative tracts and works of fiction, does not bother to describe the facts against which it is constituted and ranged, precisely because those facts, that world, are taken for granted as a starting point for whatever work the document is designed to do. Instead, Q offers extravagant ideals that, while not conforming to the facts of its context, nevertheless require those facts for its own counterfactuality to be appreciated. Possibly the greatest weakness of Theissen's analysis and that of other itinerancy advocates is the assumption that Q's context is described or implied accurately in Q itself, an assumption that implicitly involves an understanding of textual codification as a passive vehicle for the recording of facts and interpretation of facts, rather than as an act in its own right or as a contribution to the social dynamics it reflects.

Q tends to be described, especially by advocates of the itinerancy or Cynic hypotheses, as socially radical. But *radical* is too frequently assumed to be an essential and self-evident category; radical vis-à-vis *what* is not specified. When context for Q is offered, it is normally described in terms broadly sociocultural, with minimal emphasis on economic factors. Part of this lopsided emphasis is an understandable reaction to the paucity of economic data for Q's presumptive context, first-century

Galilee. Part, however, is due to a reified understanding of Q as a religious document and of religion as a purely (or at least predominantly) cultural phenomenon, to the exclusion of such mundane and distasteful matters as day to day subsistence. Such a preunderstanding is no doubt a major factor in Theissen's (inadvertent?) restriction of Q's setting to a wholly self-referential setting in the church. In order to avoid these problems, a new analysis of Q should focus on the fabric of everyday life, rather than simply describing the *ideas* circulating when Q was composed. For it is the changes in daily life that will have required a revision of current ideas and hence stimulated the composition of a new document such as Q.

For this reason, the intuition many scholars seem to have had that Q's production as a document is related to some kind of crisis, or at least perceived crisis, is probably correct. The appropriate context for Q will not be found in static descriptions of its apparent setting but rather in the shifts and ruptures that characterized everyday life—and significant disturbances to ordinary expectations of how everyday life is best lived—in the time and place in which Q was composed. In consequence, when Q's setting is imagined to embrace a wider world than the Jesus movement itself, there is a tendency to identify Q's context with moments, events, or characterizations of epochs that have come to be appreciated as of major historical significance. For instance, Roman domination is often blamed for nearly every novelty of first-century Palestinian religion, including the impulses that led to the movement or group behind Q. This domination, which in the case of the Jesus movement must be applied to Galilee somehow, is imagined in terms similar to those applicable to Judea, and in terms of the factors that are held to have led up to the First Judean Revolt of 66–70 C.E. The situation in Galilee is collapsed with that of Judea, as both are "Jewish" responses to Roman domination. This vague designation of oppression is then interpreted with reference to whatever aspect of social life the researcher intuits to be most significant. For Theissen, Q is a response to Caligula's effort to enforce his own deification in Judea (Theissen 1991:206–21). For Paul Hoffmann, it is the effort of a "peace party" to counteract the forces of violent nationalism, the Zealots and their ilk, who sought military liberation from Roman rule (1982:74–78, 308–11, 326, 331–33). And for others still, the character of Roman oppression is economic. The imposition of Roman rule, it is claimed, laid upon an already overtaxed people the burden of additional tribute, which meant that the Jewish people of Palestine suffered under double taxation: temple and other local dues were compounded by Roman taxes.[1]

What such approaches do, then, is conjecture a crisis behind Q (probably correctly), then look for a crisis, and when they have found a more or less obvious one—Roman oppression still serving as the best catchall category—they use that crisis to interpret Q. The most conspicuous single crisis event against which to locate Q from our perspective in the twenty-first century, in the broad period under consideration, is of course the First Judean Revolt itself and the events leading up to it. The inherent attraction of this event as a background for Q has in some cases led to the conclusion that Q is itself to be dated after the revolt and was in some measure composed as a response to it (Myllykoski 1996:175–99). But whether the revolt or some rather less dramatic and obvious milestone is selected against which to measure Q, the events scholarship tends to focus on—because they are interesting and because ancient literary sources focus on them—are usually singular, dramatic, and pertain to elite-level political events.[2]

Unfortunately, the assumption of crisis is not a very good methodological foundation on which to launch an investigation into the proximate context of the Q document. This caution is fairly straightforward: such a procedure relies to far too great an extent on a retrospective appreciation—whether on the part of the historian or in the available ancient literary sources—of what might constitute so subjective an entity as a crisis. We cannot be certain that events we perceive as critical, from a distance of two thousand years, would necessarily be coextensive with what people at the time would have regarded as significant. Events we may have no inkling of, because of the incomplete nature of the historical record, could have had a huge impact on daily life. Conversely, many of the events that historical interpretation valorizes, in part because they are viewed in retrospect and hence in terms of their ultimate significance, may have had minimal impact on most people. The Caligula episode, for instance, is viewed in retrospect as a focal instance of the collision course of Rome with Judea, foreshadowing the ultimate conflict that would take place several decades later; to some extent, our main source for the event, Josephus, also writing after the destruction of Jerusalem, presents it to us similarly (*War* 2.197–98; see *Ant.* 18.270). Does this mean, however, that the entire episode would not have been viewed by those people who lived before the events of the 60s as just another political event in a turbulent time? Would it call forth a movement or inspire an already extant movement to codify its overall views in a document? Indeed, the very sorts of events that the historical-literary record preserves for us, and to which we tend to be most attracted—that is, singular, dramatic, and political events—are precisely the kinds of events we would least expect to have an impact on everyday life in the countryside, especially in the kind of persistent way that would generate a movement. The First Judean Revolt is something of an exception: a war can affect the whole populace in ways that other political events may not. Most elite-level political events, however, especially given the sharp divide between urban·and rural society in antiquity (see MacMullen 1974:1–56), may have gone unnoticed in the countryside: one must establish how and why an event now deemed to have historical significance would have impressed itself as of vital and world-changing importance to its contemporaries before positing that event as a cause behind changes of thought or the formation of (relatively) novel movements.

Similar doubts may be raised for similar reasons about such cultural contexts as the phenomenon of encroaching Hellenism: there is no particularly good reason to imagine that the people immersed in the phenomenon would have had the foresight (or precognition) to have recognized its long-term implications and hence its importance for their own time. Likewise, those who posit a Cynic-like Jesus movement or one that embraced "open commensality" in table fellowship do not imagine such a movement as a response to discrete historical or political events but instead focus their descriptions of context on broad cultural phenomena such as intellectual effervescence (Mack 1993:68), the sterility of certain cultural options (Vaage 1994:13), or excessively rigid and "oppressive" social hierarchy (Crossan 1991:43–71). Such efforts at contextualization, as with the notion of encroaching Hellenism, fail to explain why, *at this time and among these people,* such incremental cultural changes were noticed and resisted.

How, then, is one to locate the putative crisis to which Q responds, the disturbed or shifting context out of which it arises? If one accepts the near-consensus position of scholarship that Q is a product of Galilee and is to be dated before the First Judean Revolt, some broad and relatively concrete description of the organization of social life in Galilee before the war is needed to serve as a context in which either significant historical events or incremental cultural or other changes would have had a discernible and definite effect. Such a description would, of course, serve to contextualize Q and to underscore the features of daily life that it takes for granted. But it would also highlight the sorts of changes that may seem inconsequential in retrospect, but would have seriously affected the lives of Q's purveyors.

What is thus at issue in the following pages is an attempt at a description of everyday life in Galilee and particularly of changes to everyday life and expectations about it that might have occurred around the early to middle first century. The focus in this description will be first and foremost political-economic, working on the assumption that the organization of social life will preeminently revolve around production or acquisition of the necessities of life, especially in the case of those for whom the availability of such necessities is relatively tenuous, the rural poor. As a result, actual economic behavior will constitute the first sphere of inquiry, with the deliberate and creative organization of social life around these economic factors being considered only subsequently. Such an approach will, one hopes, avoid ethereal questions about the cultural essence of Galilee, which continue to be a major source of controversy in much scholarship on the early Jesus movement. The paramount issue is not cultural continuity between first-century Galilee and Israelite biblical traditions, cultural or political discontinuity with Jerusalem and Judea, the extent to which Galileans identified themselves as Jews and what this identification meant for them, whether Jewish theocratic ideals were in conflict with contemporary economic trends (as though such ideals were invested with immutable content), or whether Pharisaic or apocalyptic ideologies were in wide circulation. The conflation—even identification—of such cultural effects with more concrete economic and social matters is one of the major weaknesses of the itinerancy hypothesis and remains a widespread characteristic of scholarly reconstructions of the context of the early Jesus movement.

The argument to be offered below is fairly simple, although it ranges across a variety of data and phenomena. Imperial Roman development of the noncoastal hinterland attempted to bring Galilee into the orbit of empire in order more effectively to siphon off its surplus product in the form of tribute, taxes, rents, interests and loans, and a variety of other devices. Because of the limitations of transportation technology and the absence of a highly monetized market-oriented economy (see Finley 1973:126–27, 166), the primary way in which this development was made possible was through the foundation of cities proximate to the hinterland to be exploited and accessible to potential trade outlets. The (re)foundation and expansion of Sepphoris in 4 B.C.E. and the foundation of Tiberias sometime in the neighborhood of 17 to 23 C.E. are the known and notable instances of this conduct in Galilee during the reign of Antipas. These foundations had a decisive effect on Galilean economic production and organization (as was precisely their intention).[3] This effect in turn was socially disruptive on a day-to-day basis, and, among other things, changed the character of rural social organization and hierarchy. It is against such a context that Q reacts.

Village Occupations and Production

The primary occupation of the populace of the Roman Empire was agriculture (Hanson and Oakman 1998:103). Only a tiny percentage of the people, disproportionately represented in evidentiary data and in historical reconstruction, earned their livings or performed what work was required of them in any other fashion; an equally tiny percentage were absolved by wealth from work entirely, but of these, most held their wealth in agriculturally exploited land (1998:104). Those vast numbers who were unfortunate enough to dwell in the countryside, in villages on the land, or as slaves in larger villas were engaged exclusively in agriculture or the support of agriculture. Production from the land was central to all wealth in antiquity, including that of the state.[4] This situation applied to Galilee as much as the rest of the empire. Josephus presents Galilee as a land under cultivation to an extraordinary degree:

> For the land is everywhere so rich in soil and pasturage and produces such variety of trees, that even the most indolent are tempted by these facilities to devote themselves to agriculture. In fact, every inch of the soil has been cultivated by the inhabitants; there is not a parcel of waste land. The towns, too, are thickly distributed, and even the villages, thanks to the fertility of the soil, are all so densely populated that the smallest of them contains above fifteen thousand inhabitants. (*War* 3.42–43)

The statement is an exaggeration in several respects: not only are the population figures ridiculous, but a significant portion of the land in Galilee is not cultivable. The basic point made by Josephus, however—that the entirety of the territory of Galilee is a generally productive and fertile region and that it was (relatively) densely populated and intensely under cultivation—is accurate enough.[5] Elsewhere, Josephus suggests that there are a total of 204 cities and villages in Galilee (*Life* 235), an estimate that Horsley, at least, is prepared to accept, arguing that since sites for fifty villages in the wider region of Sepphoris alone can be identified from literary and archaeological evidence, a figure of approximately two hundred for the whole of Galilee is not unreasonable (Horsley 1995a:190–91; 1996:89). If so, the land was densely populated indeed, with, on average, very little distance between settlements.

While in terms of topography, and hence also of agricultural variations as well as of administration, the region is divided into two or possibly three sectors—Lower Galilee, Upper Galilee, and what Josephus calls "the Valley," that is, the basin of the lake[6]—the whole area is nevertheless intensely productive, although in varying ways. Both soil and rainfall are felicitous for crop production (Aharoni 1979:27). Lower Galilee stretches, according to Josephus, from the Plain of Esdraelon's village of Xaloth in the south to Bersabe in the north (*War* 3.39; see *Life* 227)—that is, from the northern boundaries of Samaria and the region of Scythopolis northward to the Beth HaKerem Valley, approximately level with the northern tip of the lake.[7] East to west, the area extends from the lake to the immediate hinterland of the coastal cities (unless one excludes the lake basin as another region).[8] This area is marked geographically in the east by a series of rugged plateaus covered by volcanic basalt, while the western area is gentler, a series of limestone ridges with deep basins running from west to east in a slightly northward direction and sloping upward from the sea. The area is essentially foothill country between the Great Plain to the south and the Lebanon mountain ranges to the north. The climate in this whole area is conducive to vegetation in large measure because of the generous supply of water. Rainfall here, in contrast to the more arid south of Palestine, is plentiful, and increases as one moves north. The average annual rainfall for Lower Galilee is from 500 to 700 mm (see Pritchard 1987:59), and there is frequently snowfall in the winter as well. This precipitation was absolutely necessary to ensuring fertility in antiquity; the absence of rain, or of the right kind of rainfall, could affect crop yield, tree yield, or the filling of cisterns for water storage (*m. Ta'an.* 3.1-2). This rainfall, concentrated in the winter and early spring, was insufficiently consistent. the water needed to be stored for purposes of irrigation, as the references to cisterns illustrate.[9] Moreover, this lopsidedness of precipitation meant that violent rainfalls could cause significant soil erosion, especially in the steep inclines of the upper hill country.[10] Nevertheless, the gross fall of water was generally sufficient for irrigating the basins of the Lower Galilee, which are thus a source of rich vegetation, enhanced in a large area to the south and southwest of Tiberias by volcanic alluvia (Clark 1962:346; Pritchard 1987:59).

Crops

In particular, this region is marked by the production of two main kinds of crops: grains and fruit-bearing trees. Of the former, wheat (σῖτος; *triticum durum, triticum savitum*) was the most common and the most central; barley (κριθή; *hordeum sativum*) can be grown in the more arid conditions to the south, such as Idumea, but makes an inferior bread, deemed appropriate only for the very poor.[11] Galilee, because of its sufficient availability of water, did not require barley as a staple; its main grain product was wheat.[12] The aniconic (imageless) coins of the Agrippas, those designed for their Jewish subjects, show heads of wheat

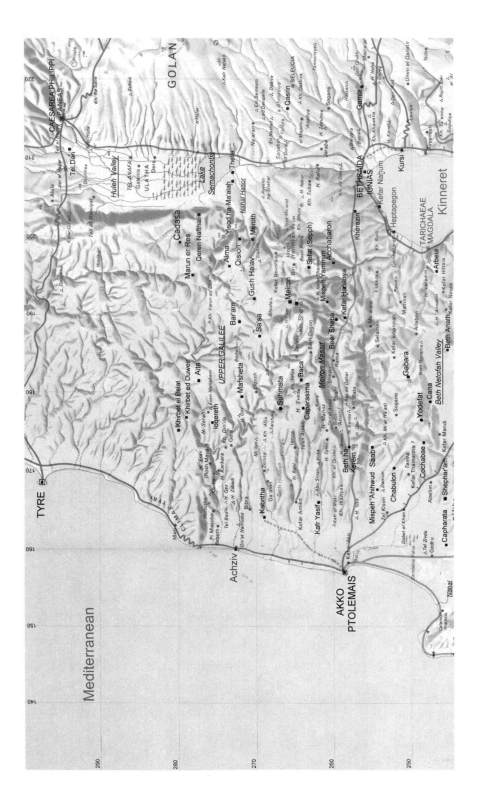

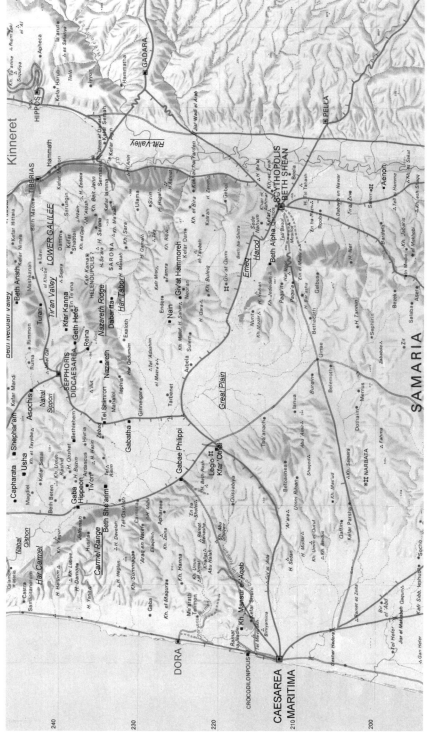

Figure 1: A topographical map with the Upper and Lower Galilee regions indicated.

on one side, illustrating the perceived centrality of the product (Meshorer 1982:52–59, 79; plate nos. 9–16); the Mishnah mentions wheat eighty-eight times, over against only forty-seven times for barley (Safrai 1994:108). In the Murabba'at documents, values for various other agricultural products were expressed in terms of wheat.[13] Wheat was also therefore the main source of food, taken (obviously) in the form of bread; aside from festive occasions, ordinary dining practices involved two main meals per day, both of which revolved around bread:

> The ancients ate two daily meals during the week and three on the Sabbath. Breakfast, eaten in the third or fourth hour of the day, consisted of bread dipped in olive oil or bread with some type of vegetable. The poor made do with bread and garlic while the wretchedly poverty-stricken ate "dry bread" which they dipped in salt. Supper, eaten during twilight, was the main meal of the day. This evening meal included bread and some cooked food such as an egg, or some type of cooked legume flour or paste.[14]

The Mishnah seems to regard standard daily human consumption to be approximately the bread made from one-half of a *kab* of wheat (approximately 0.525 kg; or a whole *kab* of barley): this makes up the two meals of an ordinary diet, not including other products going into the meals.[15] If one factors in other products, the weekly consumption of grain per person would be at least about 2 *kabs* (2.1 kg).[16] Safrai, assuming an average annual yield of 600 kg per acre, calculates that wheat cultivation of 0.32 acres is necessary to sustain the average person, which means, because of alternate crop rotation, that the average family would need to consume at least the wheat of 0.625 acres of cultivable land per person.[17] Adding to this figure on the basis of seed requirements (generously assuming a 1:5 yield, on which see below) translates into a requirement of 0.69 acres per person, and thus subsistence for a family of four, six, or eight would require the unencumbered (that is, with no taxes or other dues) availability of at least 2.76, 4.14, or 5.52 acres of cultivable land.

Safrai's yield figures, however, are unrealistic, apparently in the neighborhood of 1:10.[18] Excluding obviously exaggerated figures, literary sources and comparative evidence suggest a usual expectation of about 1:5 seed to product yield.[19] Talmudic traditions cited by Hamel suggest a standard yield of 1:5,[20] and perhaps a yield of 1:6 in better locations of the Galilee.[21] Figures for grain from Italy suggest yields of about 1:4 (Columella, *On Agriculture* 3.3.4); for exceptional districts of Sicily, about 1:8.[22] Hamel further cites *P. Ness.* 82 and *P. Ness.* as giving yield figures for wheat that translate into a ratio of 1:6.75–7.2 in the first instance and 1:4.28, 1:3.7 in the second. The latter is deemed to be standard, the former exceptional if believable at all. Yields in medieval Europe tended to be between 1:3 and 1:4 (Hamel 1990:130–31). Arab yields in modern Palestine before the twentieth century tended to be about 1:5 in the best years (Hamel 1990:132). Interesting confirmation of these lower yield ratio figures may come from another source: Julius Caesar in 59 B.C.E. provided land grants to veterans in the amount of ten *iugera* for a family of three or more children (Finley 1973:81), which amounts to about 6.25 acres, and this amount is deemed by Finley to be at the razor's edge of subsistence even with a tax exemption, such that eventual failure was a certainty (Finley 1973:81, and 226, n. 56). A calculation of 4.5 acres for subsistence for a family of six, therefore, assumes too high a yield of produce, even if one makes the obviously counterfactual assumption that most land is wholly unencumbered by rents, tithes, local dues of various kinds, debt payments, and taxes. Working from yield figures of half that assumed by Safrai, that is, 1:5,[23] necessary minimum land allotments double, making them comparable to Caesar's land grants: subsistence for a family of four, six, or eight would require the unencumbered availability of at least 5.52, 8.28, or 11.04 acres of cultivable land. This is a minimum figure, failing to take bad years and crop failures into account (except as an average), and assuming—falsely—the absence of various dues, debts, tithes, and taxes. Thus Ben-David, assuming actual consumption of only one-third of gross yield (the remainder devoted to seed and various dues) and noting that a peasant's farm in 1909–23 comprised six to nine people for 8 to 10 hectares of land (19.768 to 24.71 acres), supposes for the Roman period that a family of six to nine people will work a farm of about 7 hectares (17.297 acres; Ben-David 1974:44, 46). This is about double the figures just given. Such a plot would, assuming the general accuracy of the figures given, gross about 2,625 kg of grain product.[24] This range of figures for subsistence—and their variability—should be kept in mind in what follows.

In antiquity, then, the most important crop in terms of cultivation and consumption was wheat, which the Galilee produced in abundance. Of the three main soil types in the Roman Mediterranean world—bare mountain, limestone hill, and alluvium—Lower Galilee possessed significant amounts of the latter two: its hillside land could be used for trees and mixed crops (including grains), and its alluvial valleys primarily for grain (Hamel 1990:102). The valleys or basins between elevations, receiving runoff from higher land, would have been devoted primarily to wheat (Golomb and Kedar 1971:139), while cultivation of the higher ground was accomplished normally in strips that rise gently along the slopes, although to a lesser extent also through terracing, which was common on graded limestone in antiquity but was not used extensively or well in the Galilee because small holdings made the effort prohibitive (Golomb and Kedar 1971:138).

The wheat was sown on plowed land in the early winter, around December, to take advantage of the rainy winter growing season and hoed in the spring for thinning and weeding.[25] It was harvested in late spring or early summer, just before the onset of the hot days. Safrai describes the processes that followed harvesting:

> After harvesting the wheat, the farmer would bring it to the threshing-floor (*goren*). There he would smooth out the heap of wheat, thresh it, scatter it to complete the separation of chaff from seeds, and sift it. The final result of all this was a pile of seeds. The farmer did not grind these himself, but sold them in this form or stored them. . . . The final stage is the *merihah* or smoothing out of the pile of seeds. This was necessary to measure the seeds. (Safrai 1994:116; see *m. Šabb.* 7.2)

Although in terms of transport it would have been more economical to wholesale flour rather than wheat, normally the unground seeds were wholesaled, because of the difficulty of storing flour (Safrai 1994:117; see *m. Ma'aś. Š.* 4.1). The grinding of the wheat was normally done by women or servants;[26] Hamel describes it as "long, painful, and dreary," taking at least two to three hours per day, usually in the morning before sunrise, using either a hand mill or, more elaborately, a two-way mill operated by two women (as may be referred to in Q 17:34 and *Apoc. Zeph.* 2:2-4), or a rotary mill operated by one woman and capable of grinding about 4 lbs. (1.82 kg) of grain into flour in one hour.[27]

In addition to wheat, Galilean agriculture, because of the suitability of its soil and climate for trees, was marked by fruit production (Josephus, *War* 3.516–17). The most important of these products was the olive, which Hamel describes as the "bread and butter" of the Palestinian peasant (1990:10). As well as being eaten fresh with bread, or as preserves (sliced and salted), olives were fundamentally important for their oil, which served dietary needs in the absence of animal fat and to which nearly all of the olive harvest was devoted. The olive grows well in rocky soil and can endure dry conditions if necessary but grows best in temperate climates. While new trees grow very slowly, once mature they produce heavily for hundreds of years (Safrai 1994:118; Trever 1962:596; see Josephus, *War* 3.517 and *m. Šeb.* 1:8). Olives were planted at a density of forty-four to forty-eight trees per acre or greater (*m. Šeb.* 1:6-7). Hamel states that a grown olive tree in full production could generate 8 to 10 liters of oil per year (1990:10). Safrai, conversely, citing the Mishnah, Tosefta, Palestinian Talmud, and Cato's *De re rustica*, argues

for a much smaller yield: between 1.8 and 5.5 liters per tree per harvesting.[28] Hamel's figures may be the result of mistaking yield figures of
fruit for yield figures of oil, since the lower ranges of Safrai's figures are
about 20 percent of Hamel's, which corresponds to the (approximately)
20 percent oil content of the olive (Safrai 1994:122). In any case, Safrai's
figures are based on ancient literary data from a variety of sources, and
there is little reason to doubt them, although his upper range is probably too optimistic.

The lower range of Safrai's figures would suggest the necessity of
about one-quarter acre of olives per individual if the olives were to supplement one's grain intake in the fashion described by Safrai: a half-*log* of
oil per week, enough for two whole meals (but presumably spread over
several), or 18.5 liters every two years.[29] This means that a family of
four, six, and eight, would require one, one and a half, or two acres of
trees under cultivation in order to maintain dietary norms as they are
perceived by the Mishnah. A village of four hundred people would thus
require one hundred acres of trees and the equipment to press this
amount of olives: between 37,000 and 52,800 kg of fruit every two years,
for between 7,400 and 10,560 liters of oil.[30]

Archaeological evidence demonstrates the availability of such equipment, often multiple presses, in many villages, as well as larger cities.[31]
The presses normally consisted of an angled beam with the lower end set
in a stone socket and the upper end weighted with removable stone
weights; a pit with a grooved basin was set in the ground underneath the
bar, toward its lower end (for greater leverage), a stone wheel placed
above on the bar itself, and baskets of olives piled between the two
stones, with boards against their sides to keep them vertical; the force of
gravity was then used to press the oil out of the olives and into the cavity
of the pit below.[32]

In the lower Galilee, olive trees were planted mostly on the hillsides,
not in the valley basins where wheat is most effectively grown. Although
olive cultivation, or that of other fruits, would have been more profitable
than that of grain,[33] and although Galilee was renowned for its oil production, especially Upper Galilee, dietary requirements for grain were
greater in volume than for oil. Thus, in surveyed sites in Samaria the area
apparently cultivated for olive groves is normally about half the size of
that devoted to grain (Safrai 1994:108). Olives were also grown over or
alongside grain (intercultivation) or the trees used as trellises for
grapevines.[34] During the Hellenistic period, it appears that in spite of the
Galilee's oil-producing potential Judea imported grain from Galilee, not
oil.[35] Later, however, during the Roman period, it is obvious that Galilee
did export oil, at least to Jews living outside of Palestine, where Galilee

and Judea had something of a monopoly on oil that diaspora Jews required to be ritually clean; thus olive oil would have been an excellent cash crop for export, and at a premium.[36] Bearing in mind both the evidence adduced by Safrai and Ben-David for the export of oil during the Roman period, on the one hand, and Horsley's cautions against the anachronistic presumption of a market economy, on the other, we should probably conclude that Galilean production of oil was not in a static condition in the period under consideration. Production and use shifted over time, moving from local subsistence production to production for export over several centuries, in consequence of the changing religious status of Galilee (which thus provided the oil with a definite market for export) as well as under the pressure of financial burdens brought about by Roman domination or other political phenomena (which created demands above and beyond the requirements for local self-sufficiency).

In addition, other food products were part of regular dietary intake and were available in Galilee, including beans or other vegetables, figs, wine and grapes, and fish.[37] Meat was only rarely consumed (Hamel 1990:25–29). Vegetables were a major part of the standard diet but receive little attention because they were ill regarded as an agricultural product (Hamel 1990:9). Normally, sufficient vegetables for the consumption of one's family could be grown on a plot of a few hundred square meters; they were not grown for export or sale (Safrai 1994:144–46, 355, 366). Figs, likewise, were grown mostly for consumption, and fig products were regarded as a standard part of diet; so also various other products, including dates, the carob, various other kinds of fruit, and industrial crops such as flax, silk, hemp, and cotton (*m. Ketub.* 5:8; Hamel 1990:9–10, 21; Safrai 1994:136–45, 146–63). Especially important were grapes, grown primarily for wine (Hamel 1990:10, 22; Safrai 1994:126–36, 368). Diversification of produce helped to ensure survival: if and when one crop failed, another's yield might prevent ruin or starvation; diversification also distributed the workload (as well as ensuring a recurrent yield of different products), since different products matured at different times and required different kinds of labor at different times. In addition, land requirements for fruit products, especially oil and grapes, were not as extensive as for grain; these could in fact be intercultivated with grain (depending on the scrupulousness with which the farmer observed the law of diverse kinds).

The physical plant required for all of this work is fairly extensive. In addition to requiring the availability of fields of the sizes discussed above, treatment of the fields, involving plowing, weeding, and burning off stubble, would at least have required possession of plowing instruments, and, where fields were on hillsides, other kinds of treatment, and hence equipment, were required to ensure relatively level (by terracing or some other method) cultivation as well as perhaps irrigation, depending on the character of the land and climatic conditions.[38] On moderately sloping land, stone enclosures were also used, not only for the partition of fields but also to prevent erosion and to retain the level (Golomb and Kedar 1971:138; Hamel 1990:116). In addition, one needed harvesting equipment (hand sickles), threshing floors, storage units for the seed, and milling instruments for processing the grain.[39] References to mills in the Gospels appear to assume the general use of more elaborate and larger mills, but the Mishnah assumes the frequent use of transportable and privately owned hand mills—saddle stone bases anchored to the ground with plaster, with a rough handheld basaltic rock used to crush grain against the surface—as primary milling instruments.[40]

Larger estates, one can only surmise, used larger rotary mills, perhaps driven by animal power rather than people; more elaborate mills may also have been held in common by villages, but with all of the references to women grinding, and to hand mills, it seems safest to assume (against Hamel) that more primitive hand mills were in frequent use among smallholders (Postan 1966:99). As long as technologically primitive milling techniques remained the norm, its practice did not require communal equipment.[41] Oil presses, conversely, were demonstrably held communally much of the time. Literary sources indicate that olive presses were held to be proper to the village as a whole and were deemed to have been sold when the village as a whole was sold.[42] Archaeological evidence supports such a conclusion: presses that have been discovered in towns and villages have tended to be located for communal use rather than being spread around private locations.[43] Likewise, threshing floors were used communally by the whole agricultural village.[44] This public use and public location is probably what made the threshing floors ideal locations for the collection of tithes (or any other dues, for that matter).[45]

All of these features affect the layout and physical characteristics of any agricultural (grain-based) settlement. The setup among freeholders normally involved living in small villages immediately proximate to the land held and worked. Contrary to Josephus, archaeological evidence suggests village populations were fairly small,[46] ranging from only a few dozens in the smallest settlements to larger towns of one thousand or more persons, leaving aside the two Galilean cities of note, Sepphoris and Tiberias.[47] If the size of the village populations was fairly moderate, Josephus's figure of 204 cities and villages in Galilee could be accurate, reflecting a tendency to proliferate smaller settlements (with fairly stable holdings) rather than expand existing settlements. In the cases of larger villages and those built on steep ground, terracing was sometimes used to create level areas. Thus Capernaum was based on three main and distinct elevations, with the town's main buildings at the highest elevation, further public areas at a lower elevation, and a mainly residential sector to the west (Avi-Yonah 1975–78: v. 1, 299; Meyers, Strange, and Meyers 1981). Likewise, Tiberias appears to have been organized along the natural contours of the terrain (Avi-Yonah 1975–78: v. 4, 1180). Some towns and villages were walled, and size does not seem to have been much of a factor: the decision to fortify seems to be based on other considerations. Minor fortifications often accompany agricultural installations outside of the village as well (*m. 'Arak.* 9:5).

The village, therefore, would consist of a population cluster surrounded by fields and other agricultural land, sufficient to meet the needs of the actual population of the village itself (Horsley 1996:120). What was not a feature of the fields themselves (irrigation, terraces, enclosures of various sorts) was held in the village, sometimes in common (oil presses, cisterns), sometimes in individual houses (probably milling instruments), and sometimes shared by groups of individual houses. Other devices, such as threshing floors, were held in common outside of the village limits (*m. B. Bat.* 2:8). Houses were clustered together around common courtyards, and the courtyards and their appurtenances were deemed to be the common property and common responsibility of the households around them.[48] The fields, then, extended outward from the perimeter of the village; people did not normally live on the land they worked but traveled the short distance to it from their homes in the village. A corollary of this practice was that land closer to the village was worth more than land farther from it;[49] obviously this is a result not only of the further distance one would have to travel to work such fields but also (and primarily?) because of the distance one would subsequently have to transport finished produce. This difficulty of course would have placed limitations on the amount of actual physical space a village could comfortably cultivate and would have generated a disposition to a merely local orientation to production, since the cultivation of surplus, at least in the case of wheat, would have increased the size of land under cultivation and generated diminishing returns— hence, again, the large number of small villages, rather than a smaller number of larger villages. Archaeological remains indicate that offshoot settlements would develop around villages; such settlements represent a way of more effectively exploiting more distant land (Safrai 1994:67–73). We might expect, because of natural differences in the quality of the land, as well as the variations in value caused by proximity (or its lack) to the village, that within any given village, even a small one, there would have been variations in prosperity and variations in sizes of holdings. We cannot conclude from the communal nature of some aspects of village life that rural Galilee was marked by some sort of primitive communism; Mishnaic regulation of sales, ownership, and debt makes this very clear.

On the other hand, specialization in products other than grain may have generated surplus sufficient to motivate at least local specializations and trading patterns. It is often difficult to tell, at least from archaeological evidence alone, the ultimate intentions and dispositions of farming activity:

> Archaeological evidence shares this deficiency. Field-survey can show the survival of small-unit farming, as in Tuscany and the Molise, but it cannot distinguish an owner-occupier from a tenant. To make matters worse, peasants do not leave monuments. Their farmsteads, built of perishable materials, have not survived. The normal 'small site' of the archaeological field-survey turns out to have a relatively elaborate construction inappropriate to a basic peasant cottage. Its owner might have controlled perhaps 50 to 80 iugera or 12 to 20 hectares and produced cash crops for the local market. (Garnsey and Saller 1987:76)

If Lower Galilee, where agriculture focused on grain, was to develop trading patterns, these patterns would have to devolve from production in addition to the grain yield for the local population, and would require nearby markets (on which see below). The matter is further complicated in regions other than Lower Galilee. Upper Galilee clearly specialized in olive and fruit production, probably in addition to grain production for local needs.[50] The area along the western side of the lake is also sometimes considered a distinct region—the Valley—for reasons primarily geographical, which had an impact on production.[51] According to Josephus, this area was rich in figs, olives, and grapes, and of course fish from the lake itself (*War* 3.516–21). Fishing requires the ownership of fairly extensive equipment: nets, boats, and so on (Wachsmann 1995); fishing rights were owned by the local rulers, and contracted out to brokers, who in turn employed wage laborers (Hanson 1997; Hanson and Oakman 1998:106–9). Such features place the region bordering the lake in a different category from the inland basins around Sepphoris. Where cash cropping was employed, and when it was employed, we can also expect that a major source of subsidiary income for poorer farmers was working on other people's larger estates, especially during peak periods like the harvest (Finley 1973:107).

Social Organization

The point of all of this discussion is to present an overall picture of those material circumstances of early Roman Galilee that are more stable than the specific and historically malleable features of the social organization of those circumstances, to which we now turn. What emerges is a Galilee that is dominated first by wheat production, depending on the region in question, and secondarily by olives and grapes, that is, in all cases, direct crop production from the land.[52] Life in the countryside was normally of a standard peasant sort, rather than dominated by estates: people lived together in small villages from which they worked nearby moderately sized tracts of land,[53] primarily in a self-sufficient and maintenance-oriented (as opposed to profit-oriented) manner (although these circumstances were subject to change). The manner of life implied by all of this involves a high concentration of work: the amount of land required to feed a family comfortably is extensive enough to employ all of its members during peak periods, and the absence of economies of scale meant that concentration of holdings did not significantly diminish the labor-to-product ratio. The various domestic duties of women, in addition to their participation in agricultural work, would also have occupied a significant amount of time. On the other hand, although agricultural labors would have been spread across the year as evenly as possible, the off-peak periods for major crops (wheat, olives) would probably have allowed for periods of considerable leisure (Finley 1973:31).

Such a life, in work or in leisure, would have been lived in close association with one's neighbors. People chose to live together, in villages and towns, rather than alone on their own (private) plots. The houses in villages were small and crowded together (minimizing wasteful occupation of arable land), with shared courtyards and often with shared equipment (Safrai 1994:67–69). Even where equipment was privately owned, the work may have been done with one's fellows, whether family or neighbor, as seems to be the case with grinding (see above). The villages were apparently self-regulating, even where they lacked formal administrative apparatus, and were as self-sufficient as they could be, possessing and working their own land, and on it producing, if possible, the entirety of the different products needed to sustain life. There would thus have been very little division of labor among villages and probably very little within them either (see Xenophon, *Cyropaedeia* 8.2.5). The tremendous risk involved in peasant agriculture—production for subsistence, especially when one's produce is in part devoted to the next year's seeding, is highly susceptible to climatic factors, and year-to-year variations in yield might have a significantly deleterious effect—would to some degree have been offset by village communalism, where those with better fortune or greater resources could assist—with loans, hospitality, or some other kind of charity—those whom weather, soil, or economic deprivation conspired against. Once again, however, this is not to say that there were not discernible economic strata within any village or network of villages, nor that these strata would not have easily translated into a rigid social hierarchy.[54]

This overall picture thus offers a description of a rural Galilee (excluding Sepphoris and Tiberias) intensely under cultivation, densely populated, and dotted with settlements, but it does so without invoking either mind-boggling population estimates or anachronistic and inappropriate concepts of cosmopolitanism or urbanity. Outside of the main cities—recent cities at that!—Galilee was, like all ancient hinterland, devoted to agricultural production. One can quite properly argue that Galilee was not culturally isolated from the currents of Hellenism in the Roman period, but, if so, some notion other than urbanization (in the strictest sense) is required to express this cultural influx.

Trade, Travel, and Transport

Trade or any other form of the movement of goods in antiquity was determined and curtailed by the contemporary technological limitations on transport. Too frequently, discussions of trade, of import and export of goods, even of taxation and payment of debts, assume a monetized economy (allowing the transportation of value without requiring the transportation of actual goods) or ease of travel (allowing the transportation of actual goods), neither of which can be taken for granted in rural districts of the early Roman period. In the case of rural Galilee, transport of goods was further complicated by geography. A consideration of these physical limitations on the possibilities of transport will allow a more realistic reconstruction of actual trading patterns and their social importance.

Whether or not, as Horsley would have it (1996:83–84), self-sufficiency was a major interest among villagers, trade in bulky items was severely curtailed by the technological limitations on transport, which was physically difficult, slow, and expensive. In Finley's graphic description:

> The ox was the chief traction animal of antiquity, the mule and donkey his near rivals, the horse hardly at all. All three are slow and hungry. The transport figures in Diocletian's edict of maximum prices imply that a 1200-pound wagon-load of wheat would double in price in 300 miles, that a shipment of grain by sea from one end of the Mediterranean to the other would cost less (ignoring the risks) than carting it seventy-five miles. (Finley 1973:126; see Evans 1991:110, 147–48, n. 23)

Draft animals hauling produce are expensive to keep on hand or to rent, move slowly, and, with each passing day, consume more of the produce they are supposed to be carting.

Contemporary writers not only confirm these limitations but show a general awareness of their consequences. Thus Columella, for instance, describes location as a major variable in the desirability of land:

> After these two primary considerations he [Porcius Cato] added, as deserving no less attention [than climate and fertility], the following: the road, the water, and the neighbourhood. A handy road contributes much to the worth of the land: first and most important, the actual presence of the owner, who will come and go more cheerfully if he does not have to dread discomfort on the journey; and secondly its convenience for bringing in and carrying out the necessaries—a factor which increases the value of stored crops and lessens the expense of bringing things in, as they are transported at lower cost to a place which may be reached without great effort; and it means a great deal, too, to get transportation at low cost if you make the trip with hired draught-animals, which is more expedient than looking after your own. (Columella, *On Agriculture* 1.3.3–4; see Varro, *De re rustica* 1.16.2; 1.16.6)

The shocking absence of any kind of rational economic calculations among Greco-Roman writers (Finley 1973:110–11) makes the explicit appearance—even among such obtuse commentators as Cato—of consideration of the cost of transport that much more arresting. Interestingly, even cash crops and industrial produce, such as flax or hemp, are affected by the high cost of transport. Pliny, describing rushes along the coast of Cartagena suitable for rope-making, adds that "the cost of carriage prohibits its being transported any considerable distance [*longius vehi impendia prohibent*]" (*Natural History* 19.30). Columella argues that "it is not profitable to establish vineyards for food unless the plot is so close to a city that conditions warrant the selling of the raw grapes to marketers, as we do other fruit" (*On Agriculture* 3.2.1).

Very important for our purposes is the fashion in which these strictures were overcome. Most easily and naturally, they were dealt with by marine transport of one kind or another, wind and water currents being less hungry and more potent than oxen: shipping a load of grain down a river or even across the Mediterranean was faster and less expensive (whether in terms of money or of the actual produce being shipped) than moving it over land (Finley 1973:126). Thus the best way effectively to exploit the land was to concentrate on land with easy access to good waterways, as most of the ancient agronomists attest. Thus, at least at first, the "civilized" Roman world, at least its eastern end, tended to inhabit the fringes of the Mediterranean, drawing on only a thin belt of hinterland for produce, while the interior was ruled by "barbarians," with nearly all the great urban centers within a few miles of the coast

(1973:30). This pattern, however, changed over time, especially in Western Europe: the empire slowly grew inland (1973:31–32). In addition, of course, rivers allowed for cheap and effective water transportation. The result was the much greater desirability of land close to rivers and a tendency for cities to spring up along these waterways, supplied by them and providing markets for land adjacent to them. Strabo thus describes the cities of Italy in terms of their access to the Tiber (*Geography* 16.2.46).

The problem with water transport, of course, is that it normally requires the cooperation of nature: one cannot control the availability of rivers for access to the hinterland, nor the seasonal vicissitudes of water and wind currents. And only a tiny proportion of potentially arable (or otherwise productive and populated) land was accessible to boats. The result was that transport, where waterways were unavailable, was only via the slow, difficult means of land transport and effective only over short distances and with relatively restricted loads. It thus tended to be local, regionally restricted and autonomous, its substance underexploited by the empire. This is not to say that land transport was not used. All cities required transport of food produce from their immediate hinterland, as well as other products from even farther abroad:

> No city was self-sufficient. All supplies, of food or materials for ship-building, house-building, and industry—such as wood, stone, wool, metal, and potter's clay—had to be brought in either from the surrounding countryside, or from overseas. Land transport was always necessary in the first case, and often in the second, since many cities lay miles inland from their ports. For example, Argos and Corinth are about 5 miles from the coast, and Athens is 7 miles from the Piraeus. (Burford 1960:3)

The older view was that heavy transport was severely limited by the character of the throat-and-girth harnesses available to the ancients, which tended to ride up the horse's throat and choke it if it applied its full strength. This problem, and the failure to apply multiple yoking in any effective way, meant that animal power was never used to its fullest possible extent, was capable of an absolute maximum load of eleven hundred pounds, and did not replace the use of human beings as the primary manner of bearing loads. Even if this view were correct—and it is not, most importantly because the primary draft animal of antiquity was the ox, not the horse—such limitations have more of an effect on very heavy items, such as stone, metal, or even timber, rather than produce (1960:1–3). Indeed, in the case of produce, bulk—the transport of large volumes of grain seed or oil, whether carried by pack animals or placed in a wagon—would always have been a more significant factor than weight in retarding transport.[55]

The difficulty for moving produce, then, is not lack of power so much as lack of speed, not so much the expenditure of energy on weight as on distance. It was ineffective and uneconomical, except in the instance of rare, extremely small, or specialized items, to transport goods for any significant distance over land. Indeed, for peasant villagers, access to pack animals and carts cannot be assumed, nor can the leisure to take several days of travel in order to market one's produce. We have already seen evidence that even in so restricted an area as a village and its environs, the effect of distance was such that fields were valued differently according to their distance from the village. If any further proof is needed of the way in which ancient life revolved around the restrictive character of distance, a study of Romano-British walled towns has shown that their relative spacing was based on the optimum distance of a settlement from its "tributary area" (that is, its dependent countryside = χώρα, or smaller settlements), and larger settlements on which it in turn was dependent for markets or specialized products (Hodder and Hassall 1971). The study concludes:

> As suggested by the fixed lattice [a model used in this study], the approximate distance along the main roads from the major unwalled settlements to the edge of their tributary areas is 8 miles. . . . The average maximum distance to the hypothetical locations of the minor unwalled settlements on the other hand, is about 4 miles from the edge of their tributary areas—again probably rather more on the ground. Approximately this distance has often been noticed as being the maximum distance to market preferred in societies with primitive means of transport. . . . These minor settlements may have acted as the local markets, while the function of the major unwalled and the walled centres would have been to provide specialist services to lower-order central places, although also providing the same range of services as the lower levels in the hierarchy. In any case, as a testable hypothesis, *the whole observed locational pattern might be seen to be based on the maximum distance easily travelled to and from the local market in one day.* (1971:404, emphasis added; see Finley 1973:127)

In other words, settlement patterns reflect and partially compensate for the difficulties involved in ground transportation. At least under Roman rule and after some centuries of it, regular settlement patterns evolved in the way most conducive to maximal contact between the largest settlements and the interior they served (or which served them). The same pattern is true of Roman Palestine as well.[56]

This pattern of evolution suggests two important conclusions. First, in the absence of access to waterways for transportation, villages and other small settlements were, because of the difficulties involved in land transport, restricted to exploiting agriculturally an area whose perimeter was no more than 5 miles (8 km) from the village in any direction. This figure is a maximum: working a field 5 miles from one's village would involve considerable hardship. Moreover, a tiny fraction of such a huge area would easily be sufficient to meet the dietary needs of even a larger village. In a densely settled Galilee, villages were far closer together: only larger towns (such as Capernaum) would have been this far apart, thus facilitating traffic between their own tributary areas, that is, the villages that used them as markets. A second point, however, is more important. As long as the inland settlement pattern is restricted to larger towns about 8 km apart, the economy will remain purely local. Again, we can expect inequities to arise due to varying natural advantages, due to exploitative economic practices (insofar as they may have been applied in trading, loans, and so on), and local class variations. Nevertheless, the local centers comprised by larger towns, at least according to the model offered by Britain (and as far as can be told from the size of the towns), would have been capable of producing their basic dietary needs from their own fields. Where they would have differed from smaller settlements is in providing additional services and local markets, which would in turn have generated sufficient surplus to support such middle-range specializations (Finley 1973:107). Thus produce would not have escaped from the local economy: towns and villages would have existed in a sometimes symbiotic, sometimes parasitic relationship, in which the larger settlements did exploit their hinterlands but provided services in return, and at any rate were in little position to export surplus out of the region. The existence of larger cities within a reasonable distance from a cluster of such towns would be necessary to expand the economy in an outward, extra-local direction.

If we move from the abstract to the specific and concrete, we see that several features of the Galilean countryside invite modification of these conclusions. First, in Galilee, there *is* access to waterways for the region described above as the Valley. Second, however, the terrain generates even more restrictions on transport than is usual, steep hills and massifs between towns forcing roads to be circuitous and extending the actual distance to be traveled, and normally precluding the use of carts or oxen.[57] Thus the transportation of produce in this area must be carried by mules or humans and can be transported economically only short distances. In addition, certain patterns of movement are reinforced by the specific shape of the terrain: (1) the Valley is geographically isolated from most of the rest of Lower Galilee; (2) the use of the lake for transportation makes the towns along its shores very easily accessible to each other; (3) for the remainder of Lower Galilee, the topography runs east-west, rather than north-south, cutting it off from Upper Galilee but facilitating access to the coast; (4) there were few Roman roads in Lower Galilee, and none (known) in Upper Galilee;[58] and (5) we cannot assume the ordinary availability to peasants and small villages of draft animals, even mules, nor, for that matter, of boats to take advantage of the lake.[59]

Actual patterns of Galilean trade, as far as they can be discerned, help flesh out this picture. First, as might be expected, trade in basic products tended to be local and subsistence-oriented. It was also relatively specialized, mainly limited to those items whose character makes them difficult to produce everywhere. Pottery is the most obvious instance of such a product: it is relatively cheap and broadly necessary, but cannot be made everywhere (at least not well), because good potting clay is not ubiquitous (Adan-Bayewitz 1993). And, as it turns out, the most sophisticated and precise study of Galilean local trade currently available focuses on pottery. David Adan-Bayewitz has painstakingly analyzed the distribution of pottery throughout Galilee deriving from two known centers of pottery production, Kefar Ḥananya, marking the "border" between Lower and Upper Galilee, and (to a much lesser degree) Shikhin, possibly about 1.5 km to the north of Sepphoris.[60] These two centers were identified from literary sources as producers of pottery, and this identification, as well as the locations of the erstwhile settlements, was confirmed archaeologically.[61] The clay in the neighborhood of these sites, and the pottery known to have been manufactured on site, was analyzed using neutron activation analysis, which measures a wide array of elements found in pottery specimens; the composition of pottery from one location normally has a distinctive and fairly consistent chemical signature that can be contrasted with that derived from pottery known to have been manufactured elsewhere (1993:42–47). Pottery from a variety of sites scattered throughout Palestine was sampled, with a view to identifying the proportion of Kefar Ḥananya ware in any given location.

The results were striking. While it is clear that pottery was a major industry of Kefar Ḥananya, the vast majority of its wares was discovered very close to home. With a few significant exceptions (see below), the farther one gets from the manufacturing center, the lower the proportion of Kefar Ḥananya ware one finds and the greater the proportion of other types (see 1993:212). The vast majority (anywhere from about 80 to 100 percent) of pottery shards inventoried closely proximate to Kefar Ḥananya, such as Meiron (9.7 km away), Rama (5.1 km), Hazon (4.5 km), and Kefar Ḥananya, itself derive from Kefar Ḥananya.[62] This set of

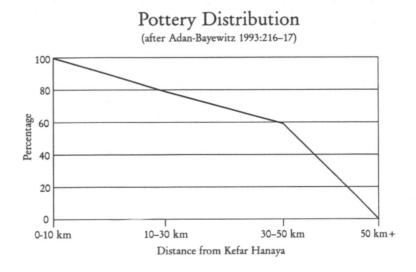

Figure 2: Approximate relationship between percentage of Kefar Ḥananya ware at various sites as a function of distance from its manufacturing center.

towns very nearly falls within the 8 km (5 miles) radius suggested above as a comfortable distance to travel and exchange goods. The heavy concentration of Kefar Ḥananya ware within this radius (or slightly beyond) should come as no surprise. Nor is it especially surprising—although it is certainly remarkable, given the specialized character of pottery manufacture and the quality of the clay available to Kefar Ḥananya—that these figures do indeed drop off significantly as the distance from the area increases. In towns about 25 km away, such as Yodefat (23 km) and Sepphoris (26.5 km), the proportion of domestic ware from Kefar Ḥananya drops to 76 percent and 74 percent, respectively, while those even farther away have a still smaller proportion (Khirbet Zabdi [36.5 km], 59 percent; Jalame [45.5 km], 56 percent). By about 50 km away, the proportion drops off to nothing. There are noteworthy exceptions to this very regular pattern. First, the towns of the Golan show smaller proportions of the ware than their distance alone would warrant: Kanaf, 30.3 km away, has 12 percent; 'Ein Nashut, 41.3 km away, has 21 percent; and Gamla, 44.5 km away, has 11 percent. Second, and conversely, Hammath Tiberias, 23.2 km away, shows a much higher proportion of domestic pottery from Kefar Ḥananya than one might expect: 97 percent.

These results do not entirely speak for themselves; they are susceptible to some varying interpretation. Clearly, the data contradict Safrai's image of marketing; Safrai suggests that the common picture of producers coming to town to market their goods should be supplemented by inclusion of caravans that left the city and traveled from town to town during the week, selling items and buying surplus produce (1994:423). Were such means used for the marketing of any bulk items, including pottery, we would expect a much more even distribution of Kefar Ḥananya ware over a greater radius: the longer radii of such caravans, including their cities of origin—rather than the more limited areas within easy walking distance of each other—should have about the same proportions of this ware. Horsley is thus doubtless correct to interpret Adan-Bayewitz's results as suggestive of very limited marketing of basic items:

> One reference in the Jerusalem Talmud (*Ma'aś.* 2.3, 49d) seems to portray Kefar Ḥananya potters as peddlers (*rokhlim*) of their own products, going around to four or five villages before returning home for the night. But Adan-Bayewitz's own study of all the rabbinic references to the term *rokhel* reveals a specific type of itinerant peddler who carried products of light weight and relatively high value such as cosmetics or spinning goods in their baskets. Significantly, the term is never used in connection with pottery. So pottery would not have been marketed by middlemen such as peddlers. The distribution pattern of Kefar Ḥananya pottery taken together with rabbinic references to the transport and sale of pottery and other goods thus suggests limited social interaction among Galilean villages or between villages and the two major cities of Sepphoris and Tiberias. The distribution of the pottery itself apparently would have entailed interaction primarily between the potters of Kefar Ḥananya and their customers. (Horsley 1994a:107)

Adan-Bayewitz offers slightly different conclusions, which fit the data more completely:

> There is good reason to suspect that the marketing of Kefar Ḥananya ware by itinerant potters was probably not an important means of distribution. The predominance of Kefar Ḥananya ware in cities and villages 25 km. from the manufacturing centre cannot easily be explained except in terms of central-place marketing. The relevant rabbinic texts, few as they are, include no hint of marketing by itinerant potters. Moreover, potters are not included in the list of occupations which involved frequent dealings with women, although *rokhlim* are mentioned. (Adan-Bayewitz 1993:233, citing *t. Qidd.* 5.14)

Itinerant peddlers, as far as can be told from the literary evidence, transported, as Horsley suggests, cosmetics and spinning goods, all relatively light and high-value items that could be carried easily by one person;

pottery, conversely, is bulky, relatively inexpensive, and not frequently replaced (Adan-Bayewitz 1993:232–33). It was evidently marketed in part by the producers themselves, carried to market in a bundle or on a carrying pole, or perhaps on a pack animal.[63] According to the Talmud, when potters traveled to other villages to market their goods, they did so only to four or five settlements nearby, and then returned home the same night (Adan-Bayewitz 1993:232, citing *y. Ma'aś.* 49d). This certainly matches the distribution patterns of local pottery discovered in the Golan, which attest to overlapping spheres of small-scale production serving quite restricted areas.[64] Such practices would explain the way the distribution pattern drops off with distance and may help to confirm Horsley's assertion that the pottery trade was quite limited and local.

But the preponderance of Kefar Ḥananya ware in towns along a 25 km radius also indicates that the cookware was marketed some significant distance beyond the 8 km radius of easy daily travel. Given the distances involved, this marketing was probably performed by middlemen (Adan-Bayewitz 1993:233). Thus Adan-Bayewitz suggests that in addition to a considerable degree of local marketing by its producers, Kefar Ḥananya ware was also distributed through central marketing: transported to a central location (or set of locations) by producers or middlemen and sold to consumers there. Such a practice would explain the fairly surprising extent of large proportions of this ware (Adan-Bayewitz 1993:219, 233). Thus Kefar Ḥananya, at least at a regional level, was involved in specialized trade of manufactures, and this trade went somewhat beyond merely local relationships. Indeed, it is equally clear that Kefar Ḥananya marketed to Galilee's two cities, as well as its scattered towns, and this in spite of the fact that Sepphoris had a pottery-producing town in the immediate neighborhood (Shikhin).[65] On the basis of these data, Adan-Bayewitz, in sharpest contrast to Horsley, concludes that:

> It should be noted that the predominance of Kefar Ḥananya cooking ware at Sepphoris and, presumably, Tiberias represents the first archaeological evidence of the dependence of these Galilean cities on the manufactured products of a rural settlement. It also represents the first well-defined archaeological evidence for continual urban-rural commercial interaction within Roman Galilee. It may also be noted that the distribution pattern of Kefar Ḥananya ware does not seem consistent with the picture, common among scholars, of the exploitation in the early Roman period of the Galilean peasant by the urban wealthy. The present evidence, of an important local manufacturing centre in rural Galilee, is also inconsistent with the conception that rural Galilee in the early Roman period was exclusively agricultural. (Adan-Bayewitz 1993:219)

These peculiar conclusions, however, are no more founded on the data than those of Horsley. While Adan-Bayewitz is quite correct to point, against Horsley, to the distances involved and to the contacts with Sepphoris and (probably) Tiberias, he is incorrect to presuppose the applicability of a modern market model for squeezing more general conclusions out of these data. In particular, Adan-Bayewitz's conclusions assume five things: (1) that cities *should* be manufacturing centers, as they are today; (2) that trade and exchange (whether monetary or in kind) are an instrument for the generation of capital, as they are (at least in appearance) today, rather than labor and the (more or less legalized) seizure of goods (tribute, rent, booty, etc.) being the main generators of value; (3) that the distribution of Kefar Hananya pottery is a direct function of trade and, moreover, of free trade;[66] (4) concomitantly, that the benefit of such trade will accrue to the producer, along the model of medieval artisanal production; and finally (5) that Kefar Hananya's production of pottery was the town's major means of support, to the exclusion of agriculture.[67]

Setting such anachronisms aside, rather different conclusions suggest themselves. First, what these distribution patterns show is that trade even in specialty items was regional. Confirming this conclusion is one of the exceptions to the distance rule noted above, which is the significantly diminished proportion of Kefar Hananya ware discovered in the Golan: the ware manufactured in Galilee was marketed for Galilee.[68] Second, even as specialized producers, the potters were governed by distance and the difficulty of overland trade. Thus one of the reasons Kefar Hananya was able to market its pottery throughout Galilee was its advantageous central location.[69] It is also likely that the disproportionate amount of Kefar Hananya ware found at Hammath Tiberias is partially a function of the availability of marine transport and perhaps also a function of the political centrality of Tiberias for the region. Third, the presence of Kefar Hananya ware in the cities is simply further evidence of the cities' overall dependence on the countryside for their goods, including manufactured basics. This does not mean that the cities were not centers of specialization; their markets were indeed the place one might find the specialty products of a variety of local centers all in the same place. But we should not assume that simply because the cities were settings for larger markets, the goods in question were produced on site. The very large percentage of Kefar Hananya ware in Hammath Tiberias, out of proportion to its distance from the town (in terms of distance alone, one would expect about 75 percent rather than 97 percent), not only reflects the accessibility of marine transport along the lake but additionally points to Tiberias as a marketing center for specialized products: Adan-Bayewitz's data suggest that the city served as a point of concentration for the goods of the hinterland to an extent that made it an exception to the consistent rule of proportion diminishing with distance. Access to the lake for transportation could only have facilitated this tendency.

What is especially informative in regard to the role of the cities in the distribution of goods is the pattern of pottery finds at Sepphoris. Here, while the common cookware was to a large degree from Kefar Ḥananya, a significant proportion of the pottery (45 percent) found was from Shikhin, in the immediate neighborhood (Adan-Bayewitz and Perlman 1990:162). One must note the importance of the fact that the majority of Sepphorean cooking ware (74 percent) was from Kefar Ḥananya in spite of there being a pottery producer close by.[70] This datum serves as a further indication that the cities functioned as concentration points for specialized rural products, manufactured and otherwise. But what is really striking is the marked differences of function of the pottery from the two different locations. Sepphorean cookware is predominantly from Kefar Ḥananya, while the 45 percent of pottery deriving from Shikhin was comprised predominantly of storage vessels (Adan-Bayewitz and Perlman 1990:158, 162, 164, 167–70). This indicates not only that Shikhin's pottery production specialized in storage vessels rather than cookware but much more importantly that Sepphoris was a large consumer of such vessels, which of course invites speculation as to what the vessels contained! As Adan-Bayewitz and Perlman conclude:

> Regarding Sepphoris as supplier, the literary sources provide useful background for our evidence. These texts indicate that Sepphoris was the most important market centre in central Galilee during the Roman period. The city is said to have had an upper and lower market and its own standards for weights and measures; on a lead weight recently discovered by the Joint Sepphoris Expedition, a market inspector is mentioned and a colonnade depicted, providing archaeological evidence for the Sepphoris markets. It is reasonable to assume, therefore, that Sepphoris was an important market centre for the pottery of both Kefar Ḥananya and Shikhin, and that *many of the Shikhin storage-jars, manufactured so close to Sepphoris, were filled with products and sold in the markets of that city.* (Adan-Bayewitz and Perlman 1990:170, emphasis added)

In particular, if the large storage jars were filled with grain, we have further evidence of Sepphoris draining produce from the countryside.

These observations suggest a number of general conclusions about trade in Galilee. First, manufacturing, even of extraordinarily basic (that is, relatively cheap and in general demand) items, was a very limited enterprise. Kefar Ḥananya did not have a monopoly on Galilean cookware but was the major supplier of this necessity in its region. Specialized production was necessary, not only because of the restrictions of skill and equipment but also because of nature (that is, the presence of better clay in Kefar Ḥananya). Nevertheless, this production for the whole region was undertaken by a mere village and evidently was not allowed to interfere with its continued agricultural activities.

Second, we have no grounds for concluding that this trade was especially profitable for its producers; in fact, a continued focus on agriculture in Kefar Ḥananya, along with the failure to develop this industry in urban locations,[71] would suggest that it was not. Rather, pottery manufacture, as a result of the presence of appropriate clays, developed opportunistically (that is, because it could), and, as more of the village's resources (in terms of time and the development of appropriate equipment and skills) were devoted to it, came to be a necessary compensation for agricultural shortcomings.[72] Any pressure on the village's agricultural resources would necessitate a corresponding increase in the devotion of resources to pottery manufacture; in a tribute system, such pressure could come in the form of simply increasing demands for so-called surplus produce, while even in a market system (which is too much to expect from antiquity), it could come from high and increasing demand for the pottery itself.[73] In either case, the village was as much a subject of this task as a beneficiary of it. We cannot assume, in the absence of a strong market economy, a monetary profit beyond those needs for decent subsistence as might have been provided by exclusively agricultural work.

Third, the pottery was apparently marketed locally by the producers themselves—if our literary sources are to be trusted, probably by short-distance traveling salesmen (not *rokhlim*)—and does have a monopoly (or nearly so) in the limited 8 km radius of casual local interaction. It was probably marketed regionally, however, by middlemen who were responsible for its transport, and who, although they worked outside of the 8 km local radius, were also influenced by the contemporary limitations on land travel, remaining within a 50 km radius and evidently working less prolifically as distance increased. It is difficult to say how, precisely, the ware was marketed at these distances. Central place marketing is convincingly argued by Adan-Bayewitz, but since the proportions of ware are normally a function of distance rather than the size of a settlement, it is difficult to argue for any singular central place; instead we should assume that middlemen transported the pottery to a variety of different locations from which they were locally marketed and that these middlemen may have dealt with products other than pottery as well (Adan-Bayewitz 1993:229). On the other hand, disproportionate quantities of Kefar Ḥananya cookware at Hammath Tiberias quite possibly attest to concentration of this ware in Tiberias, as the high quantities of Shikhin vessels in Sepphoris attest to the concentration there of the contents of those vessels. What emerges, the cities as market centers notwithstanding, is that Tiberias and Sepphoris were large consumers of rural products, without having been significant suppliers of much of anything.

Thus, fourth, we have some concrete evidence of urban siphoning of rural products, whether manufactured goods or produce, with trade attested only insofar as it signifies the physical transportation of these products. Indeed, the presence of a village that specialized in manufacturing storage jars so accessible to Sepphoris (Shikhin, rather than in a central location, like Kefar Ḥananya) suggests that its industry evolved to meet Sepphorean needs and hence that the presence of Sepphoris had a decisive effect on the surrounding neighborhood. Furthermore, its presence attests to that city's demand for vessels to store produce, which in its turn suggests a chronic practice of collecting and accumulating produce necessarily grown elsewhere.

Thus, at the very least, and in contrast to Horsley's conclusions, there appears to have been a fairly elaborate network in place, in spite of technological and geographical difficulties, to channel produce and other goods to the main cities, as well as throughout the region. By extension, other sorts of ordinary intercourse evidently could have taken place on a routine basis between close-by settlements, and so for the inhabitants of one village to have dealings on a frequent and even casual basis with those of another is unlikely to have been unusual or worth remarking. Indeed, the presence of some limited regional trade (that is, within a 25 to 40 km radius, diminishing with distance) in such specialty items as cookware indicates that travel in the Galilean hinterland beyond one's immediate neighborhood was also acceptable.[74] The pottery trade was an inverse function of distance much more because of the limitations of cartage than the sheer distance itself. A person traveling lightly could easily traverse much of Galilee in a very short time.

The situation is similar, and rather more straightforward, in the case of olive oil. Like pottery, this product requires a measure of specialization: although a staple, it cannot serve the majority of dietary needs, and it necessitates an appropriate climate (ideally, one not requiring irrigation), a prior commitment (because of the length of time it takes the trees to mature), and a not-inconsiderable physical plant (since it was the oil that was marketed, not the olives, hence making presses a necessity). Thus, as was the case with pottery, oil was one of those isolated ancient items that was both a basic need and yet required a more-than-basic apparatus to produce. As Josephus describes it, the marketing of oil may have been a feature of at least the Upper Galilean economy. Describing, as is his wont, the treachery of John of Gischala (from Upper Galilee), Josephus complains that:

> He next contrived to play a very crafty trick: with the avowed object of protecting all the Jews of Syria from the use of oil not supplied by their own countrymen, he sought and obtained permission to deliver it up to them at the frontier. He then bought up that commodity, paying Tyrian coin of the value of four Attic drachms for four *amphorae* and proceeded to sell half an *amphora* at the same price. As Galilee is a special home of the olive and the crop had been plentiful, John, enjoying a monopoly, by sending large quantities to districts in want of it, amassed an immense sum of money, which he forthwith employed against the man who had brought him his gains. (Josephus, *War* 2.591–92; see *Life* 74–75)

This text actually does not indicate—in spite of its frequent citation as evidence of a thriving oil trade and thus perhaps a significantly commercialized economy—that there was a large-scale and regular trade in olive oil from Galilee to Syria or elsewhere (see Horsley 1996:68). The text from *War* only describes the delivery of all of the local oil (that is, apparently, only what oil was on hand in Gischala) to the frontier; the slightly different account in *Life* describes the oil as destined only for the town of Caesarea Philippi. In neither case is the oil shipped any significant distance. Moreover, Josephus presents this act as a consequence of the war: he specifies that the extraordinary circumstances had driven the price of oil to remarkable heights, because they had prevented the inhabitants of a nearby portion of Syria from "obtaining oil from their countrymen" (that is, fellow Judeans). While such a result could attest to the war's interruption of commerce—by preventing the movement of producers (marketing their produce to consumers), consumers (traveling to the producers), or middlemen, between mutually hostile territories—Josephus actually describes the high oil prices as the consequence of much more specific and directly political factors. Either the border was closed (*War* 2.591: he "obtained permission to deliver it up to them at the frontier"), or, more specifically, the Jews in Caesarea Philippi were deliberately confined within the city (*Life* 74). Such a restriction would entail the inability of Caesarean Jews to travel even locally, and thus their having to make do with whatever oil was already in this predominantly Gentile town. Hence the issue of the religious purity of oil, combined with the extraordinary and unique circumstances that confined local Jews to the town itself, caused the tremendous increase in price. Horsley goes so far as to argue that such a price increase, moreover, would have been a function of the cost of overland transport anyway, or at least that this cost would have eaten into John's profits (Horsley 1996:68). Josephus does, however, regard John's actions to have netted him "an immense sum of money." Nevertheless, Horsley is correct to point to the high cost of land transport, insofar as this story implies that shipping such a distance would only be undertaken as a profitable enterprise under such extraordinary circumstances of scarcity.

This is not to say that olive oil was not ever traded or transported under ordinary circumstances. What Josephus's account does suggest, for instance, is that there was a sufficient oil surplus to sell, that there were means of transporting it, and that there was demand for it, although special and probably unique factors pushed this demand to unreasonable heights. The very extraordinary characteristics of this episode simply indicate the ordinary limits to this trade. Particularly, they indicate that while trade in oil probably was a feature of the Upper Galilean economy, trade over such distances as that between Gischala (Gush Ḥalav) and Caesarea Philippi (about 32 km as the crow flies) would have been profitable chiefly or only under conditions that allowed extravagant increases in price. Thus we probably have a picture here—under ordinary circumstances—of a specialized industry much like that of pottery: regional distribution limited by the constraints of distance and the shortcomings of land transport.

The production of olive oil, however, was less specialized than that of pottery. Not only was the whole region of Upper Galilee apparently involved in some degree of oil production, much of Lower Galilee was as well, as were the neighboring regions; and in fact oil as a staple was produced even in less advantageous locales.[75] So it makes little sense to imagine that the Upper Galilee's apparent oil surplus was used to supply the dietary subsistence needs of Palestine or Syria: the cost would have been prohibitive, and the demand would simply have been insufficient. The image of a thriving commercial economy makes little sense. The very locales to which Galileans would most easily ship oil are precisely those that were quite capable of producing that oil themselves. However, Horsley's insistence on the entirely local character of the Galilean economy and its complete self-sufficiency may be exaggerated. Subsistence grain production evidently did accompany the cultivation of olives, and it is possible that the oil presses that have been discovered were initially used for purely local demand. But Josephus's story attests to a surplus, and the oil generated in the Upper Galilee would have been superior in quality and, as the story indicates, in religious virtues as well. Moreover, larger towns would have had to obtain their oil for all purposes from somewhere: thus a plausible urban demand and evidence that surpluses were generated (at least at those times when, as Josephus puts it, "the crop had been plentiful"), suggest, minimally, that the basis or potential for trade in this product existed for the villages of the Upper Galilee.

What confirms this observation and adds interesting detail is the fact that Josephus describes John of Gischala's transactions as monetary transactions involving, specifically, Tyrian coin (*War* 2.591). This detail is especially interesting in light of the fact that a significant proportion of the coinage discovered in Galilee was from Tyre or other Phoenician cities.[76] Indeed, this preponderance of Phoenician coin is sometimes cited as an indication of strong trade ties between Galilee and the coastal cities (Meshorer 1976:57). Such trade ties would make a measure of sense: geographically, Upper Galilee is more accessible to the coastal cities than it is to cities further to the south in Galilee or in the rest of Palestine. In terms of distance, the coast is no farther from, say, Gischala, than are the cities of Lower Galilee. And in terms of geography, the coast is more accessible to Upper Galilee than anywhere else: the east-to-west flow of the terrain makes the transportation of goods from Upper Galilee to the coast a matter of greater ease (one simply follows the contour of the land downward) than would be the case for transport to the Golan (which would involve crossing over mountains) or to anywhere in Lower Galilee (which would involve continual negotiation up and down a series of east-to-west ridges blocking one's route). Moreover, the Phoenician coastal cities were centers of maritime shipping (Kapelrud 1962; Horsley 1996:85–86)—the only economical way to transport produce in antiquity—and thus the relatively short distance from, say, Gischala, to Acco or Tyre was, in economic terms, the most expensive portion of the distance from Gischala to Egypt, Italy, or Greece.

John's shipping of oil overland from Gischala to Caesarea was profitable only because of the extraordinary circumstances of war, but shipping it about the same distance from Gischala to Tyre would have been useful under even the most ordinary conditions, both because the city itself would have generated a high demand for produce (and had either the money or the power necessary to acquire it) and because its accessibility to the Mediterranean would have allowed an extension of trade otherwise impossible. Literary evidence also attests to the links between the produce of Upper Galilee and the consumption or trade of Tyre. Acts 12:20 states that the people of Tyre and Sidon sued Agrippa for peaceful relations, "because their country depended on the king's country for food," while the Talmuds describe oil caravans coming from the Galilee to the Phoenician coast (Safrai 1994:417–18). The now-standard picture of fairly close relations between Upper Galilee and Phoenicia is almost certainly correct. This also suggests, as does the overall picture painted by the Gospels, that political borders were not much of a barrier to travel except in times of war (see Acts 12:20; *War* 2.591).

The evident export of oil to the coast, however, does not in itself answer the question whether the Galilean economy was "open" or "closed" in the early Roman period.[77] While it is clear that oil and perhaps other produce went from Upper Galilee to the Syrian coastal cities, it is by no means likely that the Lower Galilee was implicated in this trade. Although its geographical position made it accessible to Phoenicia (Ptolemais or Acco), its production seems to have been oriented more or less to mixed subsistence, at least at the beginning of our period. Trade in even such a specialized item as pottery appears to have been regionally limited. Kefar Hananya is situated directly on the border of the two Galilees, and it is for this reason that it could supply them both. The preponderance of Tyrian coinage in Lower Galilee as well as Upper Galilee, moreover, does not indicate direct trade with Tyre. As Horsley points out, Tyrian currency served as a kind of standard in the area: it was minted in abundance, had an excellent and stable metal content, and silver and gold coins could not, of course, be minted locally, or even regionally.[78] Thus the presence of particularly Tyrian coinage does not necessarily indicate trade with Tyre, even though it does indicate some monetization of the economy. Moreover, even in Upper Galilee, it is by no means clear that the movement of goods was necessarily profitable for those goods' producers. As was noted above regarding pottery, the advantages of the movement of goods could and probably did accrue to the cities where they were consumed or traded rather than to the countryside where they were produced. Horsley draws attention to the overtly political background to such exchange, repudiating the anachronistic presumption that the movement of goods in antiquity is the same thing as modern trade, that is, open, free market, and motivated by the self-interest of the free parties who engage in them. He contends:

> The principal "surplus product" of the Galilean or Judean peasantry, however, was under the control of the Herodian or high-priestly rulers and/or the Roman government in the form of taxes, tithes and offerings, and tribute. Trade between Judea or Galilee and Tyre was thus under the control of the very rulers who expropriated the agricultural products of the peasantry and who desired the luxury goods Tyre had to offer—as mediated perhaps by traders working for the Judean or Roman rulers. Tyre, of course, with its shortage of land from which to draw agricultural produce, was dependent particularly on imports from nearby agricultural areas with a "surplus," such as Galilee.[79]

These are extraordinarily important points. The fact that some exchange took place between, say, Upper Galilee and Tyre should not imply that the Galileans initiated this contact on their own behalf, that it was in their own interest, or that any impressive benefit accrued to them as a result. It is difficult to imagine where in the Upper Galilee one would find sufficient demand for Tyrian products to overcome the peasant tendency to minimal effort that normally limits cash cropping and trade to whatever is required for subsistence, or who in Upper Galilee would have had the power and resources to initiate the infrastructure and organization that allowed this contact to persist. Tyre may very well have required the produce of Upper Galilee, but it is difficult to see why the exchange need have been reciprocal; when other powers had control of this region, Tyre was forced to negotiate with them in order that they allow and organize—and, if necessary, force—the shipping of goods down to the coast. And these powers, unlike independent villagers scattered through the hill country, would have had more than sufficient demand for Tyrian products, including, among other things, money.

These observations suggest that, at least insofar as the two Galilees were a collection of more or less self-governing villages, trade, especially open trade, need not have been a major factor in their economies. Some trade in basic but specialized necessities undoubtedly took place, and surplus product may have been used to acquire the odd luxury or imported good, especially from the Phoenician coast. But the Galilees were marked, in spite of what movement of goods took place, by a closed economy. Political force, however, would have oriented production, especially in Upper Galilee, toward cash crops. Military force is not quite as constrained by the same limitations as trade: whoever happened to rule (or dominate) Upper Galilee at any given time had the means to ensure its inhabitants' compliance. The casual development of free and open trade as a result of market forces is an unrealistic and anachronistic depiction of village life. Where the transport of goods became a major factor of the region's economy, we can only conclude that it was as a result of political decisions and political force; how such changes could have been organized and enforced is addressed below.

At the same time, however, there is also some evidence that by the later Roman period the entirety of the Galilee, including Lower Galilee and the Valley, was immersed in a variety of forms of trade. The Mishnah itself is filled with considerations pertaining to the treatment and sale of large herds of livestock, produce, cash crops, and so on, while it dismisses those who live on the land as the intractable *'am ha-'ares* (people of the land). Obviously, as the Mishnaic traditions developed and by the time they were codified, some significant portion of Galilean economic life was controlled by rather well-off farmers and townspeople who worked for profits and who owned considerable property. Likewise, specialization of crops and shortages of staples in some regions indicate a more "open" economy, at least among some sectors of the population (Safrai 1994:416–17). Archaeological evidence confirms this picture. Unusually large and elaborate buildings at Capernaum, especially the synagogue, "indicate a large, prosperous Jewish community supported by trade, fishing, and agriculture" (Tzaferis 1989:215). It is notable that these remains date from significantly after our period and that one of the buildings is a synagogue: the Mishnaic image of profit-oriented townspeople taking advantage of the Galilee's fertility immediately suggests itself. Thus there appears to have been a change in trading patterns over time, a movement from a closed economy to a (more or less) open one, a movement from a village-based economy incapable of sustaining the major cities to a regionally interdependent and profitable network of exchange, a movement from direct military imposition of exchange from outside to one undertaken by larger landowners and wealthy figures within the region. Safrai sums up the situation:

> As we have already seen, the trade system was rather limited during the Second Temple period, with the most important commercial institution of the time in the rural sphere apparently being the travelling salesman. The local market served, in addition to its commercial functions, as a convenient meeting place on Mondays and Thursdays. Such seasonal or temporary markets are usually good indicators of a small amount of commercial activity and the unimportant role of such activity in everyday life. The situation changed, however, somewhere at the end of the Second Temple period or immediately afterwards. The sources from that time provide a picture of a developed trade system functioning at various levels. (1994:423)

These conclusions—at least if we reject Safrai's (and others') assumptions that such developments occur, as in a free-market economy, simply because opportunities present themselves—raise the question why and how such changes occurred, what kind of tributary apparatus was initially applied by the cities to the countryside and what its effects might have been, how trade was organized and encouraged, how the flow of wealth moved from one set of rulers to another, and where the producer figured in all of this. And this set of questions immediately raises the closely related issues of monetization and of taxation.

Coinage, Monetization, Debt, and Taxes

The circumstances pertaining to monetization are less ambiguous than those associated with trade. The use of regular coinage—money rather than barter—demonstrably increases from almost nothing in the Hellenistic and early Roman period to a regular device for exchange by middle to late Roman times (see Kloppenborg 2000:233). First, throughout the Roman period, economic systems in which money was a major factor in exchange were rare, especially in rural areas (Finley 1973:107; Crawford 1970:40). Crawford specifies:

> If, therefore, the use of coined money as a means of exchange was largely limited to the cities of the Empire, its use there was probably an accidental consequence of its existence and not a result of government policy. Certainly a city did not *need* coined money, as the history of Babylon and other Eastern cities shows. The view that the cities of the Roman Empire came only by accident to adopt coined money as their means of exchange is corroborated by the absence of government reaction to the forms and structures individually created. (1970:45)

These conclusions are probably only partially correct. Although the creation of coinage may have been accidental at first, there were good reasons for the increased production of coinage or a monetized system, especially intensifying as the size of the empire increased without a corresponding rise in the technology of transport: coinage is the best form for the long-distance transportation of extracted value.[80]

The main administrative uses for hard money were the payment of taxes to the government and the payment of troops by the government.[81] In addition, urban life in antiquity required the use of money at all social levels (Crawford 1970:42 and n. 16). Both literary and archaeological evidence support this claim. Various decrees, inscriptions, letters, and historical accounts reveal the significance of money in urban locations.[82] All of the cities that have been excavated have yielded large numbers of coins, including various denominations of the low-value copper coinage required for everyday transactions.[83] Ordinarily, however, coins were not a regular feature of rural life. In the countryside, when coinage is found, it tends to be silver, and thus in higher denominations—representing "hoards" or accumulated value—than are required for use in everyday, commonplace transactions (Crawford 1970:43). At an excavated villa near Capua, Italy for instance, only thirty coins were found, all but one of which were struck fifty to one hundred years before occupation began, and this in spite of the fact that during the period of the villa's occupation Augustus had struck enormous issues of orichalcum and copper in (relatively) nearby Rome (Crawford 1970:43–44).

> This does not suggest that coinage played in the life of the occupants of the villa the sort of rôle that a rapid turnover of coins would suggest, the sort of rôle that is suggested by the occurrence at Pompeii of coins of every denomination struck within a few years before the destruction of the town. It can of course be argued that a countryman would go into town to purchase his wants and that he could partake of a market economy as much as a town dweller. But the emphasis of Cato's *de agricultura* is on producing what is needed and buying only what was absolutely necessary; it is summed up in the phrase . . . the head of a household should be a seller, not a buyer. Small, recurrent purchases do not form part of the picture. If this was true of a farm run for profit it was probably even more true of peasant farms. Cicero's claim that ordinary farmers had no spare cash undoubtedly rang true. (Crawford 1970:44)

Papyri remains confirm this picture of rural life: rent is often paid in livestock or produce.[84] Only extraordinary expenditures or efforts to hoard large values (see Matt 13:44; Luke 15:8; Matt 25:25) would require coin: hence the rural preference for high denominations. Actual money, as opposed to produce or other goods, was used to buy such objects as houses or fields, or to repay loans and other types of dues.[85] It may also have been used while traveling, to avoid having to carry bulky goods to pay one's way (see Matt 10:9), as well as in times of crisis, when liquidity was necessary to preserve or transport one's wealth.[86] When used for these desultory purposes, the money may have been acquired in the first place by making loans, by selling produce to the government (in Egypt) or to whomever else could pay cash for it, by selling property, or by renting out one's slaves.[87] Presumably hiring out oneself for labor, as attested in parables attributed to Jesus, was a comparable source of hard money for the less affluent.[88] Obviously, any developing need for money or the sorts of activities or products for which money was used—the payment of money dues, the payment of loans, the purchase of fields, travel—would require one to engage in that limited range of activities that generated money.

The point is worth reflecting on when one comes to consider the situation in Palestine, and in Galilee particularly. Here, the use of money demonstrably increased from the first century onward, and alongside of this trend, the kinds of transactions for which money was a requirement. Safrai argues that the use of (copper) city coins was widespread throughout Palestine, even in rural areas, and refers to finds of foreign city coins in such towns as Capernaum, Migdal, Gush Ḥalav, Meiron, and elsewhere

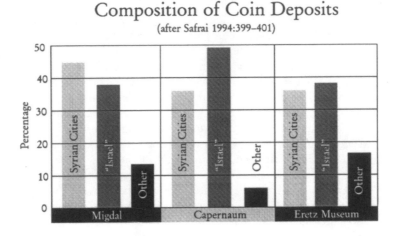

Figure 3: Sources of coins from three different locations, as described by Safrai.

(1994:399). Among such Galilean finds, Phoenician city coinage is normally most common, followed by various Palestinian issues, with a stable but usually quite small portion coming from Transjordanian cities (including the Golan and Arabia);[89] oddly, Galilean coins are present, but are not especially abundant. But Safrai does not pay sufficient attention to the dating of these coins. In the case of Migdal, for instance, which Safrai cites, there are no coins in the hoard earlier than 74 c.e. (Meshorer 1976:54, 57). Another hoard, found at Huara, has a similar range (1976:57). Since both of these collections represent deliberate hoarding rather than natural accumulation and contain coins dating well into the third century, we must assume that the distribution of dates does not reflect directly the relative abundance of coinage throughout the time period covered by the hoards. But the stark paucity of first-century copper city coins, not only in hoards but in general, does reflect a relatively unmonetized Galilee in the first century, at least as regards the daily transactions for which copper coinage would be required.

This is hardly surprising: silver and gold coinage, which could be minted only in select locations, traveled widely and quickly, even into the countryside. But copper coinage, which in the Roman period was normally minted locally, by individual cities, did not tend to travel very far, probably because of its limited value (Meshorer 1976:57). Tyre was sufficiently proximate to Palestine for its high-denomination coinage to circulate throughout Palestine and was close enough to Upper Galilee for one to assume that a certain portion of copper coinage leaked into the region, an assumption confirmed by the archaeological evidence.[90] But throughout the Maccabbean and Herodian periods, Galilee had no local mints. Copper coins minted in Jerusalem would have had to travel an unusually long way before circulating in Galilee; even Tyrian copper coins would have had to travel some considerable distance before arriving in Lower Galilee or the region around the lake. It should be clear, then, that the establishment of a mint in Tiberias (apparently coincident with the establishment of the city itself) was intended to provide the Lower Galilee, and especially the perimeter of the lake, with the kind of low-denomination copper coinage that could be used for ordinary transactions.[91] The fact that such local Galilean coins are relatively sparse even in Galilee itself indicates that the economy was not already monetized and that it was not easily or quickly monetized by Antipas.[92] The foundation of Tiberias itself, however, eventually served as a stimulus to the use of copper currency, and so the coins of Antipas can be found in Hammath Tiberias, Meiron, Gush Ḥalav, Nabratein, Arbel,

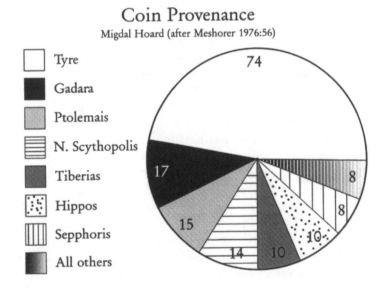

Figure 4: Sources of coins found in the Migdal hoard. Numbers in the graph indicate the actual number of coins.

and Capernaum (Meshorer 1982:205, n. 28). This was the intention: the fact that the issues were aniconic is an indication that they were not intended either for foreign trade, or for strictly governmental or Tiberian use but were for the Galilean (Jewish) population at large.[93]

Thus the establishment of a local Galilean mint at Tiberias and the increasing evidence for the use of money from the first century onward are of a piece: the Galilean economy was not especially monetized by the time Antipas came to power but became increasingly so from that point onward, and did so as a result of, or at least with the encouragement of, deliberate political policy. The simultaneous foundation of Tiberias and of a Galilean mint is no coincidence: an effort to urbanize corresponded to an effort to monetize. Monetization was unquestionably in the interests of the wealthy and ruling classes, as well as the Romans: it allowed value to be removed from Galilee without the burdensome requirement of transporting bulky items overland (Freyne 1995:38); as a result, the wealth of this very productive region could be tapped effectively and relatively cheaply. It allowed land to be purchased and hence concentrated into fewer hands.[94] It allowed Galilee, a region not immediately on the coast, to be brought into the economic orbit of the empire. By facilitating the easier exchange of one type of product for another, it encouraged economic specialization such as cash cropping, which was of no discernible benefit to the local peasantry but which benefited both the local upper classes, by generating greater profits, and the wealthy of the rest of the empire, by orienting production toward trade and luxury consumption rather than subsistence. At the political level, a ruler like Antipas or his successors could conveniently allow the Phoenician cities to retain their virtual monopoly on, say, olive oil exports from Upper Galilee because the revenue from such sales in the form of money could be easily directed to other locations and converted into whatever goods the rulers required, or it could be used to pay tribute to Rome.

In order for all of this to happen, however, more than a convenient supply of money is required: demand must also be generated. In England, as the Middle Ages drew to a close, as well as in the global imperial situations of the nineteenth century, alienation of land was used, often in combination with legally required cash dues, to create a free labor force: the mere availability of employment for cash wages was normally insufficient to motivate wage labor, so large numbers of people had to be placed in a position where they needed the money such employment could provide in order to survive. For quite different economic reasons— that is, to monetize and internationalize subsistence economies, rather than to generate a free labor force—and somewhat less effectively, the Romans employed similar techniques. The generation of extra local debt and the effective collection of dues worked in tandem and in mutually reinforcing ways to create a demand for currency, which in its turn necessitated sales—of produce, property, or labor—to obtain that currency, which in their turn fostered further monetization, in a slowly accelerating cycle (see Hanson and Oakman 1998:123).

In an influential article, Martin Goodman has suggested that the availability of liquid capital to the Judean upper classes fostered the usury that was a principal cause of the unrest leading up to the war of 66–70 c.e. (Goodman 1982). In the absence of other outlets for investment, "the exceptional influx of wealth into the economically parasitic city of Jerusalem" could only be invested profitably in the form of interest-bearing loans (1982:419). Thus unconsumed wealth (in money) from temple dues, pilgrimage income, and Herodian spending generated debt simply by being available to peasants for loans in difficult times, against the security of their land or their person (1982:427). Goodman draws our attention to some provocative phenomena, but his thesis is at odds with what is known generally about capital in antiquity. Finley states outright that the ancient economy did not have "excess capital seeking the more profitable investment outlets we associate with colonialism" and further notes that in the absence of mechanisms for the creation of credit, money lending was limited by the amount of cash actually on hand (Finley 1973:141, 158; Crawford 1971). This latter point may be irrelevant for wealthy moneylenders based in Jerusalem: as Goodman quite correctly points out, the city, as the final destination of a variety of money dues (both civil and religious) and of pilgrim travelers, would have had immoderate amounts of available coin (Freyne 1995:39). But the notion of profitable investment of this coined wealth—the use of money to generate more money and the assumption that wealth *is* money—is uncomfortably modern. Indeed, it assumes a stability and fixed value to money that was simply not the case in antiquity. Rates of exchange between copper and higher-value coins fluctuated widely (Crawford 1970:43), and, as Josephus attests (*War* 6.317), the value of money could be depreciated (and, presumably, appreciated) by circumstances. Wealth as always in antiquity is land, and land in turn generates further wealth. Goodman is certainly correct that the copious amounts of money flowing to Jerusalem would have allowed for loans in money, especially loans to the less affluent of Jerusalem itself. But the main reason to lend money, whether in Jerusalem or Galilee, would have been the longing to acquire land, rather than an interest in abstract financial return. Indeed, loans would have been a singularly inept means for generating stable profits: it is only when the borrower fails to repay that any significant gain is made, whether in the form of exorbitant late-payment penalties or, more realistically, in the seizure of the lands or persons pledged against the loan. But for the very same reasons, money lending would have been an extraordinarily effective means for acquiring land. This observation should direct our attention to the effects of money lending and indebtedness, rather than simply their preconditions. Goodman emphasizes only one side of the overall process: not only did liquid wealth fuel debt, but debt fueled liquid wealth, that is, the overall monetization of the economy.

It is something of a commonplace that debt levels were increasing among free rural smallholders throughout the first century and that this increase resulted in the concentration of land among wealthy creditors.[95] The largest body of evidence for this trend comes from the Gospels themselves, which are replete with descriptions of tenant farmers, absentee landlords, and the supplications of insolvent debtors (for example, Matt 6:12; 18:23-34; 20:1-15; Mark 12:1-11 pars.; Luke 12:16-20; 16:1-17; *GThom.* 21). Josephus, similarly, records the burning of the public archives during the revolt against Rome, commenting explicitly on its class basis: "They next carried their combustibles to the public archives, eager to destroy the money-lenders' bonds and to prevent the recovery of debts, in order to win over a host of grateful debtors and to cause a rising of the poor against the rich, sure of impunity. The keepers of the Record Office having fled, they set light to the building" (*War* 2.427). This event offers reasonable grounds for concluding that the situation in the decades preceding the war was difficult and probably worsening for those obligated to take out loans (see Goodman 1983:59). Papyri and inscriptional remains tend to confirm this inference. The wording of loan documents from the period offers some indication that foreclosure was a major motivation behind lending. Exorbitant and punitive interest rates (the usual penalty for late repayment was a fine of half of the principal or more), clauses explicitly anticipating execution of the loan on the debtor's property or person, and records of complaints about lenders overzealously exacting repayment unfairly or above and beyond the terms stipulated, all indicate that usurious lending and subsequent foreclosure were preponderant social phenomena.[96] This evidence also shows that these phenomena were problematic, that they were and were regarded to be causes of hardship and conflict.

The introduction of the *prozbul,* attested both in rabbinic literature (*m. Šeb.* 10:1-9; *m. Giṭ.* 3:3) and in an earlier (55–56 C.E.) papyrus (Benoit, Milik, and de Vaux 1961:101–3), demonstrates that loans were prevalent enough and economically important enough to warrant overriding the injunctions of Torah. Significantly, the Mishnaic *prozbul* laws apply only to loans in which land is offered as collateral (*m. Šeb.* 10:6). In other words, it is only agricultural loans that are of sufficient economic import to merit such provisions; other lending and borrowing is left to the wiles of those involved.

The abrogation of the sabbatical provisions of Torah guarantees that debtors are unprotected from the seizure of their securities, at least in the case of land. One can only agree with Goodman that the bounty of coin in Jerusalem accelerated this process, insofar as it made coin easily available for loans. But it should also be noted that much of the time agricultural loans were made not in cash but in produce. The farmer who suffered a bad harvest did not so much need money as extra produce from those who possessed larger tracts of land, to feed himself and to provide seed for the following year. Several of the literary and documentary remains attest to such practices of loans in kind;[97] many more, however, do attest to loans in money (see *m. B. Bat.* 10; Hunt and Edgar papyrus nos. 62–67, 69–70). Whether the loans were made in produce (by those with sufficiently large holdings to weather bad harvests) or in coin (by those who had sufficient coin on hand or saleable produce), they would slowly have stimulated a monetization of the economy, with all of its attendant effects.

A smallholder who went into debt because of a bad harvest, if he received coin, would then use that coin to buy produce from his more successful neighbors (that is, those with better and larger plots), putting those neighbors in the position of selling surplus produce for cash. Moreover, if the loan was made in cash, there is every indication that it was expected to be repaid in cash. Thus the hapless borrower, regardless of the sufficiency of his subsequent harvests, would have to sell his extra produce to generate the money required to repay the loan or, conversely, would have to hire himself out to wealthier neighbors, who in their turn would have to use his labor for the surplus cash cropping that would generate the cash to pay him. If the original payment was made in produce and subsequent harvests fell short, the debtor, if he was to make payment, must sell (for money) some of his own assets—property, equipment, labor—in order to buy (for money) the produce to repay his creditor. In either case, the local economy was quite effectively monetized in a variety of locations.

Moreover, if we assume that the primary debtors in this cycle were those who possessed small, subsistence-oriented tracts of family land, it is easy to see how indebtedness led to concentration of land. If, as Fiensy claims, the average family plot was in fact six to nine acres (1991:92–95), and if the figures offered earlier in this chapter for subsistence levels are correct, most families lived on the razor's edge of starvation and failure most of the time. Village communalism and local charity probably made up for ordinary shortcomings by distributing produce. However, extraordinarily bad harvests, which left little to be distributed, or external demands for cash or extra produce, would have forced smaller landholders to take out the kind of loans on which interest was calculated and penalties for late payment imposed (Goodman 1987:56). Repayment of such loans would then have cut into the tiny margins on which such individuals survived. When such loans were made, foreclosure was bound to follow eventually. This cycle, then, in addition to outright military or political seizure, led to the progressive concentration of landholdings attested for our period,[98] and these in turn further monetized the economy, in their generation of surplus produce, in the necessity to pay hired laborers, and so forth.

This whole cycle, I would contend, itself conducive to monetization, was set in motion by the creation of a greater demand for surplus or, more specifically, for cash. This increased demand was of course fostered by political processes, that is, the increased demand for dues of various types, particularly taxes, from the small peasantry. Here, the evidence suggests two apparently contradictory conclusions, which, however, may be reconciled. The first conclusion is that taxation was undoubtedly felt to be burdensome in the time of Herod the Great, in the tetrarchies under his sons, and under direct Roman rule. Most of our evidence on this matter comes from Judea, but general conclusions about the character of taxation in Galilee might carefully be extrapolated.

According to Josephus, Herod's death was taken as an opportunity to complain about his capricious and excessive taxation.[99] Archelaus, attempting to curry favor with his new subjects, therefore entertained requests that he reduce yearly payments and eliminate certain sales taxes.[100] It should be noted, however, that the real focus of these outbursts was not so much the rate of taxation as the manner in which it was exacted. The degree or burden of the regular tribute is not addressed; instead the focus is on the use of servants to collect it, the capriciousness with which it was assessed, its ultimate disposition in foreign cities, and even, in the case of sales taxes, the consistency or effectiveness with which it was collected ("ruthlessly exacted" [Josephus, *Ant.* 17.205]). After Archelaus left for Rome, the entire country appears to have broken out into open, if scattered, revolt and brigandage: "And so Judea was filled with brigandage. Anyone might make himself king as the head of a band of rebels whom he fell in with, and then would press on to the destruction of the community, causing trouble to few Romans and then only to a small degree but bringing the greatest slaughter upon their own people" (17.285; see 17.250-98; 17.269; 17.271-72; 17.273-84; *War* 2.39-79; 2.56-65). Whether this outburst was motivated by burdensome

taxation or not is unclear. The Roman response was particularly fero-
cious in Galilee and resulted in the complete destruction of Sepphoris
(17.286–98; *War* 2.66–79; see Schürer 1973:330–35).

More obviously related to taxation were the revolts that accompanied
the deposition of Archelaus and the imposition of direct Roman rule,
accompanied as it was by a census and direct Roman tribute:

> The territory of Archelaus was now reduced to a province, and
> Coponius, a Roman of the equestrian order, was sent out as procu-
> rator, entrusted by Augustus with full powers, including the inflic-
> tion of capital punishment. Under his administration, a Galilean,
> named Judas, incited his countrymen to revolt, upbraiding them as
> cowards for consenting to pay tribute to the Romans and tolerating
> mortal masters, after having God for their lord. This man was a
> sophist who founded a sect of his own, having nothing in common
> with the others. (Josephus, *War* 2.117–18; see *Ant.* 18.4-10; Schürer
> 1973:332, 381)

At about the same time, Tacitus records general dissatisfaction in Syria
and Judea with the levels of tribute (*Annals* 2.42). And the First Judean
Revolt, as well, appears to have been at least partially motivated by
Roman extraction of tribute: Florus forcibly extracted seventeen talents
from the temple treasury for the imperial service, and, in fact, tribute
was in arrears at the time the war broke out (Josephus, *War* 2.293).
Agrippa's speech at the commencement of hostilities makes payment of
back tribute a central issue: "But your actions are already acts of war
against Rome: you have not paid your tribute to Caesar, and you have
cut down the porticoes communicating with Antonia. If you wish to
clear yourselves of the charge of insurrection, re-establish the porticoes
and pay the tax" (*War* 2.403–4). And, finally, literary portrayals of tax
collectors cast these figures in an unequivocally and invariably bad light,
as voracious, unclean, and immoral.

The second conclusion, apparently contradicting the first (that taxation was felt to be burdensome), is that Roman levels of taxation were
not appreciably higher than those prior to Roman domination. According to 1 Macc 10:29-32 and as reiterated by Josephus (*Ant.* 13.48–51),
Seleucid tribute on the land was one-third of grain produce and one-half
of orchard produce, in addition to the regular tithes paid to Jerusalem
and the temple. Roman tribute, if anything, was less stringent:

> Gaius Caesar, Imperator for the second time, has ruled that they
> shall pay a tax for the city of Jerusalem, Joppa excluded, every year
> except in the seventh year, which they call the sabbatical year,
> because in this time they neither take fruit from the trees nor do
> they sow. And that in the second year they shall pay the tribute at

Sidon, consisting of one fourth of the produce sown, and in addition, they shall also pay tithes to Hyrcanus and his sons, just as they paid to their forefathers. . . . As for the villages in the Great Plain, which Hyrcanus and his forefathers before him possessed, it is the pleasure of the Senate that Hyrcanus and the Jews shall retain them with the same rights as they formerly had, and that the ancient rights which the Jews and their high priests had in relation to each other should continue, and also the privileges which they received by vote of the people and the Senate. (Josephus, *Ant.*14.202–3, 207–8)

Rome did add a poll tax to Judea after 6 c.e., but this imposition would not have affected the client kingdom of Antipas in Galilee. Nor were Herod the Great's massive building projects funded entirely on the backs of his subjects: Emilio Gabba has argued convincingly that the additional revenues required for such products were acquired from Herod's own wealth in landholdings and, interestingly, in mining and tax farming outside of his own domain (1990:162–63). In spite of all of his building activity, he was thus able, it appears, to maintain the tax rates established by Rome at the death of Caesar, yielding approximately one thousand talents annually for the entire realm.[101] Thus,

it certainly appears that the amount collected was the result of a re-ordering of the previous variegated fiscal system and that the collection was carried out with the usual brutal methods: this in itself is enough to explain the obvious complaints which were raised in Jerusalem and Rome after the death of the King. The accusations of excessive exploitation of the kingdom and of consequent general misery, which are often accepted by modern historiography, seem, however, to be without foundation. Taxes were levied directly—on products of the soil, through payment of a proportional or fixed quota (there does not appear to have been a poll tax: this was introduced later by the Romans), and indirectly—on sales and certain trade, particularly transit trade activities, by means of excise duty and tolls. It is possible that the collection methods later imposed by the Romans replicated at least part of the system in force under Herod. (1990:161–62)

Gabba's summary indicates precisely how our discrepancy is to be explained. It is not that the tax burden had increased in terms of total demand, at least until the time of Vespasian (Suetonius, *Vespasian* 16.2), but rather that it was being exacted more efficiently and effectively than it had been in the past. Finley points out that taxation, the bulk of which fell on the land, was bearable, in spite of accelerating rates of gross intake (1973:55, 89–90). Instead of raising tax rates, as Gabba notes, ever-increasing amounts of tribute and government income were generated by administrative means, that is, either "by various schemes designed to bring marginal and deserted land into production, by confiscations and by requisitioning devices, for example, for road construction and the imperial post" (Finley 1973:90; see SEG XIX 476), or by large-scale money lending by the same individuals who were responsible for collecting the taxes that made the loans necessary in the first place (Finley 49–50). Since the Roman tax burden lay disproportionately on those who worked the land, that is, the peasantry, the effect of this extension of taxation into areas not yet within the orbit of the imperial economy was to place further pressure on an already encumbered peasantry. Thus Finley summarizes:

> It is in the nature of things that the peasant, independent or tenant, has a fragile hold on his land: he has little margin when times are hard. The combined effect of the various developments I have been examining—increasing taxation, depredations and devastations, depression in status as symbolized by the establishment in law of the category of *humiliores* [of humble rank]—were to drive him either into outlawry or into the hands of the nearest powerful landlord (or landlord's agent). And the latter, as we saw in the case of the tenants on the imperial domain at Carthage, meant protection and oppression at the same time. (Finley 1973:91)

While the circumstances here encapsulated by Finley do not necessarily pertain directly to first-century Galilee,[102] the general implication was correct that additional tax burdens on the peasantry would have had the effect of shaking them loose from control of the land.

Josephus's complaint that Herod's sales taxes were exacted "ruthlessly" reveals less concern about the official existence of the taxes than about the fact that they were enforced. When Josephus and other sources describe the actual collection of taxes, in Judea or elsewhere, what emerges is that, as with all other kinds of ancient economic contact, proximity is a prerequisite. Physical contact is necessary to determine the amount of taxes to be collected, and in order to actually, physically, collect them (MacMullen 1974:36–37). Josephus, speaking of Judea in the period immediately before the war, describes the manner in which the Roman tribute was obtained: "the magistrates and the members of the council dispersed to the various villages and levied the tribute. The arrears, amounting to forty talents, were rapidly collected. Thus for the moment Agrippa dispelled the menace of war. . . . The king . . . sent the magistrates and principal citizens to Florus at Caesarea, in order that he might appoint some of their number to collect the tribute *in the country*" (*War* 2.405, 407). What is especially notable here is that the city—Jerusalem—collects its tribute from the villages immediately adjacent to it. As with transport, easy economic contact is restricted to the immediate neighborhood. The collection of dues from "the country," on the other hand, must take place at a later time and under direct Roman supervision. While this example derives from Judea, not from Galilee, the general point should be clear: the taxation system at the time worked best in situations of close physical proximity.

What emerges, then, is that political power must be based, physically, fairly close to its sources of revenue in order to obtain that revenue. Even the use of military force, armed servants, contracted tax collectors, and other traveling emissaries decreases in efficiency the farther it reaches beyond its power base. Under normal circumstances, a hinterland community, especially one with an unmonetized economy, while theoretically subject to the taxes levied by its rulers, was often in an easy position to slight those demands simply because of the difficulty of and the cost involved in the physical removal of its produce. This is not to say that taxes were not collected but simply that they were collected much more regularly and efficiently from areas close to cities than they were from areas far from cities. Other types of dues would be even more affected by the same considerations: tithes paid to a local priesthood could be easily maintained, but those dues, especially money dues, destined for Jerusalem are less likely to have been honored.[103] Such a hinterland community, in its ability to avoid a variety of dues and to be largely unmolested by the demands of tax collectors (who would gravitate to centers more likely to yield higher profits, that is, those within easy transportation distance from larger cities) and its relative segregation from Mediterranean trading patterns, would, as long as these circumstances continued, have been able to maintain a certain autonomy and the basic patterns of smallholder village life. On the other hand, the moment these circumstances change and the community is subjected to intensified tax demands, whether in money or in kind, the peasants' tenuous hold on the land is threatened, and they begin a cycle of debt, monetization, loss of land, tenancy, and further monetization, all of which serve to benefit the local elites and the imperial administration. By the political imposition of taxes, the region in question is drawn into an empirewide orbit of money and trade, and must redirect its own local resources accordingly.[104]

The Cities and Urbanization

It is obvious that the sole events in first-century Galilee that would have achieved these effects are the foundation of cities within the Galilean hinterland. Two such cities were founded by Antipas: Sepphoris and Tiberias. Moreover, these cities were founded at the very beginning of the period we have been considering, and, indeed, shortly before the rise of the earliest Jesus movement and the composition of Q. It has become the standard view in scholarship on antiquity that the cities were sites of consumption, not of production.[105] As a result, the normal attitude of the countryside to urbanites was fear and hatred; tensions and conflict mark the contacts between city and countryside (Horsley 1996:118–30; MacMullen 1974:28–41). We have already seen how Sepphoris and Tiberias relied even for such basic manufactured goods as pottery on small towns and villages such as Shikhin and Kefar Ḥananya. The cities' complete dependence on the countryside for agricultural goods, which they were of course incapable of producing, is even more obvious. These goods could be obtained through outright seizure, forced services, taxes, rents, interest on loans, or fees for various services offered by the cities, including market and exchange services (see Horsley 1996:119–20; MacMullen 1974:34–35, 52–53; SEG XIX 476).

If we take this notion of the consumer city seriously, the impact of the foundations of Sepphoris and Tiberias should become clearer. Jonathan Reed has already described at some length the effect such large new cities would have on the countryside surrounding them: "After their founding as major centres by Herod Antipas, the agricultural practices of the Galilee were not only completely realigned, but were also stretched. Lower Galilee could no longer be considered as a series of villages, hamlets, and farms. The entire agricultural focus turned to feeding Sepphoris and Tiberias. . . . [N]ow entrepreneurial farmers and landowners, who grew a single cash crop on a larger scale for the granaries at Sepphoris, became necessary" (1994:214–15). But mere urban consumption of the produce from nearby villages is just the beginning. The effect of the new cities should not be measured only in terms of what they took because they had to but also in terms of what they took because they could. In addition to requiring a complete reorientation of the Galilean economy toward surplus production and cash cropping (with attendant stimulation of trade and monetization) simply to feed their inhabitants, Sepphoris and Tiberias would have also formed a practical and proximate home base for those, including Rome and the Herodian government, who wished to plunder the agricultural wealth of this underexploited region. The new settlements could serve as concentration points or collection centers for tax demands on the countryside, for loans to Galilean freeholders, and eventually for the income of absentee landlords from their rural estates.[106]

It is difficult to conclude that this policy was anything but deliberate. Towns had to have access to fertile hinterlands to survive (Finley 1973:126, 139), but, conversely, fertile hinterlands could not be adequately exploited without the presence of towns. The entire history of the incorporation of the Middle East into the vast Hellenistic and then Roman empires is the story of the establishment of new cities by conquerors. In Palestine, the Roman proconsul Gabinius is reported to have established or rebuilt Samaria, Azotus, Scythopolis, Anthedon, Raphia, Adora, Marisa, Gaza, Apollonia, Jamneia, Gamla, and perhaps others (Josephus, *Ant.* 14.88; *War* 1.166; see Issac 1990:152 and n. 3). Roman client kings likewise established cities, as did the Flavian emperors (Issac 1990:154–58). Even where the client kings exercised a measure of autonomy, their own interests in founding administrative centers for themselves would have likewise served the demonstrable tendency of the whole empire toward urbanization.

Gottwald refers to the political-economic organization behind the Hellenistic and Roman empires as the "foreign tributary mode of production" (1993:7–8). Its establishment of a network of metropolis-periphery relationships is to be distinguished from that of modern imperialism insofar as the main source of surplus in the ancient tributary mode of production derives from force, the application of military and political power to directly remove others' assets, rather than from uneven market transactions.[107] But in order for local rulers and profiteers to exercise this power economically and effectively—and thus to enrich themselves and to enable Rome to expect consistently high levels of tribute, as well as simply to circulate the goods of the countryside among the empire's wealthy consumers—physical proximity was required, and hence a policy and consistent practice of "urbanization" (the founding of cities of significant size, spaced throughout the hinterland in order effectively to tap its resources).[108]

So, as a piece with this general imperial practice, all of Herod the Great's successors engaged in the building of cities in their new, smaller, realms. Philip built Caesarea Philippi; Antipas did not restrict himself to Galilee but also built or rebuilt Betharamphtha (Livias, Julias) in Perea (Josephus, *Ant.* 18.27; *War* 2.168). Strictly speaking, Antipas did not found Sepphoris: the city had been the major urban center of Galilee for decades or longer. Antipas merely reestablished the city in about 3 B.C.E., only a year after it had been destroyed by Varus (Josephus, *Ant.* 18.27; *War* 2.168). Horsley even suggests uninterrupted continuity of occupation during this period (1995a:167). Clearly, Antipas rebuilt Sepphoris on a grander scale than it had hitherto existed (*Ant.* 18.27); nevertheless, in so doing, he altered only the magnitude of its impact on Lower Galilee. Only a year had gone by since it had last been standing, and, at any rate, the rebuilding of Sepphoris took place a good deal before the public activity of Jesus or the composition of Q, and, apparently, at some distance from the setting of these events. The (re)foundation and expansion of Sepphoris, while of a piece with Herodian and Roman policy, and necessary for the exploitation of Lower Galilee proper, probably did not have much impact around the rim of the lake, which was not only rather distant but was also somewhat geographically isolated. Nor is it likely that Upper Galilee was much affected by this new foundation, for the same reasons.

Thus it is very interesting, both in terms of Antipas's political-economic policy and its impact on the region of primary interest for Q, that several years later he established a completely new foundation, in a region not easily accessible to Sepphoris, in a region that was accessible to the Valley (that is, because of the availability of water transport, the whole area bordering the western edge of the lake, as well as being in easier contact with Upper Galilee), and, moreover, even made this new city his capital. Antipas founded Tiberias around 19 c.e.—after more than twenty years with Sepphoris as his royal ornament—on the southern edge of the lake. From here, because of the character of the local geography, Antipas had access to large sections of Galilee formerly untapped by Sepphoris. Reed sums up the situation:

> The major urban centres along the Levant—Caesarea Maritima, Scythopolis, and Tyre—form a rough triangle. Galilee lies beyond the immediate reach of each of these major urban centres. Only Scythopolis lies within twenty-five km of Galilee. *But with the founding of Sepphoris and Tiberias, no area of Galilee lies outside a twenty-five km radius of these two minor urban centres.* Therefore Tiberias and Sepphoris must be seen as minor urban centres, dominating the agricultural landscape of the Galilee, but not large enough to attract substantial international trade. (1994:218, emphasis added)

This suggests that the Roman partition of Palestine was a very wise strategic move: by parceling off political jurisdictions, in an economy based on tributary extraction of surplus, Augustus thereby ensured, with such fragmentation at a political level, a far more concentrated and penetrating economic exploitation. The foundation of Tiberias, then, should be seen as a deliberate part of Roman-Herodian policy and one that had a decisive and dramatic effect on the surrounding countryside, which had, prior to this foundation, lived in relative smallholder autonomy, protected by geography and the constraints on ancient transport from severe exploitation by Roman or Hellenistic powers based even as close by as Sepphoris. The moment the brand-new city of Tiberias went up, however, there would have been a sudden and dramatic effect on the countryside around the lake, and, to a lesser degree, in Upper Galilee. In particular, we would expect this region to experience a drift of goods toward the city (with attendant social effects at the village level), a (forcible) reorientation of agriculture toward urban consumption, progressive monetization of the economy, more frequent use of hired labor, greater efficacy in the extraction of taxes and other dues, incremental concentration of land with resultant tenancy and loss of smallholdings, cash cropping and specialization, greater trade, and a noticeable polarizing of the divide between the relatively wealthy and the very poor—in short, an incremental reduction, at a variety of levels, in the rural peasantry's standard of living.[109]

Social Effects on Galilean Village Life

The various effects of these relatively sudden changes unquestionably had a significant impact on the social organization of the villages, forcing as much of a concomitant reconfiguration and reconsideration of social roles as of economic behavior (Kloppenborg 2000: 231). It is obvious that the villages were not communistically oriented prior to Roman-Herodian rule and the establishment of Tiberias. Whatever else he may have done, Antipas did not dismantle paradise. Class differences and distinctions had long existed in the villages, in spite of their relative autonomy and their subsistence orientation.[110] Houses were of different sizes and quality (see Overman 1993:41). Some land was better than other land, because of its agricultural character or merely because of its relative proximity to the settlement. Plots were different sizes. Some specialization of produce had already begun centuries before: orchards and oil presses were not the prerogative of everyone, nor did they benefit everyone. And some export trade to the Phoenician coast, including grain, is attested from Ptolemaic times.[111]

One should thus not be misled by the rhetoric of Q itself nor by the panegyrics on smallholder life offered by Horsley, Fiensy, and others:[112] the old-fashioned ideals and practices of the pre-Herodian period did indeed both conceal and foster class distinctions and did indeed benefit a relatively elite sector of the local populace. It is worth pointing out that Q takes for granted the legitimate existence of rich and poor, of creditors and debtors, as well as the more obvious distinctions between men and women, children and parents. Those with greater resources could increase their wealth and their access to luxury items by exporting their surplus to the coast, a practice we know took place. They could afford to devote less of their time and personal labor to the maintenance of their lands and perhaps even hire some of their fellow villagers as laborers during peak periods. They could serve as patrons or benefactors at a local level and thus bolster their social status and local prestige. Finally, in consequence of all of these factors, their political position within the village would be one of leadership.[113] This kind of phenomenon must necessarily have been somewhat variegated: more or less absent or unofficial in tiny settlements, exaggerated or formalized in larger ones, and shared by a greater or smaller number of prominent families (Schürer 1979:184–90). In the case of larger villages and towns, with several prominent families, with diverse economic circumstances and plot sizes, with some specialization, with some occasional hiring of labor or perhaps tenancy, and with at least nominal attachment to an outside power (Egypt, Syria, Judea, depending on circumstances), a local administrative apparatus was required. The necessarily limited political affairs of such communities were conducted by a collection of elders, some of whom, perhaps, from time to time bore the title of κωμαρχής (village leader) or something similar (see SEG XXXIII 1359; Hunt and Edgar 1988: v. 2, 35), their legal affairs settled by magistrates (see SEG XIX 476, ll. 20–21; Josephus, *Ant.* 18.37), while their total polity and community life was expressed in gatherings of village assemblies (see Horsley 1994a:113; 1995a:222–37; 1996:131–53; Kee 1999).

Under such circumstances, even the most de facto autonomous of towns required various official and witnessed bills of sale, petitions, contracts, marriage agreements, wills, and so forth, as well as an apparatus for the administration of justice. Thus, in addition to local strong men and affluent families, a small class of literate administrators was essential to the smooth functioning of the region even prior to Roman-Herodian city building. Such a role was normally filled by the so-called village clerk, the κωμογραμματεύς. We have extensive evidence from Egypt for the presence and function of these figures (SEG XXXIII no. 1359; Hunt and Edgar 1988: v. 2, 34–39, 250–59, 392–93; Westermann and Hasenoehrl 1934:135, 143, 147, 149; Westermann, Keyes, and Liebesny 1940:105–6), and some indications that they were a feature of Palestinian village life as well (see Josephus, *War* 1.479; *Ant.* 16.203). As their title indicates, their primary task was writing: composing various official documents for those unable to write (for example, Hunt and Edgar 1988: v. 1,171); forwarding petitions to appropriate officials (for example, 1988: v. 2, 35; 2, 251–59); ensuring the execution of legal responsibilities (for example, 1988: v. 2, 255; Westermann, Keyes, and Liebesny 1940:105–6); and serving as witnesses (for example, Westermann and Hasenoehrl 1934:135, 143), middlemen (for example, 1934:147, 149), or accountants (for example, Westermann, Keyes, and Liebesny 1940:105–6) for persons with extensive business dealings.

These administrators would not be found in every settlement and could not have been very numerous even in larger settlements.[114] Thus a single scribe might very well have serviced a cluster of villages, and inhabitants of smaller settlements, when seeking justice, preparing documents, or pursuing other official business, had to travel to the nearest settlement that had a scribe. These duties did not occupy the scribes full-time. They were as engaged by agricultural production as their fellow villagers and were drawn from the local peasantry itself,[115] with whom they probably, to some degree, identified. At the same time, however, their roles involved a measure of prestige and power, at least within the village and its immediate area.[116] These administrators thus occupied a middle position between the average smallholder and the larger landowners who dominated village life and whose interests the scribes tended to represent. They therefore formed something of a rudimentary retainer class, who mediated between the ordinary people and the upper classes, and who, in so doing, sought to maximize their own power and privileges.[117]

The relative loss of local autonomy brought about by Antipas's administration would probably have affected the social roles and the perceptions of these village scribes more than anyone else. As Kautsky notes regarding peasant responses to change,

> They [peasants] must become aware of changes affecting their conditions for better or for worse if they occur quickly enough to provide an opportunity for comparison with preceding conditions. Thus, crop failure, particularly when not accompanied by a reduction of taxes, or an increase in taxes imposed upon them are obviously felt by peasants and are likely to be resented. As Barrington Moore puts it: "Economic deterioration by slow degrees can become accepted by its victims as part of the normal situation. Especially where no alternative is clearly visible, more and more privation can gradually find acceptance in the peasants' standards of what is right and proper. What infuriates peasants (and not just peasants) is a new and sudden imposition or demand that strikes many people at once and that is a break with accepted rules and customs." (Kautsky 1982:307, quoting Moore 1966:474)

The foundation of Tiberias probably did in fact have a dramatic and immediate effect on the settlements within its immediate orbit, if only insofar as Antipas forced its settlement (*Ant.* 18.37). But the incremental deterioration of smallholders' circumstances, as it has been described in this chapter, took place primarily through a series of processes that were relatively slow, cumulative, and methodic: debt, monetization, trade, and the gradual loss of title to the land (without necessarily the loss of its occupancy). If Kautsky and Moore are correct, not much of a reaction is to be expected from the peasantry under these circumstances.

Those who, however, were the victims of relatively sudden change, of new impositions and demands that did indeed "break with accepted rules and customs," were the few and scattered individuals charged with the administration of a now-defunct system. With the transfer and central-ization of wealth and power to the new cities, the mediating status of these individuals is lost. Their patrons and masters have transferred their allegiances (and residences!) to the cities,[118] leaving the scribes behind to make do—alongside the peasantry—in the countryside, away from the centers of power. The scribes have been transformed into local clerks charged with little more than supervising the intensified exploitation of their compatriots.[119] This new situation, in addition to involving a con-siderable curtailment of function and a loss of prestige, also places these figures in a tenuous position among their neighbors. Still charged with a mediating position, they must now serve the villagers as functionaries for and representatives of not the local strong men or leading families, who may serve both as respected community patrons and as nearby sources of power and authority in cases of conflict, but of the distant and hated city. Like the tax collectors who figure so prominently in the narrative stories of Jesus, they are forced to play the role of the enemy within.[120] Aban-doned by their patrons, perhaps resented by their charges, with consid-erable loss of power and diminution of roles,[121] these individuals both increasingly identify with the progressively exploited peasantry yet are alienated from them and, indeed, participate in their exploitation.

Of course the relative autonomy of the village as a whole (not only that of its administrators) was affected, and this is nowhere more evident than in the gradual transformation of the role of synagogues. As Horsley argues, the synagogue as a Galilean institution predates any identifiable remains of synagogue buildings (Horsley 1995a:222–37; 1996:131–53). The tendency over the centuries was toward a more exclusively Jewish character and a more explicitly religious function. This is reflected archi-tecturally from the third to fourth centuries c.e., as what appear to be simply public buildings are increasingly marked by distinctively reli-gious designs. But literary evidence (the New Testament and rabbinic literature) indicates that these changes may have come earlier, as rabbis and other religious leaders came to dominate these assemblies. In first-century Galilee, before the war, it is probable that the term *synagogue* retained its primarily political connotation of local assembly, at least in the cities (see Josephus, *Life* 277–82.). The gradual transformation of these institutions into bodies whose purposes were restricted to what we moderns would call religious, however, attests to their relentless removal from practical functionality. The local assemblies atrophied and came to serve little purpose beyond the affirmation of communal identity made in religious worship. The founding of cities affected relative prosperity, and the surrounding communities undoubtedly felt this. Economic changes of this sort, even incremental ones, did indeed breed resentment, as is evident from the persistence of the rural-urban divide,[122] the continuation of widespread banditry, and the willingness of Galileans to participate in the war against the Romans.

Other major changes were cultural. Several scholars have appealed to the routine anthropological distinction between the great tradition and the little tradition in attempting to chart these changes. These terms, however, are routinely misapplied in such scholarship, either to refer to the distinction between the actual behavior of the ruling classes (great tradition) and the ideal values that characterize the society (little tradition; for example, Fiensy 1991:23), or to distinguish between the elite documentary compositions (great tradition) and the oral traditions that preceded them (little tradition; for example, Horsley 1996:172–75). The little tradition in fact is simply the popular reflection, appropriation, and distortion or subversion of high culture;[123] it is not a preexisting authentic culture over which the upper classes ride roughshod to accomplish their nefarious aims. The little tradition is always, by definition, inferior. On the other hand, an intensified ideology of patronage would have been accelerated in first-century Galilee by the more sharply hierarchical character of the relationship between city as city and country as country. Such an ideology would have served the interests of the urban elites by reorienting and fragmenting class (or, if one prefers, regional) loyalties:

> Patronage works by distributing resources and services preferentially to some of the poor but not others, and the ideal rural client (from the patron's perspective) is concerned with his own interests to the exclusion of those of his fellows. It may be that we should see the ideology of patronage as subverting village solidarity in some areas of the ancient world. Patronage provides an alternative or a supplement to reciprocity within kinship groups and between status equals. (Garnsey and Woolf 1989:157; see Libanius, *Oration* 47.19, 22)

The process is actually reciprocal: as village solidarity is eroded, opportunities for elite patronage increase, which, in their turn, further erode village solidarity.

It is first and foremost, as I have argued, the village scribe—the κωμο-γραμματεύς—from the previously (de facto) autonomous towns newly within the sphere of Tiberias (the Valley) who will have been aware of these changes, most affected by them, most resentful of them, and thus most inclined to react to them in some fashion. While perhaps alienated from the populace by virtue of their involuntary complicity in the new order, what sources exist suggest that there was enough general resentment of the social, economic, and cultural changes enforced by the new regime for these scribes to imagine that their indignation was generally shared by their fellow villagers and thus that their response to the situation would be shared as well. As numerous studies have shown, dependent peasantries only rarely rise in open revolt, even when conditions are deteriorating. More typically, the response to deterioration in conditions—and it should be stressed that most innovations initiated by the elites bring deterioration (for the peasant, that is) with them—is a variety of forms of relatively passive resistance: "foot-dragging, dissimulation, desertion, false compliance, pilfering, feigned ignorance, slander, arson, and so on" (Scott 1989:343). We should thus expect a response of roughly this sort—a kind of bullheaded passive resistance—from the general population of the Valley in response to what appears to have been an event of major political and economic import, the founding of Tiberias. We should further expect that among those in a position to be most vocal and creative in their resistance will be the village scribes, a class of persons dramatically uprooted in their social and professional standing by the extended process set in motion by Antipas, and, moreover, a literate class, trained in the administration of village life.

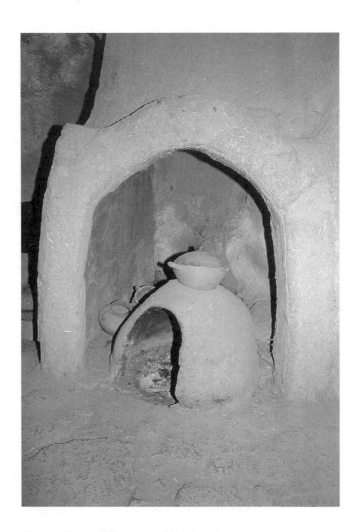

Oven, internally coated with salt
"Salt is good; but if salt has become insipid, with what will it be seasoned?" (Q 14:34)

5.
Q's Rhetoric
of Uprootedness

I HAVE RECOUNTED the various twists and permutations of the itinerancy hypothesis and its history in the foregoing pages. This basic theory has been and remains the main scholarly approach to Q's social history and to its rhetoric of inversion and upheaval. The development of this hypothesis and its intimate association with the cultural politics of its desultory advocates betrays a certain timeliness, which one might suspect has had as much or more to do with the enormous popularity of the hypothesis as does the cogency of its treatment of the evidence. In fact, its treatment of the evidence is not especially cogent: none of the documents normally adduced for traces of early Christian wandering radicalism—especially the *Didache,* Q, and the *Gospel of Thomas*—provides unequivocal or even compelling evidence of the phenomenon. Several of these documents—not all—do refer to travel, but what animates these discussions is the problem of hospitality, as well as the question of the status and renumeration of an emergent clergy. These are exactly the kinds of matters we would expect to crop up in the ordinary course of the church's evolution: a phenomenon as unique or dramatic as itinerancy is superfluous. At the very least, the documents in question do not compel itinerancy to explain their contents—other readings are possible. Moreover, the hypothesis is broadly unrealistic, a fatal flaw in a viewpoint that aims to be at least protosociological. There is no especially good reason offered for why people in first-century Palestine suddenly decided to take on the role of roving beggars nor for why they rationalized that role in the terms offered by the Jesus movement, Theissen's various excessively broad and vague "factors" notwithstanding. No explanation is offered for how such traveling might be funded, where the surplus for travelers' support would come from, or how people might react to them or their impositions. In spite of possible Cynic parallels, the thesis appears to draw its real force from a credulous appropriation of the image of the ancient Hebrew prophets. Too little attention, on the other hand, is paid to the Hellenistic literary precedents for presenting a god or hero as itinerant (Herakles, Asklepius or Hippocrates, Apollonius, and so on); as a result, Jesus' own peripatetic behavior in the Gospels is normally granted unquestioned assent.

The foregoing discussion has also addressed the concrete context in which the earliest Jesus movement appeared: Galilee before the war. Here again, nothing very extraordinary need be posited. A Roman policy of urbanization, pursued in other locations as well, was adopted in Galilee by Herod Antipas, the Roman client king. The intention of this policy was to allow more effective reach into the hinterland to be tapped more effectively, to the benefit of the imperial administration and of the regional upper classes. The foundation of Tiberias, in particular, formed the basis for a more effective incorporation of the region to the immediate west of the lake into the economic orbit of the Roman Empire. The result for the smallholders in that hitherto relatively autonomous area was a more effective collection of taxes, a progressive monetization of the economy, increased trade, increased cash cropping, and increased consolidation of holdings and consequent tenancy. The economy of what Josephus called "the Valley" (*War* 3.35–40) was thus rather suddenly and forcefully pushed from a local and subsistence-oriented organization to an open, outward-oriented market economy (or protomarket economy, to avoid overstating the case). These changes were to the obvious detriment of the small peasantry, instituting the beginning of a cycle of incremental deprivation. Even more affected than the ordinary peasantry, at least in terms of immediate, visible, and dramatic consequences, was the small class of local administrators, a retainer class for an older order that was suddenly defunct. These figures had the most to lose, at least at first glance, from the changes taking place, and had a certain amount of education and administrative experience.

In such a context, itinerancy is by no means absolutely precluded. Indeed, the trading patterns of the Galilee as discussed in the last chapter, both before and after Antipas's administration, suggest that travel within the region was not especially remarkable. And economic dislocation of a sort certainly was taking place, although, arguably, not in a way commensurate with Theissen's catastrophic generalities. But the mere physical possibility of itinerancy does not make the evidence for its actual occurrence any better, nor does it make the overall hypothesis, as it is presented, any more realistic. The economic and concomitant social dislocations described in the last chapter do not form much of a platform on which to erect a thesis of wandering radicals: as the primary discernible social disturbance of the general time and place of Q's composition (and that, presumably, of the first stages of the sayings tradition), which might plausibly constitute its primary *Sitz im Leben*, it is simply not reflected in the rhetoric and ideology of wandering radicalism as reconstructed by Theissen. What this suggests is that a more fruitful and less circular direction for research would, as I have already argued, begin with this situation, the evidence for which is independent of Q itself, interrogate its relationship to the composition of Q, and assess Q's arguments, rhetoric, and ideology in terms of that relationship.

The Immediate Setting of Q

Thus the first question of import for linking the composition of Q to the situation described in the last chapter is that of the immediate circumstances of Q's composition: where and when it was collected and written down, and by what kinds of people. The internal evidence provided by Q itself suggests an immediate setting in Galilee before the war, probably among the towns and villages of the upper rim of the lake, and further suggests that the cultivation and composition of the Q traditions was undertaken by persons with the characteristics of the village scribes (κωμογραμματεύς), that is, by rural scribes who were moderately, but not spectacularly, educated. Such conclusions would place Q's tradents squarely in the midst of the socioeconomic changes and dislocations surrounding the foundation of Tiberias and would suggest that these events did indeed constitute the formative social matrix out of which Q arose.

The geographical location of the people responsible for Q, and thus probably also the location of Q's composition, is normally fixed in Galilee, and with fairly good reason.[1] Of the places named by Q, a preponderance are Galilean or Phoenician: Bethsaida (Q 10:13), Capernaum (7:1; 10:15), Chorazin (10:13), Sidon (10:13-14), and Tyre (10:13-14). Jerusalem (4:9; 13:34), Nineveh (11:32), and Sodom (10:12) are also mentioned, but their significance is intertextual—symbolic or thematic—rather than immediate; they occur in the context of references to epic or mythic events: Jesus' temptation by Satan, personified Wisdom's lament over the course of history, the biblical-epic Jonah story, and the biblical legend of the destruction of Sodom.[2] As Reed elucidates it, "The mention of Jerusalem in the lament in Q 13:34-35 provides an example: here Jerusalem is not merely the capital of Judaea, nor the city perched along the Kidron Valley, nor even that point in Palestine where thirty-one degrees north latitude and thirty-five degrees east longitude intersect. Rather Jerusalem is personified as a character in the Q community's reading of Israel's epic" (1995:18).

The only places mentioned in Q as real places known, and of immediate significance, to the (fictive) speakers and (real) "hearers" of Q are Galilean towns and villages on the northern rim of the lake, as well as perhaps the two Phoenician cities of Tyre and Sidon.[3]

The significance of the mention of these Galilean towns is compounded by their relative obscurity, especially that of Chorazin. Chorazin, in fact, plays no role elsewhere in the gospel tradition.[4] Thus the appearance of these towns in the text of Q is unlikely to have been a consequence of any general repute or firm place within the traditions about Jesus they might have possessed. In any case, as a sayings collection, Q is not under the same obligation as the narrative Gospels to lend its contents verisimilitude by specifying the (Galilean) locales in which Jesus must have appeared. Contrast, for instance, Q's various references to actual places with the flawless atopicality of the *Gospel of Thomas*.[5] Moreover, the extreme localization of these references (the three Galilean towns mentioned are within about 5 km of one another) contrasts sharply with what is found in the narrative Gospels, which tend to scatter topical references (comparatively) widely throughout Galilee, Gaulanitis, Samaria, and Judea.

On the other hand, these local Galilean references, including the references to Tyre and Sidon, are, for the most part, restricted to a single pericope: the woes on the unrepentant cities (Q 10:13-15) that conclude the so-called Mission Charge: "Woe to you, Chorazin! Woe to you, Bethsaida! For if the wonders performed in you had taken place in Tyre and Sidon, they would have repented long ago, in sackcloth and ashes. Yet for Tyre and Sidon it shall be more bearable at the judgment than for you." Tuckett therefore cautions: "The evidence is, of course, not conclusive, above all since it is virtually confined to one unit, the woes in Q 10:13-15. Hence the place names there may indicate that only that individual tradition, rather then [*sic*] the whole of Q, stems from such a locale" (1996:102). The situation is complicated further by the literary stratification of Q. If indeed Q is to be divided into more or less discrete instructional and polemical compositional layers along the lines suggested by Kloppenborg, this unit certainly belongs to the secondary stratum (see p. 7 in this book).[6] Since the peculiar types of inversionary ethical injunctions and encomia on detachment from cultural norms—the supposed social radicalism—that characterize Q's inversionary rhetoric are largely restricted to the first stratum of Q, it is disconcerting that practically the only material that allows a localization of the Q traditions is from its second stratum. Although most recent studies of the relationship between Q's strata and the history of their development have assumed a social continuity between them, this assumption—although probably correct—has yet to be demonstrated. And to the best of my knowledge no one has shown or even argued that such a social continuity would also necessarily imply geographical continuity in the group's location. In consequence, one could conceivably argue that Q 10:13-15 tells us only where one of Q's traditions came from, and a secondary tradition at that, potentially unrelated to the layer from which the radical or inversionary ethos of Q is derived.

Several factors, however, militate against such a conclusion. Q's links to other writings likely to have derived from Syria, such as Matthew and the *Gospel of Thomas,* might reinforce the suggestion of a Galilean provenance.[7] In addition, Jonathan Reed has ingeniously noted the geographical significance of the sign of Jonah pericope (Q 11:29-32), arguing that:

> One of the most neglected aspects of the study of the Sign of Jonah pericope is that Jonah was not only a northern prophet, but a Galilean prophet, and that there were local traditions which attest to his significance in the Galilee. The importance of the Galilean connection is not only obvious for the saying if it is authentic, since Jesus' activity is surely to be placed in the Galilee, but also because his first followers who compiled and created Q should be placed there. (1996:134; see 135–36)

The (supposed) site of Jonah's tomb was in Galilee, at Gath-Hepher, only 3 km (2 miles) outside of Sepphoris along the road to Tiberias. The subsequent reference in the Q woes against the Pharisees (11:47-48) to building tombs for the prophets is possibly an allusion to this site in particular. Reed believes that the reference to Jonah in Q 11:29c is original to the tradition about Jesus' response to requests for a sign and has been deleted in the parallel Markan version (Mark 8:11-12; see v. 12). Regardless of which of the two versions of the core of this pronouncement is original, it is clear that the various additions to it made prior to, and during, its incorporation into Q (that is, 11:30, and 11:31-32) either create, or intensify, the focus of the pronouncement on Jonah. This suggests, then, a Galilean origin not only for the original core saying itself but for its subsequent elaboration into the cluster now comprising Q 11:29-32.

These observations suggest another point. Q 7:1, one of the few doubly attested narrative overtures in Q, records Jesus entering Capernaum; thus the Q references to the northern rim of the lake are not entirely restricted to 10:13-15. But what is especially interesting about this reference is that, as a narrative clasp between the initial Q sermon (Q 6:20-49) and the story of the centurion's boy (παῖς) (Q 7:1-10), the description is likely to be a redactional creation: indeed, if one follows Kloppenborg's stratification of Q, the phrase is virtually certain to derive from the hand responsible for the second redaction of Q.[8] The redactionally formulated 11:31-32, likewise, may betray a Galilean provenance in its emphasis on the Galilean prophet Jonah. Moreover, the woes of Q 10:13-15, so replete with references to the northern shore of the Sea of Galilee, are almost certainly representative of the latest stage in the composition of the Mission Charge, and are linked to the Mission Charge by a redactionally formulated connector (Q 10:12).[9] Again, if one follows the conventional stratification of Q, these additions must have been made at the stage of the Q^2 redaction, because the earliest portions of the Mission Charge (Q 10:2-11, 16) were already incorporated in written form into Q^1 (Kloppenborg 1987:192–97, 243; contrast Uro 1987:98–116). Thus any later additions to the Mission Speech could not have occurred in oral transmission but are products of the redactor of Q^2, who, apparently, at this stage incorporated 10:13-15 and composed 10:12.[10]

Thus all of the texts that actually mention northern Galilean place-names are late redactional creations or additions of the second-stage compositor, and the emphasis on Jonah may belong, in part, to this stage as well. While this observation does not help us directly to locate the first stage of Q, it at least indicates that at one stage in its development, the people responsible for Q were probably located at the northern rim of the lake, especially around Capernaum, which is singled out for attention twice. The place-names are a product of this group's interests, not merely a reflection of the original provenance of some of the traditions incorporated into Q. In other words, because of the redactional character of the indications of locale that appear in Q, we cannot attribute their appearance merely to the fact that some desultory Jesus traditions must (of course) have had their origin in Galilee.

Two further considerations suggest that the two main strata of Q derive from roughly the same geographical area, although on this question any conclusive verification is almost certain to remain elusive. First, Matthew's and Luke's appropriation of Q in virtually identical forms and the document's subsequent disappearance indicate that if Q did indeed have a three-stage compositional history,[11] it probably circulated beyond its immediate composers only after that composition had reached its final, that is, tertiary, form. This evidence of very limited circulation of Q's first and second stages matches what we know of the production and publication of texts in antiquity: normally that circulation is quite restricted, and usually it moves along social links already established, at least at first (Harris 1989). The fact that Q failed to survive apart from its incorporation—in its final form—in Matthew and Luke indicates that even the final text was not widely distributed. It is all the more certain, then, that earlier versions of the text were of very restricted currency. It therefore seems safe to assume that the use of an earlier version of Q, and indeed its treatment as a foundational document, by those who redacted Q, indicates that a single group was responsible for its various stages.

A second, admittedly peculiar, argument may be offered for the identification of the site of Q^1's composition with that of Q^2. The literary
evidence is unanimous in suggesting that Jesus lived in Galilee and that
a major portion of his public activity took place along the northern
shores of the lake. Without adopting the (mythic) Lukan model of the
gradual and systematic spread of the Christian movement outward from
its origins, it must be said that it appears unlikely that a group based at
the northwestern side of the lake, a group that viewed Jesus as a founding figure, would have drawn traditions about him from outside of this
geographical area. Obviously, this consideration is not probative, but it
does serve to underscore the likelihood that the people responsible for
Q^2 were, more or less, the same people who were responsible for Q^1.
Thus a northern Galilean location—probably in the neighborhood of
Capernaum—is indicated for both major stages of the document's literary history.

This conclusion already solves the problem whether Q is the product
of a rural or an urban environment. In a sense, the question is anachronistic: to the extent that every ancient city was dependent on its villages
and towns, to the extent that urban centers of necessity dealt largely
with agricultural produce, and to the extent that neither Sepphoris nor
Tiberias was exceptionally large, even by the standards of the day, everyone in Galilee, including the residents of Sepphoris and Tiberias, lived in
a rural environment. Thus Jonathan Reed's attempt to associate Q's use
of natural imagery with the bucolic romanticism of urbanites such as
Virgil, expressing a desire to flee the confines of the city rather than a real
intimacy with the natural world, is, in spite of some attractive features,
not convincing.[12] Indeed, the references to urban life in Q are sufficiently
limited that larger cities are probably not in view at all:

> The particular amalgamation of urban imagery in Q provides con-
> siderable information about the Q community's perception of the
> city. None of the amenities that urban life offered, such as the baths
> or the theatre, appears in Q. Although Q betrays an awareness of
> the city, the Q community does not seem to have scaled the social
> hierarchy of the city very high. Rather, the blend of images portrays
> a familiarity with those features of and places in the city open to the
> lower classes and those coming from outside the city: gates, plazas,
> streets, the agora, banks, and, in the worst case, courts and prisons.
> (Reed 1995:28)

Of course, this same description of Q's urban imagery could suggest two
alternative conclusions, namely, that the people responsible for Q did
not live in one of the two larger Galilean cities but rather encountered
them as strangers, visitors, travelers; and that the setting in which the Q

people did live lacked at least some "of the amenities that urban life offered," that is, was a smaller town than either Sepphoris or Tiberias.

The fact that Q fails to show any interest in the ultimate disposition of Tiberias or Sepphoris, even to the point of failing to single them out for criticism or to mention them at all, is hardly indicative of an origin in these cities, despite some creative suggestions that have been made.[13] We are thus compelled to surmise that the people responsible for Q— while they certainly lived in a settlement of sufficient size that relatively complex transactions were a commonplace and while they may have had some experience of Sepphoris or Tiberias as visitors[14]—lived in a town or village settlement of more moderate size. Even Reed, in spite of an inclination to stress the urban features of Q, draws similar conclusions, which are worth quoting in full:

> To summarize: an analysis of the place-names in Q strongly suggests the importance of Capernaum to the Q community; and the remaining place-names, especially Chorazin and Bethsaïda, the negative comparison with Tyre, and a suspicious view of Jerusalem confirm more broadly a Galilean perspective. The particular amalgamation of agricultural and urban imagery, especially the positive example of nature, makes good sense in the recently urbanized Galilee. Although I would not go so far as to locate the entire Q community in the cities of Sepphoris and Tiberias themselves based on spatial imagery, contact with these cities—illustrated primarily in the market and judicial imagery—on the part of the Q community is certain. Although perhaps more likely at home in such larger Galilean villages as Capernaum, or other sites on the north shore of the lake, the Q community perceived the major cities of Galilee with some apprehension—because they were visited by the members of the Q community. (1995:30)

Capernaum thus presents itself as the most attractive single possibility for the location of the people responsible for Q at both major stages, but any of the towns, of varying size, in this general region at the north of the lake would also suffice (see also Kloppenborg 1991:86). Such a location would of course place Q's composers at the center of the socioeconomic impact generated by the relatively novel foundation of Tiberias. Capernaum is situated in an area formerly not easily accessible to large-scale trade or other contacts; thus we can expect it to have maintained a considerable autonomy, and, most likely, some status as a major local center, until the founding of Tiberias suddenly brought it and its immediate neighbors into the orbit of the broader Roman-Herodian political economy.

The Dating of Q

The date at which Q was composed is not as easily unraveled as its place of composition. Against those who argue for a very late date for Q (Hoffmann 1982; Myllykoski 1996), several features of the text suggest that Q was completed before the war and indeed that its compositional history begins at a very early date. Most obviously, and unlike Matthew and Luke, for example, Q betrays no overt awareness of the destruction of the Temple by Titus in 70 c.e. Indeed, there are no references to war whatsoever in minimal Q, at any stage of the document's composition. Compare the irenic backdrop of Q's apocalypse to that of Mark:

Q 17:26, 30	Mark 13:7-8
And as it was in the days of Noah, so it will be in the days of the son of man. They ate, they drank, they married, they were being married, up to the day when Noah entered the ark, and the flood came and destroyed them all. . . . So will it be on the day when the son of man is revealed.	When you hear of wars and rumors of wars, do not be alarmed; this must take place, but the end is still to come. For nation will rise against nation, and kingdom against kingdom; there will be earthquakes in various places; there will be famines. This is but the beginning of the birth pangs.

There is no good reason at all to imagine that these passages reflect the same or similar circumstances: Q urges awareness in the face of normality; Mark urges circumspection in the face of cataclysm. The temptation narrative is equally lacking in military overtones or any other indication of knowledge of the First Judean Revolt—indeed, it seems to reflect no specific political situation whatsoever (so Kloppenborg 1987:254–56). As far as Q 4:9-12 is concerned, the existence of the temple requires no comment or explanation. Likewise, other possible tertiary glosses to Q, such as 11:42c and 16:17, promote a nomistic (Torah-focused) orientation (Kloppenborg 1990b; see 1996b:49) without reflecting on the significance of the temple's absence for such an orientation. Q 13:34-35 is unlikely to be a "'prophecy' after the fact" because it envisions not a rebuilding of Jerusalem or its sanctuary but a repentance on the part of the city ("you will not see me until . . . you say: blessed is the one who comes"): the sanctuary is not destroyed but given by God back to his impenitent people ("behold, your house is forsaken"). Admittedly, these observations represent an argument from silence, but such a silence is significant enough when one reflects on the Galilee's direct involvement in the war, as well as the Q people's bitter denunciations of Jerusalem. Indeed, the whole general force of Q's rhetoric—

layer by layer and from beginning to end—requires the normality of life to make its examples convincing: its arguments tend to be buttressed by appeal to ordinary experience rather than by pointing out extraordinary events.

These observations may be pushed a little further: there are reasonable grounds for suggesting a date for Q quite early in the prewar period rather than toward its end. The redactional complexity of Q and of its traditions—once one has settled on a model of Q's development that involves the stratification of written layers rather than oral aggregation of units—suggests a relatively long history and hence one whose initial steps must have been quite early. The distance, at least in tone, from Q^1 to Q^2, and again from Q^2 to Q^3, is sufficiently ample to indicate the lapse of several years. If the latest stage of Q was composed prior to 66 C.E., we are probably safe in guessing that its earliest written phases could be no later than the 50s. Even the second, redactional, layer of Q is also likely to have been composed no later than the 50s. This conclusion is suggested, albeit tenuously, by Q^2's thematic links to the earliest of Paul's letters, 1 Thessalonians. Regardless of the actual causes for this language, 1 Thessalonians and Q^2 share a strong authorial (that is, not traditional or ancillary) interest in current persecution; past, epic persecution of the prophets; and apocalyptic judgment in consequence of these actions. This set of motifs is representative, of course, of the deuteronomistic view of Israel's history (the view that Israel's history is marked by disobedience and divine calls for repentance), which is widely acknowledged to be a major factor in the redaction of Q^2 (Steck 1967; Lührmann 1969; Kloppenborg 1987). The main elements of this perspective, however, are far less prevalent in Paul's letters, even where apocalyptic expectation is emphasized. The text of 1 Thessalonians not only contains references to apocalyptic judgment scenarios (1:9-10; 4:13-18; 5:1-7) but also shares with Q—in sharp contrast to Mark—the concern that the continuation of ordinary life not dampen expectation of the imminent end. Moreover, in 1 Thess 2:14-16, Paul provides a thumbnail sketch of the deuteronomistic condemnation of Israel that thoroughly matches Q^2's redactional interests:

> For you, brothers and sisters, became imitators of the churches of God in Christ Jesus that are in Judea, for you suffered the same things from your own compatriots as they did from the Jews, who killed both the Lord Jesus and the prophets, and drove us out; they displease God and oppose everyone by hindering us from speaking to the Gentiles so that they may be saved. Thus they have constantly been filling up the measure of their sins; but God's wrath has overtaken them at last [or "completely," εἰς τέλος].[15]

Regardless of the actual situation—in Thessalonica or Judea—prompting the hope for such harsh reprisal, the motifs used to describe and rationalize this situation are nearly identical to that found in Q^2. Note especially how closely the already-accomplished consummation of judgment in Paul, "God's wrath *has overtaken* them at last," matches that of Q 13:34-35, "your house *is forsaken*." If there is any single New Testament text that most closely matches the style (not genre, obviously) and thematic content of the redaction of Q (Q^2), it is 1 Thessalonians! Interestingly, this use of emphatic deuteronomistic language largely drops out of Paul's writings after 1 Thessalonians and is not especially marked in other New Testament epistolary literature.

Paul's rather uncomfortable use of deuteronomistic language in 1 Thessalonians may indicate that such language was being used in Christian circles generally, at around the same time, to rationalize negative experiences.[16] The evidently temporary (judging by its subsequent desuetude) application of deuteronomistic theology within at least some branches of the Christian movement to desultory situations of disapproval might thus—if we are to date it at all—be situated roughly in the period in which 1 Thessalonians was composed (sometime between 41 and 51 c.e.), which in its turn might have implications for dating Q^2.[17] Further support for such an early dating of Q^2 may be found in the use to which John the Baptist is put by the redaction of this stage. John is not, at this point, a figure drawn from the epic of Jesus' own story but rather appears in Q as an independent folk hero whose commensurability with the Q group's program, behavior, and founder (Jesus) is used to inflate the group's sense of legitimacy (Arnal 1995a:176). What is important here is that this use reflects an oral, folk esteem for John, not his preservation in the literary record of later Christians or even of disciples of John himself. While we need not suppose folk memories to be short (witness Robin Hood), the only folk appeal to the memory of John of which we may be certain—Q excepted of course—is that recorded by Josephus surrounding the defeat of Antipas's army by Aretas sometime before 37 c.e. (*Ant.* 18.116–19). Thus, as with 1 Thessalonians and the deuteronomistic theme, the only datable manifestation of this motif derives from the period around the early 40s c.e.

A final indication of how the various layers of Q are to be dated, that is, that the compositional layer of Q is to be dated very early, is the complete absence of christological reflection in the first stratum of Q. Although Q^1 does show interest in the status and significance of Jesus, especially evinced in Q 6:46's appeal to him as "Lord, Lord," the first stratum of the document is entirely lacking in any reflection on Jesus' supernatural significance or his relationship to God: he is simply and only a wise man, whose words, like those of all wise men, must be obeyed if one is to live wisely and well.[18] Given not only that all subsequent forms of Christianity of which we are aware from the New Testament attribute to Jesus in their different ways a religious—that is, supernatural and extraordinary—role but also that Q[2] pursues this trajectory as well and so reveals that the Q group had no animus against this mode of inflating Jesus' authority, the complete absence of such reflection must indicate an extremely early and rather isolated phase of the Jesus movement as a whole. Jesus is nothing more than a sage: we are not even informed that his sayings belong to the past. In light of this, Ivan Havener's observation, in connection with Q, that "the rationale for preserving and transmitting Jesus' sayings existed *before* his death" (1987:42, emphasis original), while outrageous in its implications, is surely pertinent. There is simply no thematic indication in Q[1] that Jesus is perceived to be a figure from the past, even the recent past. This is not to argue that Q[1] dates from the period before Jesus' death but to say that it is surely a very, very old composition.[19]

The Q People as Village Scribes

The final question pertaining to Q's immediate context is that of the identity of its purveyors. While much has been made of the prophetic identity of these figures, or their Cynic-like character, these designations do not help us identify the social sectors from which they might have been drawn in the first place; the labels are simply not socially descriptive. The only evidence we possess for who these individuals might have been comes from the document itself: its presupposed world of experience and its own essential complexion. The latter consideration especially suggests purveyors who at the very least were literate: Q was indeed a written document.[20] More than this, its written form was not the result of simple transcription of orally circulating material but involved the organization and arrangement of material in the form of carefully constructed arguments.[21] Ronald Piper's work on the argumentative clusters that comprise much of the hortatory, sapiential material of Q[1] (including Q 6:27-36, 37-42, 43-45; 11:9-13; 12:4-7 and 22-31), has revealed a consistent compositional pattern, which is complex, painstakingly structured, and repetitive: "Characteristic of these collections too is the pattern of progressing from general to specific application, the location of the interpretive key at the conclusion of the argument, the use of (usually multiple) rhetorical questions at the center of the collection, the change in imagery as the argument progresses, and the dominance of the appeal to experience and reason" (Piper 1982:416; see 1989). The argumentative techniques of Q^1 involve primarily the constituent arguments of Wisdom literature: clusters of imperatives followed by supporting motive clauses or aphorisms, the use of persuasion by analogy (Q 6:43-45), doubled rhetorical questions (6:32-33, 39, 41-42; 11:11-12), appeal to common experience (6:47-49), observation of general human behavior (6:32-33; 11:33), arguments from lesser to greater (11:11-13; 12:6-7, 24-28), *imitatio Dei* arguments (6:35), and possibly even such intentional rhetorical forms as enthymemes (6:20-22) and elaborations (6:27-36).[22] In many of the argumentative clusters, as Piper has shown (1982:416), some behavioral application is spelled out explicitly toward the end of the argument.

This sort of intellectually sophisticated, suasively oriented construction, and the careful composition of Q^1 within the parameters of a known ancient literary genre underscore the conclusion that Q is not merely a literate document but is also literary (see esp. Kirk 1998). Nor does the picture change for the other strata of Q, which retain the overall generic characteristics of Near Eastern and Hellenistic Wisdom literature, and which show numerous signs of careful composition and deliberate rhetorical technique, including chreiai and elaborated chreiai (Kloppenborg 1987:317–28; 1991:91–94, 99–100; Mack and Robbins 1989:31–67; see Kirk 1998). Moreover, each layer actually shows increasing comfort with the use of literary traditions, an increasing tendency to textual exegesis. At the first stage of the document's composition, ordinary experience is normally invoked to support argumentative points; no Old Testament texts are quoted, nor even alluded to, outside of a very general reference to Solomon's splendor in Q 12:17.

By the secondary redaction, the group is appealing primarily to a deuteronomistic understanding of the epic tradition, and the revised document includes a number of textual allusions (for example, Q 7:22) and prooftexts (for example, 7:27), as well as references to biblical events (for example, 10:12) and characters (11:30-32; 13:28). By the time of the tertiary emendation of Q, written texts are a basis for authoritative revelation (Q 16:17), and (textual) exegetical proficiency is the mark of wisdom (4:1-13); note that two of the three Q^3 texts contain actual references to written textuality (Q 4:4, 8, 10, 12: "it has been written"; 16:17: "one stroke"[23]). One might finally observe in connection with the literary status of Q that the document produced at the level of Q^1 evidently came to serve as a kind of foundational or authoritative document for the group that produced it, as attested not only by its preservation (within that group) but by its continual emendation to suit the group's changing situations.

Thus any description of Q's tradents that fails to take this feature into account—including any itinerancy hypothesis that forces us to imagine wandering beggars carrying scrolls and writing implements from town to town (see Douglas 1995:120)—is guilty of ignoring one of the most telling pieces of evidence: these people communicated and preserved their ideas in writing. Moreover, writing was not simply a passive vehicle for the recording of the oral life of these traditions (against Kelber): it was a major—and evidently comfortable—vehicle or medium for promoting the ethos and agenda of these people. What they wrote down was composed, not recorded, and composed according to the dictates of the style, rhetoric, and to some degree the content of the broader category of writings we may call Wisdom literature.

The immediate conclusion to be drawn from these observations is not only that Q's tradents were literate in a world where literacy was relatively rare (Harris 1989) but that their literacy was more than merely functional: these individuals were not simply capable of writing down words—thus, taking dictation, copying decrees, keeping accounts, and so on—but were relatively proficient at the production (composition, authorship) of texts, and literary texts at that. On the other hand, the genre of text these individuals evidently preferred and the rhetorical techniques they employed within it were, although literary and cultivated, more or less rudimentary, especially when compared to some of the "high literature" of antiquity (Kloppenborg 1991:84–85). Alongside extended historical writings, developed biographies, or apocalypses, Q can appear rather disorganized, simplistic, or primitive. We are thus dealing, in the case of the Q tradents, with persons who are educated and who think of themselves as—and are—learned beyond the ancient norm but who, at the same time, do not occupy the pinnacle of the learning antiquity had to offer.

John Kloppenborg's suggestion, therefore, that the persons responsible for Q were scribal figures, and, more particularly, were village scribes (κωμογραμματεύς), makes a great deal of sense. They were middle- or lower-level administrators who dealt with local "administrative infrastructures which saw to the collection and disbursement of various revenues and to the administration of justice" (Kloppenborg 1991:85; 2000:196–97). Indeed, it is difficult to see who else in first-century Galilee would have been likely or able to produce a document such as Q^1, or Q as a whole, other than the village scribes sketched in the previous chapter (so also Kloppenborg 1993:25). Not merely the form but the values and contents of Q^1 support such a conclusion:

> In accord with scribal values, the Sayings Gospel places a premium
> upon both clarity of perception, especially when it comes to matters
> of guidance (Q 6:40, 41-42), and good speech, the characteristic mark

of good thinking (Q 6:45). Guidance and moral example are also the subjects of the sayings on judging (Q 6:37-38), scandal (Q 17:1-2), and forgiveness (Q 17:3b-4). This reflects the self-consciously "public" character of the scribal pursuit: although the scribe necessarily requires leisure not at the disposal of the peasant or hand-worker, the scribe's responsibility is ultimately to the public and public approbation in the form of honour and fame crowns the sage's achievement. (Kloppenborg 1991:83)

Also buttressing such a conclusion are the indications in Q, at both major levels of redaction, of familiarity with teaching situations (especially Q 6:39-49; Batten 1995, 1998; Kloppenborg 1991:83) and with the processes and mechanisms of law courts (especially Q 6:29, 37-38; 11:31a, 32a; 12:11-12, 57-59; 22:30; Piper 1995). In addition, Q shows a predilection for coupling male examples with female examples, a stylistic tendency that I have argued is characteristic of legal and other types of regulatory language.[24] This apparent familiarity with the administration of justice and apparent comfort in appropriating its language, style, and imagery support the characterization of the Q tradents as village scribes. One final observation on the language and imagery of Q—this time more typical of the second stratum than the first—helps corroborate this identification, and that is the strong interest in the language and imagery of delegation. Perhaps the most prominent single motif in Q^2 (with the possible exception of that of judgment), the theme of representation or delegation forms the most common basis of the appeals to experience one finds in the constituent material of Q^2. The notion of one person speaking for or acting for another serves as the primary theological metaphor for the relationships between God, Jesus, and the Q people themselves (see Q 7:8; 10:16, 22; 12:8-9, 42-46; 14:16-24; 19:12-26; 22:29-30). There is a clear homology, or structured correspondence, between this kind of (theological) language and the (social) roles of the retainer class, to whom, of course, the village scribes belong. At the very least, the ubiquity of this theme for Q^2's theological constructs demonstrates habitual exposure to and experience of the phenomenon of delegation, and suggests that this experience leads those who have generated these images to identify naturally with the delegate rather than the one who does the delegating. This emphasis, then, accords well with the experience and perhaps worldview of the village scribe—a retainer who habitually acts on behalf of the law, the state, and powerful patrons.

In sum, the immediate circumstances of Q's composition place its development squarely in the midst of the events devolving from the foundation of Tiberias shortly before, or during, the early 20s C.E.

Internal evidence suggests that the document was composed, at least in its first two major stages, in Galilee, probably at the northern edge of the lake, and quite conceivably in Capernaum itself, which, as Kloppenborg notes, would probably have had a sufficient density of bureaucrats to allow for such developments: "it seems doubtful that a single village could have sustained the Q group. The Q people, however, may have flourished in a network of villages, perhaps even in association with the lower administrative sectors of a larger center. . . . One might also consider the larger towns like Capernaum in Galilee or Bethsaida Julias in Gaulanitis, whose commercial interests would have supported a relatively substantial bureaucracy" (1991:86). The date at which its formative layer was composed is no longer determinable, but an earlier date, such as the 30s or 40s c.e., seems preferable to a later one. Even the second layer of Q, to the extent that any evidence whatsoever can be adduced, may be ascribed to the 40s or 50s. Thus the time over which the document was composed was probably the period in which the long-term and structural effects of Galilee's gradual incorporation into the Roman-Herodian orbit—increased trade and monetization, more effective extraction of taxes and other dues, increasing debt, incrementally increasing tenancy and land consolidation, and the restructuring (and revaluing) of village and town administrations and social organization—were beginning to be felt with a vengeance. And, finally, the persons apparently responsible for the document, village scribes involved in the administration of formerly autonomous village life, are the persons identified in the previous chapter as those with the most (or apparently the most) to lose from the new world order heralded by Antipas's foundation of Tiberias. All of this implies that the immediate context of Q's composition was precisely the set of circumstances outlined in the last chapter. It remains to be seen what Q's composers made of those circumstances, and to what extent Q's program represents a response to them.

Travel in Q

Because of the general dominance of the itinerancy hypothesis and the centrality of Q's Mission Charge for most social descriptions of the Q people, the first issue that presents itself in an attempt to decipher Q's inversionary language is the question of travel. Q[1] does indeed include references to travel, as well as possible indications of homelessness. It is this combination of references—viewed synthetically[25]—that makes Q a fertile source for theories of early Christian radical itinerancy, against the background of which Q's other injunctions are then assessed.

The first thing to observe in this connection is that Q, again at all of its stages, presupposes a complex social life and a complex set of inter-personal interactions, in which even the most conventional and structured relationships persist. The sapiential instructions in Q are most obvious in this regard. Different socioeconomic classes are assumed to be present among the document's addressees, with the result that exhortation is made about both giving (Q 6:30) and receiving (10:7), both borrowing (12:57-59) and lending (6:34-35); the wealthy are directly addressed (12:33-34; 16:13), as are the poor (6:20-21; 12:22-31; Arnal 1995b:481, 484). An ongoing involvement in structured and sedentary village life is presupposed (Horsley 1993:211–12; 1995b:43; Tuckett 1996:306). In Q[1], we are dealing with a document that can offer the following types of injunctions at the same time:

> Do not treasure for yourselves treasures on earth, where moth and gnawing deface and where robbers dig through and rob, but treasure for yourselves treasure in heaven, where neither moth nor gnawing defaces and where robbers do not dig through nor rob. For where your treasure is, there will also be your heart. (Q 12:33-34)[26]
>
> Therefore I tell you, do not be anxious about your life, what you are to eat, nor about your body, with what you are to clothe yourself. Is not life more than food, and the body than clothing? Consider the ravens; they neither sow nor reap nor gather into barns, and yet God feeds them. Are you not better than the birds? (Q 12:22-24)

Q[1] is thus clearly a document that—at least fictively—addresses itself to the range of social classes in its general purview; it does not restrict itself to the poor or outcast (in spite of the impression given by such programmatic texts as Q 6:20-22). As Tuckett states,

> A number of other passages in Q imply that the people addressed are, if not well-to-do, at least not destitute. Warnings about storing up treasure on earth (Q 12:33f.) or against serving mammon (Q 16:13) only make sense if directed against those who have a certain amount of money or possessions. Similarly, the exhortation to lend to those who ask without expecting any return presupposes an audience who have the wherewithal to give money away. One must not therefore make the situation presupposed too uniform. (1996:360)

Proponents of itinerancy tend to treat the ordinances apparently offered to the wealthy by Q[1] as though they were general statements of principle, while they treat those addressed to the poor as specific injunctions with direct application (for example, Theissen 1978:12–13; Patterson 1993:159 and n. 7). Given the undeniably specific character of the other advice directed by Q¹ to those in comfortable economic positions (the material on giving and lending cited above), such a reading is not only arbitrary but demonstrably false. Q addresses itself, at least in part, to the relatively wealthy. Indeed, one might turn the tables on itinerancy advocates and tentatively advance the hypothesis that Q¹ is primarily addressed to the affluent; that it is the statements apparently directed to the poor that articulate general principles, using the imagery of poverty as a rhetorical device (see Bloomquist 1997) rather than because destitution is a reality for the Q tradents or their intended audience. For instance, the text on anxiety quoted above (12:22-24; see vv. 25-31) appears as though it is addressed to people who are in a position to worry about such basic necessities as food and clothing: a situation of the utmost poverty is thus implied (so Horsley 1993:258; Theissen 1978:13). But the advice given is idealistic in the extreme, even offensive, and, if meant to be taken seriously, actually suggests a situation in which living without care is possible, that is, one of general prosperity: "It does not seem very likely that idealizations of poverty and detachment would have had much appeal to beggars, day workers or small holders; instead, these are the views of intellectuals who utilize such idealizations as a counterbalance to what is perceived as a bankrupt or failing culture" (Kloppenborg 1991:88). One wonders, therefore, whether the two texts quoted in parallel above are not of a thematic piece, that is, whether they both advocate, to the affluent, a general emotional detachment from their wealth. Q 12:22-31 is actually an effective argument only in such a context. It is not especially credible or useful to tell people who are naked and starving to "consider the ravens," but for those to whom the necessities of life have never (or only infrequently and temporarily) been denied, this argument matches their own experience (that is, of finding the world relatively bountiful), and may therefore serve as a quite resonant suggestion to tone down concerns about the accumulation of wealth.

Relations with family probably persist in both major strata of Q as well: Q 11:11-13, from Q¹'s sapiential material, is addressed, fictively or not, to those who have children, and apparently whose children live with them: "what man *among you* (τίς ἐστιν ἐξ ὑμων), if his son asks for a loaf of bread, will give him a stone?" (Q 11:11). Richard Horsley has noted that two Q¹ texts often adduced for an antifamilial ethos in Q— 9:59-62 and 14:26—actually suggest the opposite: the texts work in a rhetorically effective way only on the supposition that family relations continue within the group to whom Q is addressed (Horsley 1988:198, 200; see Arnal 1995b:481 and n. 40). Both of these texts are hyperbolic examples—focal instances—of the kind of radical commitment required of those who follow Jesus. Q 14:26-27, exhorting the hearer to hate parents, is, like the (independent) version in *Thomas* 55, juxtaposed with a statement about taking up one's cross in order to be a worthy disciple. David Seeley has shown that the cultural and argumentative context for the cross saying is best found in Cynic-Stoic notions of discipleship, stressing that the true student will be sufficiently committed to the truth taught by his master (Jesus) that in the pursuit of this truth he will despise any consequences (including the loss of his own life), consequences that are, in fact, predictable in a world in which the truth is despised (Seeley 1991:133–35; 1992:225–30, 232–33). Unless we imagine that itinerants are deliberately to seek crucifixion, it is clear that this injunction is simply intended to serve as a rather extreme example of the potential cost of—and thus the commitment required for—seeking true wisdom. The point of the cluster of examples in Q 9:57-60 (or 9:57-62)[27] is the same: following Jesus requires unconditional commitment, even at the cost of responsibilities otherwise deemed unquestionably inescapable. Obviously the rhetorical force of these focal instances is completely lost unless those to whom they are addressed—that is, members of the group itself, since the interest in following Jesus is taken for granted in these sayings—have close family relationships and persist in maintaining them. They are not being told, literally, that they must give these things up any more than they are being enjoined to commit suicide (14:27; Horsley 1988:298). Rather, they are being told that these family connections, which are at the apogee of value comparable to their very lives, are of less importance than their mission to advance the wisdom of their teacher, and the importance of this wisdom is thus dramatically (and hyperbolically) underscored. At the level of Q^2 and Q^3, incidentally, the situation does not much change. Q^2 17:34-35 implies that those who have heeded the Q^2 call to repentance are indistinguishable in their activities and locations from those who have not. Even Q^3, which adds so little to the Q document, and the bulk of which is set in the wilderness, approves the diligent tithing of spices (Q 11:42c), a practice unlikely to be of any relevance or concern to a wandering beggar.

The apparent stability of this set of complex, socially involved, and apparently sedentary contexts militates against a traveling lifestyle among the people Q envisions for its audience, and it equally precludes any kind of isolation of the people responsible for Q from the ordinary life of larger villages and small towns. Since much of the exhortation in Q^1 is very clearly directed to insiders (concerning, as it does, Jesus' disciples or those who are "worthy" of him),[28] it seems reasonable enough to conclude that the sedentary and rather ordinary lifestyle envisioned in general by the text applies as much to its tradents as to its audience.

The only direct and unequivocal reference to homelessness in Q, at any stage of its development, is limited to the single saying in Q 9:57-58: "Someone said to him, 'I will follow you wherever you go.' And Jesus said to him, 'Foxes have holes, and birds of the air have nests, but the son of man has nowhere to lay his head.'" As already noted, in its immediate Q^1 context, the saying has more to do with absolute commitment than with literal homelessness. The following saying (9:59-60) exhorts a would-be follower not so much to leave home as (shockingly) to value his commitment to Jesus over basic filial responsibility. The final saying in this triptych (Q/Luke 9:61-62), if indeed it derives from Q, is clearest of all: a statement of general principle that one must not be distracted from the crucial task at hand. The fact that this set of sayings is immediately followed by the Mission Speech in Q^1 makes the cluster appear to be a programmatic introduction to a longer discussion of the practices involved in wandering discipleship (Kloppenborg 1987:200–201; Patterson 1993:133–34, 134, n. 61; Schürmann 1994:83). But such an interpretation relies entirely on a particular reading of 10:2-16 in light of itinerancy, which, of course, begs the question. The situating of the Mission Speech—which itself makes no reference at all to homelessness!—after this set of chreiai only denotes that the Mission Charge itself pertains, like 9:57-60 (61-62), to the issue of discipleship and how one is to understand and undertake the commitment of being "worthy" of Jesus.[29]

The individual saying on homelessness (9:57-58) is actually quite opaque and does not have a clear referent. If the version in *Thomas* 86 reflects a more original form of the saying,[30] the statement was not originally made in rejoinder to an interlocutor's interest in discipleship but as a general observation. This text is one of the few synoptic instances in which "son of man" may be a generic designation, rather than a titular reference to Jesus (Bultmann 1963:28; contrast Hoffmann 1982:90–91; Schürmann 1994:82–83). Thus if the text does not bespeak itinerancy in Q, neither does it at an earlier stage of the tradition, circulating as a loose saying: what it denotes, rather, is the conviction that human beings are helpless to an extent shared by no other creature on earth. If, however, as Kloppenborg argues, Q 6:22 was originally part of Q^1,[31] "son of man" *is* used in this text to designate Jesus, and so, at the time the "foxes have holes" saying was incorporated into Q^1, the reference was already understood to refer to Jesus, specifically (Kloppenborg 1987:192). Its association, secondarily, with the pair of chreiai that follow it would have already suggested such an interpretation.[32]

What is so interesting about this history of transmission is what it implies for almost any version of the itinerancy hypothesis. Several analysts have already drawn the conclusion that Q itself and Q's Mission Speech in particular cannot reflect the perspective of itinerants but of a settled "community" that made use of older material, originally transmitted by itinerants, in new rhetorical contexts and with new implications.[33] The history of 9:57-58 suggests that this conclusion is only partly accurate. The Q[1] Mission Speech apparently is not addressed to missionaries themselves. Moreover, the collection of chreiai that precedes this speech, especially if one counts 9:60-61 as originally part of Q, clearly is concerned with the theme of commitment, and perhaps, more specifically, the theme of commitment in the face of familial criticism.[34] The follower is not enjoined to be itinerant; only Jesus himself is presented as "having no place to lay his head." And what this phrase is deemed to mean in its Q[1] context—actual homelessness, the absence of family for Jesus as in the two following sayings, or simply a general lack of welcome, that is, rejection—remains less than clear. But the saying, in fact, once it is detached from its immediate literary context, implies itinerancy even less than it does within the confines of Q. Without the immediate context of Q 9:59-60 (61-62), the voluntary aspect of the homelessness described in vv. 57-58 is nowhere in sight. And without the larger context of Q[1] as a whole, "son of man" does not obviously refer to Jesus or to any other single person but would, quite naturally, be taken simply to mean human beings. Thus the point of this Wisdom saying, circulating in isolation, is that not some but all human beings, and not willingly but perforce, have no natural sanctuary. There is no especially good reason to regard such a sentiment as the invention of itinerants, particularly when the itinerant's asceticism is voluntary and hence a display of religious virtuosity, something absolutely not to be imputed to human beings in general.

Of course the main impetus for associating Q with any form of itinerancy, at any stage of its development or of the development of its traditions, is the Mission Charge of Q 10:2-16. The text in its current form is a product of both major redactional layers of Q. Q 10:13-15 clearly interrupts the flow of the thought and the form of the preceding material: it is directed to outsiders, not to those sent; and like other Q[2] texts (7:1-10; 11:31-32; 13:28-29) emphasizes not only the theme of judgment and rejection but also of invidious comparison of Israel with Gentiles.[35] One might also note the distinctive retrospective, rather than prospective, sense of these verses: given the miracles performed, Tyre and Sidon would have repented long ago. These sayings, then, were added secondarily to a collection that already existed in Q[1] by the hand responsible for Q[2] (Kloppenborg 1987:199–203; see Braun 1991:291).

The Q[1] version of the Mission Charge allows for at least a few inferences. The explicit analogy of those "sent" to day laborers in v. 3 is complemented by what appears to be an implicit analogy to other types of travelers and to the parameters of official local hospitality that they might reasonably expect. Both the Mishnah and the Tosefta have closely parallel texts, which are, surprisingly, routinely ignored by itinerancy advocates. The Mishnah, describing how one is to practice charity, states that "A poor man that is journeying from place to place should be given not less than one loaf worth a *pondion* [from wheat costing] one *sela* for four *seahs*. If he spends the night [in such a place] he should be given what is needful to support him for the night. If he stays over the Sabbath he should be given food enough for three meals" (*m. Pe'ah* 8:7). The Tosefta, somewhat later, offers clarifying amplification of these injunctions (while simultaneously abbreviating the language):

> Do not open yourself [that is, give charity] to *a poor person who wanders from place to place* [beyond] a dupondius' worth [of bread] from [wheat costing one *sela*] for four *seahs*. If he sleeps there, give him what is due to a sleeper: oil, and beans. If he stays over the Sabbath [that is, if he stays a week], give him food for three meals: oil, beans, fish, and vegetables. These things are said for instances in which you do not know him. But for instances in which you do know him, you are even to go ahead and clothe him. Now, *if he goes around from door to door, you are not obligated to him for anything.*[36]

In comparing Q's Mission Speech to these texts, what is missing from Q is as remarkable as what is present. Utterly lacking in Q is the concern expressed by the Mishnah and Tosefta about the provisions required for those who stay various lengths of time: overnight ("if he spends the night," "if he sleeps there") or a week ("if he stays over the Sabbath"). Unlike the travelers described in the *Didache* and unlike those wandering paupers (beggars?) at issue in the Mishnah and Tosefta, the Q travelers do not stay overnight. Thus the reference in the Mission Speech to entering houses (Q 10:5) is almost certainly not an indication that lodging is sought but instead that these individuals are seeking a general welcome and table hospitality (a supposition supported by 10:7b, which imagines food offerings as an indication of acceptance).

The two main features that Q shares with these injunctions are also notable. First, these texts all evince a practice of wandering and the expectation of hospitality in the form of rations. Moreover, that hospitality appears to have an official character: it represents what the traveler may be expected to receive from the village in which he is found, not from individual persons. The rations to be provided (a small loaf of bread for the day; oil, fish, and vegetables if the wanderer stays longer) are not especially prodigal, but they are—and are meant to be—sufficient for subsistence, indicating that such charity is not expected from each and every person in the village but from the village as a whole. Thus the image suggested by vv. 8-10 that acceptance or rejection of the Q "messengers" occurs at the level of the "city" as a whole makes sense not only in terms of the social homogeneity of small settlements (Kloppenborg 1991:90) but apparently also in terms of the concrete strategies actually used (at least according to the Mishnah and Tosefta, albeit at a later date) among villagers and townspeople for dealing with strangers, and invoked in this speech. Thus the direct juxtaposition of instructions for behavior toward a household (vv. 5-7) with instructions for behavior toward a village (vv. 8-11), while almost certainly a form-critical aporia, was probably viewed as completely continuous advice within the context of Q. What all of this tells us is simply that the Q^1 messengers viewed themselves as addressing themselves to—and in return being addressed by—the settlement as a corporate entity, and in its relatively official manifestation. Visits to houses are hence deemed to be commensurate with official and public visits to, appeals to, and acceptance or rejection by the whole settlement in which the house was located.

On the other hand, the relative paucity of the rations corporately provided by villages (according to the Mishnah and Tosefta, that is) may in part account for Q's stipulation to "eat what is set before you" (v. 8). While v. 7 encourages the workers to accept hospitality as their due (their "wages"), v. 8 warns them not to spurn hospitality that is not all that it could be, that is, to accept whatever it is that any given town has to offer. The important thing is not what is given but that anything is given at all, sage advice when one considers that the people who live in these villages are not especially well off, and that, if anything, given the circumstances recounted in the last chapter, their livelihood is probably shrinking. The concern here thus seems to have little to do with issues of Jew or Gentile or purity (see *Thomas* 14, where purity does seem to be an issue) and more to do with how to receive hospitality when it is offered.[37]

Second, the text from the Tosefta includes, as does Q 10:7c, an injunction against going from door to door. The Tosefta's stipulation that one is not required to extend charity to a poor person if that person has been going from door to door probably does not represent any kind of specific critique of begging so much as an assumption that such a person's needs will thus already have been addressed, and so no (further) charity is required. This stipulation, therefore, confirms the impression that the charity or hospitality in question in the Mishnah and Tosefta is official: it is offered instead of, or as an alternative to, the charity of individual households. Again, the parallel may suggest useful lines of interpretation for the injunction in Q 10:7c. The point of this prohibition is not to avoid greed or to prevent the messengers from pestering individual householders (against Mack 1993:129–30). Rather, the point is—at least insofar as the Tosefta's parallel sheds light on the assumptions and implications the Q Mission Charge—that the messengers are addressing themselves to the village or town as a corporate entity rather than to the individual households that comprise it. In other words, a mission of individuals to individuals is not in view. By way of confirming the relevance of this parallel for such an interpretation, it is notable that this prohibition (10:7c) is associated both thematically and by juxtaposition with the twin injunctions to accept (10:7a,b) and to receive graciously (10:8b) whatever hospitality may be offered. Thus the argumentative progression of the multiple sayings concatenated in these two verses is: (1) accept what you can get on such journeys, because you deserve it (10:7a,b); but (2) the point of the journeys is official business, that is, involves dealings with the village or town as a unit, and is not orientated toward establishing individual connections (10:7c, see 10:8a); and so, therefore, (3) even if the official pickings could be better, accept what you are given, because the real point is whether or not you will be welcomed at all, not how much you can accumulate or how comfortable your hosts will make you (10:8b).

Several scholars imagine that the shift within the Q Mission Discourse between instructions pertinent to approaching houses (vv. 5-7) and those applicable to approaching cities (vv. 8-12) represent an aporia indicative of different historical stages in the activity of the people responsible for this unit (Braun 1991:288–89; Hoffmann 1982:288, 296, 298–99; Uro 1987:106). This is almost certainly correct, as the absence of the additional city-oriented material in the Markan parallel attests. But any claim that the city stage came prior to the house stage is certainly incorrect (against Mack 1993:129–30). As most commentators argue, it is clear that the instructions for entering households represent a core element of the speech, probably combined with the equipment rule to form the earliest nucleus of the charge as a whole.[38] And what is equally clear is that at or by the time the instruction was incorporated into Q, the focus was now entirely on cities as such (Braun 1991:289), on the public character of the mission. Thus the Mission Speech as it now appears in Q (at both main strata of the document), focusing on official and collective reception and subsuming the household instructions within that program, represents the logic of the people responsible for Q, or at the very least the logic they accept and endorse.

What are the Q[1] village scribes doing? Apparently, at least immediately prior to the incorporation of the Mission Charge into Q[1], they are

Development of the "Mission" Speech

	Text	Ideological Orientation	Medium and Stage Added
Stage 1	Q 10:4ab, 5-6, 8-9; equipment rule framed positively?	proclaiming the kingdom? travel instructions?	*oral:* original core
Stage 2	addition of 2, 4c, 7	additional behavioral specifications	*oral:* early oral additions
Stage 3	addition of Q 10:3, 10-11; references to "city" in v. 8; negative framing of equipment rule?	"official" orientation; provisions for rejection	*written?:* pre-Q¹ additions
Stage 4	addition of Q 10:16; association of mission speech with Q 9:57-62	formal conclusion; increasing pessimism about mission; rationalization in terms of Jesus' unique authority; generalization to theme of commitment	*written:* Q¹ redaction
Stage 5	Q 10:12-15	deuteronomistic polemic; mission relegated to the past	*written:* Q² redaction

Table 2: This table summarizes the stages through which the Mission Speech developed, and indicates in summary form the agenda promoted at each stage.

making short trips to adjacent towns in some kind of official or quasi-official capacity. In other words, they are acting, as we might expect, like administrators, even if what they are doing is not part of their authorized job description. In the performance of administrative duties, it appears that normally subordinates traveled to superiors and not the other way around. Thus the village scribe may indeed have been expected to venture to, say, Tiberias from time to time but would not normally venture out to the nearby villages, at least not in the course of his official duties. If a villager needed paperwork done, that was a reason to come into town, not for the scribe to venture out to the village. So in this sense, in terms of the performance of their official duties, the activity described in

Q 10:2-11, 16 is decidedly unauthorized (see Table 2). But the approaches made, from (newly peripheralized) center to periphery (such as from, for example, Capernaum to Chorazin) were made in an official mood or were intended to have an official tone. They were thus local, public, and corporate in intention. Persons were actually traveling, but not as beggars and not for long distances. The official aura of the injunctions and the apparent satisfaction of these emissaries with bare acceptance rather than some sort of acquisition or remuneration may allow us hints of what the Q^1 (or pre-Q^1) people were trying to accomplish.

Obviously they were not taking these trips to procure a good supper. If bare welcome, signaled and symbolized by any degree of hospitality (see 10:8), was sufficient, the main point of these trips was surely ideological persuasion, the effort to convince one's neighboring towns to join the reign of God (10:11). This effort was not made by ragged bums preaching in the town square but by official emissaries addressing themselves to the local leadership: another village administrator (κωμάρχης), or the local strong man. The intention, then, was not to behave like wild-eyed roving prophets (a literary type if there ever was one) but to use a combination of bureaucratic position and reasoned persuasion to generate a network of villages and towns that adopted—officially, as it were—the ethos of the Q people. The overtures were not made to individual persons as such but to the political-administrative apparatus already in place, in the form of presenting themselves in the town square and there making approaches to whatever officials or leaders could be found. Q^1 is able to gloss over the juxtaposition between house instructions and village instructions so easily not only because social solidarity makes the two essentially equivalent but also because for Q they were literally equivalent: as far as they were concerned, welcome by the village or town was being welcomed by its chief man. This also implies that the agenda promoted by Q^1 was intended to be enacted politically or administratively as well as disseminated in this fashion. And that in its turn suggests that the ethos, agenda, or program of the reign of God was itself a political and administrative policy, rather than the sort of thing we moderns would regard as self-evidently and obviously religious.

One should finally note that even at the stage at which Q^1 was finally pieced together, these individuals were not especially optimistic that their plans would come to fruition. That the network they proposed to establish came to naught is evident enough in the Q^2 woes against Capernaum, Chorazin, and Bethsaida. But already in Q^1 there are indications that things are not proceeding according to plan. Although the majority of the Q^1 Mission Speech focuses on how to approach towns and what to make of a positive reception (so vv. 2, 4-9), it is the later additions that discuss how to respond to rejection (vv. 10-11) and that express trepidation about the enterprise as a whole (v. 3). Moreover, the juxtaposition of the Mission Charge (10:2-11, 16) with the sayings on discipleship (9:57-62)—a juxtaposition that must come from a very late stage in the composition of this material, probably Q^1 redaction itself—reinforces the sense of hardship associated with this work and actually may represent a first step in the direction of converting these injunctions from literal instructions into metaphorical exhortations to perseverance in discipleship.[39]

The Rhetoric of Uprootedness in Q

Of what, exactly, this scheme, ethos, agenda, or program might have consisted is another question, and it is the question that brings us face-to-face with Q's imagery of inversion and uprootedness, imagery that scholarship has normally explained in terms of the legacy of radical itinerants. If, however, the Q people were not wandering beggars, were not itinerant radicals, were not the settled converts of such individuals, what caused the inversionary and radical tone of their language and hence presumably of their program? To what ends is this rhetoric applied in their efforts to persuade their fellow administrators of the cogency and attractiveness of the reign of God?

If one examines Q's rhetoric as rhetoric, that is, in its rhetorical (literary) context and as an effort at persuasion, the document's apparent concern with poverty as such and especially with outright destitution is somewhat attenuated. While a great deal of its rhetoric is inversionary, that rhetoric does not necessarily either reflect or exhort poverty: rather, it uses poverty alongside other images of social inversion as a metaphor to communicate the repudiation of social hierarchy as the Q tradents experienced it. In other words, the terms and especially the dichotomies of the contemporary social structure (and its ideological rationalizations) were taken up and either dissolved or inverted in Q's rhetoric. The image of poverty is used in Q^1 to this end, as is a variety of vignettes involving loss or depreciation of social standing (loss of wealth, honor, status, prestige). These images are of a piece. While they do indeed reflect the diminished status of the Q^1 tradents as a result of the socioeconomic phenomena outlined in chapter 4, their primary and intended purpose is to provide loci for arguments whose the cumulative effect is the subversion of local and translocal hierarchy as it is being manifested, in novel (and evidently disagreeable) forms, for these individuals and for their occupational caste generally.

The point, then, was not to promote the specific inversions that appear in Q^1 so much as to advocate a persuasive way of viewing the

Galilean social body in which the bases for an unfamiliar social hierarchy—that is, that being promoted by urbanization—were corroded. In general, all of this rhetoric focuses on a single basic idea: the eschewal of any and all forms of social mediation. The theme of poverty or loss of status, the denigration of strict reciprocity, and so forth are, within the context of Q^1 and of the program it advances, simply suasive forays into this theme, in the form of (logically or rhetorically) convenient examples or focal instances.[40]

This pattern is perhaps most clear in the stereotypical argumentative clusters described by Piper, which probably formed the backbone around which Q^1 was constructed.[41] As Piper has noted, each one of these speeches uses a very conventionalized argumentative structure to convey its point:

1. A saying used as a general opening
2. Arguments directly in support of this opening assertion
3. Rhetorical questions or new illustrations
4. Final argument and application (Piper 1982:416; see Table 3)

Piper's Argumentative Clusters

	Description	Example: Q 11:9-13
Step 1 General Opening	categorical assertions and/or imperatives	I tell you, ask and it will be given to you, seek and you will find, knock and it will be opened to you.
Step 2 Supportive Arguments	motive clauses, usually keyed to a future state of affairs	For everyone who asks receives, and the one who seeks finds, and to the one who knocks it will be opened.
Step 3 Rhetorical Questions and/or Illustrations	illustrations from ordinary behavior, sometimes framed as rhetorical questions	What person of you, if his son asks for a loaf of bread, will give him a stone, or if he asks for a fish, will give him a snake?
Step 4 Specific Conclusions; Application	application of general principles to specific setting: in this example, prayer	If you, then, though you are evil, know how to give good gifts to your children, how much more will the Father from heaven give good things to those who ask him!

Table 3: A breakdown of the structure of Q^1's argumentative clusters, as determined by Ronald Piper.

Thus, speaking from the rhetorical perspective of the pre-Q¹ compilers of these speeches, the intended point of each argument will be found in its concluding exhortations. Collecting together the exhortations Piper identifies as concluding each of these speeches (1982:416), we arrive at the following:

> Be merciful, as your Father in heaven is merciful. (Q 6:36)

> Remove first from your eye the log, and then you will see clearly to cast out the speck . . . [from] the eye of your brother. (6:42b)

> The good person brings forth good things from a good treasure. But the evil one brings forth evil things from the evil treasure. For from an abundance of the heart the mouth speaks. (6:45)

> If you then, though you are evil, know how to give good gifts to your children, how much more will your Father from heaven give good things to those who ask him. (11:13)

> Do not fear, you are worth more than many sparrows. (12:7b)

> Therefore do not be anxious, saying What shall we eat? or What shall we drink? or What shall we wear? For the Gentiles seek all these things; for your Father knows that you need them. But seek his kingdom, and these things shall be yours as well. (12:29-31)

Not a one of these concluding points is at all inversionary: they exhort mercy, fair judgment, good deeds, trust in prayer, and—perhaps the most radical conclusion of the lot—avoiding obsession with material goods. These conclusions are sufficiently banal that one can easily imagine them circulating as part of the stock and utterly conventional sagacity of local scribalism long before the specific and peculiar agenda of Q¹ had developed, indeed, plausibly enough, before Jesus came on the scene at all.[42]

However, when we turn to the opening lines of each cluster, the resultant picture is very different (Piper 1982:416):

> Love your enemies and pray for those who abuse you: thus you will be sons of [God]. (Q 6:27, 6:35b)

> Judge not, and you will not be judged; for with the judgment you judge you will be judged. (6:37)

> There is no sound tree which bears bad fruit, nor again an unsound tree which bears good fruit. (6:43)

> I tell you, ask and it will be given to you, seek and you will find, knock and it will be opened to you. (11:9)

> Nothing is covered which will not be revealed and hidden which will not be made known. (12:4)

> Therefore, do not be anxious about your life, what you shall eat,
> nor about your body, what you shall put on. (12:22)

These assertions and imperatives are rather more peculiar. Here the
familiar radicalism and inversion of Q^1 is most apparent. One is encouraged to love enemies (6:27), eschew judgment entirely (6:37), seek anything in the conviction of receiving it (11:9), and trust in God even for
bare subsistence (12:22).[43] Q 12:4 invokes an inversionary scheme, which
seems to imagine divine intervention or at least a world turned upside
down. Not every single one of these introductory sayings is self-
evidently radical—the inversionary saying in 12:4 could be applied in a
variety of ways, and as for the proverb about sound and unsound trees in
6:43, as Bultmann says (in his usual pithy manner), "No one wants to
maintain that the saying rises above the standards and outlook of secular wisdom."[44] But all of these statements are categorical, and all envision
radically revised or novel circumstances in which their validity will be
apparent. In this sense, like the first three beatitudes, their rationale
works along the lies of an enthymeme, directing the hearer's attention to
the unstated premise lurking behind the ostensible conclusion.[45] This
premise cannot be, as Carruth (1995:108) thinks is the case regarding the
Beatitudes, that "you" (that is, those being addressed) fall into the categories under discussion, because most of these sayings make the direct
address (that is, to "you") quite explicit; the premise is thus in no way
unstated. Rather, it seems that the unstated premise to which all of these
peculiar sayings direct the hearer's attention—and direct it in large measure precisely because of their apparent unconventional character or even
counterfactuality (for example, 6:37a; 11:9; 12:4)—is that there will be
circumstances in which each assertion is valid.[46] It is notable that several
of the sayings (6:27, 35b, 37; 11:9) take the form of imperatives (implying future action) followed by motive clauses specifying results that are
described in the future tense. The failure, enthymeme-like, to state those
circumstances explicitly is an interesting rhetorical strategy, inviting—or
at least leaving open the possibility for—the hearer to imagine or consider what those circumstances will be. Unfortunately, the modern
exegete is left in the same position, unsure whether the implicit trans-
formations required by the logic of these sayings are to be characterized
in terms of an attitude (and are thus Cynic-like), a social program (and
are thus reformist or revolutionary), or some kind of direct divine
intervention (and are thus "eschatological"[47]).

It is notable that the sayings that conclude these clusters are no less
attested, as isolated sayings, than are the radical sayings that open the
clusters.[48] Thus, clearly, the rhetorical organization of the material does

not reflect—at least not directly—its tradition-historical provenance. We can only conclude that the argumentative relationship between the opening and closing sayings of these clusters represents a deliberate and motivated decision on the part of the people responsible for them. The compositions, then, were organized with a view toward subsuming these radical or inversionary sayings into coherent and persuasive arguments that asserted fairly commonplace conclusions (using fairly commonplace examples and images). The inflammatory, mysterious, or inversionary aspects of the rhetoric of the constituent material were thus effectively domesticated: they became general principles supporting (relatively) conventional observations.

The people responsible for these argumentative clusters, therefore, were not interested in the same inversionary agenda that stimulated the opening imperatives. The people behind the Q document, as one might have already determined from that document's apparent setting, are not withdrawn from the social world of their contemporaries and are not promoting the complete dissolution of that world. But the use of these originally isolated exhortations as persuasive statements of general principle from which to launch rather more focused and innocuous compositions betrays an implicit openness to the inversionary rhetoric they represent. That is, provided it is expressed metaphorically or in terms of general wisdom, the lexicon of social dissolution remains powerful enough to serve as a persuasive basis for these persons. Just as the overall argumentation of these clusters mitigates the radical character of some of their constituent elements, so the radical character of the constituent elements mitigates somewhat the banality of the arguments they serve. The presence of these inversionary sayings within the clusters makes it clear that the conventional arguments offered at this stage are not intended to procure entirely conventional results; the use of eccentric premises to attain rather subdued conclusions is indicative of a certain subversive ethos, a countercultural spirit, behind those conclusions, however subdued they may be. While there may be an intelligible and even constructive social agenda behind Q[1], the easy application of a rhetoric of uprootedness to this agenda should serve to warn us that the program is reactive, that it is offered at least in part as a response and rejoinder to some kind of social alienation on the part of its advocates.

The Q[1] Beatitudes (Q 6:20b-23b)[49] offer another salient example of essentially the same process. As the opening teachings of the first recension of Q, they serve a programmatic function for what follows: they are more an assertion of Q[1]'s overall viewpoint than an argument for it, but they influence the tone of all that follows.[50] This programmatic function, as well as the bare content, of the Q version of the Beatitudes encourage the view that Q is addressed to, if not actually written by, the destitute and miserable, and dominated overall by an interest in them.[51] This view is further bolstered by the wording of the first beatitude, which honors not simply "the poor," but the πτωχοί (beggars) (see Hanson 1995). The distinction between πένης (poor man) and πτωχός (beggar) is made much of by some commentators, as denoting a distinction between the merely poor (that is, those who have to work for a living) and the utterly destitute (Crossan 1991:270–73, citing Aristophanes, *Plutus* 535–54; see Crossan 1998:321). Thus, in blessing the πτωχοί, Q 6:20b is doing more than simply blessing those who are not wealthy: it is blessing the destitute, the beggars, the "unclean, degraded, and expendable classes" (Crossan 1991:273).

This reasoning does not entirely stand up to scrutiny, in part because the structural role of the Beatitudes for the entirety of Q¹ is not given sufficient consideration, nor is the process by which they came to fill this role. The first point that must be stressed is that this cluster of Beatitudes, even in its Q¹ form, is composite and went through several stages of development. Classically, Bultmann pointed to the distinction in both form and content of the fourth of the Q Beatitudes from the first three: "It is essential to see that Lk. 6:22 or Matt. 5:11f. is a new element of the tradition which is clearly distinguished from the older element Lk.6:20f. or Matt.5:3-9 in form (second person and detailed grounds of blessedness) and content, arising *ex eventu* and for that reason created by the Church. It is in this second set that we first have a direct reference to the person of Jesus" (Bultmann 1963:110).[52] We do not need to trace the process by which these elaborations were added; it is sufficient to note that all of the additions were probably made subsequent to this saying's association with the other three beatitudes, but (excluding v. 23c) prior to their attachment to the following instructions on love of enemies and forgiveness.[53]

What this indicates, among other things, is that already prior to their incorporation into Q¹, the Beatitudes, as a single unit, had come to refer to something other than literal poverty or destitution: they were used, rather, to enunciate a set of paradigmatic inversions of basic social positions in support of a final conclusion to the effect that adherence to "x" program (that is, ἕνεκεν "x") would be beneficial in spite of apparent disadvantages. As a result, the "reign of God" in the first beatitude also comes to have this self-referential sense: it too becomes denotative of the specific program ("x") marked by ἕνεκεν/ἕνεκα.[54] Even the juncture of the first three beatitudes indicates that something other than voluntary itinerancy is at issue. Regardless of the setting of the blessing on the poor or on the hungry, their association with the blessing on those who weep is certainly indicative of a general and principled inversion (the world turned upside down) rather than of a specific and practicable one accomplished by choice, such as voluntary itinerancy. Itinerants may choose to be poor and even perhaps hungry, but they do not choose weeping as a feature of their lifestyle! Indeed, strictly speaking, weeping is not a socioeconomic index at all; thus even the very early clustering of the first three beatitudes represents a shift away from the strictly socioeconomic force of the first and second beatitudes taken in isolation.[55] The point has become general and relatively abstract. The addition of a fourth (persecution) beatitude, attracted by the influence of the third (weeping) beatitude, further shifts attention away from the strictly economic character of the first two blessings and sharpens and elaborates the reference to weeping: "those who weep" are weeping, we are to imagine, because they are reviled, cast out, or reproached. Under the influence of this motif, then, the last beatitude is elaborated and amplified to express this theme more clearly and to specify the motivations behind the reproaches, influencing, as a result, the tenor of the entire list of blessings.

Thus the thematic progress of the Beatitudes in the course of their development was (1) economic inversion, (2) general or abstract inversion, (3) a specific social inversion (involving esteem or repute), and (4) social inversion as a result or consequence of adherence to a specific program (see Table 4). Such a progression of course matches to some degree what has already been noted in the development of other Q^1 blocks. The composition of Piper's pre-Q^1 argumentative clusters follows the same course rhetorically (synchronically) as the Beatitudes follow tradition-historically (diachronically): that is, they are based on radical sayings, which are used to express inversion in the abstract, in the service of some specific type of social exhortation (often involving esteem or repute). The fourth stage, on the other hand, not present at the stage in which the pre-Q^1 clusters developed, is, however, paralleled in the Q^1 redactional juxtaposition of the Mission Charge (step 3: a specific set of social behaviors, concerned with welcome, that is, esteem or repute) with the discipleship sayings of Q 9:57-62 (step 4: the social destabilization that occurs as a result of adherence to a program).[56]

And within the overall context of Q^1, as its programmatic introduction, the Beatitudes serve a similar literary and rhetorical (synchronic) function to that served by the opening lines of Piper's argumentative clusters: they establish a general or abstract inversionary tone (stage 2, above) that is used as a basis upon which to develop further arguments. Thematically, however, this incorporation into the totality of Q^1 means that they function in terms of diachronic stage 4, that is, as denotative of

Development of the Beatitudes

	Text	Source/Literary Features	Social Characteristics of Those Blessed
Stage 1	3 loose beatitudes	oral tradition; Jesus?	profound and specific economic deprivation
Stage 2	serialization of beatitudes	unknown	generalized economic deprivation
Stage 3	addition of original persecution beatitude	unknown; scribal elements?	social deprivation; economic deprivation as a result of social deprivation
Stage 4	modification of persecution beatitude: addition of ἕνεκα/ἕνεκεν (on account of) clause (Q 6:22c)	Q^1 tradents, prior to Q^1 composition	social deprivation as a result of adherence to a particular program
Stage 5	association of four beatitudes with speech on love of enemies (Q 6:27 ff.)	Q^1 redaction	those who advocate a social program based on inversion of ordinary values
Stage 6	addition of Q 6:23c, "for so their fathers did to the prophets"	Q^2 redaction	sectarian adherents, with deuteronomistic rationalization

Table 4: This table summarizes the stages through which the Beatitudes developed and indicates the social characteristics of those addressed.

social inversion that stems from advocacy of a certain program. This is natural enough: it corresponds to the final stage in the development of these beatitudes in their Q^1 form. This is all to say that although the Beatitudes as a unit already show in their aggregational development an orientation toward the theme of uprootedness as a consequence of certain choices, they function rhetorically within Q^1 as generalizations promoting the principle of inversion and as identifications of that comprehensive inversion-in-principle with the reign of God or the Son of Man. Thus all of what follows in Q^1 has the character of specific applications of 6:21-23, just as many of the constituent clusters attempt specific applications of the general principles with which they open. Carruth is at least partly correct when she argues that the authority of Jesus as the speaker is presumed here, not developed:

> Enunciating a number of beatitudes does not prove a case, but it does intensify the sense of the speaker's authority by showing that he or she can illuminate the situation of the hearers in a comprehensive way. Here in the exordium of the sermon, where rhetorical principle emphasizes the establishment of the speaker's character, Jesus is shown to be one who overturns common wisdom and lays down a different way of perceiving one's situation. The acceptance of this new wisdom will depend in large measure on the authority attributed to Jesus by the audience. (1995:108–9)

Apparently Jesus was a sufficiently authoritative character for the people responsible for Q^1 (or their fictive or putative audience) that an effort was made to assimilate or subsume material already circulating under his name. Carruth may, however, be reversing cause and effect. The association of Jesus with such inversionary sayings may have been part of the reason he was selected as a speaker in the first place. These inversionary sayings have a powerful suasive force of their own, and, to the extent that Q^1's agenda was in fact subversive and that its tradents identified themselves as uprooted or their audience as responsive to such rhetoric, such material—if it could be successfully integrated into the program at hand—must have been extraordinarily attractive in its own right, Jesus himself notwithstanding.

The inversionary logic of these beatitudes is the logic of the categorical opening statements of Piper's clusters and is partly attractive simply because of its categorical, black-and-white, and arresting view of reality.[57] The sayings are memorable and powerful precisely because they are not subtle, not casuistic. But even more so, they are powerful because of the way they force the hearers to imagine for themselves the circumstances under which the sayings might be true. It is for that reason that I described these opening sayings above as enthymeme-like in their rhetorical effect. What the Beatitudes do—as the opening for Q^1 as an integral document—is invoke that speculation in the most general, explicitly inversionary, and comprehensive way possible. Appropriately enough, the beatitudes are enthymemes, in their formal characteristics, and not simply in terms of the logic they depend upon (Carruth 1995:107–8). As such, the reader-hearer is left to supply the premises that will make the main assertions of these sayings come true. She is warned (or promised) that the arguments to follow will be inversionary, but not how they will be inversionary. She is warned that the arguments that follow will depend on and articulate a condition known as the reign of God but is not told the terms and prerequisites of this condition; transformation is promised but not described. Not only is the serialization of blessings attendant upon harkening to wisdom a known introductory strategy within the genre of wisdom instructions (Kloppenborg 1987:188), but their formulation as enthymemes[58] is perfectly appropriate to Q^1's subsequent rhetoric and tone. Moreover, it serves to hook the reader-hearer, inviting not simply speculation and consideration about the character of this future inversion but also curiosity about the remainder of the document (How will these promises be fulfilled?), the assumption that the arguments that follow do indeed fulfill the agenda of general inversion (these ideas are what it is that will make the poor, hungry, and so on happy), and possibly also assent in advance (by forcing the audience to imagine the topsy-turvy world in which such sayings would be true, the audience creates that world, at least in the imagination, making what follows all the more plausible).[59]

In sum, then, within the context of Q^1 as a document, the Beatitudes are not indicative of beggary among the audience or speakers. The use of "poor men/beggars" in the first of these blessings is not as significant as it has been made out to be: in Hellenistic literature, "poor man" and "beggar" are used interchangeably, and for the New Testament, "beggar" is the usual term for poverty (Bammel 968:894 and n. 79; 902 and n. 155; see BAGD 728). The set of conditions that these sayings outline is decidedly not prescriptive, and hence their inversionary rhetoric is only imperfectly accounted for by itinerancy hypotheses. In the form in which they appear in Q, the Beatitudes have already been considerably domesticated and now serve rhetorically to promote an abstract sense of inversion that both thematically situates or reinforces the material that follows and actively attempts to engage the audience prior to the commencement of what promises to be an unconventional project. By the time we arrive at the redaction of Q^1, this project, invoking the Jesus traditions and (apparently) Jesus himself, is already being viewed retrospectively. The composition of Q^1, in time with and thematically of a piece with the evolution of the individual traditions harbored by the group, may have been in part a response to the failure of an earlier agenda (and hence a desire to collect such traditions in lieu of the mission to disseminate them) represented by the initial formulation of Piper's argumentative clusters, the Mission Speech (as a unit and in its Q^1 form), and the initial serialization of the first three beatitudes and especially their juncture with (the original form of) the fourth beatitude. For the persons represented by Q^1's development, then, the uprootedness expressed in the Beatitudes is not economic and is not voluntary; it is metaphoric, rhetorical, and deliberately vague. It is invoked only in the service of more specific points that are considerably less radical (and less mysterious) and that focus on social esteem to a considerable degree. Thus the economic uprootedness evoked by some of the Q^1 material appears, rhetorically, to be yoked to the service of a redactional and preredactional Q^1 interest in social uprootedness. That interest, in turn, seems to center on—or to have once centered on—a specific social vision in which esteem, honor, and local standing are of paramount importance. It is to the specific points served by these arguments, to the specific social vision and agenda they were intended to promote, that we now must turn.

The Social Project of the Q Tradents

The agenda to which Q^1 harkens as the basis for its own group identity can be identified with some plausibility if we return to the specific applications that concluded each of the argumentative clusters noted by Piper. These applications include exhortations to be merciful regarding the failings of others (Q 6:36), to exercise clear and objective judgment (6:42b), to act and speak good things corresponding to one's reputation (6:45), to trust in God's care (11:13), to avoid fear (12:7b), and to forebear from concern for material goods (12:29-31). Obviously the last three items form a coherent set with a single coherent theme: you can avoid the pursuit of material goods, even necessities, by placing your trust in God (or the reign of God, Q 12:31), who will then provide them for you. There does seem to be a relationship here between the commitment or attitude enjoined and the promised results. People are not actually told that under all circumstances God will simply provide them what they need. Rather, they are told that if one relies entirely on God (what precisely this means, as usual, is unspecified), these providential results will follow (see especially 11:13b: "to those who ask him"; 12:31: "but seek his reign, and these things shall be yours as well").[60] What is enjoined, then, is a redirection of the commitments, values, or interests of those addressed (addressed fictively, at least in the context of the document), from material goods (economic greed) to God (commitment to the collective values of the social body, at least as they are understood by the Q people).[61] Of course the economic inversions of the first two beatitudes effectively underscore such an appeal. Material benefit is to be subordinated to the value of community, to ancestral values (as they are understood by the people responsible for Q).[62]

There remains the question, however, what is intended by the first three exhortations on judgment and whether they fit the agenda expressed by those on trust in God. These former arguments, with their focus on judgment and their language of brotherhood, are normally understood to be addressed to an in-group (Horsley 1995b:43; Kloppenborg 1987:185, 188, 238–39; Piper 1982:416–18). That is, the group responsible for Q is exhorting its own membership to be fair and peaceable with one another. As we have already seen, however, the range of social roles addressed by Q¹ indicates that the persons responsible for the document were not limiting themselves to a sectarian enclave, at least not in theory. The insider form of address in Q¹ (for example, "brother," Q 6:41-42) is perfectly appropriate to a general address to everyone at a local level, at least so long as sectarian lines have not yet been drawn. Moreover, if, as I have argued, the people responsible for Q¹ were involved in the general administration of justice, an address intended to circulate among themselves would nevertheless be an appeal with broad implications for the entire local population. If these exhortations are addressed to the local community at large, in which mechanisms for judgment and the acquisition of esteem are already in place, their significance will obviously be rather different than if they were intended to regulate sectarian or in-group behavior.

It is also notable that—in spite of the grand idealism of their opening injunctions (Q 6:27 "love your enemies"; 6:37 "judge not")—the applications of these first three argumentative clusters do not forbid judgment but actually assume its continuation and offer guidelines for how it is to take place. Judgment is to be merciful, clear, objective, and based on deeds and words rather than prior reputation. All of the injunctions are thus thematically of a piece, insofar as they all advocate a certain type of justice in which mercy and overt (good) deeds are of central import and are accorded the role of central and basic juridical ideals (see Piper 1995:58–60). The examples used in the course of making these arguments are significant. At least in part, actual judicial practices are in mind: one is to sustain injury generously, rewarding one's enemy with additional benefit (prayer, the other cheek, your shirt, and the principal to one's debtors) in lieu of seeking formal redress (Q 6:28-30; see 12:58-59). Piper believes that such advice is indicative of a complete loss of confidence in official legalities and represents a warning that it is better (for oneself) to give up a great deal, informally, than trust in a rapacious legal system (Piper 1995:59–66). But these exhortations are not actually showing a broad disdain for the legal system as such (with its various stipulations that have nothing to do with the actions described in Q); they focus instead on its adversarial aspects.

Several of the examples these clusters use, moreover, are drawn from without the legal sphere but share with the forensic examples the focus on conflict or, more specifically, on situations in which unequal social roles might impart some form of competitive advantage: begging (6:30), leadership (6:39), teaching (6:40), and so forth. This phenomenon suggests that what motivates these arguments is less an impulse and exhortation to flee specifically legal institutions of all and any kind than an interest in avoiding conflictual or competitive relationships entirely. The whole paradox of the exhortation to love your enemies is that such a practice (in the abstract, at any rate) leaves no enemies left to love. Giving to all who ask leaves no one left in need. Within all of the formal situations with which a scribe, particularly, will have contact—legal claims and loans, but also master-pupil relationships, leadership, and the assessment of conduct in general—a kind of pragmatic (and latently conservative) ethos of dependability and ethical transparency, combined with a spirit of communal generosity, is enjoined. One is to return to a simpler assessment of social behavior in which the good are good, the bad are bad, and in which being good means acting for the benefit of all rather than attempting to accrue benefit to one's self.

The claim that Q^1 militates against a limited-good view of the world (Douglas 1995:124–25) is probably quite mistaken: rather, these arguments presuppose a universe in which value is limited (exactly what one would expect of an ancient document such as Q) and thus one in which gain, whether in honor or in material goods, is made at the expense of others, or, more accurately, made at the expense of the group. The injunctions to avoid the pursuit of material gain or the (active) retention of honor at the individual level thus aim to inhibit the loss of these items at the communal level. The perception of limited good in this instance is probably correct: the new links of the villages at the northern end of the lake to the imperial order represented by Tiberias may have allowed individual gain among the local upper classes but would simultaneously have meant loss for the villages themselves, corporately speaking. A reassertion of old-fashioned values and the transparency of moral judgment is applied to the effort to shore up or return to the social autonomy of the past, in which social relationships were conceptualized and acted upon at the level of the villages and towns, and not in relations with the Roman imperial order, the Herodian dynasts, or the city of Tiberias. The wealthy are thus encouraged in these speeches to cease their predatory behavior, to abandon the (in some measure newly acquired) techniques of personal gain, in favor of an ethos of communalism that would have fostered local independence and self-sufficiency, and would have employed values conceived as ancestral and self-evidently authentic.

The values of honor and shame, of course, when applied to the new situation of the northern Galilean villages, could reinforce the moral economy of the Roman-Herodian system: an extended social hierarchy based on status, reputation, and thus powerful (that is, Herodian or imperial) patronage rather than genuine good deeds or (local) community benefaction. The effort to align these values away from social status and toward communal service appears radical; in fact, it is only a rhetorical effort to return to earlier (local) standards for the assignment of status. Thus the seemingly radical opening injunctions of Piper's clusters are illuminated somewhat. While these injunctions are subordinated to the argumentative focus of each of the clusters, each serves additionally, on its own, to reinforce the tenor of the specific conclusions drawn, insofar as they all show a tendency to undercut honor-shame considerations in their own right. "Love your enemies," for instance, is not simply the first step toward the conclusion "be merciful" but is also, on its own and in its own right, an attack on the honor-shame edifice that "be merciful" was also intended to undercut. Thus the cluster's argument is ultimately directed against the same institutions and circumstances that its more radical opening line attacks directly.

Both threefold sets of arguments militate against acquisitiveness in the interests of something like social solidarity: in the last three arguments, material interests—with the acquisition of property and other excessive economic benefits in mind—are subordinated to a realm of plenty signaled by God's providence, that is, to whatever self-evident collective interests are signaled by God or to whatever corporate body *God* stands for as a cipher. In the first three sets of arguments, similarly, the acquisition of honor, prestige, reputation, or power—evidently conceived of as at the expense of others—is set over against an understanding of justice in which the community's interests prevail, in which the trees that bear good fruit are the trees that are deemed good, in which everyone is marked by judgment in the same way, and in which mercy rather than hostile competition marks relations between individuals. Verses 6:37-38 sum up both poles of the argument: "And judge not . . . you will not be judged. For with the judgment you judge you will be judged, and with the measure you measure will it be measured to you." To the extent that basic and informal reciprocity is at odds with the values of honor, extended hierarchy, and the acquisition of superfluous value, Q^1's arguments promote a retreat from the social effects of economic urbanization.

These propositions are confirmed by the contents of the remainder of Q^1. The original document as a whole is devoted to a rhetoric that denigrates any and all formal hierarchy, and that appeals to naturalistic imagery to reinforce that denigration (see Kloppenborg 1991:82; 1993:27). It is in this respect that the Q people and the Q program most resemble Cynicism. But, as with Cynicism, the appeal to nature and to logical transparency and unaffected behavior does not actually constitute a rejection of all human processes or of all artificiality; rather, it is a potent rhetorical strategy for attacking novel structures felt to be artificial, in favor of a falling back onto older patterns of behavior that assume the appearance, by contrast, of nature, of transparency, of lack of affectation (Kloppenborg 1991:84). The entirety—or nearly the entirety—of Q^1 proposes an ethic of local communalism, in large measure by the elimination of competitive behavior based on social hierarchy, a hierarchy that Q criticizes by appeal to nature and natural behavior, and by appeal to an incipient leveling of that hierarchy expressed by inversionary language. Q^1's reign of God is both the paradisaical state of affairs that will arise out of this program and the symbolic expression of the social force (the force of custom, collective values, God) that will ensure its completion. Q's suasive program, in combination with the inherent and obvious rightness of its goals, will put an end to the extended social and economic hierarchies by which some locals gain tremendously at the apparent expense of everyone else. As a result, the establishment of God's reign will ensure that the poor are blessed, that the hungry will be fed, that those who now weep will laugh. Inversion, for Q, denotes leveling, which in its turn is actually denotative of the resumption of a former social hierarchy deemed to be natural.

Thus, for instance, as Kloppenborg has argued, the parables in Q^1 support a similar program of local leveling:

> The entire section from Q 15:4 to 17:6 deals with reconciliation and peace-making in a social situation where the categories of honour and status threaten stability by valuing the large, the numerous, the male, the elder, the "just" and the powerful over their opposites. . . . no shepherd will let one sheep go astray, even if there are still 99 left. . . . no woman will ignore the loss of one drachma, even if she still has nine left. Why then in community relationships should there be differential valuations according to the standards of gender or standing or honour and why should those standards be permitted to destroy and dishonour the one or the weak? Like the ethics proposed by Q 6:27-35, this section of Q imagines the reduction of local conflict by a re-evaluation of the values (protection of honour) operative in Palestine (and indeed Mediterranean) village culture. (1995a:316–17)

This characterization requires supplementation or correction in only one respect. The situation to which this ethos stands opposed is not a static one; Q^1 is not simply an enlightened but unaccountable attack on the conventional values of the day. Rather, the conventional values of the day are attacked to the extent that they promote and support the economic and social changes wrought by the Herodian foundation of

Tiberias. As discussed in the last chapter, these changes generated a dis-location—or relocation—of the previously operative local village hierar-chy and set of values, in which the persons responsible for Q had been heavily invested. The mere oppression and exploitation of the poor, a practice millennia-old, comes to the attention of these figures only to the extent that its recent intensification was caused by the extension of the social world of northern Galilee that ensured that the region would be subsumed, in a dependent and peripheral role, within the larger world of the Roman imperial order. This increase in the capacity and hence extent of exploitation—the siphoning off of local surplus product—was matched, moreover, by a notable and significant reduction in the status of the village scribes who comprised the original Q tradents. Thus they have thrown in their lot, as persons dispossessed by the new order, with those who have been dispossessed by every other regime in the past, οἱ πτωχοί, οἱ πεινῶντες, οἱ κλαίοντες (the poor, those who hunger, those who weep), and who were now even more (incrementally) intensely exploited. Such persons had little to gain from a return to the good old days, but in the imagination of the Q tradents, such a return would mark a renewal of prosperity, of peaceable and just local relationships, with no city, no artificiality, no false allegiance to alien values, to abet competition and strife.[63]

The ideology behind this program and set of interests is expressed most obviously in the notion of the reign of God (so Vaage 1994:55–65), but more broadly in a general set of suppositions about God and the relationship of God to the circumstances that Q addresses.[64] It has already been noted that in Q, God and the values associated with God are tied very closely to communal values. We are unquestionably dealing here with a self-consciously Jewish group that views its audience's Jew-ish identity as self-evident and sees in ancestral religious allegiance a cipher for the social unity and solidarity of the local audience it addresses. What makes this so interesting is that Q's program, when viewed in terms of its theology (an approach that I have avoided so far), dis-plays an arresting structural homology (see Holmberg 1990:136; Theissen 1982c:187–90) with the social situation of its tradents and with the social and political ideals they endorse. The main ideological rationale offered in Q[1] for its ethos, its inversionary rhetoric, and for the specific behav-iors it exhorts is the immediacy of God's providential care. Q[1] both argues and assumes that access to God is direct and unmediated by any formal structures, such as temple, holy text, or even purity considera-tions.[65] This theological position of course makes excellent social sense. To the extent that the formal structures for the mediation of God's prov-idence are themselves the ideological apparatus of the ruling classes and involve differential gradations according to wealth, status, or proximity to the redemptive media of the city,[66] a theological focus on such structures would have had the effect of tying the northern Galilean villages that much more closely to the city and the values of the city. Thus Q's focus on unmediated access to God directly (and intentionally?) bypasses the very ideological apparatuses that serve to universalize and justify the interests of the cities and of the imperial order (in its Judean manifestations).

But more than this, the promotion of an ideology of divine immediacy parallels, at a metaphysical level, the conception of status and social hierarchy promoted by Q, and opposes that promoted by the new Herodian order. It has been noted by several studies that, commencing in the Hellenistic period, there was an ideological tendency to distance God from the mundane world, probably as a result of the alienation of the centers of political power from their traditional national locations (see especially Smith 1983). Such a trend was manifested, for instance, in apocalypticism, which posited a series of mediating figures between earth and heaven, such was the incredible spiritual and moral distance between the two realms; the causes of earthly events are neither transparent nor localized (Koch 1983:26). Thus the metaphysical world, in which the center of power was far distant and approached indirectly through a series of angelic patrons, matches a political situation in which, as a result of the great empires of the Hellenistic and Roman periods, the center of power was no longer local but distant, and in which such power could be approached, indirectly, only by the patronage of a series of intermediaries. The increasing extension of hierarchy (as a result of the incorporation of local political entities into great empires) is matched by the structurally homologous alienation of the deity from immediacy and earthly affairs. What is so striking about this is that Q's theology in such a context serves as a structural homology to social circumstances in an almost identical—although exactly opposite—way: its theological emphasis on the immediacy and nearness of God, God's accessibility through nature and direct contact, for instance, is a structural homologue to and a symbolic articulation of the social consequences of the Q program, a program that eliminates all extra-village or extra-local political structures. Hence, just as the whole set of external social structures and contacts is eliminated, so the distance of God is eliminated. The emphasis on the immediacy of God is but a symbolic ideological articulation of a vision that harks back to local autonomy.

The initial promotion of the Q^1 agenda appears to have been undertaken along the lines suggested by the Mission Charge in its original form, that is, not itinerancy but short day trips to the villages and towns of the region (all of which would have been affected similarly by the foundation of Tiberias) in order to appeal to their administrative infrastructure to support the Q program. The appeals, the seeking of a welcome, are public and official because they are made to the local leadership and made on behalf of the village as a whole. The effort is a clearly political one, in which village leadership is encouraged to ignore the administrative apparatus of the new city and the values disseminated by it. Q^1's emphasis on leadership and judgment, as well as on the voluntary relinquishment of financial gain and other types of power, confirms this focus. The program was intended to be enacted administratively and officially, if it was to be enacted at all.

Such a program, a kind of nativistic renewal movement with a strong Luddite dimension[67]—an imagined return to the gloried (if fanciful) past as a response to the economic pressures and social injustices of the present—was doomed to failure on two obvious grounds. The first, that it understandably failed to capture the imagination of the common people, is aggravated by the second, that it equally understandably failed to capture the imagination of the local powerful and wealthy it aimed to convert. The scribal figures behind Q were unquestionably caught in the difficulties of social realignment: they had appropriated a local folk hero, Jesus, as a spokesperson for their fictive address to a segment of the population that had no real investment in the good old days and from whom, presumably, the Q tradents had been somewhat distanced or alienated even before the onset of the new Herodian economic order. Their actual address to the upper classes and local leadership, although it attempted to play on symbols of common identity, did not sufficiently take into account the degree to which the socioeconomic changes may have worked to the benefit of these classes and the extent to which the religious ideology of Judaism could be harnessed to those interests, as well as against them. The initial Q project, in short, was a failure.

The consequences of this failure can be seen not only in the later literary stages of Q's development—especially the bitter polemic of Q^2—but even in the process leading up to the formation of Q^1 itself. Even at the level of Q^1, the focus is no longer directly on the agenda just described or on its promulgation (see Table 5). Rather, compositions that reflect that agenda and the interest in its promulgation (such as the Mission Speech or Piper's argumentative clusters) have been incorporated into a larger document whose overarching theme has shifted to reflection not so much on the program itself as on the consequences of allegiance to that program. If one inspects the discrete speeches that comprise Q^1, it quickly becomes obvious that a strong

General Model of Q's Literary Development

	Ideology	Source or Description	Example 1: Beatitudes	Example 2: Mission Speech	Example 3: Piper's Clusters
Original Oral Tradition	"radical wisdom" of the "reign of God	Jesus? other floating traditions ascribed to Jesus	scattered beatitudes	mission speech "core": Q 10:4ab, 5-6, 8-9	opening imperative or assertion
Oral Additions or Changes	tendency to specify applications of, or to reinforce, original oral material	scattered oral tradition, probably emanating from followers or admirers of Jesus	serialization of beatitudes; addition of original persecution beatitude	addition of 10:2, 4c, 7	serialization of multiple imperatives; composition of motive clauses?
Pre-Q¹ Scribal Additions	appropriation of "radical" oral traditions in short (written?) compositions designed to support a scribal agenda; a distinct sense of "mission"	initial scribal use of Jesus traditions in the interests of a specific program	addition of ἕνεκα or ἕνεκεν (on account of) clause to persecution beatitude	addition of 10:3, 10-11; and minor changes	composition of Piper's speech clusters
Q¹ Redaction	increasing pessimism; mission replaced with internal attitudinal and commitment issues; authority of Jesus inflated	primary literary composition of Q	juxtaposition of beatitudes with speech on love of enemies	addition of 10:16 and juxtaposition with 9:57-62	collection of speech clusters and incorporation into Q¹
Q² Redaction	deuteronomistic and polemical; sectarian	secondary literary redaction of Q	addition of 6:23c	addition of 10:12-15	incorporation of entirety of Q¹ into Q²

Table 5: The oral and literary stages through which Q material progressed, indicating the ideological orientation and the social characteristics of the material's tradents at each stage.

interest in commitment has been redactionally attached to nearly all articulations of ethos. Thus the opening beatitudes have been supplemented by—and hence reinterpreted in terms of—persecution "for the sake of the son of man"; the "Sermon" has been concluded by a series of sayings on the effects of commitment; the Mission Charge has been prefaced with a series of illustrations of the high cost of discipleship; promises of God's providential care have been prefaced with a prayer, suggesting that the provision of such care is a consequence of group identity, not a general principle; exhortations to avoid anxiety have been prefaced with sayings encouraging fearless preaching; and the collection as a whole has been concluded with a series of sayings emphasizing the need to follow the advice given and the high personal cost that may result (13:24; 14:26, 27; 17:33; 14:34-35). Thus interest in a social program has modulated into an incipient group-formation that understands its identity in terms of its commitment to the program, to the reign of God. The point is no longer the advancement of the program but commitment to the group that endorses it.

Conclusions

In sum, the agenda of Q^1 (or indeed of any later stage in the document's development) does not seem to evince itinerancy at all. The document's rhetoric of uprootedness is a device used in the service of a much more specific social agenda that can be characterized, in brief, as essentially Luddite. A new social order, perceived to be unjust and unappealing, was criticized in terms of the values and conditions of the past. The critique is simultaneously progressive and reactionary: it harks back to a past that was no more genuinely beatific than the authors' present, but simultaneously it uses that past as a lever to offer serious class-based criticisms of the present order. Traditionalism is used against itself. The uprootedness evinced by Q also reflects a realignment of the social interests of the scribal figures responsible for Q and the change their own status had recently suffered. The extension of hierarchy resulting from the progressive incorporation of local political entities into the structures of the whole empire finds its ideological reflection in cultural effects that mirror its extended pyramidal structure, such as patronage ideology or any religious paradigms—temple, Torah, purity—for which mediation is a central aspect. In reaction to this process and its ideological corollary, Q^1 radically flattens and simplifies the ideological pyramid, reducing it to only two levels: "us villagers" and God. Q^1 furthermore suggests in its program that all other structures of mediation or structural hierarchies in human life are false; the effect of this, culturally, is to pretend (or intend) that the social pyramid of Galilee is (naturally or essentially) freestanding and hence out of the orbit of the newly felt extended imperial structures placing pressure on local relations. What is at issue here is not a rejection of native traditions (see Kloppenborg 1993:26) but an effort to revive those traditions, to apply a brand of nativistic revival against the encroachments of imperialism.[68]

The validity of these conclusions could probably be tested by comparing Q, and the social situation it presupposes, to other imperial situations, especially within Roman antiquity (but also cross-culturally). Such a study is beyond the purview of this work but does suggest several specific directions for further research. First, the question of the historical Jesus has not been addressed here at all, and one need not suppose any direct continuity between Jesus himself and the Jesus movement as represented by Q, especially if the figure of Jesus has been used by Q simply because he was a current local folk hero. However, if some of the materials used in Q^1 do indeed go back to Jesus,[69] even if used in an idiosyncratic way by Q, they may serve as evidence that Jesus himself was engaged in some form of reaction to circumstances similar to those that actuated the Q people. The best way to pursue this suggestion, in all probability, would be to analyze the independently circulating narrative traditions about Jesus, many of which appear in Mark and several of which were incorporated into Q^2 and Q^3 as well. These apparent folk traditions about Jesus, when juxtaposed with the more focused use of Jesus by scribal interests in Q and probably also the *Gospel of Thomas* (see Arnal 1995b:489–92), may reveal a common core. The nonscribal use of the figure of Jesus, and hence perhaps Jesus himself, may thus also be an example of nativistic reaction to the consequences of Herodian-Roman policy. Second, the Pharisaic-Rabbinic movement in Galilee might be queried as a similar, if rather more successful, nativistic response to new imperial circumstances. With Q, this movement shared a primitivizing or nativizing tendency, but unlike Q it cast that appeal to ancestral traditions in terms of extended structures of mediation, and hence was more appropriate to the changed circumstances. Third and finally, one would expect, if the conclusions suggested here are at all correct, that other areas of the empire would manifest, by the same token, similar movements as they too were incorporated into the imperial order. One should expect to find, in other words, at various times throughout the Roman Empire, the rise of radical primitivistic or nativistic movements in such places as North Africa, Gaul, Britain, and so forth. Such movements would then provide perhaps the best comparative context for the rise of the earliest movement of those who followed Jesus.

NOTES

Introduction

1. Especially notable are the several books of John Dominic Crossan and Burton Mack. Both are productive reconceptualizations of Christian origins that are partly driven by recent studies of Q. See also the comments of Kloppenborg 1996a:325. A dramatic example of the more common tendency to dismiss such scholarship without much consideration, and thus to fail (or refuse) to benefit from its insights, is to be found in Meier 1994:178–81.

2. See Crossan 1998:111:

> Q was quite acceptable as long as it was nothing more than a source to be found within the safe intracanonical confines of Matthew and Luke. But now the Q *Gospel* is starting to look a little like a Trojan horse, an extracanonical gospel hidden within two intracanonical gospels. If certain scholars have held all noncanonical gospels to be late and dependent, what will they do with a noncanonical gospel that is not only very early and independent but on which two intracanonical gospels are themselves dependent?

3. Allison 1997:4. Generally, for Allison's critique of Kloppenborg, see 1997:4–8, and for his alternative proposal see 1997:8–40.

4. Kloppenborg 1987:169. Compare Allison's "critical" observation that "Q 11:31-32 compares Jesus with both Solomon, a wise man, and Jonah, a prophet" (1997:5), a point also made by Kloppenborg (1987:133–34)! Kloppenborg actually goes so far as to note that "in second-temple Judaism 'wisdom' was not simply a matter of abstract cosmological knowledge, but included repentance (Sir 17:24; 44:16, 48; Wis 11:23; 12:10, 19). Solomon is represented as a repentance preacher, chastising kings for their sins (Wis 6:5; cf. 11-19). Hence *both* σοφία [wisdom] and κήρυγμα [preaching], especially when associated with Jonah and Solomon, contain connotations of the preaching of judgement" (Kloppenborg 1987:133–34, emphasis original). That the secondary, polemical, layer of Q is also concerned with wisdom, albeit in a rather more developed form than the primary layer, underscores precisely that Kloppenborg does not assume "wisdom" and "apocalyptic" to be

incompatible, as does, of course, the simple fact that the second stratum built upon the first!

5. Q texts are cited by Lukan versification, without prejudice to the original wording or order of the Q text in question.

1: Itinerant Preachers and the Didache

1. See Audet 1958:1, 24–26; Giet 1970:15–16; Jefford 1989:1; Mattioli 1980:17–18; Niederwimmer 1989:33–36; Rordorf and Tuilier 1978:11–12; Shepherd 1962:841. The text was first published by Archbishop Philotheos Bryennios, its discoverer, in 1883 as Διδαχὴ τῶν δώδεκα ἀποστλων ἐκ τοῦ ἱεροσολυμιτικοῦ χειρογράφου νῦν πρῶτον ἐκδικομένη ὑπὸ Φιλοθέου Βρυεννίου ("Teaching of the Twelve Apostles"), (Bryennios 1883). On the date of the Didache, see further below. The manuscript itself is actually dated: it was written June 11, 1056 C.E.

2. Didache 11:3-6. Text from Lake 1912–13:326; Lietzmann 1962:12; Niederwimmer 1995:32–33.

3. See Harnack 1884, esp. 93–138. Harnack repeats this treatment substantially in 1904–5 (see v. 1, 417, n. 2). The following summary of Harnack's views is drawn primarily from these two key works.

4. Text from Audet 1958:240; Lake 1912–13: v. 1, 330; Lietzmann 1962:14.

5. On the racism of mainstream nineteenth-century linguistic theory, see Olendar 1992.

2: The Sayings Tradition and Itinerant Preachers

1. He considers and ultimately rejects the possibility that such itinerants were also responsible for the miracle traditions (1983:261–63).

2. He cites synoptic tradition as follows: (1) homelessness: Mark 1:16; 10:28ff.; Matt 8:20; 10:5ff.; 10:23, 44; 23:34; (2) rejection of family: Mark 1:20; 10:29-30; Matt 19:10-11 (which praises castration!); Luke 8:19-21; 11:28ff.; 14:26; (3) disdain for possessions: Mark 10:17ff.; 10:25; Matt 6:19ff.; 6:25-34; 10:10, 42; Luke 6:24-25; 10:5ff.; 16:8, 19-31; Acts 4:36-37; (4) defenselessness: Matt 5:38-41; 10:17ff.

3. He cites Acts 1ff.; 9:10; 10:1ff.; 11:20ff.; 21:3-4, 7; and Gal 1:22. In addition, Matt 8:14; Luke 8:2-3; 10:38ff.; and Mark 14:3ff. are cited as evidence that families formed the original nuclei of these sedentary "communities" (conceding that the term community may be misleading).

4. He cites texts of three basic types: (1) regulations for behavior: Mark 1:44; 10:2ff.; 10:13ff.; 11:15ff.; Matt 5:17-23; 6:1-6; 6:16-17; 17:24,

26; 19:2; 23:1-3, 13ff.; (2) structure of authority: Mark 14:7; Matt 16:19; 18:18; 23:8ff., 34; 1 Cor 9:13-14; Gal 2:11-12; 3 John; *Did.* 11:2, 6, 9, 12; 13:1-4; 15:2; (3) acceptance and rejection of membership: Matt 28:19; 1 Cor 1:17; 18:15ff.; *Did.* 7; 11:1. He also notes (1978:19) that both Matthew (19:21) and the *Didache* (6:2) imply that not everyone need be "perfect" (τέλειος), perfection being a function, apparently, of radical itinerancy and divestment of possessions.

5. Theissen qualifies this statement in an interesting way, claiming that even a completely reductionistic understanding of religion as an epiphenomenon must still take seriously the religious response itself, its own self-understanding, and the effects of that self-understanding.

6. Theissen claims that in some instances (for example, Matt 11:28; Mark 10:52; Luke 5:1ff.) the primary texts offer direct indications that poverty or marginality in some way preceded an itinerant life following Jesus. See 1982:30–31.

7. He cites Josephus, *Ant.* 15.96; 16.2; 17.307, 318ff., 321, 355; Josephus, *War* 1.361; 2.591; Josephus, *Life* 24, 119; Diodorus Siculus 2.48.9; Acts 12:20ff. He also notes the role played by the Pharisees in legitimating the claims of the native aristocracy, as well as pointing to the way that overpopulation and taxation exacerbated and contributed to this crisis (1978:40–45).

8. But note also that Theissen draws back from a reduction of social phenomena to direct economic causes, especially by pointing to the much-cited observation that it is usually not the destitute who cause trouble in periods of economic crisis but rather those more in the economic middle range, who are most affected, adversely or positively, by changes (1978:39–40; compare 46).

9. See, for example, the comments in Kloppenborg and Vaage 1991:9: "At the same time that Lührmann's book set in action a renewal of the literary description of Q, a parallel revolution in its historical evaluation was announced by Gerd Theissen in his 1973 article on 'itinerant radicalism.' With this essay, specific attention began to be paid to the social history of Palestinian Christianity and, as before, Q was at the centre of things. As with Lührmann, Theissen's preliminary insights required further explication and elaboration by others."

10. Mack 1988b:87, n. 7, characterizes the assumption that both Jesus and his immediate followers (especially those represented by Q) were prophets as "the current scholarly view."

11. Boring 1982:58. Here Boring incorrectly characterizes Harnack as separating apostles, prophets, and teachers, who are charismatic, universal, and itinerant missionaries, as over against the bishops and deacons, who represent the settled groups. Harnack in fact felt that teachers as a

distinct class were not itinerant. Boring goes on to critique Harnack on some minor points but appears to accept the overall accuracy of his reading of the *Didache* (58–59).

12. Boring 1982:127–36, 179–80 (see also 233–34). Boring cites as prophetic oracles Q 6:22-23; 10:3, 4, 5-12, 13-15, 16, 21-22; 11:29b-30, 39-52; 12:8-9, 10, 11-12; 13:34-35; 16:17; 22:28-30. As texts reformulated from a prophetic perspective, he cites Q 6:20b-21; 10:2(-16), 23-24; 11:14:23, 29a, 31-32; 12:2-3, 4-7 (2-12), 22-23, 51-56, 57-59; 13:23-30; 17:22-37. See also Aune 1983:240.

13. Robinson 1971. In agreement with this critique, see Hoffmann 1995:188.

14. Boring 1982:140 (original emphasis); see 180–81. Boring notes, in fact, that there are "historicizing" (that is, sapiential) tendencies in Q alongside the prophetic "contemporizing" forms, but he believes that the latter predominate and that the overall form of Q (beginning with a prophetic "call"—the baptism and temptation—and proceeding on to a collection of oracles) likewise suggests a relationship to Christian prophecy.

15. This basic characterization, says Aune 1983:215 (see 213), applies also to Matthew and the *Didache*.

16. See Patterson 1993a:129–34. For a summary and brief critique of the applicability of the basic itinerancy model to *Thomas*, on the grounds that the direct evidence of homelessness is ambiguous, see Arnal 1995b:480–82. For the text of *Thomas*, see Layton 1987.

17. Note that it is unclear that all of these sayings do in fact offer a critique of wealth; in some instances (for example, 109), Patterson is forced to argue that the saying is intended ironically. It is also notable that of all the motifs Patterson adduces in support of itinerancy, the critique of wealth is easily the best attested. Such a motif, however, does not in its own right evince itinerancy.

18. On this matter see esp. Patterson 1993a:151–53. He also posits the possibility of female itinerants (1993a:153–55).

19. I cannot, however, resist citing Stevan Davies's recent article in *Neotestamentica* (Davies 1996), which argues that the Gospel of Mark is literarily dependent on *Thomas*. The paper makes a surprisingly good case (largely on the basis of demonstrable Markan dependence on redactional features discernible, for instance, in *GThom.* 13 [see Mark 8:27-33] and 65-66 [see Mark 12:1-12]). If its thesis is correct, this would date even developed versions of *Thomas* to a period prior to that of any other extant writings about Jesus.

20. It is worth speculating (as Patterson in fact does, 1993a:212–14) that the different trajectories of secondary theological reflection

undertaken by *Thomas* and Q (*Thomas* in a gnostic direction, Q in an apocalyptic direction) owe their distinction to the initial difference between the documents' tradents. The *Thomas* itinerants tend toward a radical and somewhat individualistic self-justification in the form of Gnosticism, while the Q people, representing the householder orientation, seek legitimation within the more communalistic and conservative framework of apocalypticism. For a methodologically similar but substantively different explanation of the same phenomenon, see Arnal 1995b:492–94.

21. See Patterson 1993a:172–78. Where Patterson does depart from Harnack (in addition to dating the *Didache* much earlier—probably the end of the first century—than Harnack did) is in attempting to stratify the text of the *Didache*. He argues that chap. 11 stems from an earlier period than chaps. 12–13 and that the latter attest to the itinerants' greatly diminished status. We can thus see even within the *Didache* evidence of a historical process toward the marginalization of the power and status of the itinerants.

22. Patterson 1993a:192 notes an affinity between the *Thomas* version of saying 25, "Love your brother [not 'neighbor'] like your soul," and the consistent use of the term "brethren" for the itinerant preachers in 3 John. This is obviously a rather strained and flimsy connection.

23. See Crossan 1996:118. His case in point is *Did.* 1:3b-4, which parallels Q 6:27-29 in consisting of a set of (similar) injunctions, the first set phrased in the second-person plural and the second in the second-person singular. See Crossan 1996:122.

24. Patterson 1993a:154–55, citing esp. Castelli 1986:61–88, and the figure of Xanthippe in Xenophon's *Ephesaica*.

25. This latter reference does not occur in the published forms of Crossan's paper but was part of the original speech in Ottawa, June 7, 1993. Otherwise, see Crossan 1996:120–21.

26. For a survey of these views and a critique of—and alternative to—the suggestion that Q is self-consciously critical of the subordination of women, see Arnal 1997a:78–83.

27. Schüssler Fiorenza 1983:145–46. Schüssler Fiorenza attributes Theissen's assumption on this matter to a reading of Luke 14:26 as if the wording here reflected the original tradition, which it clearly does not (see Luke's rendering of Mark 10:29b at Luke 18:29b).

28. Jacobson 1995:379. He cites Q 10:5-7; 12:51-53; and possibly 7:6; 10:7; 12:42; 13:29; and 14:23 as indications that, for Q, the focus of activity was on households (375).

29. Jacobson 1995:364, 369. Jacobson views Q 16:13, the statement that it is impossible to serve both God and "mammon," as antifamilial

because the locus of economic activity in Q's environment would have been the subsistence household. He regards viewing this text as a warning against amassing wealth to be anachronistic.

30. Richard Horsley and Burton Mack are the most notable exceptions. See the discussion later in this chapter.

31. Again, there are exceptions, most productively, perhaps, John Kloppenborg and Ronald Piper, in addition to Mack and Horsley.

32. Blasi 1986:246. Other—and I might add, better—sociological work on the early gospel traditions has also raised the issue of the earliest Christian movement as a sectarian organization and has attempted to set its characteristics within a broad cross-cultural typology of sectarianism. See, in this respect, Scroggs 1975 and Stark 1986.

33. For a succinct summary of the application of the itinerancy hypothesis to Q, see Kloppenborg 1993:12–18. For further discussions of itinerancy, see also Kuhn 1980 and Schmeller 1989.

34. See also Kloppenborg 1993:17, citing White 1986:256 and Schmeller 1989:94.

35. This is the main thrust of Schottroff 1986. See also Stegemann 1984:155, 161–64.

36. Schottroff 1986:40–42. See her cutting remarks both about these philosophers of renunciation themselves (whom she characterizes as privileged armchair ascetics) and about those scholars who propose them as a model for understanding early Christian itinerancy (whom she characterizes as interpreting the Q material from their own position of affluence).

37. And this is so regardless of the reason for their deprivation. Even if the fourth and final Q beatitude, the persecution beatitude, shifts the focus of the cluster specifically to Jesus people who are persecuted for that very reason (and hence, presumably, also poor, hungry, weeping), the cluster still assumes that these people are already in this state, and not by their own choice. This is clearest perhaps because of the juxtaposition of weeping with poverty, hunger, and persecution. No reconstruction of itinerancy suggests that the charismatics were voluntarily sad on top of everything else!

38. Such asceticism on the part of the wealthy, it should be noted, probably serves to universalize their own experience (which thus includes both economic extremes) while marginalizing the experiences or perspectives of those who have no such choice; it serves as a way for the wealthy and powerful to lay claim to, and hence defuse the rhetorical potential of, an entire sector of human experience of which they might otherwise be ignorant. In addition, by adopting the supposed garb, experience, and attitude of the poor, the ascetic retrenches cultural

conceptions of poverty and serves to naturalize it as a phenomenon.

39. Stegemann 1984:151–61. See also Kloppenborg and Vaage 1991:9; Kloppenborg 1993:16.

40. Stegemann 1984:156–57. All other materials evincing itinerancy, he argues, are either from Q, which Stegemann thinks is a special case, or from Matthean or Lukan redaction of Mark, a problem that Theissen ignores because of his indiscriminate use of sources.

41. It is interesting that some of the Cynic-advocates in question do not accept Kloppenborg's stratification as given (1987), in spite of claiming it as a starting point. Rather, they tend to adapt the stratification to their own claims that Q^1 (as opposed to Q^2) is Cynic-like. Thus material that appears to cohere with Cynic interests tends to be assigned to the earliest stratum regardless of where it might appear in Kloppenborg's original schema. Mack is rather limited in his alterations, while Vaage is quite extensive.

42. Some critics of the Cynic hypothesis, however, have suggested precisely the reverse. As noted above, Stegemann believes the "Cynicizing" of the sayings tradition is the work of Luke. Freyne (1997) has suggested that, in Q, Cynic-like elements date from a later period (or stratum), in which the people responsible for the document had moved to an urban setting where such influences would be commonplace and would make more sense. So also Horsley 1989:118. A hint of this is also offered in Betz 1994:474 and n. 127. Perhaps the most interesting and detailed study of this particular issue is Marshall 1997. Marshall offers a close tradition-historical analysis of the sayings material in *Thomas* that is paralleled in the synoptic tradition; by using *Thomas* as an independent control on the redaction or oral alteration of the synoptic material, he is able to show, with considerable probative force, that the most significant parallels between the sayings tradition and ancient Cynicism are secondary to the tradition.

43. The most striking instance is Vaage's book, which nominally proceeds on the basis of Kloppenborg's reconstruction (see the claims in Vaage 1994:7, 107), yet which includes a long appendix ("Appendix One," 107–20) expressing considerable disagreement with the specifics of Kloppenborg's reconstruction in *Formation of Q* (1987), usually on grounds (such as thematic generalizations) that undercut the methodology by which the stratification was arrived at in the first place. The sources of disagreement are—no surprise!—those texts susceptible to a Cynic reading that Kloppenborg has, on consistent methodological grounds, assigned to later redactional strata of Q, most especially Q 7:24b-26, 28a, 33-34; and Q 11:39-48, 52. In both of these cases, there is clearly an antecedent oral (or even possibly written) development in

which the material aggregated—this is never denied by Kloppenborg (see Kloppenborg 1987:115–17, 139–47). But a complex prehistory neither requires nor even hints at a likelihood that the sayings originated from an earlier literary stratum of Q. Likewise, Burton Mack wishes to attribute the whole persecution beatitude (Q 6:22-23) rather than just 6:23c ("for so they used to do to the prophets who were before you") to the secondary stratum of Q, presumably since such a view would mesh perfectly with Mack's (overly schematic?) reconstruction of the progressively increasing mythologizing and social self-identification that he detects behind nearly all developments in earliest Christian "myth-making." See Mack 1993:83 (see also his attribution to the tertiary layer of Q, for similar reasons, of Q 10:21-22; 12:5; 13:34-35; 16:16-18 [89, 94, 98, 100]). Unfortunately for this rather too-neat scenario, the "association of the beatitudes with the admonition to love one's enemies [this latter an uncontested Q^1 argument] presupposed that 6:22-23b was already part of the beatitudes" (Kloppenborg 1987:187); for such an association relies on (1) the shared theme of hatred and mistreatment, and possibly (2) a catchword connection between 6:22 ("when they hate you") and 6:27 ("to those who hate you") (Kloppenborg 1987:178), both of which are only present in the persecution beatitude, rather than the three preceding ones.

44. Vaage 1994:3–7, 10–14, critiques such an orientation and cites Smith 1990 extensively in his introduction as a methodological model.

45. I should give credit where it is due: Vaage is usually more consistent than this, assiduously avoiding language of identity and specifying, as part of the overall framework of *Galilean Upstarts* (1994), that the comparison is proceeding on the broad grounds of ethos, ethics, ideology, critique, and appeal to founder figures ("memory"). What he has apparently not realized, however, is that according to Smith the point of these specifications is not to pile up evidence for either identity or some kind of absolute comparability but rather to restrict the scope of the comparison. That is, if we are comparing Q and Cynicism on the grounds of, say, ideology, the conclusions or fixed questions residing behind and motivating the comparison will themselves have to do with Q's ideology and our understanding of it, not with the broader topic of Q and Cynicism.

46. See, for example, Cameron 1990:60: "John and Jesus are both characterized as Cynics: the one 'ascetic,' the other 'hedonistic' . . . act together to bless the community of Q."

47. See Horsley 1989; 1991b; 1991c; 1993:209–326; 1995b; Kloppenborg 1990a; 1991; Reed 1995; 1996. Especially significant is Piper 1995, in which a local and genuinely socially descriptive interpretation is

offered of the "love your enemies" argument in Q, quite at odds with that of Vaage. See also Arnal 1995b:480–89. For an explication of these and similar views, see chap. 3.

48. It should be made perfectly clear, however, that a discussion of the tendentious impetus behind such scholarship is, per se, by no means intended to constitute an argument against it. It is a too-popular (and destructive) fallacy in our field that congenial views are necessarily false.

49. Another classic instance of precisely the same phenomenon is the appropriation of Herman Hesse (1877–1962), the German late Romantic and avid Easternist, by the generation that grew up in the 1960s.

50. Note, most obviously, Tuckett 1996:390, who explains the itinerancy he deems to lie behind Q in terms of a sense of eschatological urgency: "What is at stake in Q is the preaching of the imminent arrival of the eschatological kingdom of God."

51. Nowhere is this more evident than in Downing's popularizing treatment of his version of the Cynic hypothesis (1987a), esp. 1–3, 6, 33–50. Downing treats the economic problems of the contemporary United States, United Kingdom, and France as "threats to freedom" (that is, as cultural, psychologistic, and individual problems, obstacles to self-actualization) to which, apparently, the Cynic-like early Jesus movement offers useful rejoinders in its exhortations to openness, generosity, and love, which exhortations originally addressed analogous threats to freedom in antiquity. See also Crossan 1991:421; Downing 1987a:163–64.

52. The following comment (Robinson 1996a:46), addressed to the Jesus Seminar but directly pertinent to the Cynic hypothesis, strikes me as especially revealing: "What concerns me most about the Jesus Seminar is that it tends to make Jesus into a queer duck rather than a serious person worthy of a hearing. . . . In a similar way the Jesus Seminar has not communicated to intelligent people a Jesus worthy of consideration, but often only conveyed the offensiveness of uncritically negative biblical scholarship."

53. To make this assertion somewhat clearer, one could say that the itinerants or Cynics proposed to lie behind Q and the early sayings tradition could just as easily exist in a far away land as in the past: temporal distance here is interchangeable with spatial distance. The point is not that historical study has eschewed the "great man" approach to the past in favor of broader social description—for such a result, we could only be grateful. Rather, in line with developments in the popular imagination, history is increasingly offering snapshots rather than moving pictures; disjointed, if richly described, vignettes rather than linear progressions or sequences that have clearly definable results or that can be seen as necessary preconditions for subsequent events. Instances have replaced

sequences in the historical imagination. On the atemporality of post-modern sensibilities (or its spatialization of time), see especially Jameson 1991:154–80.

54. The reconstruction is itself denaturalizing as well: it presents self-evidently "religious ideology" through the filter of less spectacular and apparently secular models, often deliberately so. The movement away from a focus on apocalypticism as a contributing originary factor, which we see very clearly in the Cynic hypothesis, reflects a distinctively post-modern tendency to undercut categories, in this case the category of religion as Other.

55. The same fictive construct, of course, was used by early modern and Enlightenment political theorists who wished to distance their political theory from the concrete realities of the societies in which they lived.

56. See Gitlin 1997:21: "Roberts cites a study of the fate of the *Louisville Courier-Journal* since it was bought by Gannett, the longest chain. The overall news space did go up, but much of the increase consisted of features, soft news and wire copy. The average local news story shrank. Wire service copy—almost always the most rudimentary and least probing—went up by an astounding 76 per cent."

57. Decades-old treatments of Jesus, or of the earliest Jesus movement, tended to present Jesus as a replacement of the (hypocritical, jealous, or antiquated) dominant groups, that is, the Pharisees. Jesus and his earliest followers are presented as having authority, as offering a serious message with world-changing ramifications, rather than as disseminating a merely provocative nonmessage to marginal people for no other reason than the intrinsic value—or fun!—of so doing. Obviously the shift in the seriousness accorded scholarly subject matter is, among other things, a reflection of the lack of seriousness with which scholars sometimes (unwittingly?) cast their own discipline and intellectual activities broadly.

58. Theissen's "ecological factors" and "socio-cultural factors" (1978:31, 33–46, 77–95; see 32–41; 1982a:33).

59. Downing 1987a:26–27. He adds (27), "We are just rather better equipped with doles and lotteries and displays of mindless affluence on television to make the excluded believe they belong, this must all be preserved for one day it could be theirs."

60. See Vaage 1994:85: "At least there is [as a result of Cynic-like criticism] a sense in which the dominant social order was thereby rendered not inevitably supreme, though this is never expressed in any more positive or constructive terms. The social critique championed by the woes in Q was thus not tied to particular utopian desires for a specific cultural 'restoration' or 'renewal.' It may be that the sheer press of established

ways was such that, practically speaking, all the Q people could hope for was to unsettle things a bit."

61. See Mack 1993:68: "What if we acknowledged that the compact and convoluted history of foreign conquests in Galilee had created disaffection for many Galileans, and a predisposition for social and cultural critique? What if the mix of indigenous, Hellenistic, Jewish, and Roman cultures had disturbed the social equilibrium enough to challenge the traditional diffidence of the people in Galilee?"

62. The first-person plural here is intended to be inclusive: the totalistic ideology of our social relations directly affects and is rendered equally opaque to even those groups that are marginalized by it. It should be noted too that "the white male" is also an identity, participating in identity politics. At any rate, the impulse toward self-definitions based on such identity is itself a product of our dominant ideological vision of the world, a vision that itself pretends to be universal and to some degree is successful in making itself universal.

3: *The Problem with Itinerant Preachers*

1. The Cynic analogy, properly applied, is not at all an explanation for the rise of earliest Christianity, and so is immune, to a certain degree, to materialist criticism that as an explanation it is idealist. Nevertheless, the focus of this hypothesis, at least in the forms currently extant in New Testament scholarship, is far too much on ideology detached from concrete social setting. The cultural is emphasized at the expense of the social.

2. White (1986:261) associates much current sociology of the Jesus movement with a Weberian model, and says: "Too much of Weber's model, virtually a theology of its own it would seem, was built on his Ritschlian neo-orthodox presuppositions. Even if basic concepts such as *charisma, prophetic religion,* or *routinization* are to be retained, one cannot from the historical perspective simply assume that either early Judaism or early Christianity was a patented form."

3. He characterizes them as "three different *procedures*" from which social data may be derived as part of a "process of inference" (1978:3, emphasis added).

4. Many of the people I would describe as pioneers of sociological examinations of antiquity and of the biblical texts in particular have been more rigorous than Theissen in their discussion of theoretical issues. Norman Gottwald, in his work on the origins of the Israelite epic tradition (*The Tribes of Yahweh,* 1979), has offered considerable justification for his use of a structural-functionalist model. So also has G. E. M.

de Ste. Croix for a Marxist model in his *Class Struggle in the Ancient Greek World* (1981).

5. Horsley is obviously quite capable of providing just such a detailed social history: he does so in *Bandits, Prophets, and Messiahs* (1985). In his work on Q, however, he fails to relate the aspects of this social history to concrete and specific features of the text of Q.

6. One might as well try to understand contemporary black Muslims, the group that calls itself the Nation of Islam, in terms of African social circumstances in the 1500s, to which the movement refers rhetorically and that obviously are greatly constitutive of its self-understanding, but which actually have almost no sociological relevance whatsoever for the current shape of this movement.

7. Note also that Paul does not here restrict himself by any means to this trinity of roles but extends the discussion to "deeds of power" and the "gift" of healing. 1 Corinthians 14:19 makes clear Paul's motivation in assigning preeminence to apostles, prophets, and teachers, and in playing down more obvious charismatic and ecstatic manifestations of the spirit: "In church I would rather speak five words with my mind, in order to instruct others also, than ten thousand words in a tongue." Against the applicability to Paul of Harnack's typology, see also Greeven 1952.

8. For examples and discussion of ἔρχομαι (come) used with this sense, see BAGD 310–11.

9. Draper 1991:350 and n. 14. For more extended argumentation, see Draper 1999. It is in fact unclear to me just which section "on prophecy" he is referring to. I assume that he is focusing on chap. 11, and hence the material to which he refers as a later addition is 11:7-12. It remains uncertain what relationship we are to assume between this material and the instructions on prophecy in chap. 13. Probably Draper assumes that they were added to the text at the same point (along with chap. 12?), since he describes the advice given about prophets as "self-contradictory."

10. Draper 1991:349. Note that Draper here is constructing an argument quite at odds with what I am claiming: he believes that the text of the *Didache* has become composite as a result of extensive glossing to an already unified written work. But his description of the evolution of "community rules" quoted here is at least as helpful for my case as for his.

11. The Two Ways material appears also in *Barnabas* 18–20; *Doctrina apostolorum; Canons of the Holy Apostles* (or *Apostolic Church Order*); and *Apostolic Constitutions* 7.2.2-6; see the Qumran Manual of Discipline (1QS 3.13—4.26). For a clear and recent summary exposition of the differences among these versions and of their literary relationships, see Kloppenborg 1995b:88–92. Note also the literature cited there, and see, among others, Audet 1958:122–63, and esp. his synoptic chart, 138–53; Crossan

1996:121–23, and esp. his synoptic chart, 125; Horsley 1991a:207; Jefford 1989:22–29; Niederwimmer <1989:48–64> 1998:30–41.

12. To illustrate the difference I am invoking here between stratification and use of anterior traditions, note that Q is probably a genuinely stratified document, but each of the literary layers of the document itself makes use of anterior tradition.

13. Niederwimmer (1998:42–52) treats the redaction of the *Didache* similarly, that is, as a bringing together of various older materials by a single "author," rather than a composition in discrete redactional stages. See also Niederwimmer 1977:147–53.

14. Obviously, this latter observation is not directed against Draper's hypothesis, which asserts no such thing, but against the possibility of claiming that the discussion of prophets in 11:7-12 reflects an earlier written redaction of the *Didache*, modified later by inclusion of (at least) 11:3-6.

15. Patterson 1993a:174–77; 1995:317–18; Jefford and Patterson 1989–90. Niederwimmer's views (1977) are similar but not identical.

16. Draper 1995:298, 302–7, although for different reasons, sees the same agenda at work here. He associates the effort to specify community roles as part of what Werner Kelber would identify as a process of textualization. See esp. 307: "The emergence first of oral and then of written text provided the organizational change by which the community of the *Didache* overcame the severe problems that were left behind by the quarrel over Torah. The ambiguity of roles that is so clear in the instructions of the *Didache* is transformed by the emergence of an authoritative text."

17. Niederwimmer (1977:152) regards 13:4 as a postredactional gloss.

18. Niederwimmer (1977:151) regards 11:1-2 as redactional.

19. This stage, as well as its preredactional accumulation (listed here as step no. 3), are treated together by Niederwimmer simply as pre-*Didache* "community rules." Although he regards most of chap. 11 as traditional, in agreement with the proposal offered here, he does not regard chap. 13 as traditional and, moreover, breaks up chap. 11 rather differently than I do, that is, regarding 11:4-6 as part of the longer (traditional) block extending to the end of the chapter. Breaking up the material in this way causes him to overlook the strong degree of structural and stylistic similarity between 11:3-6 and 12:1-5, and so he fails to conclude, as I would think appropriate, that these two sections stem from the same hand. See Niederwimmer 1977:151 and n. 16.

20. Note that the discussion of bishops and deacons is associated with "prophets and teachers" here: "apostles" are not yet part of the equation. Yet when apostles are raised, "prophets" are mentioned in conjunction with them. This supports the claim that 15:1-2 belongs

with 11:7-12 and 13:1-7, that this hand is unaware of the material in 11:3-6, and that the hand responsible for 11:3-6 is already aware of 11:7-12; 13:1-7; and 15:1-2.

21. Niederwimmer (1977:151–52) agrees that chap. 12 is redactional, as well as 11:3, but thinks that the advice in 11:4-6 is traditional. He also believes that chap. 13 stems from the hand of the redactor. As noted above, this reconstruction ignores the tremendous similarity between 11:3-6 and 12:1-5; it also has the redactor rather implausibly repeating in chap. 13, information that has already been given in a more specific form.

22. Note that in this material bishops and deacons do not receive a significant amount of attention—the reader is simply encouraged to respect them, and because of their links to prophets and teachers, at that—nor is their authority contrasted in any way with that of prophets and teachers. It should also be noted that the perspective from which bishops and deacons are discussed is the same as that of prophets: as third parties under discussion, not as embattled advocates of the rules being articulated.

23. Note in the text quoted above the conflation, like that in the *Didache,* of prophecy with teaching: the activity of prophecy is supposed to take place in such fashion "so that all may *learn.*"

See also Rom 12:6-8, in which *leaders* (ὁ προϊστάμενος) are distinguished from prophets. Meeks (1983:134) believes this title is more indicative of a patronage function than of actual leadership. But he acknowledges that since such patrons are charged to "admonish," some kind of leadership function is built into or implied by their role. Malherbe (1983:98) also argues that the term cannot denote an office.

24. Note that although there is an apparent parallel between the injunctions against false teachers in the Pastorals and the concern in the *Didache* about false prophets, the *Didache*'s concerns with false prophets are decidedly not dogmatic ones.

25. As suggested by the fact that 12:1-5 is a later redactional creation. Note that 13:1 picks up once again the theme and language of "true prophets," which is the main concern of 11:7-12.

26. The idea, in other words, could be more clearly phrased as what to do if a true prophet arises among you. See BAGD 389, on the range of meaning of the verb κάθημαι. The term literally means "sit," although BAGD cites *Did.* 13:1 as an instance of the figurative meaning "reside" or "settle." Obviously "reside" is the meaning implied by 12:3, but since the material in 13:1 (if original to the preredactional stage) stems from a different hand, the two similar phrases need not have meant the same thing when each was written. If the Didachist modeled 12:3 on 13:1, however,

he probably did take the κάθημαι in 13:1 to mean "settle." It would appear, however, that "prophecy" was an institution in desuetude by the time this redaction took place (see also the Pastorals), and so the author misconstrues the references to prophets as an exceptional or external phenomenon. Note also that if the κάθημαι in 13:1 simply means "sit," its point of reference could very well be liturgical, given the apparent liturgical functions of prophets. Hence, the text is referring, very specifically, to prophets who wish to sit in worship as prophets; it could even be the case that the "firstfruits" to be accorded them are specified only for this special context. This speculation has the additional advantage of accounting for the interpolation of this material into liturgical instructions (that is, those on the Eucharist in 10:1-6 and 14:1-3).

27. Even the reference to the provision of "money, clothes, and all of your possessions" (13:7) focuses on "firstfruits" and qualifies the injunction with "as it seems best to you."

28. A major weakness with his claim is that the institution of bishops and deacons is justified with reference to the very prophets (and teachers) that Draper thinks are more recent intrusions!

29. By contrast, Crossan (1996:119) describes them, without argumentation, as "by definition, prophets on their way to found new Christian households or communities elsewhere and are supported by already established ones on their way."

30. It is notable that Patterson (1993a:178–88) adduces James as evidence of itinerancy. What may be at issue in James, however, is cross-fertilization among different assemblies in the same locale. See Malherbe 1983:101.

31. Second John prohibits the extension of hospitality to such persons (2 John 10–11), while 3 John complains that hospitality has been unfairly denied (3 John 10) and exhorts hospitality for "the brothers." See Malherbe 1983:103–10. That ordinary travel is at issue here, rather than true itinerancy as Patterson (1993a:188–95) would claim, is indicated by the author's need to point out explicitly that these travelers do not accept hospitality from non-Christians (3 John 7). In other words, they will only stay with fellow Christians along their way. Itinerant missionaries, one imagines, would not be in any position to presume on the hospitality of nonbelievers!

32. The view of the issue as nearly entirely internal is in sharp contrast to most treatments. Niederwimmer (1977:153) nicely gives voice to the usual reading of the text, especially 11:4-12: "The first impression shows: wandering charismatics and local sedentary Christians represent two independent and clearly distinguished forms of Christian existence. The problem is the relation of both groups to each other."

33. See, for instance, Braun 1991:295–302; Hoffmann 1982:237–63; Mack 1988b:84–85 and n. 6; Patterson 1993a:159 and n. 5; Tuckett 1996:355–67, 390–91; Uro 1987:129; Vaage 1994:17–39, esp. 38. See also the general comments of Uro 1987:21–23, and the literature he cites (nn. 98–109).

34. See my comments above on the mythologizing import of such a characterization. Note also Borsch 1975 for the argument that Jesus himself was not actually itinerant.

35. So Kloppenborg 1987:192, citing, among others, Bultmann. See also Koester 1971:170–71, n. 34.

36. The latter is present only in Luke, prompting some scholars to deny that it was originally in Q. See Kloppenborg 1988:64 and the literature cited there. Kloppenborg, noting that this saying fits well with Vassiliadis's criteria for inclusion in Q (see Vassiliadis 1978), concludes that "[o]f all the Lukan Sondergut, this has the strongest probability of deriving from Q." For the opposite conclusion, see Moreland and Robinson 1993:503.

37. I am excluding from consideration, thus, according to Kloppenborg's stratification hypothesis, Q 10:12-15, 21-24. (Note, however, that Catchpole [1990] believes that this text, essentially, constitutes a unity.) These secondary, redactional sayings, particularly vv. 12-15, promote an almost formal sense of mission (a city-to-city, miracle-working call to repentance), but this mission is almost certainly fictitious, a literary conceit evoking the deuteronomistic understanding of the Q people's plight that characterizes this second, redactional layer of Q. (On the "failure" and fictitious nature of the Q^2 "mission," see, among others, Kloppenborg 1987:167–68, 196, 325; 1991:92–96.) Thus these additional sayings confuse the intentions of the original speech by conflating it with an idealized scenario that does not actually accord with the tradents' behavior.

38. See Arnal 1995b:481 and n. 40; Horsley 1988; 1993:228–31, 231–40; Piper 1995:55–66.

39. This suggestion is in sharp contrast to the more usual understanding that these prohibitions promote among the missionaries, either literally or symbolically, the condition of radical dependence on God. See, for example, Braun 1991:296–98; Catchpole 1990:168–70; Hoffmann 1982:312; Laufen 1980:252–53; Schultz 1972:415; Tuckett 1996:386–90; Uro 1987:125.

4: The Socioeconomics of Roman Galilee

1. Horsley 1993:29 is typical in this regard: "The pressure came from the double burden of taxation, the many dues for the cultus and priests, and the tribute to Rome. Neither the Romans nor the Jewish aristocracy were about to forgo their income by reducing their demands. Instead they collaborated in the effective exploitation of the largely peasant producers."

See also, for example, Crossan 1991:209, 212 (taxation a factor in revolt; see 4, 21–22); Frend 1984:55, 57 (tribute resented); Freyne 1980:183 (two separate systems of taxation, each making full demands without taking the other into account); Gottwald 1993:18 (taxation multilayered); Horsley 1995a:139–40, 201 (taxation multilayered); Jeremias 1969:124–26 (taxation resented); Schürer 1973:372–73 (Roman taxation "oppressive").

2. Note that Freyne (1997:67) criticizes Crossan's reconstruction of the milieu of Jesus for its "atopicality," precisely on the grounds that singular characteristics of the contemporary and specific Galilean political order are absent from it: "Antipas was a fact of life in the Galilee of Jesus, and I find his almost complete absence from Crossan's book strange but predictable in the light of Crossan's tendency to atopicality."

3. Freyne 1997:68, 70, 79–83; 1995; Reed 1994:213–15; and Edwards 1992 have, in different ways, helpfully drawn attention to the effects of the establishment of these two cities. My observations in what follows are dependent on and indebted to the original insights of these three authors. Horsley's recent book on Galilee (1996) develops theses very similar to those that will be presented here, but these similar trains of thought were developed independently; I had arrived at these general conclusions about early first-century Galilee, its political economy, the tributary mode of surplus extraction (on which see Gottwald 1993), Roman policy, and the implications of the ancient urban-rural divide, before having looked at Horsley's excellent book.

4. Ste. Croix 1981:10–11; Duncan-Jones 1982:33; Evans 1981:428; Finley 1973:89; Jones 1974:30–31; Rostovtzeff 1957: v. 1, 192–93. Garnsey and Saller (1987:43) offer a description of the Roman economy as one of classic premodern "underdevelopment":

> The Roman economy was underdeveloped. This means essentially that the mass of the population lived at or near subsistence level. In a typical underdeveloped, pre-industrial economy, a large proportion of the labor force is employed in agriculture, which is the main avenue for investment and source of wealth. The level of investment in manufacturing industries is low. Resources that might in

theory be devoted to growth-inducing investment are diverted into consumption or into unproductive speculation and usury. Demand for manufactured goods is relatively low, and most needs are met locally with goods made by small craftsmen or at home.

5. So also, for example, Freyne 1980:5, 15; Hoehner 1972:65; Oakman 1986:19; Richardson 1996:133; Schürer 1973:341.

6. For this division, see Josephus, *War* 3.35–40, and for description of the parameters of these regions and their main characteristics see also Adan-Bayewitz 1993:27–31, incidental to locating the site of Kefar Ḥananya, which marks the division between Upper and Lower Galilees; Freyne 1980:9–15; also, among others, Fiensy 1991:55; Kloppenborg 2000:213–14; Richardson 1996:132. *M. Šeb.* 9:2, describes the distinction in terms of agricultural differences: "Galilee is divided into upper Galilee, lower Galilee, and the valley: from Kefar Ḥananya upwards, wheresoever sycamores do not grow, is upper Galilee; from Kefar Ḥananya downwards, wheresoever sycamores grow, is lower Galilee; the region of Tiberias is the valley."

7. Adan-Bayewitz 1993:27; Freyne 1980:9. Xaloth was in the Great Plain (modern Iksal, according to LCL 2.587, n. "b"), about level with Mount Tabor. Freyne associates Bersabe with a site proximate to Kefar Ḥananya in the Beth HaKerem Valley and believes that this valley, and its continuation in the deep gorge of the Ammud stream, is the geologic marker of the boundary between Lower and Upper Galilee. Clark 1962:346 describes the distinction as marked by the plain of Ramah, roughly on a line from Capernaum to Ptolemais.

8. Josephus, *War* 3.38 (LCL 2.587), describes the east-west range of Lower Galilee as extending from Tiberias to Chabulon, "which is not far from Ptolemais on the coast" (ἧς ἐν τοῖς παραλίοις Πτολεμαῒς γείτων).

9. Freyne 1980:5; Hamel 1990:102–3. Buttressing literary references to cisterns is the discovery of numerous cisterns from the early to middle Roman periods in excavations of Sepphoris. See Meyers, Netzer, and Meyers 1986:15; Strange 1992:341.

10. Freyne 1980:5; Hamel 1990:103, 106–7. The story of Honi the circle-drawer (*m. Ta'an.* 3:8) illustrates these conditions and the delicate balance between drought and flood.

11. In fact other grains were cultivated in ancient Palestine as well—foxtail, spelt, emmer, durra, millet, rice (Hamel 1990:11; Safrai 1994:117–18)—but "wheat and barley not only bore the biggest grains and yielded the most flour but also were the most suitable for bread" (Hamel 1990:13). The problem with barley is that it could not be easily husked without prior roasting, which operation destroyed much of the gluten

content of the grains and thus made its dough inelastic (Hamel 1990:13). On barley as a source of inferior bread, see BAGD 450, which refers to Appianus, *Illyr.* 26.76, where inferior soldiers receive κριθὴ ἀντὶ σίτου; and see Josephus, *Ant.* 5.219, who refers to a κριθίνην ὑπ' εὐτελείας ἀνθρώποις ἄβρωτον. In *m. Sanh.* 9:5 it is suggested that a three-time criminal offender is to be put into prison and fed only barley "until his belly bursts"; and the amount of barley required to be left on the threshing floor for the poor is double that of wheat (*m. Pe'ah* 8:5).

12. See Pritchard 1987:59, and, indirectly, Safrai 1994:108–9. One can only guess, but it is possible that Josephus so highly esteemed the productivity of Galilee because, in contrast to less irrigated regions to the south or northeast, proportionately little of the land was used for grazing or for the production of animal feed (barley and other inferior grains). It must thus have seemed that "every inch of the soil" was under direct cultivation.

13. See *Mur* 90 (DJD 2:218), which lists produce in one column, followed by a parallel column that gives equivalences in wheat, using the formula ἴσ(ον) (πυρου) ιγ, and so on, literally given as "ισ4" (and see editors' commentary on this practice, 219); see no. 96 (228–29); and see Hamel 1990:126, n. 178. For the relative value of wheat to barley in different regions and at different times, see chart 6 in Ben-David 1974:102.

14. Safrai 1994:105. The bread was in fact very hard and dry and was used for scooping up a vegetable or oil pulp, which in its turn helped soften the bread and make it more palatable. See Hamel 1990:12, 14–15.

15. See, for instance, *m. Pe'ah* 8:7: "A poor man that is journeying from place to place should be given not less than one loaf worth a *pondion* [from wheat costing] one *sela* for four *seahs.*" Safrai 1994:105 works this out to a loaf of 0.525 kg: "The price for a *seah* of wheat is one-quarter of a *sela* = *dinar.* The *pondion* is one-twelfth of a *seah.* Thus, a loaf is one-twelfth of a *seah* or one-half of a *kab.* A *seah* of wheat, therefore, is 6.3 kilograms. Thus, the Mishnah is describing a loaf that weighed 0.525 kilograms." See also *m. Pe'ah* 8:5; *m. Ketub.* 5:8; *t. Pe'ah* 4.8. Safrai 1994:107 suggests that this figure of (the equivalent of) about one-half of a kilogram of wheat per day applies to nearly everyone: "The rich consumed more, but the addition would mostly [*sic*] likely not have been in terms of grain, but rather additional fruits, wine, meat and other luxury items."

16. So Safrai 1994:110 (see 106), based on *m. Ketub.* 5:8. This estimate is probably rather low, since it assumes the availability of these other products, an assumption that may not pertain accurately to the condition of the rural poor or to all times of the year. Two *kabs* would make eight ordinary meals, that is, enough for four days, not seven. Safrai is

assuming six additional meals comprised of oil and vegetable products, or of figs. One should therefore take the figures offered here as a minimum. Evans 1981:432 suggests that minimum intake to sustain life is between 190 and 235 kg per year; if Safrai's figures are augmented to include seven days of intake rather than four, weekly consumption is 3.675 kg per week, or 191.1 kg per year, on the low end of Evans's range.

17. Thus Safrai 1994:110. This figure is based on the figure of 0.525 kg required per day, not on the weekly figure that incorporates other types of food products. Nevertheless, the figure is probably a minimum, given that Safrai admits that his yield figures are rather optimistic. Safrai gives his figures for the *dunam*, not the acre, which I have translated here on the basis of the equation 4 *dunams* = 1 acre. The figures he gives are an annual yield of 150 kg per *dunam*; basic dietary needs require the annual yield of 1.28 *dunams*; with alternate fallow, this translates into about 2.5 *dunams*.

18. Safrai does not give yield ratios directly, but his figures work out to a cereal product of 1,482.6 kg per hectare; Hamel 1990:135, working on the assumption of a 1:5 yield, puts cereal product at 750 kg per hectare. Or again, Safrai suggests a product of 150 kg per *dunam*, while Ben-David (1974:78, 106) implies a yield of 77 kg per *dunam* (a *Beth-Se'atajim* = 1568 m², a fivefold yield on 20 *Beth-Se'atajim* would be 2,057 kg). Therefore Safrai appears to be assuming an average yield about double that of Hamel or Ben-David. Safrai depends on Feliks 1963 for his figures. Note that Garnsey and Saller 1987:77–82, however, agree with this higher yield figure, arguing that Columella's low yield figures (see below) are idiosyncratic; see Hanson and Oakman 1998:104.

19. Mark 4:8 (seed to product yields of 1:30, 1:60, and 1:100) and *Thomas* 9 (yields of 1:60 and 1:120) are examples of such inflated and essentially meaningless figures. Varro and the Talmuds also give similarly unrealistic figures from time to time, ranging from 1:45 to 1:100. *M. Pe'ah* 5:1, which suggests that the same amount of grain should be left for the poor as is set aside for seed, implies a ratio of 1:45. Modern farming yields ratios of 1:30 to 1:40 under the very best of conditions. See Hamel 1990:126–28.

20. Hamel 1990:127 and n. 189, citing *b. B. Meṣi'a* 105b, which implies yield ratios of 1:3.75 and 1:7.5 (4–8 *se'ahs* per *kor*). See Oakman 1986:28; Reed 1994:212, n. 40.

21. Hamel 1990:129 and nn. 201, 203, 204: *y. Pe'ah* 7.4.20a: a *se'ah* of Arbel (that is, from the Arbel plain, 6 km northwest of Tiberias) generates 6 *se'ahs* of various grades of flour and bran; *y. So,tah* 1.8.17b; 9.14.24b: a *se'ah* of Arbel produces 6 *se'ahs* of various grades of flour and bran; *b. Ketub.* 112a: a *se'ah* of Judah produces 5 *se'ahs* of various grades

of flour and bran. Note, however, that these texts describe flour yield, not grain yield. Volume increment takes place at milling, depending on the quality of the grain: hence actual grain yield figures would be somewhat lower.

22. Cicero, *Actionis secundae in C. Verrem*, 3.18.47; 3.47.112; see Hamel 1990:131, n. 218. Actually, there seem to be two main sets of credible figures, not quite compatible with each other. Cicero suggests around an eightfold yield, while Columella suggests about fourfold. Likewise the *P. Ness.* papyri suggest a similar discrepancy. See Evans 1981:429–31. Evans argues that this discrepancy, which, suggestively, involves a doubling or halving of the figures in question, may be only an apparent contradiction: the result of yield figures being calculated on the basis of ground actually sown (which would then yield the 1:8 figure), or on the basis of ground actually possessed, half of which would normally be fallow (thus giving the 1:4 figure); or perhaps the lower figure refers to intercultivation. This ingenious suggestion is probably incorrect: statements about yield in the ancient literature are based directly on land sown, as they sometimes explicitly refer to seed-to-yield ratios. The discrepancy is thus probably to be explained some other way: differing soil productivity, yield being measured by flour rather than grain, or discrepant sowing practices.

23. This figure is an average, not a norm: in the Galilean valleys yields probably fluctuated between as low as 1:3 and as high as 1:8. So Hamel 1990:133. In fact, there are indications that sometimes yield was 1:1 or less, that is, barely enough for next year's seed; hence some tenancy contracts introduce penalties for noncultivation (Hamel 1990:130 and n. 210). See *Mur* 24b, lines 11–13 (DJD 2:125), and 24c, lines 10–11 (DJD 2:128–29). The Mishnah also includes such penalties: *m. B. Meṣiʿa* 9.3 (362): "If a man leased a field from his fellow and he let it lie fallow they assess how much it was likely to have yielded and he must pay the owner accordingly, for thus such a lease prescribes: 'If I suffer the land to lie fallow and do not till it I will pay thee at the rate of its highest yield'"; *m. B. Meṣiʿa* 9.5 (362–63): "If a man leased a field from his fellow and it was not fruitful, and there was only enough produce to make a heap, he must still cultivate it. R. Judah said: What manner of measure is 'a heap'!—but, rather, he must cultivate it even if it yields only as much grain as was sown there."

24. Assuming, with Hamel 1990:136, 150 kg of seed sown per hectare, with a 1:5 yield. Seven hectares would thus yield 5,250 kg of grain, if under continuous cultivation. Alternating fallow would yield half that figure, viz., 2,625 kg. Note also the various yield figures given by Ben-David 1974:106.

25. The land was sometimes plowed twice or more, partly in order to minimize weeds: once in the late summer or early fall after threshing and winnowing, and again in December, just before sowing. See Hamel 1990:109–10, 113–15, who notes that the postharvest plowing was sometimes neglected. See also Duncan-Jones 1982:329.

26. See, among others, Q 17:35: "Two women will be grinding at the mill"; *Apoc. Zeph.* 2:2-4: "I also saw two women grinding together at a mill." Most clearly and explicitly, however, see *m. Ketub.* 5:5: "These are the works which the wife must perform for her husband: grinding flour and baking bread and washing clothes and cooking food and giving suck to her child and making ready his bed and working in wool. If she brought him in one bondwoman she need not grind or bake or wash." See also *m. Ṭehar.;* and Hamel 1990:112.

27. Hamel 1990:112 and n. 102. Grinding at a hand mill on a saddle stone allows for the grinding of about 1 lb. (0.454 kg) of grain into flour per hour.

28. Safrai 1994:122: 20 to 60 liters per *dunam,* which roughly equals 80 to 240 liters per acre, which, at a (low?) density of forty-four trees per acre translates into 1.8 to 5.5 liters per tree annually (recognizing, however, that a reasonable yield can be expected only every other year).

29. Safrai 1994:106, citing *m. Ketub.* 5:8. A half-*log* is 0.178 liters, which in two years or 104 weeks adds up to 18.512 liters, which requires about ten trees. Safrai estimates that a family of seven would require 64.8 liters of oil per year (this is almost exactly the same amount I have calculated: 18.5 liters every two years = 9.25 liters per year per person, multiplied by seven persons = 64.75 liters). Ben-David 1974:112, by contrast, estimates a half-*log* to be about 0.14 liters.

30. Safrai 1994:123–25, discusses various estimates of oil press capacity, concluding that estimates based on traditional Arab presses are methodologically questionable. Basing his own figures on the capacity of the storage pits of actual ancient presses (an average of 40 to 50 liters), and recognizing that the content of these pits was 75 percent water, he arrives at an average pressing capacity of 10 to 12.5 liters of oil per turn. Thus 900 turns of a standard press (or 450 turns of two such presses, or 300 turns of three, and so on) would be required to supply our hypothetical village. Safrai further notes that Arab presses, which are more sophisticated than those of antiquity, take about an hour for one complete turn and argues that ancient presses would therefore have taken between one and two hours for a complete turn. Of course, different types of presses will produce at different rates: a screw press is faster than a beam press relying on weights (see Safrai 1994:124). With such rates, 900 to 1,800 hours of press-time is required to supply a village of four hundred

persons. If, with Safrai, we assume a ten-week season and a press-week of between eighty and ninety-eight hours (the first figure is Safrai's, assuming a fourteen-hour day with observance of sabbath; the second figure is an extrapolation deliberately failing to account for observance of the sabbath), reasonable press-time for a single press in season would have been from 800 to 980 hours. A little less than double this output is required unless the press was operating at the fastest rate indicated, that is, one turn per hour. Otherwise, to be adequate for the supply of a village of four hundred, the press would have to be worked during the night (unlikely but conceivable?), or two presses would have to be operating (more likely), or olive yield would have to be planned so that only half of the trees under cultivation yielded each year (so that the two-year total yield was in fact spread over two seasons, rather than occurring all at once).

31. See the survey of sampled sites offered by Adan-Bayewitz 1993:52–59, in which several locations are identified as including oil presses: 'Ein Nashut (multiple), Rama (multiple, one excavated), Gamla (multiple), Sepphoris (multiple), and Beth She'arim (single). See Hamel 1990:10, n. 14. On presses being found at Sepphoris, see Strange 1992:343. See Michael Avi-Yonah 1975–78 for presses found at three locations: Beth She'arim, v. 1, 231; Chorazin, v. 1, 299; Nazareth, v. 3, 922. There is some extensive material on the technology of presses written in modern Hebrew: see in particular Frankel 1984.

32. See the diagram in Trever 1962:596; see Safrai 1994:119; Hanson and Oakman 1998:117–18. For a description of the items of an olive press, see *m. B. Bat.* 5:5. For a description of the process of pressing, see *m. Țehar.* chaps. 9 and 10.

33. So Safrai 1994:356 calculates that a vineyard would be four times as profitable as an identical area dedicated to wheat, and an olive grove 2.5 times more profitable.

34. Intercultivating trees with grain would presumably be a useful check on soil erosion. Under the law of diverse kinds, it is forbidden to sow wheat under hanging grapevines, but it is not forbidden to sow wheat under trees, nor to grow grapevines over or around trees. See *m. Kil.* 6.4: "If he trained the vine over part of a fruit tree he may sow seed beneath the rest, and if new tendrils spread along the rest of the tree they must be turned back."

35. So Freyne 1980:338, n. 34, citing Eupolemus (ca. 150 B.C.E.), as recounted in Eusebius, *Praep. Ev.* 9.33.1. This text mentions agricultural supplies coming to Jerusalem from various sources: wheat comes from Galilee, while oil comes from Judea. Freyne believes that the importation of wheat rather than oil is more a product of halakic considerations

(a question of being uncertain about the ritual purity of Galilean oil at this time, before the region had been officially integrated into Judea) than an indication of low oil production. This is possible, but it is equally possible that Judea was self-sufficient in oil at this time and that where grain growing was possible, Galileans did so, having no real market for surplus oil.

36. See Safrai 1994:122–27, arguing for olive oil as an export crop; and see similarly Ben-David 1974:111–12. Josephus's account of John of Gischala taking advantage of war conditions to inflate artificially the price of olive oil (*Life* 74–76) is revealing in this regard, demonstrating both the abundance of oil in Upper Galilee (the price of oil in Gischala was one-tenth its price in Caesarea Philippi) as well as the demand for pure oil (which evidently now included that from Galilee) elsewhere. It is notable also that the Mishnah includes provisions for retaining the purity of Galilean oil from contamination by the *'amme ha-'areṣ*, including locking press-workers inside the pressing area (*m. Ṭehar.* 10:1)! Horsley (1996:68–69, 102–3) concedes that some export of surplus oil occurred, but never as a "business" or in exchange for grain, on the model of a market economy; rather, what oil was exported was used as payment of taxes, rents, or whatever other demands were forced on the populace over and above subsistence. He is probably correct to note that the activities of John of Gischala reported by Josephus are described as ad hoc but fails to explain the strong Mishnaic concern with workers contaminating the oil supply.

37. See *m. Ketub.* 5:8: "If a husband maintained his wife at the hands of a third person, he may not grant her less than two *kabs* of wheat or four *kabs* of barley [every week]. . . . He must also give her half a *kab* of pulse and half a *log* of oil and a *kab* of dried figs or a *mina* of fig-cake; and if he has none of these he must provide her with other produce in their stead."

See also *t. Pe'ah* 4.8, which stipulates that during the week hospitality for a poor traveler should include oil and beans; on the Sabbath it should include oil, beans, fish, and a vegetable. On various Palestinian food products (in addition to grain and olives), see also Strabo, *Geography* 16.2.41; 17.1.51, on the palm, balsam, and other Judean products. Strabo, *Geography* 16.2.45 also refers to the fish in the Sea of Galilee and to surrounding trees: "At the place called Taricheae the lake supplies excellent fish for pickling; and on its banks grow fruit-bearing trees resembling apple trees."

38. Hoeing was frequently used in addition to plowing, because of the primitive character of available plows, which were not capable of creating furrows but more or less simply scratched the ground. The

Mishnah regards plowing instruments as essential: like a pillow, when held in surety they must be returned for use (*m. B. Meṣiʿa* 9:13: "he must give back a pillow during the night-time and a plough during the day-time"). Cisterns may have been needed, or channels to collect runoff, or dams to divert water flow for collection and to create new strips of cultivable land by collecting eroded soil from runoff from higher fields. Because of irrigation considerations, land higher up on hills was less desirable than land lower on their sides or in the valleys between them: water would wash down from top to bottom, bringing with it eroded soil. The majority of the land, at any rate, was not artificially irrigated. See also *m. B. Bat.* 4:8: "If a man sold a field he has sold also the stones that are necessary to it, and the canes in a vineyard that are necessary to it, and its unreaped crop, and any reed-thicket that covers less than a quarter-*kab*'s space of ground, and the watchman's hut if it was not fastened down with clay, and ungrafted carob trees and young sycamores." In general, see also *m. B. Bat.* 2:1; Ben-David 1974:83–91; Golomb and Kedar 1971:139; Hamel 1990:113, 117–18; Postan 1966:97.

39. Specialized equipment was needed for threshing: flails, oxen, or a *tribulum* (a flint-studded board driven over the floor by animals). See Burford 1993:140–42; Postan 1966:99. The grain was normally winnowed from the threshing floor. On storage of seed, see Luke 12:18: "I will pull down my barns and build larger ones"; and Q 3:17: "and he will gather his wheat into the barn."

40. The Q text that refers to hanging a millstone around someone's neck (Q 17:2) is described by Matthew (and see Mark 9:42) as a μύλος ὀνικός, a donkey millstone. See BAGD 529, "μύλος" (mill); and "ὀνικός" (donkey), 570. On the other hand, the fact that Mark and Matthew feel it necessary to stipulate the kind of millstone in order to convey its largeness may in fact suggest the more common use of hand mills. The author, that is, cannot take it for granted that his audience will assume that a millstone is very large. The IQP regards the Lukan wording, λίθος μυλικός (millstone), in this instance, to reflect the original wording of Q (Robinson, Hoffmann, and Kloppenborg 2000:474–75).

On the Mishnaic assumption of the use of hand mills, see *m. Moʿed Qaṭ.* 1:9 ("They may set up an oven or stone or hand mill during mid-festival. R. Judah says: They may not roughen the millstones for the first time"); *m. B. Meṣiʿa* 9:13 ("If a man takes away the mill-stones, he transgresses a negative commandment, and he is culpable by virtue of taking two utensils together, for it is written, *No man shall take the mill and the upper millstone to pledge.* They spoke not only of the mill and the upper millstone, but of aught wherewith is prepared necessary food, as it is written, *For he taketh a man's life to pledge*"); *m. B. Bat.* 2:1 ("The hand-mill may not be kept at such a distance that the wall is less than three hand-breadths from the lower mill-stone or four from the upper mill-stone"). For a description of these implements, see Richardson 1962a:380.

41. In contrast to medieval Europe, for instance, in which the use of the waterwheel for milling was a feature of most manors. Rome and Constantinople had water mills, and horse- or donkey-driven mill-houses have been found in larger centers, such as Pompeii or London. See Postan 1966:99. The references in Q and *Apoc. Zeph.* to women milling together, however, do suggest a communal practice of milling, regardless of the actual equipment used.

42. *m. B. Bat.* 4:7: "If a man sold a town, he has sold also the houses, cisterns, trenches, vaults, bath-houses, dovecotes, olive-presses, and irrigated fields, but not the movable property." This list serves as a helpful précis of the standard features that were often an intrinsic part of a town or village. Prior to this text (*m. B. Bat.* 4:5), a discussion of the sale of presses indicates that they could be privately owned. Since, however, they are included as part of the sale of a town, and since they are specifically exempted from the sale of a courtyard (*m. B. Bat.* 4:4), it is clear that privately owned though they may be, nevertheless they are located for communal use (and these communities and community locations can evidently also be privately owned). See also Safrai 1994:124.

43. See, for example, Avi-Yonah 1975–78: v. 1, 231: an oil press was discovered beside the city gate on the northern side of the hill at Beth She'arim. Apparently the same layout was used at Tiberias in the Byzantine period: Hirschfeld 1992:41–42 shows the location of an oil press just inside the Byzantine walls on Mount Berenice, and proximate to a gate in the wall and to the church built during the reign of Justinian. Or again, two oil presses discovered at Chorazin were located in a public, that is, nonresidential, area (the town center was on a terrace at the highest elevation and included most important public buildings; a second area was on the lowest terrace to the south, and this is where the presses were, along with a cistern; a third sector, to the west, was residential and densely populated). On Chorazin, see Avi-Yonah 1975–78: v. 1, 299.

This is not to say that no oil presses were privately owned. Peter Richardson (personal communication) has pointed to a press discovered on the western portion of the site at Gamla that was likely privately owned. The point here is that in most small villages, the oil press was not a household feature (like milling equipment) but was a sufficiently elaborate and central installation as to be used by the community as a whole.

44. On the threshing floor, see *m. Pe'ah* 5:8; *m. Kil.* 2:5; *m. Sanh.* 4:3 (on threshing floors as round); *m. Mid.* 2:5 (on threshing floors as round);

m. Kelim 15:4-5. See especially *m. B. Bat.* 2:8: "A permanent threshing-floor may not be made within fifty cubits from the city. None may make a permanent threshing-floor within his own domain unless his ground extends fifty cubits in every direction; and it must be far enough from the plantations and ploughed land of his fellow for it to cause no damage." Safrai 1994:75 notes that archaeological evidence for threshing floors is rare because little actual construction was involved: a flat rock or pounded-earth surface, evidently rounded (on which see also Richardson 1962b:636), would suffice. However, he does point to a threshing floor found about ten meters from the cluster of buildings of Khirbet Levad, which was apparently used by the small settlement's residents (Safrai 1994:75, and see fig.19 on 68).

45. See Josephus, *Ant.* 20.181, 206 (see *Life* 80); and see Freyne 1980:284; Hamel 1990:148–49: the system of tithing "required the close supervision of village threshing floors by priests" (149); Jeremias 1969:106–8 (citing *b. Ketub.* 105b, which describes the priest who patrols the threshing floor); Schürer 1979:262–63. It is irrelevant to my point whether these dues were scrupulously paid or not, or how the laws regulating their collection changed over time; the point is simply that the (theoretical? occasional? institutional?) collection of dues from the threshing floors makes perfect sense in light of the communal nature and use of these floors.

46. Smaller, indeed, than village populations would have been in the same region early in the twentieth century, in spite of, or rather because of, the greater prosperity of the Galilee in the Roman period. Broshi 1979:6 explains that in times of relative peace and prosperity the number of settlements increases, while their size decreases. In other words, hard times tend to lead to a concentration of settlements: fewer in number but greater in size.

47. Horsley 1996:44–45, offers overall population estimates (150,000 for all Galilee, with 15,000 of that in Sepphoris and Tiberias combined) suggestive of an average town or village population of less than seven hundred. He arrives at his figures by working from the physical size of Tiberias (40 hectares) and Sepphoris (60 hectares) and assumes a density comparable to that known for Pompeii (about 125 to 156 people per hectare) rather than a more congested city like Ostia (about 435 people per hectare). On the physical space occupied by Sepphoris and Tiberias see also Broshi's table (1979:5). Horsley thus arrives at an overall figure for Galilee by assuming that, as is usual in agrarian societies, there must be at least ten people on the land to support any one nonproductive person in the cities. Thus the overall population of Galilee will be about tenfold that of Sepphoris and Tiberias combined, that is, 150,000 people

or thereabouts. If we divide this figure, less the supposed population of the two cities, by the number of other settlements in Galilee, that is, 202, the average population of a settlement is somewhat less than seven hundred persons. This does not mean, however, that the typical settlement will actually possess this many persons, since a number of atypical larger sites would distort the overall picture. Thus while larger villages like Capernaum may have had one thousand to seventeen hundred or so people in early Roman times (downgraded from the fifteen thousand of some earlier estimates!; see Horsley 1996:114; Reed 1994:211–12; and, for discussion of the classification of Capernaum as a "village" versus a "city" see Corbo 1975:217–18), Horsley 1996:109 estimates that the standard village would have been comprised of about four to five hundred persons. For a sense of how current population estimates drastically reduce the numbers formerly estimated for Palestine, see the chart in Broshi (1979:3), where he compares his population estimates of various dwellings to those of Avi-Yonah. And for an example of the former tendency to exaggeration, see Golomb and Kedar 1971:136, who appear to accede to the Josephan statements that would place the overall population of the Galilee alone around 1.5 to 2 million!

Horsley's estimates are flawed in a number of different ways, however. He cannot be sure that some sectors of the urban population are not involved in agricultural production, and he certainly cannot be sure that the ratio of nonproductive city dwellers to the rest of the population is only 1:10 (only that it is at least 1:10). These factors might cancel each other out. His low density figures for these cities, however, are rather more problematic: as Reed (1994:214) notes, walled cities tend to be more densely populated, and there is some evidence from Sepphoris that multistoried dwellings may have been used (Strange 1992:349–50). Thus Reed, at any rate, prefers a population density of three hundred persons per hectare for the area within the city walls. This, according to Reed, would upgrade the population of Tiberias and Sepphoris to about twenty-four thousand persons each, and the population of the countryside would thus have to be scaled up accordingly. Reed's calculations here are to be preferred to Horsley's: the latter simply assumes, on no particularly good grounds, that the density of these cities would be the same as that of Pompeii. We might thus assume that the average village could have been inhabited by anywhere between four to eight hundred persons, with larger towns like Capernaum supporting even more. Some room should also be allowed for the existence of intermediate-sized towns, with populations in the low thousands.

48. There is a significant amount of Mishnaic regulation of matters pertaining to courtyards. See *m. B. Bat.* 1:1; 1:4-6; 3:7; 4:4. For a sense of

the overall size, design, and situation of such houses, see the various diagrams, photographs, and descriptions in, for example, Meyers, Strange, and Meyers 1981; Corbo 1975; Safrai 1994:64–67.

49. See *m. ʿArak.* 9:2: "A man may not sell a distant field in order to redeem one that is nearby," the reason behind the stipulation being that the practice would be usurious, as nearer land is worth more than farther land.

50. Upper Galilee included the southern ranges of the Lebanon mountains and had rainfall in the neighborhood of 1,110 mm per annum. See Clark 1962:346; Freyne 1980:5; Pritchard 1987:58–59. The rainfall obviated the need for irrigation, which latter tends to reduce the oil content of olives. Thus the Upper Galilee made a good setting for fruit and olive production. *Gush Ḥalav* (= Gischala) means "fat soil."

51. For Josephus's description of the Valley as a distinct geographical area, see *War* 3.516–21. Freyne (1980:10) states: "The valleys on the eastern side [of Lower Galilee] are narrow and devious and communication on an east/west axis is not at all as easy as might appear at first sight. In turn this means that the region of the lake is to some degree cut off from the rest of Lower Galilee, a factor that will have to be kept in mind when discussing the likely sphere of influence of Tiberias on the hinterland." Notably, under Agrippa II the region was also administratively distinct from the rest of Galilee.

52. Witness, as already noted, the frequency of agricultural motifs on aniconic coinage; witness also the Mishnah's classification of kinds of work (*m. Šabb.* 7:2), the majority of which is related to agriculture.

53. See Finley 1973:80–81, on soldiers accepting land allotments that he thinks, even with tax exemption, were not of sufficient size. See also Finley 1973:105–6:

> The optimum size of a peasant farm is an obviously meaningless notion: there are too many variables. But let us take as a basis of discussion the Caesarian settlement, ten *jugera* (six-plus acres) for a veteran with three children. The Roman unit, the *jugum*, was the area of land one man could (hypothetically) plough in a day. Ten *jugera* of good arable would produce enough food to sustain a small family (but not an ox in addition) even with the alternate fallow system, especially when free from rents and taxes. The size of the family itself then became a major crux, first because there were few crops to spare; second, because ten *jugera* cannot keep a family employed full time; third, because, under the Greek and Roman rules of inheritance, an estate was in principle divided equally among legitimate sons (and sometimes daughters), with no trace of

primogeniture; fourth, because a peasant cannot dismiss his excess labour.

54. Indeed, local socioeconomic inequities would have translated into hierarchy just as easily as any other class distinction: whether by charity or debt, rescue in misfortune creates long-term obligations, the returns of which keep accruing to the benefactor.

55. See, for example, *m. B. Meṣi'a* 6:5, which allows damages against someone who abuses a rented ass by forcing it to carry additional bulk rather than additional weight.

56. See Karmon 1961:57: of 58 Roman settlements in the Sharon Plain, not one is more than 5 km from a paved road.

57. Safrai 1994:267 believes that these difficulties were obviated by donkey transport to the roads at which point produce could be loaded onto wagons. The Mishnah, in fact, routinely refers to asses as animals used for transport, while referring to cattle as herd animals (as in the cattle tithe or the parts of cattle included in various sales [*m. B. Bat.* 5:5]) or as used for plowing (*m. B. Meṣi'a* 6:5). On the other hand, when reference is made to wagons (infrequently: *m. Kelim* 14:4-5, 21:2, 24:2), the wording makes it clear that the yokes are intended to be attached to cattle. What this suggests to me (as does the relative frequency of reference to asses against reference to wagons) is that, naturally enough, cattle were used to haul wagons but that wagons were used only infrequently, while donkeys were used to carry produce much more frequently, at least among the relatively prosperous farmers represented by the Mishnah. On the other hand, *m. B. Bat.* 5:1 associates mules with wagons and oxen with yoke (for plowing?). Thus some wagons were pulled by mules.

58. Adan-Bayewitz 1993:234. On Roman roads from the period after the First Judean Revolt, whose general contours confirm the observations made above about the overall shape of the terrain and its impact on travel, see Roll 1994.

59. The Mishnah associates ships and their packing bags with mules and their wagons as means of transport. See the regulations for their respective sale in *m. B. Bat.* 5:1. Slaves are associated with shipping vessels in this text, so we have to assume that the owner of such a ship was relatively and distinctively wealthy. The presence of such ships should be assumed for the coast, not for the Sea of Galilee. On boats in Galilee, see Josephus, *War* 2.608, 635; Hoehner 1972:68. Mules were regularly rented: see Safrai 1994:263–67; on Talmudic texts referring to donkey-lending practices, see Safrai 1994:266. See also *m. B. Meṣi'a* 6:3, 5, etc.

60. Adan-Bayewitz 1993. See also Adan-Bayewitz and Perlman 1990. This latter study, entitled "The Local Trade of Sepphoris in the Roman

Period," analyzes the frequency of wares of different provenance (primarily, as it turns out, from Kefar Ḥananya and Shikhin) in Sepphoris only.

61. At least in the case of Kefar Ḥananya. See Adan-Bayewitz 1993:27–31. James F. Strange has identified a site 1.5 km north of Sepphoris with ancient Shikhin; so Adan-Bayewitz and Perlman 1990:168; see Adan-Bayewitz 1993:32.

62. The figures are as follows: Kefar Ḥananya, 100 percent; Hazon, 100 percent; Rama, 97 percent. Three locations in Meiron were sampled separately, yielding figures of 99 percent, 84 percent, and 69 percent. The first site dates through the Roman period (50 B.C.E.–365 C.E.), while the second and third date from the fourth and fifth centuries C.E., respectively (Adan Bayewitz 1993:205, 221–22).

63. *m. Ṭehar.* 7:1 describes a pot seller setting down a group of pots bundled or tied together. *m. 'Ohol.* 16:2 describes a pot seller walking about with his pots on a carrying yoke resting behind his shoulders. See Adan-Bayewitz 1993:232. Literary sources do not attest to the use of pack animals, but it is reasonable enough to assume they may have been used, especially for longer distances. Adan-Bayewitz (1993:232, n. 5) notes that transport in a wheeled vehicle would not have been very practical, given the terrain.

64. Adan-Bayewitz 1993:234 and n. 10. Incidentally, this small-scale production in the Golan and on the eastern side of the lake probably explains why Kefar Ḥananya pottery is not widely distributed there, in spite of easy access by water: the main market for this ware was among Jews, because of the ritually pure character of the vessels. Thus the main maritime market of these goods would have been on the west side of the lake.

65. Adan-Bayewitz is assuming, correctly I suspect, that the surprisingly high proportion of Kefar Ḥananya ware found in Hammath Tiberias reflects the situation in Tiberias itself as well.

66. Horsley 1996:66–87 has argued at length that the movement of goods in early Roman Galilee, especially from village to city, was a result of tribute rather than trade, that is, the (more or less) forced removal of goods from the countryside rather than their free and advantageous sale. This would mean that the presence of Kefar Ḥananya ware in the cities is by no means an indication that the cities did not exploit the countryside; on the contrary, it is evidence of that exploitation.

67. This is a point he himself denies later on: climatic conditions make the production of pottery difficult precisely during the olive-processing season. Potters would thus have been available for agricultural work when extra hands were most needed. Ethnographic studies tend to confirm that potters normally assist in the agricultural work of their

communities. So Adan-Bayewitz 1993:236 and n. 14. It is also worth noting that if pottery was the prime focus of Kefar Hananya, food would have to be imported, raising all kinds of difficulties not easily solved by the central marketing of the pottery.

68. Such pottery could have been regarded as ritually pure. Non-Jews in the Golan would have obtained their own pottery from local sources.

69. So also Adan-Bayewitz 1993:237: "Kefar Hananya was well situated with respect to the Galilean markets; the settlement lies on the border between the Upper and the Lower Galilee, and along the route from 'Akko to the eastern Galilee."

70. This accounts for 25 percent of the total pottery found in Sepphoris. Thus, in terms of total accumulations (rather than just cooking ware), Shikhin provided Sepphoris with less than double the amount of pieces of pottery as Kefar Hananya, 26.5 km away.

71. On Sepphoris and Tiberias failing to produce pottery, see Adan-Bayewitz and Perlman 1990:169; Adan-Bayewitz 1993:227. Finley (1973:22, 137) notes that no cities were established because of or rested their prosperity on manufacture.

72. Similarly, Adan-Bayewitz 1993:235 cites the natural presence of good ceramic resources and the absence of an adequate agricultural base as preliminary factors stimulating the specialization of Kefar Hananya.

73. Adan-Bayewitz 1993:235 acknowledges the availability of a market, that is, demand, as another preliminary factor stimulating increased specialization.

74. Note that this regional radius very roughly corresponds to the distances envisioned by the Mishnah (m. Bek. 9:2) for the limits of a single herd of cattle. Cattle are imagined to range about 16 "miles" (the measure appears to be somewhat between a kilometer and a mile) while pasturing, and the text allows for (at least hypothetically) the single ownership of herds stretching along 32 of these miles. Thus property could be spread out, regionally, over fairly significant distances.

75. Note the wide range of towns in both Galilees found to have possessed oil presses (Adan-Bayewitz 1993:52–59; Avi-Yonah 1975–78: v. 1, 299, v. 3, 922; Hamel 1990:10, n. 14; Strange 1992:343). See also Josephus's testimonial to the fertility of the area around the lake (War 3.516–17), in which he mentions olives, among other produce. On the cultivation of olives in Samaria, see Safrai 1994:108. On their cultivation in Judea, see Freyne 1980:338, n. 34, citing Eupolemus (ca. 150 B.C.E.), as recounted in Eusebius, Praep. Ev. 9.33.1.

76. See, for example, Meshorer 1976:57 (and see chart, 1976:56), noting that about half of the coins found in a hoard from Migdal were from Tyre, Acco-Ptolemais, and Byblos; and Meshorer 1982:41, noting that

the basic currency of Palestinian antiquity was the Tyrian shekel rather than the Roman denarius.

77. The terms are borrowed from Safrai 1994:415. "Closed" means that normally farmers produced for their own or local needs, with luxury or trade items being picked up from the occasional surplus. "Open" means that farmers were extremely dependent on trade and commerce, and cultivated different crops specifically for sale.

78. Horsley 1996:69. It is also worth noting that the coins of Acco are far less frequent in Galilee (Upper or Lower) than those of Tyre (Migdal: seventy-four Tyrian coins but only fifteen from Acco; Meiron: twenty-five Tyrian coins but only two from Acco), in spite of being about the same distance as Tyre from Upper Galilee, and even closer to Lower Galilee.

79. Horsley 1996:86. He also associates the rise of pottery-producing centers with the establishment of Sepphoris and Tiberias (1996:85, emphasis added): "It is surely of significance that the sudden increase in the incidence of pottery from Kefar Hanania coincides with the rise to prominence of Sepphoris and the founding of Tiberias. Not only would increased demand for cooking ware have stimulated an increasing specialization of production of pottery at Kefar Hanania, but *the Herodian administration of these cities would have been concerned to assure an adequate supply of such an essential item.*" In my view the case for this kind of influence is even stronger for Shikhin.

80. This is not say, however, against all evidence, that the Roman government had sufficient fiscal foresight to regulate the flow of money except in those instances where it was to its obvious and direct benefit to do so, such as for the payment of troops or to inhibit forgeries that might later be paid in taxes. See Crawford 1970:48. See also Finley 1973:56, 166, 196 on the Roman state's inability to maintain sufficient supplies of coin for the population's needs, and the consequently chronic liquidity problems, even among the upper classes.

81. See Crawford 1970:46. During the late Republican period, fluctuation in volume of coinage shows a direct correspondence to the number of legions in the field. For example, the only major new minting of coins of the 70s B.C.E. corresponds to the assistance sent to Pompey in Spain in 74 B.C.E.

82. Crawford 1970:42 and n. 16, citing Plutarch, *Pericles* 16; the economic activities of Cicero and his correspondents; the general plaudits received by the praetor Gratidianus in 85 B.C.E. for stabilizing the exchange rate between bronze and silver; and *OGIS* 484, an inscription of Hadrian at Pergamum, recording a petition from merchants and traders complaining about bankers charging illegal rates of exchange.

83. Crawford 1970:42–43. He notes especially Pompeii, where a significant proportion of bronze coins was found and the fact that the Roman forum and the Tiber are littered with coins, mostly bronze. On the importance of issuing a wide variety of low denominations, see Crawford 1970:41. On the minting of copper coins in Palestine, see Hamburger 1962:423–35, 427–28.

84. See, for example, Hunt and Edgar 1988: v. 1, 211–13 (papyri nos. 72, 73): rental receipts in which payment is made in pigs and in produce, respectively.

85. See Finley 1973:56. See the various "agreements" and "receipts" in vol. 1 of Hunt and Edgar 1988, in which large purchases of property or the repayment of loans provide the most frequent instances of transactions involving money.

86. Josephus makes it clear that conversion of assets to money was a safe means of liquidating wealth threatened by war circumstances. See in particular the gruesome stories recounted in *War* 5.420–21 and 5.550–51.

87. On the hiring out of one's slaves for cash, see, for example, Theophrastus, *Characters* 30.15 ["Chiseling"]: "When he collects tenant-rent (ἀποφοράν) from his slave, he demands also the fee to exchange the copper, as also when he settles accounts with a steward"; and *Characters* 30.17: "When he is travelling with acquaintances he uses their servants, and hires out his own (τὸν δὲ ἑαυτοῦ ἔξω μισῶσαι) without sharing the proceeds."

88. See, for example, the parable of the laborers in the vineyard, Matt 20:1-16. The workers are explicitly paid in cash. See also Hunt and Edgar 1988 papyrus no. 17 for an example of cash payment for labor, in this case labor at an oil press.

89. See Safrai 1994:399, who breaks down the composition of the large quantity of coins found at Migdal, thus: of 168 city coins, 89 (47 percent) were from Syrian cities, 44 were from Israel (23 percent), and 19 (10 percent) were from Transjordanian cities. On the city coins found at Capernaum, Safrai (1994:400) notes that 55 percent are from Israel (including Galilee), 38 percent from Phoenicia, and 7 percent from Arabian cities. Tyre is especially well represented in this collection, its coins comprising 22 to 27 percent of the total. A breakdown of the coin collection at the Eretz Museum of Tel-Aviv (Safrai 1994:400–401), which Safrai concedes is both eclectic and uncatalogued, nevertheless is comprised of coins from Israel (42 percent), from Phoenicia (28 percent), from Transjordan (8 percent), from cities in Syria (10 percent), and from Egypt/Alexandria (16 percent). Individual cities prominent in the collection include Tyre (15 percent), Sidon (4 percent), Antioch (7 percent), Acco (3 percent), Alexandria (16 percent), Neapolis (9 percent),

Caesarea (8 percent), Aelia Capitolina (6 percent), and Tiberias (3.3 percent).

90. See Safrai 1994:402–3, pointing to increasing numbers of Palestinian coins from the first century onward. Of city coinage in the Museum of Beirut, 5 percent is Hasmonean, 1 percent Herodian, and 11 percent from first-century Judea. Only 1 percent of its total of Palestinian coins dates to the period before the Common Era. Safrai believes this indicates that trade relations between Israel (including Galilee) and Phoenicia became extensive only from this period onward; more likely, it indicates the more extensive monetization of the Palestinian economy from this period onward.

91. On the very restricted circulation of local Galilean coins, see Safrai 1994:403, noting that the coin collection of the Museum of Beirut has a grand total of twenty-six coins from Sepphoris and Tiberias, or only 4 percent of the total collection. See also Meshorer 1982:41: "The coins minted by Antipas were not circulated beyond the borders of his tetrarchy. Indeed, only one of the tens of thousands of ancient coins found in various excavations in Jerusalem was struck by Antipas. The pieces minted by this tetrarch have been generally discovered in the excavations in and around Tiberias." On the denominations of Galilean coins, see Meshorer 1982:37–38, who argues that Antipas issued four denominations: a large denomination (see his plates 1, 5, 9, 13, 17) corresponding to a Roman *dupondius;* a half-denomination corresponding to a Roman *as* (see plates 2, 6, 10, 14, 18); a quarter denomination corresponding to a Roman *semis* (see plates 3, 7, 11, 15, 19); and an eighth denomination corresponding to a Roman *quadrans* (see plates 4, 8, 12, 16). The weights of these coins are slightly different than those of their Roman (rough) equivalents because the alloy used by Antipas (a consistently poor bronze alloy) differs from those used for Roman coins (Roman *sestertia* and *dupondia* were made from a zinc and copper alloy, while smaller coins were copper only).

92. Meshorer 1982:38, notes a hiatus in Antipas's production of coins from 21 to 29 c.e., for no apparent political reason. He speculates that "the new currency would have been superfluous. The market may have been saturated with the bronze coins struck for Judea and Samaria by the Roman procurators." Much more likely, there was insufficient demand for lower-denomination coin in the immediate region at first. See also Freyne 1995:40.

93. See Freyne 1995:40, who helpfully notes that while the royal palace in Tiberias sported animal likenesses, the coinage did not. For a good sense of how consistently Antipas's coins avoid the portrayal of anything offensive to Jewish sensibilities, see the description in Meshorer

1982:72–75, which focuses on the reed or palm-branch design. Meshorer thinks that the design, involving the plant life to be found nearby, is intended to evoke the founding of the city (74–75). For the actual coins, see his plates, consistently with reed or palm and olive wreath (see also Meshorer 1982:35–41). Likewise, the coins of Agrippa I intended for his Jewish subjects were inscribed with a canopy and wheat or barley design (Meshorer 1982:52–59).

Meshorer 1982:40–41 (see 39–41; plate nos. 1–15) also comments that "all coins struck by Antipas prior to 38 c.e. are inscribed with his title and name in the genitival form: ΗΡΩΔΟΥ ΤΕΤΡΑΡΧΟΥ ["belonging to Herod the Tetrarch" or "of Herod the Tetrarch"]. This grammatical construction adds emphasis to the ruler's possession of both country and currency." One might, if Meshorer's reasoning here is cogent, suggest that this feature, too, is indicative of his intention that the coins circulate locally (or regionally, that is, within his tetrarchy).

94. Both Fiensy 1991 and Horsley 1995a point to a shift in the Hellenistic and Roman periods from patrimonial, family-based ownership of relatively small plots of land to the purchase of land, to tenancy, and to large estates. Obviously, an unmonetized economy discourages the speculative purchase of land; indeed, it makes land virtually inalienable, except by brute force.

95. I have addressed this issue in Arnal 1995b:485–87, from which the following observations are taken. For additional articulations of this view, see, among others, Fiensy 1991:55–57; Freyne 1995:29–35; 1997:81–82; Hanson and Oakman 1998:119–20; Horsley 1989:88–90; 1993:246–55; 1995a:215–16; 1996:80; Oakman 1994:238–39.

96. See, for instance, Hunt and Edgar 1988, papyri nos. 247, 259, 277, 279, 286–87; DJD 2:101–3 (for an Aramaic loan contract dated around 55–56 c.e.); 2:240–41 (for a Greek loan contract dated around 171 c.e.); and for earlier examples, Westermann and Hasenoehrl 1934:134–43; Westermann, Keyes, and Liebesny 1940:83–86.

97. Hunt and Edgar 1988, papyrus no. 68, refers to a loan of wheat; *m. B. Meṣiʿa* 5:1 speaks of lending two *seahs* of wheat for three in repayment; and *m. B. Meṣiʿa* 5:8-9 also speaks of lending wheat and bread.

98. As early as Ptolemaic times, extreme concentration of agricultural holdings appears in an inscription that refers to whole villages as the property of a single person (see Landau 1966:59–61 [lines 21–23]). Such huge holdings are presupposed much later in the gospels, most egregiously in *Thomas* 64: "I have bought a village (*ᶜnoukōmē*)."

99. Josephus (*Ant.* 17.3068) describes complaints that Herod imposed contributions in excess of the regular tribute and that the income from

his taxes went to the enhancement of foreign cities rather than his own realm. Similar charges are recounted in Josephus, *War* 2.85.

100. Josephus, *Ant.* 17.204–5: "Some cried out that he should lighten the yearly payments that they were making. Others demanded the release of the prisoners who had been put in chains by Herod. . . . Still others demanded the removal of the taxes that had been levied upon public purchases and sales and had been ruthlessly exacted." See *War* 2.4.

101. So Gabba 1990:161 and n. 1. This figure is arrived at in part by attention to the "incomes" stipulated for the various parts of Herod's kingdom when it was divided in 4 B.C.E. See Josephus, *Ant.* 17.318–20; *War* 2.95–97.

102. The increase in taxation is measured by Finley over centuries, not decades. Indeed, Galilee is not under direct Roman rule until after the death of Agrippa I. Apart from the First Judean Revolt, which is after our period, the only Galilean "depredations and devastations" of note revolve around Varus's destruction of Sepphoris in 4 B.C.E. The distinction between *humiliores* (of humble rank) and *honestiores* (of distinction) in law is not demonstrably relevant, as it was only certainly formalized by the early second century (Finley 1973:87).

103. On the fashion in which tithing to priests took place, see Josephus, *Ant.* 20.180–81: "No, it was as if there was no one in charge of the city, so that they acted as they did with full license. Such was the shamelessness and effrontery which possessed the high priests that they were actually so brazen as to send slaves to the threshing floors to receive the tithes that were due to the priests, with the result that the poorer priests starved to death. Thus did the violence of the contending factions suppress all justice." The text indicates the local priesthood's dependence on tithes, as well as the actual physical removal necessary to redirect those tithes to Jerusalem. There is no evidence for such events taking place in Galilee, it should be noted. There is a great deal of discussion in the Mishnah, esp. *m. Šeqal.*, about various tithes and dues owed in money.

104. In a very detailed and meticulously supported article, Keith Hopkins argues that "the Romans' imposition of taxes paid in money greatly increased the volume of trade in the Roman empire (200 B.C.–A.D. 400). Secondly, in so far as money taxes were levied on conquered provinces and then spent in other provinces or in Italy, then the tax-exporting provinces had to earn money with which to pay their taxes by exporting goods of equal value" (1980:101). He adds that rents functioned in approximately the same way (104), and that the entire process was accompanied by a corresponding growth in money supply (106, 109). See also Finley 1973:175–76.

105. See, succinctly, Finley 1973:123:

> Greeks and Romans never tired in their praise of the moral excellence of agriculture, and simultaneously in their insistence that civilization required the city. They were not being self-contradictory; Strabo, it will be noticed, saw agriculture, not trade or manufacture, as the prelude to stability and urbanism. The true city in classical antiquity encompassed both the *chora,* the rural hinterland, and an urban centre, where the best people resided, where the community had its administration and its public cults.

Finley discusses several examples of ancient cities that might appear to have "carried their own weight," but that, in the final analysis, did not: Athens, Marseilles, Tarentum (see 130–34, 193–94; see also MacMullen 1974:28–56, generally).

106. See Gottwald 1993:6, 18–20, on the techniques for removing surplus from the countryside. Many of the parables of Jesus, as Gottwald points out, serve as graphic illustrations of the political exercise of power in first-century Palestine. It is interesting, by the way, that the word often used for "tribute" is the same as that often used for "rent": φόρος.

107. In drawing this contrast, I am relying on the work of André Gunder Frank (1967) on metropolis-periphery relations in modern colonialism, leaving aside the intra-Marxist question of whence the accrued and drawn-off value described by Frank actually and ultimately derives. Pearse (1989) describes the penetration of more or less traditional and autonomous peasant societies in modern times through the mechanism of urbanization, but the proximity of cities in modernity tends to stimulate free trade and market exchange through (in part) the mere availability of markets, rather than extracting rural goods by sheer force. For a helpful summary of theoretical perspectives on the metropolis-periphery relationship, see Rowlands, Larsen, and Kristiansen 1987:4–11. And for a series of discussions on the actual Roman imperial penetration of various hinterland regions, see Rowlands, Larsen, and Kristiansen 1987:87–140.

108. See Frank 1938:704: In Asia Minor, in the period "of Augustus and the Julio-Claudians, although it records a substantial beginning upon the urbanization of the areas still organized as villages and tribes, achieved much more evident results . . . in the restoration of cities previously existent. There are indications, however, that the emperors from Augustus on were as willing to further the rise of new cities as they were to restore and maintain the old."

109. See the crisp summary of the economic effects of commercialization in Kautsky 1982:34–35:

Nor does agriculture, the economic basis of the old traditional aristocratic empire, remain unaffected. If the landed aristocracy wants to buy the products newly made available by trade, whether by exchanging money or agricultural products for them, peasants, who may now pay their dues in cash rather than in kind, must contribute a bigger surplus out of their labor than was needed to support the aristocracy before. This can lead to more extensive and intensive agriculture, to peasant indebtedness, the alienability of land and its sale as a commodity, and the division of the peasantry into landed and landless segments. All these are symptoms that tend to accompany commercialization.

110. On status and class distinctions in peasant communities, see, for example, Bailey 1989:287 (on the "chief" or "big shot"); and Dobrowolski 1989:273, emphasis added: "A very significant feature of the peasant traditional culture was a strong bond of social cohesion which, *despite the existing class differentiation,* joined the population of individual settlements into well-defined territorial groupings, the village communities."

111. See Westermann and Hasenoehrl 1934:6–9, recording camel caravans traveling from Sidon to Galilee and vice versa, carrying grain between these locations.

112. Horsley 1995a:196–201 (see 1996:74–75), for instance, implies that the fundamental social distinction in village life was simply that between men and women and that even this distinction did not really amount to much.

113. At a slightly later period, perhaps John of Gischala was just such a local "strong man." See Josephus's description of him in *War* 4.84–85.

114. Philadelphia in Egypt apparently had only one village scribe, Anosis, whose duties appear also to have embraced Zenon's extensive business dealings.

115. The duties of Menches, of Kerkeosiris in Egypt in 119 B.C.E., involved the cultivation of a set parcel of land in addition to his administrative obligations (Hunt and Edgar 1988: v. 2, 393).

116. As attested by some apparent bidding for the position in Egypt. See Menches' willingness to pay high rent on unproductive land in exchange for the appointment, in Hunt and Edgar 1988: v. 2, 393.

117. On retainer classes in agrarian societies, generally, see Lenski 1984:243–48, esp. 246–47.

118. Josephus (*Ant.* 18.37–38) complains of Antipas populating the new city of Tiberias with rabble, but the text clearly indicates that these poorer individuals were brought in to supplement the population, not to comprise it entirely. What so scandalizes Josephus is not that the population of Tiberias is uniformly poor but that any of its citizenry is poor.

119. For a sense of their diminution in status as a result of falling within the orbit of the cities, note the scorn of the references in Josephus, *War* 1.479; *Ant.* 16.203.

120. Given the training and position of the κωμογραμματεύς (village scribe), and especially the evidence that they were responsible for the execution of certain legal orders, it is possible that they would have made ideal local due collectors (rents or taxes) on behalf of the cities. If so, the references embedded in the narrative tradition to tax collectors among the companions and followers of Jesus could be testimony to the involvement of village scribes in the formative stages of the Jesus traditions. This suggestion is, of course, a foray into the realm of sheer speculation, but it at least makes for intriguing speculation.

121. Including supplantation by urban bureaucrats, such as the *agronomos* attested on the weight found at Sepphoris. For a description and photograph of this weight, see Meyers, Netzer, and Meyers 1986:16–17.

122. As evinced at length in the behavior of "the Galileans" (as opposed to the residents of Tiberias) recounted throughout Josephus's *Life;* and as evinced in rabbinic segregation of and scorn for the *'amme ha-'areṣ.*

123. A case in point is Q's reference to Solomon's glory (Q 12:27), which is used as a proverbial and commonly known instance of sartorial distinction. The reference is not clearly derived from or in explicit reference to a written source, and yet it is unrealistic to imagine that interest in the figure of Solomon ultimately stems from any location other than the Hebrew Bible. In this instance, some features of this text have simply been disseminated in oral form and have thus come to assume an oral or proverbial character.

5: Q's Rhetoric of Uprootedness

1. A few of the works on Q that assume or argue for a Galilean origin include, for example, Arnal 1995b:483, 488; 1997a:93–94; Freyne 1997:87; Havener 1987:42–45; Hoffmann 1982:331–34 ("Palestinian"); Horsley 1995a:71; Kloppenborg 1991:85–86; 1993:22–23; 2000:167–71; Lührmann 1969:88 (Syria generally, with a reluctance to specify more precisely); Mack 1993:48–49; Reed 1995:18; 1996:130–31, 134–39; Schenk 1993; Tuckett 1996:102–3; Uro 1987:21–22 ("Palestinian"); and Vaage 1994:1, 3.

2. On Q's "narrative world" (as opposed to its real world), derived from sacred story and employing cities of biblical repute as negative exemplars and sites of corruption, see Kloppenborg 1990a:144, 150–54;

Reed 1995:18; 1996:130–31. Of course, as Kloppenborg stresses, there is a "real" dimension to this distrust of urban centers lurking behind the symbolic usage.

3. Unlike Jerusalem, Nineveh, and Sodom, the two Phoenician cities are not associated in the text of Q with particular mythic tropes or biblical legends, so their significance is not necessarily textually (as opposed to experientially) based. Of course, Tyre and Sidon are among the main cities of any significant size proximate to, and linked with, the northern end of Galilee. Reference to them would tend to confirm a northern Galilean origin for Q. However, the two cities may—like Jerusalem, Nineveh, and Sodom—have some symbolic force: in the context of Q, the mention they receive is associated (at least by implication) with a kind of proverbial wickedness. Reed 1995:21–22 includes Tyre and Sidon alongside the more obviously literary or imaginative references to specific locations: "Israel, Sodom, Tyre and Sidon, Nineveh, and Jerusalem can each claim an important role in the Israelite epic imagination, and they can each boast a long literary pedigree in the Hebrew Bible as well as in other Graeco-Roman and ancient Near Eastern texts."

4. Havener 1987:43: "The naming of the towns of Chorazin and Bethsaida is particularly significant, because these towns play no role elsewhere in the synoptic tradition and their mention in passing suggests familiarity with the area and, perhaps, the places from which these materials came." See also Tuckett 1996:102. The claim that Bethsaida plays no role elsewhere in the synoptic tradition is erroneous. Chorazin appears in the entire New Testament only in Q, but Bethsaida, a larger city or town, aside from its appearance in Q, occurs in Mark 6:45; 8:22; Luke 9:10; as well as in John 1:44; 12:21.

5. Saying 60 comes closest to specifying locations: "A Samaritan [was] carrying a lamb and going to Judea." The saying does not locate the event it describes, however, and is surprisingly vague. If the underlying point involves the sacrifice of the lamb, we would at least expect the Samaritan's destination to be specified as Jerusalem, rather than simply as Judea.

6. See Kloppenborg 1987:195–96, 199–200, 243. The stratification of Q proposed by Kloppenborg and independently confirmed, at least in some respects, by Piper 1989 (on which see Kloppenborg 1996b:50–51; Robinson 1991b:186) is adopted in the argument of the present chapter. The assumption of such a stratification, it may be noted, is not absolutely necessary to much of the argument, however, since the material that falls under the rubric of inversionary rhetoric derives almost exclusively from Q's putative first stratum. The material in Q's second stratum certainly attests to conflict, dissension, and rejection but is quite straightforward

in its expressions and rationalization of this phenomenon. Simple failure and consequent polemical rejoinder are sufficient explanations for this language: itinerancy is not at issue. This restriction of a particular type of language to one, and only one, supposed stratum of Q should, of course, serve only to underscore the thematic unity and distinction of each of the layers of Q as they have been reconstructed by Kloppenborg.

7. So Tuckett 1996:102. If Matthew can indeed be located in Syria, especially in southern or southwestern Syria, this may be a fairly strong argument: Matthew is likely in considerable social continuity with Q (on which see Boring 1994:587–89; Robinson 1991b:193). The provenance of the *Gospel of Thomas,* however, may be less relevant, as Q and *Thomas* are unlikely to have any literary links. One may still make a case, however, that the extent to which they share parallel traditions militates for geographical proximity.

8. It not only forms a bridge between two larger sections, suggesting relatively late incorporation into the document, but also forms a bridge between a section from the first stratum (Q 6:20-49) and a section from the second stratum (Q 7:2-10, 19-35). Hence, as a clasp, it cannot be attributed to anything but the written composition of the second stage of Q.

9. See Braun 1991:291; Catchpole 1990:162–63; Lührmann 1969:62; Kloppenborg 1987:195–96, 243; Uro 1987:100, 111–12. Catchpole 1990:164, however, entertains the possibility that v. 12 was originally part of the core of the speech, on the grounds that it "is a more natural development of what precedes it than an anticipation of what follows" (see Braun 1991:291).

10. Note also that Kloppenborg 1990a:151, provides additional support for the view that the Q^2 redactor composed 10:12, insofar as its concern with Sodom is matched by an overarching Q^2 interest in the symbol afforded by this proverbially evil town.

11. This is the standard view and is reflected in the near-verbatim agreement of some double-tradition material, as well as the similar sequences of material evinced by Matthew and Luke (on which see Taylor 1959; Kloppenborg 1987:64–80). Although some Q scholars have proposed divergent recensions as the cause for some of the differences between Matthew and Luke (Sato 1988:47–62; Lührmann [1969:105–21] has also proposed a significant expansion of the Q tradition received by Matthew), these proposals are speculative and, for the most part, gratuitous: the differences between Matthew and Luke are more economically explained by recourse to different evangelistic redactional interests and independent omissions of Q material or additions of

non-Q material. Too frequently Q^Mt looks very much like Matthew itself and Q^Lk like Luke. See Tuckett 1996:96–100.

12. Reed 1995:28–30, 36, n. 57. One attractive feature of Reed's argument is the observation that peasants are unlikely either to romanticize their own work or to extol the virtues of nature. While probably true, the observation misrepresents the use to which agricultural imagery is put in Q. In fact, the countryside is less romanticized in Q than it is taken for granted. Like the references to urban transactions also noted by Reed (see esp. 26–28), rural transactions are primarily used in exemplary ways: they are cited as familiar features of life from which argumentative conclusions may be drawn (see, for example, Q/Luke 12:18; Q 12:24, 28, 12:54-56: there is nothing especially romantic about building granaries, about ravens, about grass being burned in the oven, about rainstorms). And, as Reed himself cannot help observing, many of the "romanticized" (that is, paradigmatic or exemplary) transactions invoked by Q are not "natural" and could take place as much in urban settings as in rural ones (see, for example, Q 11:9-13). But the real problem with Reed's argument remains that, unlike Virgil's Rome, Sepphoris and Tiberias are simply not large enough to be distanced from the rural exchanges that Reed imagines are presented as alternatives to their city life.

13. Most especially by Schenk 1993. A failure to mention these cities because of their unresponsiveness to Q's message makes no sense, given the vehement denunciations of Capernaum, Bethsaida, and Chorazin. See also Kloppenborg 1991:86, who appears to want to associate Q with administrative centers (Tiberias, Sepphoris, Tarichaeae, Gabara) because of the probable density of administrative figures there. One might also note that the cultural or ethnic homogeneity presupposed in Q's bland and unelaborated references to Gentiles as negative examples (Q 6:33; 12:30) may point to a less "urban" environment. Kloppenborg 1991:87 has also suggested that the dislocations that prompted Q's radical ethos may have been a result of transfers of political jurisdiction, most notably that in which Sepphoris replaced Tiberias as the capital of Galilee in 54 c.e. (on which see Josephus, *Life* 38).

14. In this connection, Kloppenborg 1991:96 (following Cotter 1987; see Cotter 1989) notes that Q 7:31-35 presupposes the layout of a Greek city, not a Galilean village.

15. Some argumentation has been put forward to the effect that this text is an interpolation into 1 Thessalonians dating from the period around the First Judean Revolt. The same considerations that lead to a dating of Q's apocalyptic features to this period are likewise partly responsible for this interpolation hypothesis. In addition, this text appears to constitute a deviation from the ordinary formal features of

Pauline letters, that is, it constitutes the beginning of an unprecedented second "thanksgiving" section. See Pearson 1971. Thus Myllykoski 1996:175 notes that the comparability of 1 Thess 2:13-16 is not a very effective argument for an early dating of Q. However, Hurd 1962 and 1986 has shown convincingly that these verses are actually an integral part of the letter's overall structure, and are surely original.

16. I say non-Pauline because Paul appears to use the motif only in connection with a comparison between his Thessalonian converts and the churches of Judea. It appears that he has borrowed and reapplied a stereotypical presentation of the experiences of those churches from some, obviously Christian, source.

17. Note also that Richardson 1984:95–96, 100 argues for a link between the "Johannine thunderbolt" of Q 10:21-24 and the Pauline material in 1 Corinthians 1–2, believing Paul here to be commenting on and providing a "correct" (in Paul's view) interpretation of this text. Such a conclusion would tend to support my observations on the use of 1 Thessalonians tentatively to date Q^2: 1 Corinthians is the second earliest of Paul's letters, and the "thunderbolt" is a Q^2 text.

18. On the presentation, in the Q inaugural sermon (6:20-49), of Jesus as an authority on the basis of his role as a speaker of wisdom who has a personal relationship with his hearers, see Carruth 1995.

19. Literarily, there are indications in the overall design of Q^1 that some effort has been made to organize, indeed in several stages, a body of extant material. In particular, the formalized argumentative clusters noticed by Piper were not only compiled but then were collected together and framed by other material, such as the beatitudes (also secondarily associated, see *Thomas* 54, 68–69), the parable of the builders, the Mission Charge, and so on. Mack 1988a:618 and 1993:105–30 constructs elaborate developmental stages behind the compilation of Q^1, all on the basis of these kinds of literary indications of composite development.

20. For a summary of the arguments for a written, as opposed to oral, Q, see Kloppenborg 1987:42–51; Tuckett 1996:34–39. The high degree of verbal agreement between Matthew and Luke in the double tradition, surpassing even their degree of agreement with each other in the triple tradition, which we know to have been drawn from a written source (namely, Mark; see Carlston and Norlin 1971:71–72); their common sequence of individual pericopes; and the presence of peculiar phrases unlikely to survive oral transmission all serve to indicate that Q was a fixed and necessarily written document, rather than a deposit of oral traditions coincidentally used by Matthew and Luke.

21. On the careful arrangement and argumentative organization of Q^1 as a whole, see Kloppenborg 1987:342–45. See Carruth 1995 on the

literary and rhetorical techniques used in the Q[1] "sermon" (Q 6:20-49) to highlight Jesus' authority; and Sellew 1990.

22. Carruth 1995:108; Douglas 1995:118; Kloppenborg 1987:238–45, 317–19, 342–43; Piper 1982:413–14; Sellew 1990:7.

23. "Horn" or "hook": the reference is to a serif, that is, a part of a letter, or possibly accents or breathings. See BAGD 428.

24. Arnal 1997a:90–94. See Batten 1994. And see Q 11:31-32; 12:51-53; 13:18-21; 14:26-27; 15:4-10; 17:27, 34-35; see also Q 9:57-60; 10:13-15; 11:11-12; 13:18-21.

25. That is to say, the two themes do not appear together in Q; one is not used, in the document, to interpret the other. The advocate of itinerancy underlying Q must therefore read each of these themes separately, view each as a literal, if partial, description of the actual circumstances of the authors, and then combine the characterizations to produce homeless travelers.

26. I am following the International Q Project (IQP) reconstruction and translation of the text (Robinson, Hoffmann, and Kloppenborg 2000:328–32), which in this instance prefers the Matthean wording. The Lukan wording does indeed suggest voluntary (if partial) impoverishment, although, apparently, to further charity rather than itinerancy: "sell your possessions, and give alms" (see, similarly, for example, Luke 16:9, for the Lukan notion that wealth may be used to buy righteousness).

27. The IQP, unaccountably in my view, excludes Luke 9:61-62 from the original text of Q. See Moreland and Robinson 1993:503; Robinson, Hoffmann, and Kloppenborg 2000:156–57. For a contrary view, see Kloppenborg 1987:190–91, n. 80. For a summary of the scholarly positions on this question and an indication of the character of the arguments, see Kloppenborg 1988:64. Especially notable among the arguments for inclusion in Q is the suggestion that Matthew (8:21) may be showing knowledge—reminiscences—of the material from Luke 9:61 in his wording, "Now another one . . . said."

28. See Q 6:40 ("disciple," doubly attested); 14:26 (Matt: "worthy"; Luke: "disciple"); 14:27 (Matt: "worthy"; Luke: "disciple"). So also Kloppenborg 1987:238–39; Piper 1982:416–18.

29. See Kloppenborg 1987:202: "Rather than treating the specifics of instructions for mission, they [9:57-62] deal with discipleship in general, interpreting it as an emulation of the homeless and detached life style of Jesus, the Son of Man. Thus the speech shifts from a mission discourse to a discipleship instruction."

30. And it probably does: *Thomas* shows no aversion to response-chreiai (see *Thomas* 6, 12, 18, 20, 21, 24, 37, 43, 51, 52, 53, 61, 72, 79, 91, 99, 100, 104, 113, 114), and so there is no good reason to imagine that

the author has pared away the original introduction to the chreia. Rather, Q^1 or pre-Q tradition has added the narrative setting to explicate its significance, as well as, possibly, to create the double or triple set of interchanges that now appears in Q. See Kloppenborg 1987:192; Schürmann 1994:82. On the other hand, *Thomas*'s addition of "and rest" to the end of the saying is of a piece with his redactional motif of "rest/repose," and so should be regarded as secondary. See Patterson 1993:133 and n. 60.

31. Kloppenborg 1987:178 (see 173, 187), noting that the association between the beatitudes and the next Q^1 material, 6:27ff., is based on the common theme of persecution and adversity, as well as a possible original catchword connection between 6:22 and 6:27 ("when they hate you" and "those who hate you"). By contrast, see Mack 1993:73, 83; Vaage 1994:185–86, n. 2, both unconvincing on this point.

32. So Kloppenborg 1987:192, 200–201; Schürmann 1994:82. Against these views, and running against the composition-historical arguments of most commentators, the IQP, by denying a Q provenance for vv. 61-62, suggests a formation of this cluster beginning with the pair of apothegmatic units in vv. 57-58 and vv. 59-60, to which was subsequently added the Mission Charge, and only at the stage of Lukan redaction was a third example slipped in between the two chreiai and the Mission Speech.

33. Kloppenborg 1987:193; 1993:17; Uro 1987:113–15, 204; White 1986:256; Zeller 1994:125–26. The grounds for this conclusion are especially the shift between Q 10:2, which exhorts prayer that more "missionaries" (actually, "workers") materialize (implying that those addressed are not themselves missionaries), and Q 10:3, which appears directly addressed to those missionaries ("behold, I send *you*").

34. Note, in fact, that the redactor of Q^2 may have understood this cluster in the same way, that is, as part of a general injunction to replace familial affections with commitment to "the kingdom," of a piece with 14:26 (and, more generally, 14:27 and 17:33), with alienation from family serving as a focal instance of some level of social ostracism. The last line of the Q^2 material preceding this (Q^1) cluster, a block that was added at the level of Q^2's overarching redaction, is "but Wisdom was vindicated *by her children*" (ἀπὸ τῶν τέκνων αὐτῆς; 7:35), and this phrase is used at the conclusion of a description of the general disparagement suffered by both Jesus and John. It may not be a coincidence that an image of fictive family is thus associated by this redactor with earlier (Q^1) injunctions to be willing to turn one's back on actual family.

35. So Catchpole 1990:162–63; Kloppenborg 1987:196; Uro 1987:112; Zeller 1994:125. On the use of Gentiles to shame unrepentant Israel, see

also Bultmann 1994:32; Lührmann 1994:62; Steck 1967:287, n. 2; Tödt 1965:244; Wegner 1985:327–33.

36. Emphasis added. The translation into English was made for me by Rachel Urowitz (personal communication). See also the translation in Neusner and Sarason 1986:4.8 (69).

37. Against Braun 1991:289; Catchpole 1990:164–65; and most others. Given what we know about the Jesus movement and the categories through which we ordinarily view it, the inference that purity concerns are at issue is a natural one but is not supported by the text itself, where hospitality, not ethnicity, is the matter under discussion.

38. So Uro 1987:107–9, 115–16. Supporting this view is the fact that such a core is attested by the Markan parallel. Note also that the parallel saying in *Thomas* 14 specifies welcome by cities no more than does Mark: for *Thomas*, the mission grounds are the "region" and the "countryside." Hoffmann 1982:288, 296 argues that 10:5-7a was the earliest portion of the Mission Speech, appearing to regard the equipment rule as a later addition or expansion (see 313). Thus, for Hoffmann, too, the city rules are secondary, but so is the equipment rule. On the aggregational development of the oldest core of this speech, see also Braun 1991:288–91.

39. Which is how, for example, Laufen 1980:252–53 reads the equipment rule in Q 10:4: as a hyperbole intended to exhort general reliance on God, not actual travel without provisions. It is easy to see how such an interpretation would evolve, either among modern scholars or the individuals for whom Q served as a foundational document.

40. The idea of "focal instances" as applied to some of the rhetoric of Q is drawn from Kloppenborg 1995a:316–17.

41. The model of Q^1's development I am assuming here, attempting to work together the insights of Kloppenborg (1987) and Piper (1989), is one in which a set of argumentative "templates," examples of stereotypical strategies of persuasion on a variety of thematically related points, were collected and supplemented by some clarifying glosses and other commentary material, a few loose aphorisms, the Lord's Prayer, the Mission Speech, the Beatitudes as an opening address, and a handful of parables. These argumentative speeches, all deriving from the same setting and quite possibly in written form already, thus constitute the earliest stage of Q's literary development.

42. The characterization of the Wisdom tradition as necessarily conservative is something of a caricature. Nevertheless, ordinarily Wisdom literature and Wisdom sayings represent the expression of a conventional worldview (see the comments in Kloppenborg 1987:318–21). Thus it is a distinctive, albeit perhaps not unique, and characteristic mark of the synoptic and Thomas sayings tradition, and thus probably of the Jesus

tradition in general, that proverbial forms are used to convey inversionary or countercultural content. My point about the sayings that conclude (and, according to Piper, apply) the Q^1 argumentative clusters is that they lack this distinctive trait.

43. Q 12:22 appears almost identical to 12:29-31 but in fact, when carefully compared, conveys rather different ideas. The opening maxim (v. 22) addresses subsistence—life itself—encouraging those addressed not to worry about their lives or their bodies. The idea, then, is to display no concern whatsoever for the perpetuation of life. Verses 29-31, on the other hand, subtly shift the focus to bounty and especially to acquisition. The point, as the examples of ravens failing to gather into barns or the quality of lilies' adornment (vv. 24-27) make clear, is not to devote oneself to the pursuit of material goods; it is not to eschew the necessities of life altogether. Within the cluster, such a thematic shift is signaled immediately after the opening line by the rhetorical question "Is not life more than food, and the body more than clothing?" (v. 23), which entirely subverts the point—and radicalism—of v. 22.

44. Bultmann 1963:104. Here, as with Q 12:22, the opening saying is still somewhat more radical than the conclusion of the speech. As Bultmann notes (1963:84, 104), vv. 43-44, unlike v. 45, are not restricted in their focus to either individual words or individual deeds but to the entirety of personal character. Immediate and summary judgment is conveyed, not exhortation to do good deeds or to think good thoughts. Note also that this saying has been appropriated by the secondary redaction of Q (Q^2) with explicitly apocalyptic consequences, in Q 3:9.

45. See Carruth 1995:107–8. Of course, the Beatitudes are formally enthymemes, while the injunctions currently under discussion are not.

46. Thus, if one of these opening sayings (for example, 6:37), taken in isolation, were to be formulated, beatitudelike, as an enthymeme, in terms of the categories offered by Carruth 1995:108, it would look like this:

> *Unstated:* There will be circumstances under which someone will apply your own standards of judgment to you.
>
> *Stated:* Judge not.
>
> *Conclusion:* Thus you will be not be judged harshly.

47. *Eschatological* is of course the favorite explanatory category for these inversions, for the obvious reason that the term is strongly connotative of distinctively (and unique) religious ideology and interests, under the rubric of which biblical texts are typically approached. In addition, as Ron Cameron has pointed out (1991), *eschatology* is an extraordinarily

labile term and so can mean almost anything (and hence nothing): thus the failure to understand the referent of these sayings is most frequently expressed by a proliferation of references to eschatology, eschatological consummation, and the like. The virtue of the Cynic hypothesis and of Horsley's thesis of "local renewal" (1989, 1991c) is that they avoid both of these features, that is, eschatology's religious overtones and its lack of a stable referent.

48. Thus Q 6:27, an opening exhortation, is paralleled in Rom 12:14, while this cluster's concluding imperative (6:36) is not paralleled in the tradition; but 6:37, an introductory saying to another cluster, is not paralleled, while that cluster's conclusion (6:42) is paralleled in *Thom* 26. The same is true of the illustrations that appear in the midst of these arguments (for example, Q 12:27 par. *P. Oxy.* 655.1.1–17): there simply does not appear to be a consistent pattern of attestation matching the rhetorical function of each component of each speech.

49. That is, excluding v. 23c as a Q^2 gloss. See Kloppenborg 1987:173, 187, 190, 243; Tuckett 1996:179–80.

50. On the introductory function of the Beatitudes, at least for the initial Q sermon, see, among others, Carruth 1995:108–9; Catchpole 1993:80; Douglas 1995:125; Kloppenborg 1987:188–89, 188, n. 77; 1991:81; and Tuckett 1996:226: "They form the start of the Great Sermon which inaugurates Q's account of Jesus' teaching. They can therefore justifiably be seen as outlining the terms in which the whole of what follows is to be seen" (Tuckett 1996:226).

51. See, for example, Crossan 1991:273–74; Funk and Hoover 1993:138–39; Kloppenborg 1987:188: "they pronounce blessing upon a group defined by social and economic circumstances: poverty, hunger, sorrow and persecution. In Q they pronounce blessing upon the community"; Uro 1996:87–88. Tuckett 1996:226 sees them as allusions to Isa 61:1-2, thereby symbolically indicating that Jesus is the eschatological prophet.

52. It is clear that the first three Q beatitudes comprise a set marked by similarity in form μακάριοι οἱ + plural substantive (blessed are those), followed by a single-part ὅτι-clause (because) [Kloppenborg 1987:172]) and in focus (that is, apparently on socioeconomic categories). Even these three beatitudes were not originally a series but were collected on the basis of their similar form and because they all make the same basic point. The fourth beatitude ("blessed are you when they insult and persecute you, and say every kind of evil against you on account of the son of man") fails to fit this original set, not only in its focus on reputation, its connection of this concern to in-group membership (ἕνεκεν), its pronominal (rather than vocative) address to "you," and its use of "Son of Man" as a title apparently in reference to Jesus but

also in its extended form and multiple rationalizations. This fourth beatitude is composite in its own right, not only by virtue of the Q^2 gloss at v. 23c, but also, as the independent parallel in *Thomas* 69a (see 68) demonstrates, in the addition of the "on account of" clause (v. 22c) and the imperative clause (23a: "rejoice and be glad"), neither of which appears in either of the two *Thomas* parallels, indicating that the saying circulated as a bipartite unit: a blessing on the persecuted followed by a motive clause describing the rewards or results of the persecution. The amplification of the description of persecution in 6:22a,b is probably also secondary. Verse 23b ("because your reward is great in heaven") or some version of it, on the other hand, is probably original to the makarism, as it is attested in both *Thomas* versions of the saying. That is, some kind of result or reward is described as the second half of the saying. In *Thomas* 68 the result is that "no place will be found, wherever you have been persecuted," while for 69a, the reward is that they "have truly come to know the Father." Both formulations in *Thomas* are almost certainly secondary: they evince the redactional characteristics of the document as a whole, including the terminology of "place" (*pma* or *pto-pos*) and "Father" (*peiōt*). But they do indicate, as noted, that the saying circulated independently in a bipartite form with some type of result clause, the original form of which is unknown. Even in this bipartite form, however, the saying was structurally distinct from the first three beatitudes.

53. The basis for the association of the fourth beatitude with the first three is its rough formal similarity to them, as well as its thematic similarity ("blessed are those who weep, for"; "blessed are you when they revile you, and"): both of these features are clearly apparent only in the persecution beatitude's original bipartite form. Once it has been added to the end of this list, however, it serves as an interpretive key for the foregoing three beatitudes, so that by clarifying its referent (those persecuted on behalf of the Son of Man), the focus of the entire list is clarified. Thus, in final position, this beatitude has suffered considerable modification, while the others have been left relatively intact. Note also that the expansion in v. 23a, "rejoice and be glad," may have been inspired by the prior association with v. 21, "for you will laugh."

On the other hand, once an association has been made between the beatitudes and the speech on love of enemies, there is little reason to add such amplifications as we find in vv. 22-23, because they redirect the beatitudes toward a rather different thematic focus than the association with vv. 27ff. would suggest and because vv. 22-23 no longer occupy as rhetorically significant a position once the set of beatitudes is associated with the following material.

This reasoning, however, is potentially paradoxical: it could also suggest quite the opposite conclusion, namely, that the association between the fourth beatitude and the speech on love of enemies predates the various amplifications and redirections added secondarily, since the original form of this beatitude is thematically closer to vv. 27ff. than is the secondary form in which we now have it. This similarity could be a coincidence or a product of both units drawing from the same traditional fount, which one would expect to have at least some measure of thematic consistency. On the secondary character of the association, however, see Schürmann 1994:80–81.

54. On the "reign (of God)" as a self-referential cipher, see, somewhat obscurely, Mack and Robbins 1989:159–60; more clearly, Mack 1988:69–74; and, most clearly of all and with explicit reference to Q, Mack 1993:123–27: "the link between the notion of the rule of God and the pattern of Q's countercultural practices is very, very strong" (124), but "the thought had not yet occurred at the Q^1 level, as it did later at the Q^2 stage, that the location of God's kingdom was to be found precisely in the social formation of the movement" (127). See also Vaage 1994:55–65. Mack in particular is one of the few commentators to make sense of the phrase in any clear and convincing way; most accounts of its referent are (unsurprisingly) obscurantist.

55. See, in this vein, Vaage 1994:57: "It is clear in 6:20b that a share in God's kingdom means not going along with the customary understanding of misery and bliss, if only because one is convinced that present tears and hunger will soon give way." Note the logical connection in Vaage's reading between the first beatitude's meaning and the presence of the two following beatitudes. Even the juxtaposition of the first with the second beatitude mitigates the force of the former somewhat: poverty is a status and is restricted to only some people, while hunger is a state and is experienced in greater or lesser degrees by everyone; poverty is imagined to be a permanent feature of the people blessed, while hunger will be mitigated.

56. Of course the fifth step, visible at the level of Q^2 redaction but not undertaken (much) in Q^1, is to use authoritative and conventional topoi (such as apocalyptic judgment, biblical prooftexts, or the deuteronomistic schema of Israel's history) to rationalize that destabilization: "for so their fathers did to the prophets."

57. In this sense they are, formally speaking, much like conventional wisdom. A view of the world in which categories are sharply drawn is not eschewed: it is simply inverted.

58. In contrast to most of the examples cited by Kloppenborg 1987:188, n. 77, which tend to be prescriptive and have fully articulated

premises. See for instance, Tob 13:14b: "Blessed are those who grieved over all of your afflictions; for they will rejoice for you upon seeing your glory." The framing of beatitudes with dropped premises—presumably in order to foster consideration and reflection about wisdom and the good life, to invite the hearer's voluntary assent—is not unique to Q, however. See, for instance, Sir 26:1: "Happy is the husband of a good wife; the number of his days will be doubled." Here, the premise that an unhappy home life will kill you (or the like) is left unstated. It is, however, very easily inferred.

59. Any audience might be resistant to simple description of such an outlandish world; it is difficult to imagine how such a description could be or even sound realistic. But by forcing the audience to create the image for itself, not only is assent to its (mental) reality compelled but its characteristics will match the desires and resonances of each person's imagination. This basic technique—the compulsion of assent—is the way Sir 26:1 works: the imagination constructs a happy man living well at home or a haggard man unhappy at home, and one's own mind has already—in the course of merely trying to follow the argument—supplied an image that confirms the author's conclusions, and thus convinces one that those conclusions are agreeable and, indeed, self-evident.

60. Against Douglas 1995:124, who argues that this type of material in Q^1 is intended to critique a limited-good orientation. But the texts in question, at least in their Q contexts, do not suggest absolute bounty (in general) so much as the conviction that, under the right circumstances, God will provide whatever is lacking.

61. This represents a kind of Durkheimian take on the significance of religious language but should not be especially controversial. The persons represented by this document as its intended audience are self-evidently Jewish; the composers take it for granted that the behavior of "Gentiles" (τὰ ἔθνη) is not to be emulated (Q 12:30, possibly Matt/Q 6:33; see also Bultmann 1994:32; Theissen 1991:225). Thus language invoking "your Father," "God," "God's rule," and so forth is almost certainly an effort to invoke a set of collective values. Whether these values as they are understood by the Q people represent the articulation of those values in the culture at large is another question; the people responsible for Q would of course (at least at first) wish to maintain that they do.

62. This description is an effort to summarize both the actual injunctions and the consequences they would have conveyed or were intended to produce. The basic characterization offered here—that the injunctions against anxiety are ultimately more designed to affirm community values over against acquisitiveness than to be taken literally by people who are

actually destitute—is remarkably similar to Horsley's general observations about the early Jesus traditions, insofar as he describes the Jesus movement as an effort at "local renewal" (1993:167–284; 1995b:43–51). The observations on Q proffered here, however, are rather more specific than Horsley's and are more textually focused on the rhetorical intentions of Q as a document.

63. As noted at the beginning of chap. 4, Seán Freyne, Richard Horsley, and Jonathan Reed have all, in different ways, suggested something similar: Q, and the early Jesus movement in general, are responses or reactions to the socioeconomic restructuring of Galilee as a result of Roman domination and more particularly as a result of the foundation of Tiberias by Antipas.

64. I mean *ideology* here in the most narrow sense: a transcendent and universalizing projection of social relationships onto a metaphysical realm, such that those relationships, real or ideal, are rationalized and justified in their concrete or quotidian manifestations by virtue of their correspondence with essential and immutable reality.

65. See Kloppenborg 1990b:38–42; 1991:83–84; Vaage 1988:593, 599–602. Within Q itself, see Q 6:35; 11:9-13; 12:6-7, 22-31. And see especially the Lord's Prayer, Q 11:2-4: "Father, let your name be sanctified; let your kingdom come. Our day's bread give us today; and pardon us our debts as we too have pardoned those in debt to us; and do not bring us to a test." God is here addressed as though directly present.

66. See, for example, Kloppenborg 1991:83–84. On the social interests and consequences of, for example, Pharisaic piety, or of devotion to the temple, see, among others, Hanson and Oakman 1998:146–54; Oakman 1986; Saldarini 1988.

67. On which see Arnal 1997b:318–19. On Luddism as a progressive rejoinder to new conditions, using the screen of the past as a technique for illustrating the deficiencies of the present order, see Thompson 1991:515–659.

68. John the Baptist, apocalyptic movements, messianic movements, and even perhaps Gnosticism, all represent similar phenomena in the broadest sense. See Horsley 1993.

69. A fairly prevalent view: see especially Funk and Hoover 1993:549, in which eleven of the fifteen "red" sayings (that is, sayings deemed certain to have derived from Jesus himself) appear in Q.

BIBLIOGRAPHY

Note: Dates in pointed brackets (< 1966 >) refer, in the case of translations, to the date of the original language editions or, in the case of reprints, to the original date of publication.)

1. Ancient Sources

Aristotle. 1981. *The Politics.* Trans. T. A. Sinclair, revised by T. J. Saunders. London: Penguin.

Benoit, P., J. T. Milik, and R. de Vaux. 1961. *Discoveries in the Judean Desert.* Vol. 2: *Les Grottes de Murabba'ât.* Oxford: Clarendon.

Charlesworth, James H., ed. 1983. *Old Testament Pseudepigrapha,* vol. 1. Garden City, N.Y.: Doubleday.

Columella, Lucius Junius Moderatus. 1960. *On Agriculture.* Trans. H. B. Ash. LCL. Cambridge: Harvard Univ. Press.

Danby, Herbert. 1933. *The Mishnah.* London: Oxford Univ. Press.

Dittenberger, W., ed. 1903–5. *Sylloge Inscriptionum Graecarum.* 4 vols. Leipzig: Hirzel.

Hunt, A. S. and C. C. Edgar. 1988 < 1932 >. *Select Papyri.* LCL. Cambridge: Harvard Univ. Press.

Josephus. 1926a. *Against Apion.* Trans. H. St. J. Thackeray. LCL. Cambridge: Harvard Univ. Press.

———. 1926b. *The Life.* Trans. H. St. J. Thackeray. LCL. Cambridge: Harvard Univ. Press.

———. 1927–28. *The Jewish War.* Trans. H. St. J. Thackeray. LCL. Cambridge: Harvard Univ. Press.

———. 1930–65. *Jewish Antiquities.* Trans. H. St. J. Thackeray. LCL. Cambridge: Harvard Univ. Press.

Kloppenborg, John S. 1988. *Q Parallels: Synopsis, Critical Notes, and Concordance.* Sonoma, Calif.: Polebridge.

Lake, Kirsopp. 1912–13. *The Apostolic Fathers.* LCL. New York: G. P. Putnam's Sons.

Landau, Y. H. 1966. "A Greek Inscription Found near Hefzibah." *IEJ* 16: 54–70.

Neusner, Jacob, and Richard S. Sarason, eds. 1986. *The Tosefta: Translated from the Hebrew (First Division: Zeraim)*. Hoboken, N.J.: Ktav.

Pliny. *Natural History*. 1950. Trans. H. Rackham. LCL. Cambridge: Harvard Univ. Press.

Robbins, Vernon K. 1989. *Ancient Quotes and Anecdotes: From Crib to Crypt*. Sonoma, Calif.: Polebridge.

Robinson, James M., ed. 1988. *The Nag Hammadi Library in English*. 3d ed. San Francisco: Harper & Row.

Strabo. 1923. *Geography*. Trans. H. L. Jones. LCL. New York: Putnam.

Theophrastus. 1993. *Characters*. Trans. J. Rusten, I. C. Cunningham, and A. D. Knox. LCL. Cambridge: Harvard Univ. Press.

Varro. 1978. *De re rustica*. In *Varron: Économie rurale: Livre premier*. Trans. J. Heurgon. Paris: Société d'Édition.

Vermes, Geza. 1990 < 1987 >. *The Dead Sea Scrolls in English*. 3d ed. London: Penguin.

Westermann, William Linn, and Elizabeth Sayre Hasenoehrl, eds. 1934. *Zenon Papyri: Business Papers of the Third Century B.C. Dealing with Palestine and Egypt*, vol. 1. New York: Columbia Univ. Press.

Westermann, William Linn, Clinton Walker Keyes, and Herbert Liebesny, eds. 1940. *Zenon Papyri: Business Papers of the Third Century B.C. Dealing with Palestine and Egypt*, vol. 2. New York: Columbia Univ. Press.

2. Harnack, Imperial Germany, and Scholarship

"Art and Germany's Savants." 1914. *The Literary Digest* (October 24), 790–91.

Becker, Carl. 1914. "An Interview with the Muse of History" (review of George Macaulay Trevelyan, *Clio, A Muse, and Other Essays, Literary and Pedestrian* [New York: Longmans, Green, and Co., 1914]). *The Dial* 56 (Jan. 1–June 16):336–38.

Bryennios, Philotheos. 1883. Διδαχὴ δώδεκα ἀποστόλων ἐκ τοῦ ἱεροσολυμιτικοῦ χειρογράφου νῦν πρῶτον ἐκδικομένη ὑπο Φιλοθέου Βρυεννίου. Constantinople: [n.p.].

Case, Shirley Jackson. 1915. "Religion and War in the Graeco-Roman World." *AJT* 19:179–99.

Duboc, Julius. 1877. "German Comic Papers." *International Review* 4: 191–208.

Dunelm, J. B. 1885. "Results of Recent Historical and Topographical Research upon New Testament Scriptures." *The Expositor* (3d series) 1:1–11.

Fenske, Hans, ed. 1982. *Quellen zum politischen Denken der Deutschen im 19. und 20. Jahrhundert*. Vol. 7: *Unter Wilhelm II (1890–1918)*. Darmstadt: Wissenschaftliche Buchgesellschaft.

Forbes, Archibald. 1885–86. "Christmas-Tide with the Germans before Paris." *Harper's Magazine* 72 (December–May):263–74.

Hammer, Karl. 1971. *Deutsche Kriegstheologie (1870–1918).* Munich: Kösel.

Harnack, Adolf von. 1884. *Die Lehre der zwölf Apostel.* Leipzig: Hinrichs.

———. 1904–5. *The Expansion of Christianity in the First Three Centuries.* Trans. J. Moffatt. New York: Putnam.

———. 1978. *What Is Christianity?* Minneapolis: Fortress Press.

———. 1981. *Militia Christi: The Christian Religion and the Military in the First Three Centuries.* Trans. D. M. Gracie. Philadelphia: Fortress Press.

Holborn, Hajo. 1969. *A History of Modern Germany, 1840–1945.* Princeton: Princeton Univ. Press.

Kipling, Rudyard. 1919. *Rudyard Kipling's Verse: Inclusive Edition, 1885–1918.* Toronto: Copp Clark.

Moore, Charles Leonard. 1914. "German Culture." *The Dial* 57:441–43.

Nietzsche, Friedrich. 1968a. *The Anti-Christ.* Trans. R. J. Hollingdale. London: Penguin.

———. 1968b. *Twilight of the Idols.* Trans. R. J. Hollingdale. London: Penguin.

Olendar, Maurice. 1992. *The Languages of Paradise: Race, Religion, and Philology in the Nineteenth Century.* Cambridge: Harvard Univ. Press.

Otto, Rudolf. 1958. *The Idea of the Holy: An Inquiry into the Non-Rational Factor in the Idea of the Divine and Its Relation to the Rational.* Trans. J. W. Harvey. London: Oxford Univ. Press.

Schweitzer, Albert. 1981. *Quest of the Historical Jesus: A Critical Study of Its Progress from Reimarus to Wrede.* Trans. W. Montgomery. London: SCM. (First complete edition Minneapolis: Fortress Press, 2001).

Sharpe, Eric J. 1986. *Comparative Religion: A History.* 2d ed. La Salle, Ill.: Open Court.

Smith, J. M. Powis. 1915. "Religion and War in Israel." *AJT* 19:17–31.

Tuchman, Barbara W. 1962. *The Guns of August.* New York: Macmillan.

———. 1966. *The Proud Tower.* New York: Macmillan.

Wallis, Wilson D. 1915. "Missionary Enterprise from the Point of View of an Anthropologist." *AJT* 19:268–74.

Weber, Max. 1958. *The Protestant Ethic and the Spirit of Capitalism.* Trans. T. Parsons. New York: Scribner.

Weiss, Johannes. 1959. *Earliest Christianity: A History of the Period* A.D. *30–150.* Trans. F. C. Grant. New York: Harper & Row.

Wolff, Theodor, ed. 1918. *Vollendete Tatsachen 1914–1917.* Berlin: Kronen.

3. Other Works

Adan-Bayewitz, David. 1993. *Common Pottery in Roman Galilee: A Study of Local Trade.* Jerusalem: Bar-Ilan Univ. Press.

Adan-Bayewitz, David, and Isadore Perlman. 1990. "The Local Trade of Sepphoris in the Roman Period." *IEJ* 40:153–72.

Aharoni, Yohanan. 1979. *The Land of the Bible: A Historical Geography.* 2d ed. London: Burns & Oates.

Allison, Dale C., Jr. 1997. *The Jesus Tradition in Q.* Harrisburg, Pa.: Trinity Press International.

Arnal, William E. 1994. "Jonathan Z. Smith, *Drudgery Divine* (review)." *MTSR* 6:190–99.

———. 1995a. "Redactional Fabrication and Group Legitimation: The Baptist's Preaching in Q 3:7-9, 16-17." In *Conflict and Invention: Literary, Rhetorical, and Social Studies on the Sayings Gospel Q,* 165–80. Ed. J. S. Kloppenborg. Valley Forge, Pa.: Trinity Press International.

———. 1995b. "The Rhetoric of Marginality: Apocalypticism, Gnosticism, and Sayings Gospels." *HTR* 88:471–94.

———. 1997a. "Gendered Couplets in Q: From Rhetoric to Social History." *JBL* 117:71–90.

———. 1997b. "Making and Re-Making the Jesus-Sign: Contemporary Markings on the Body of Christ." In Arnal and Desjardins, *Whose Historical Jesus?,* 308–19.

Arnal, William E., and Michel Desjardins, eds. 1997. *Whose Historical Jesus?* SCJ 7. Waterloo, Ont.: Wilfrid Laurier Univ. Press.

Ascough, Richard S. 2000. "The Thessalonian Christian Community as a Professional Voluntary Association." *JBL* 119:311–28.

Audet, Jean-Paul. 1958. *La Didachè: Instructions des apôtres.* Paris: Gabalda.

Aune, David E. 1983. *Prophecy in Early Christianity and the Ancient Mediterranean World.* Grand Rapids: Eerdmans.

Avi-Yonah, Michael. 1950–51. "The Foundation of Tiberias." *IEJ* 1:160–69.

———, ed. 1975–78. *Encyclopedia of Archaeological Excavations in the Holy Land.* 4 vols. Englewood Cliffs, N.J.: Prentice-Hall.

Bailey, F. G. 1989. "The Peasant View of the Bad Life." In Shanin, *Peasants and Peasant Societies,* 284–99.

Bammel, Ernst. 1968. "πτωχός." In *TDNT* 6:885–915.

Barley, Nigel. 1995. *Dancing on the Grave: Encounters with Death.* London: John Murray.

Batten, Alicia. 1994. "More Queries for Q: Women and Christian Origins." *BTB* 24:44–51.

———. 1995. "Patience Breeds Wisdom: Q 6:40 in Context." Paper presented at the annual meeting of the Society of Biblical Literature. Philadelphia, November 19.

———. 1998. "Patience Breeds Wisdom: Q 6:40 in Context." *CBQ* 60:641–56.

Bauer, Walter, William F. Arndt, F. Wilbur Gingrich, and Frederick Danker. 1979. *A Greek-English Lexicon of the New Testament and Other Early Christian Literature.* 2d ed. Chicago: Univ. of Chicago Press.

Ben-David, Arye. 1974. *Talmudische Ökonomie: Die Wirtschaft des jüdischen Palästina zur Zeit der Mischna und des Talmud,* vol. 1. Hildesheim: Georg Olms.

Betz, Hans Dieter. 1994. "Jesus and the Cynics: Survey and Analysis of a Hypothesis." *JR* 74:453–75.

Blasi, Anthony J. 1986. "Role Structures in the Early Hellenistic Church." *Sociological Analysis* 47:226–48.

———. 1988. *Early Christianity as a Social Movement.* New York: Peter Lang. 1988.

Blass, F., and A. Debrunner. 1961. *A Greek Grammar of the New Testament and Other Early Christian Literature.* Rev. and trans. R. W. Funk. Chicago: Univ. of Chicago Press.

Bloomquist, Gregory. 1997. "The Rhetoric of the Historical Jesus." In Arnal and Desjardins, *Whose Historical Jesus?*, 98–117.

Boring, Eugene M. 1982. *Sayings of the Risen Jesus: Christian Prophecy in the Synoptic Tradition.* SNTSMS 46 Cambridge: Cambridge Univ. Press.

———. 1994. "The Convergence of Source Analysis, Social History, and Literary Structure in the Gospel of Matthew." In *SBLSP,* 587–611. Ed. E. H. Lovering Jr. Atlanta: Scholars.

Borsch, Frederick H. 1975. "Jesus, the Wandering Preacher?" In *What About the New Testament? Essays in Honour of Christopher Evans,* 45–63. Ed. M. Hooker and C. Hickling. London: SCM.

Braun, Willi. 1991. "The Historical Jesus and the Mission Speech in Q 10:2-12." *Forum* 7:279–316.

———. 1997. "Socio-Rhetorical Issues: Context." In Arnal and Desjardins, *Whose Historical Jesus?*, 92–97.

Broshigen. 1979. "The Population of Western Palestine in the Roman-Byzantine Period." *BASOR* 236:1–10.

Bultmann, Rudolf. 1963. *History of the Synoptic Tradition.* Trans. John Marsh. New York: Harper & Row.

———. 1994. "What the Sayings Source Reveals about the Early Church." In Kloppenborg, *The Shape of Q,* 23–34.

Burford, Alison. 1960. "Heavy Transport in Classical Antiquity." *Economic History Review* 13:1–18.

———. 1993. *Land and Labor in the Greek World.* Baltimore: Johns Hopkins Univ. Press.

Burnham, Clint. 1995. *The Jamesonian Unconscious: The Aesthetics of Marxist Theory.* Durham: Duke Univ. Press.

Buttrick, G. A., ed. 1962. *Interpreter's Dictionary of the Bible.* 4 vols. Nashville: Abingdon.

Cameron, Ron. 1990. "'What Have You Come Out to See?' Characterizations of John and Jesus in the Gospels." *Semeia* 49:35–69.

———. 1991. "Response to Helmut Koester, *Ancient Christian Gospels.*" Paper presented at the annual meeting of the Society of Biblical Literature. Kansas City, November 25.

Carlston, Charles E. and Dennis Norlin. 1971. "Once More—Statistics and Q." *HTR* 64:59–78.

Carruth, Shawn. 1995. "Strategies of Authority: A Rhetorical Study of the Character of the Speaker in Q 6:20-49." In *Conflict and Invention: Literary, Rhetorical, and Social Studies on the Sayings Gospel Q,* 98–115. Ed. J. S. Kloppenborg. Valley Forge, Pa.: Trinity Press International.

Castelli, Elizabeth. 1986. "Virginity and Its Meaning for Women's Sexuality in Early Christianity." *JFSR* 2:61–88.

Castelli, Elizabeth, and Hal Taussig, eds. 1996. *Reimagining Christian Origins: A Colloquium Honoring Burton L. Mack.* Valley Forge, Pa.: Trinity Press International.

Catchpole, David R. 1990. "The Mission Charge in Q." *Semeia* 49:147–74.

———. 1993. *The Quest for Q.* Edinburgh: T. & T. Clark.

Clark, Kenneth W. 1962. "Galilee." In *IDB* 2:344–47.

Collins, John J. 1993. "Wisdom, Apocalypticism, and Generic Compatibility." In *In Search of Wisdom: Essays in Memory of John G. Gammie,* 165–85. Ed. L. G. Perdue, B. B. Scott, and W. J. Wiseman. Louisville: Westminster John Knox.

Corbo, Virgilio C. 1975. *Cafarnao,* vol. 1: *Gli Edifici della Citta.* Jerusalem: Franciscan.

Cotter, Wendy J. 1987. "The Parable of the Children in the Market-Place, Q (Lk) 7:31-35: An Examination of the Parable's Image and Significance." *NovT* 29:289–304.

———. 1989. "Children Sitting in the Agora: Q (Lk) 7:31-35." *Forum* 5: 63–82.

———. 1992. "The Parables of the Mustard Seed and the Leaven: Their Function in the Earliest Stratum of Q." In *Scriptures and Cultural Conversations: Essays for Heinz Guenther at 65* (= *TJT* 8), 38–51. J. S. Kloppenborg and L. E. Vaage, eds.

Crawford, Michael. 1970. "Money and Exchange in the Roman World." *JRS* 60:40–48.

———. 1971. "Le problème des liquidités dans l'Antiquité classique." *Annales* 26:1228–33.

Crim, Keith, ed. 1976. *Interpreter's Dictionary of the Bible, Supplementary Volume.* Nashville: Abingdon.

Crossan, John Dominic. 1983. *In Fragments: The Aphorisms of Jesus.* San Francisco: Harper & Row.

———. 1991. *The Historical Jesus: The Life of a Mediterranean Jewish Peasant.* San Francisco: HarperSanFrancisco.

———. 1996. "Itinerants and Householders in the Earliest Kingdom Movement." In Castelli and Taussig, *Reimagining Christian Origins,* 113–29. (A substantially identical version of this paper appears as "Itinerants and Householders in the Earliest Jesus Movement." In Arnal and Desjardins, *Whose Historical Jesus?,* 7–24.)

———. 1998. *The Birth of Christianity: Discovering What Happened in the Years Immediately after the Execution of Jesus.* San Francisco: HarperSanFrancisco.

Dar, Shim'on. 1986. *Landscape and Pattern: An Archaeological Survey of Samaria 800 B.C.E.–636 C.E.* Oxford: BAR.

Davies, Stevan L. 1996. "Mark's Use of the Gospel of Thomas." *Neot* 30:307–34.

Dobrowolski, Kazimierz. 1989. "Peasant Traditional Culture." In Shanin, *Peasants and Peasant Societies,* 261–77.

Douglas, R. Conrad. 1995. "'Love Your Enemies': Rhetoric, Tradents, and Ethos." In *Conflict and Invention: Literary, Rhetorical, and Social Studies on the Sayings Gospel Q,* 116–31. Ed. J. S. Kloppenborg. Valley Forge, Pa.: Trinity Press International.

Downing, F. Gerald. 1987a. *Jesus and the Threat of Freedom.* London: SCM.

———. 1987b. "The Social Contexts of Jesus the Teacher: Construction or Reconstruction." *NTS* 33:439–51.

———. 1988a. *Christ and the Cynics: Jesus and Other Radical Preachers in First-Century Tradition.* Sheffield: Sheffield Univ. Press.

———. 1988b. "Quite Like Q; A Genre for 'Q': The 'Lives' of Cynic Philosophers." *Biblica* 69:196–225.

———. 1992. *Cynics and Christian Origins.* Edinburgh: T. & T. Clark.

Draper, Jonathan A. 1989. "Lactantius and the Jesus Tradition in the *Didache.*" *JTS* 40:112–16.

———. 1991. "Torah and Troublesome Apostles in the *Didache* Community." *NovT* 33:347–72.

———. 1995. "Social Ambiguity and the Production of Text: Prophets, Teachers, Bishops and Deacons and the Development of the Jesus

Tradition in the Community of the *Didache.*" In Jefford, *The Didache in Context,* 284–312.

———. 1999. "Wandering Charismatics and Scholarly Circularities." In R. A. Horsley with J. Draper, *Whoever Hears You Hears Me: Prophets, Performance, and Tradition in Q,* 29–45. Harrisburg, Pa.: Trinity Press International.

Duncan-Jones, Richard. 1982. *The Economy of the Roman Empire: Quantitative Studies.* 2d ed. Cambridge: Cambridge Univ. Press.

Eddy, Paul Rhodes. 1996. "Jesus as Diogenes? Reflections on the Cynic Jesus Thesis." *JBL* 115:449–69.

Edwards, Douglas. 1992. "The Socio-Economic and Cultural Ethos of the Lower Galilee in the First Century: Implications for the Nascent Jesus Movement." In *The Galilee in Late Antiquity,* 53–73. Ed. L. I. Levine. New York: Jewish Theological Seminary of America.

Elliott, John H. 1993. *What Is Social-Scientific Criticism?* GBS. Minneapolis: Fortress Press.

———. 1995. "The Jewish Messianic Movement: From Faction to Sect." In Esler, *Modelling Early Christianity,* 75–95.

Epstein, Isidore. 1962. "Talmud." In *IDB* 4:511–15.

Esler, Philip F., ed. 1995. *Modelling Early Christianity: Social-Scientific Studies of the New Testament in Its Context.* London: Routledge.

Evans, John K. 1981. "Wheat Production and Its Social Consequences in the Roman World." *Classical Quarterly* 31:428–42.

———. 1991. *War, Women and Children in Ancient Rome.* London: Routledge.

Feliks, Y. 1963. *Agriculture in Palestine in the Period of the Mishnah and Talmud.* Jerusalem: Magnes.

Fiensy, David A. 1991. *The Social History of Palestine in the Herodian Period: The Land Is Mine.* SBEC 20. Lewiston, N.Y.: Edwin Mellen.

Filson, Floyd V. 1962. "Troas." In *IDB* 4:712–13.

Finegan, Jack 1962. "Cenchreae." In *IDB* 1:546.

Finley, M. I. 1973. *The Ancient Economy.* Berkeley: Univ. of California Press.

———. 1991. "Ancient Society." In *A Dictionary of Marxist Thought,* 23–26. Ed. T. Bottomore. 2d ed. Cambridge: Blackwell.

Frank, André Gunder. 1967. *Capitalism and Underdevelopment in Latin America: Historical Studies of Chile and Brazil.* New York: Monthly Review Press.

Frank, Tenney, ed. 1938. *An Economic Survey of Ancient Rome,* vol. 4. Baltimore: Johns Hopkins Univ. Press.

Frankel, R. 1984. "The History of the Processing of Wine and Oil in Galilee in the Period of the Bible, the Mishnah and the Talmud." Ph.D. dissertation. Tel Aviv Univ.

Frend, W. H. C. 1984. *The Rise of Christianity.* Philadelphia: Fortress Press.

Freyne, Seán. 1980. *Galilee from Alexander the Great to Hadrian 323 b.c.e. to 135 c.e.: A Study of Second Temple Judaism.* SJCA 5. Wilmington, Del.: Michael Glazier.

———. 1988. *Galilee, Jesus, and the Gospels: Literary Approaches and Historical Investigations.* Philadelphia: Fortress Press.

———. 1992. "Urban-Rural Relations in First-Century Galilee: Some Suggestions from the Literary Sources." In *The Galilee in Late Antiquity,* 75–91. Ed. L. I. Levine. New York: Jewish Theological Seminary of America.

———. 1995. "Herodian Economics in Galilee: Searching for a Suitable Model." In Esler, *Modelling Early Christianity,* 23–46.

———. 1997. "Galilean Questions to Crossan's Mediterranean Jesus." In Arnal and Desjardins, *Whose Historical Jesus?,* 63–91.

Funk, Robert W., and Roy W. Hoover, eds. 1993. *The Five Gospels: The Search for the Authentic Words of Jesus.* New York: Macmillan.

Gabba, Emilio. 1990. "The Finances of King Herod." In Kasher, Rappaport, and Fuks, *Greece and Rome in Eretz Israel,* 160–68.

Garnsey, Peter, and Greg Woolf. 1989. "Patronage of the Rural Poor in the Roman World." In *Patronage in Ancient Society,* 153–70. Ed. A. Wallace-Hadrill. London: Routledge.

Garnsey, Peter and Richard Saller. 1987. *The Roman Empire: Economy, Society and Culture.* London: Duckworth.

Geertz, Clifford. 1985 <1966>. "Religion as a Cultural System." In *Anthropological Approaches to the Study of Religion,* 1–46. Ed. Michael Banton. London: Tavistock.

Giet, Stanislas. 1970. *L'Énigme de la Didachè.* Paris: Ophrys.

Gitlin, Todd. 1997. "Daily Papers' Credibility Crisis." Toronto (Ont.) *Now* (January 2–8) 21.

Goldin, Judah. 1962. "Josephus, Flavius." In *IDB* 2:987–88.

Golomb, B., and Y. Kedar. 1971. "Ancient Agriculture in the Galilee Mountains." *IEJ* 21:136–40.

Goodman, Martin. 1982. "The First Jewish Revolt: Social Conflict and the Problem of Debt." *JJS* 33:422–34.

———. 1983. *State and Society in Roman Galilee, A.D. 132–212.* Totowa, N.J.: Rowman & Allanheld.

———. 1987. *The Ruling Class of Judaea: The Origins of the Great Revolt against Rome A.D. 66–70.* Cambridge: Cambridge Univ. Press.

———. 1990. "The Origins of the Great Revolt: A Conflict of Status Criteria." In Kasher, Rappaport, and Fuks, *Greece and Rome in Eretz Israel,* 39–53.

Gottwald, Norman K. 1979. *The Tribes of Yahweh: A Sociology of the Religion of Liberated Israel 1250–1050 b.c.e.* Maryknoll, N.Y.: Orbis.

———. 1993. "Social Class as an Analytic and Hermeneutical Category in Biblical Studies." *JBL* 112:3–22.

Greeven, Heinrich. 1952. "Propheten, Lehrer, Vorsteher bei Paulus." *ZNW* 44:1–43.

Grundmann, Walter. 1981. *Evangelium nach Lukas.* 9th ed. THKNT 3. Berlin: Evangelische Verlagsanstalt.

Hamburger, Herbert. 1962. "Money." In *IDB* 3:423–35.

Hamel, Gildas. 1990. *Poverty and Charity in Roman Palestine, First Three Centuries C.E.* Berkeley and Los Angeles: Univ. of California Press.

Hanson, K. C., 1996. "How Honorable! How Shameful! A Cultural Analysis of Matthew's Makarisms and Reproaches." *Semeia* 68: 83–114.

———. 1997. "The Galilean Fishing Economy and the Jesus Tradition." *BTB* 27:99–111.

Hanson, K. C., and Douglas E. Oakman. 1998. *Palestine in the Time of Jesus: Social Structures and Social Conflicts.* Minneapolis: Fortress Press.

Harris, William V. 1989. *Ancient Literacy.* Cambridge: Harvard Univ. Press.

Harvey, David. 1990. *The Condition of Postmodernity: An Enquiry into the Origins of Cultural Change.* Cambridge: Blackwell.

Havener, Ivan. 1987. *Q: The Sayings of Jesus.* GNS 19. Wilmington, Del.: Michael Glazier.

Hill, Christopher. 1972. *World Turned Upside Down: Radical Ideas during the English Revolution.* New York: Viking.

Hill, David. 1976. "On Suffering and Baptism in 1 Peter." *NovT* 18: 181–89.

Hill, Michael. 1973. *A Sociology of Religion.* London: Heinemann.

Hirschfeld, Yizhar. 1992. *A Guide to Antiquity Sites in Tiberias.* Jerusalem: Israel Antiquities Authority.

Hobsbawm, Eric J. 1959. *Primitive Rebels: Studies in Archaic Forms of Social Movement in the 19th and 20th Centuries.* New York: Norton.

Hock, Ronald F. 1980. *The Social Context of Paul's Ministry: Tentmaking and Apostleship.* Philadelphia: Fortress Press.

Hodder, Ian, and Mark Hassall. 1971. "The Non-Random Spacing of Romano-British Walled Towns." *Man* 6:391–407.

Hoehner, Harold W. 1972. *Herod Antipas.* SNTSMS 17. Cambridge: Cambridge Univ. Press.

Hoffmann, Paul. 1982. *Studien zur Theologie der Logienquelle.* 3d ed. NTAbh 8. Münster: Aschendorff.

———. 1995. "The Redaction of Q and the Son of Man: A Preliminary Sketch." In Piper, *The Gospel behind the Gospels,* 159–98.

Holmberg, Bengt. 1990. *Sociology and the New Testament: An Appraisal.* Minneapolis: Fortress Press.

Hopkins, Keith. 1980. "Taxes and Trade in the Roman Empire." *JRS* 70:101–25.

Horsley, Richard A. 1988. "Questions about Redactional Strata and the Social Relations Reflected in Q." In *SBLSP,* 186–215. Ed. D. J. Lull. Atlanta: Scholars.

———. 1989. *Sociology and the Jesus Movement.* New York: Crossroad.

———. 1991a. "Logoi Prophētōn?: Reflections on the Genre of Q." In Pearson, *The Future of Early Christianity,* 195–209.

———. 1991b. "Q and Jesus: Assumptions, Approaches, and Analyses." In Kloppenborg and Vaage, *Semeia* 55:175–209.

———. 1991c. "The Q People: Renovation, not Radicalism." *Continuum* 1:49–63.

———. 1993 < 1987 >. *Jesus and the Spiral of Violence: Popular Jewish Resistance in Roman Palestine.* Minneapolis: Fortress Press.

———. 1994a. "The Historical Jesus and Archaeology of the Galilee: Questions from Historical Jesus Research to Archaeologists." In *SBLSP,* 91–135. Ed. E. H. Lovering Jr. Atlanta: Scholars.

———. 1994b. "Innovation in Search of Reorientation: New Testament Studies Rediscovering Its Subject Matter." *JAAR* 62:1127–66.

———. 1994c. "Wisdom Justified by All Her Children: Examining Allegedly Disparate Traditions in Q." In *SBLSP,* 733–51. Ed. E. H. Lovering Jr. Atlanta: Scholars.

———. 1995a. *Galilee: History, Politics, People.* Valley Forge, Pa.: Trinity Press International.

———. 1995b. "Social Conflict in the Synoptic Sayings Source Q." In *Conflict and Invention: Literary, Rhetorical, and Social Studies on the Sayings Gospel Q,* 37–52. Ed. J. S. Kloppenborg. Valley Forge, Pa.: Trinity Press International.

———. 1996. *Archaeology, History, and Society in Galilee: The Social Context of Jesus and the Rabbis.* Valley Forge, Pa.: Trinity Press International.

Horsley, Richard A., and John S. Hanson. 1985. *Bandits, Prophets, and Messiahs: Popular Movements in the Time of Jesus.* Minneapolis: Winston. (Reprinted: Harrisburg, Pa.: Trinity Press International, 1999.) Hurd, John C. 1962. "Thessalonians, First Letter to the." In *IDBSup,* 900.

———. 1986. "Paul ahead of His Time: 1 Thess 2:13–16." In *Anti-Judaism in Early Christianity,* 31–36. Ed. P. Richardson and D. Granskou. SCJ 2. Waterloo, Ont.: Wilfrid Laurier Univ. Press.

Issac, Benjamin. 1990. "Roman Administration and Urbanization." In Kasher, Rappaport, and Fuks, *Greece and Rome in Eretz Israel,* 151–59.

Jacobson, Arland Dean. 1978. "Wisdom Christology in Q." Ph.D. dissertation. Claremont Graduate School.

——. 1982. "The Literary Unity of Q: Lc 10,2–16 and Parallels as a Test Case." In *Logia: Les Paroles de Jésus—The Sayings of Jesus: Mémorial Joseph Coppens,* 419–23. Ed. J. Delobel. Louvain: Peeters and Leuven Univ. Press.

——. 1992. *The First Gospel: An Introduction to Q.* Foundations & Facets: Reference Series. Sonoma, Calif.: Polebridge. .

——. 1995. "Divided Families and Christian Origins." In Piper, *The Gospel behind the Gospels,* 361–80.

Jameson, Fredric. 1971. *Marxism and Form: Twentieth-Century Dialectical Theories of Literature.* Princeton: Princeton Univ. Press.

——. 1976. "Criticism in History." In *Weapons of Criticism: Marxism in America and the Literary Tradition,* 31–50. Ed. N. Rudich. Palo Alto, Calif.: Ramparts.

——. 1981. *The Political Unconscious: Narrative as a Socially Symbolic Act.* Ithaca, N.Y.: Cornell Univ. Press.

——. 1984. "Postmodernism, or The Cultural Logic of Late Capitalism." *New Left Review* 146:59–92.

——. 1990. "Spatial Equivalents: Postmodernist Architecture and the World System." In *The States of Theory,* 125–48. Ed. D. Carroll. Columbia Univ. Press.

——. 1991. *Postmodernism, or The Cultural Logic of Late Capitalism.* Durham: Duke Univ. Press.

Jefford, Clayton N. 1989. *The Sayings of Jesus in the Teaching of the Twelve Apostles.* VCSup 11. Leiden: Brill.

——, ed. 1995. *The Didache in Context: Essays on Its Text, History and Transmission.* NovTSup 77. Leiden: Brill.

Jefford, Clayton N., and Stephen J. Patterson. 1989–90. "A Note on Didache 12.2a (Coptic)." *SecCent* 7:65–75.

Jeremias, Joachim. 1969. *Jerusalem in the Time of Jesus: An Investigation into Economic and Social Conditions during the New Testament Period.* Trans. F. H. Cave and C. H. Cave. Philadelphia: Fortress Press.

Jones, A. H. M. 1974. *The Roman Economy: Studies in Ancient Economic and Administrative History.* Oxford: Blackwell.

Juschka, Darlene. 1998. "Symbol, Myth, and Ritual in the Work of Mary Daly, Elisabeth Schüssler Fiorenza, and Rosemary Radford Ruether." Ph.D. dissertation. Univ. of Toronto.

Kapelrud, Arvid S. 1962. "Tyre." In *IDB* 4:721–23.

Karmon, Yehuda. 1961. "Geographical Influences on the Historical Routes in the Sharon Plain." *PEQ* 93:53–57.

Käsemann, Ernst. 1969a < 1960 >. "The Beginnings of Christian Theology." In *New Testament Questions of Today,* 82–107. Trans. W. I. Montague. Philadelphia: Fortress Press. (Originally in *ZTK* 57:162–85.)

———. 1969b < 1962 >. "On the Subject of Early Christian Apocalyptic." In *New Testament Questions of Today,* 108–37. Trans. W. I. Montague. Philadelphia: Fortress Press. (Originally in *ZTK* 59:257–84.)

Kasher, A., U. Rappaport, and G. Fuks, eds. 1990. *Greece and Rome in Eretz Israel: Collected Essays.* Jerusalem: Israel Exploration Society.

Kautsky, John H. 1982. *The Politics of Aristocratic Empires.* Chapel Hill: Univ. of North Carolina Press.

Kautsky, Karl. 1953. *Foundations of Christianity.* Trans. H. F. Mins. New York: Russell & Russell.

Kee, Howard Clark. 1970. *Jesus in History: An Approach to the Study of the Gospels.* New York: Harcourt Brace Jovanovich.

———. 1999. "Defining the First-Century c.e. Synagogue: Problems and Progress." In *Evolution of the Synagogue: Problems and Progress,* 7–26. Ed. H. C. Kee and L. H. Cohick. Harrisburg, Pa.: Trinity Press International.

Kelber, Werner. 1983. *The Oral and the Written Gospel: The Hermeneutics of Speaking and Writing in the Synoptic Tradition: Mark, Paul, and Q.* Philadelphia: Fortress Press.

Kirk, Alan. 1998. *The Composition of the Sayings Source: Genre, Synchrony, and Wisdom Redaction in Q.* NovTSup 71. Leiden: Brill.

Kloppenborg, John S. 1986. "The Formation of Q and Antique Instructional Genres." *JBL* 105:443–62.

———. 1987. *The Formation of Q: Trajectories in Ancient Wisdom Collections.* SAC. Philadelphia: Fortress Press.

———. 1990a. "City and Wasteland: Narrative World and the Beginning of the Sayings Gospel (Q)." In *How Gospels Begin* (= *Semeia* 52), 145–60. Ed. D. E. Smith. Atlanta: Scholars.

———. 1990b. "Nomos and Ethos in Q." In *Gospel Origins and Christian Beginnings: In Honor of James M. Robinson,* 35–48. Ed. J. E. Goehring et al. Sonoma, Calif.: Polebridge.

———. 1991. "Literary Convention, Self-Evidence and the Social History of the Q People." In Kloppenborg and Vaage, *Semeia* 55:77–102.

———. 1993. "The Sayings Gospel Q: Recent Opinion on the People behind the Document." *CRBS* 1:9–34.

———, ed. 1994. *The Shape of Q: Signal Essays on the Sayings Gospel.* Minneapolis: Fortress Press.

———. 1995a. "Jesus and the Parables of Jesus in Q." In Piper, *The Gospel behind the Gospels,* 275–319.

———. 1995b. "The Transformation of Moral Exhortation in Didache 1–5." In Jefford, *The Didache in Context,* 88–109.

———. 1996a. "The Sayings Gospel Q and the Quest of the Historical Jesus." *HTR* 89:307–44.

———. 1996b. "The Sayings Gospel Q: Literary and Stratigraphic Problems." In *Symbols and Strata: Essays on the Sayings Gospel Q,* 1–66. R. Uro, ed. Helsinki: Finnish Exegetical Society.

———. 2000. *Excavating Q: The History and Setting of the Sayings Gospel.* Minneapolis: Fortress Press.

Kloppenborg, John S., and Leif E. Vaage. 1991. "Early Christianity, Q and Jesus: The Sayings Gospel and Method in the Study of Christian Origins." In Kloppenborg and Vaage, *Semeia* 55:1–14.

———, eds. 1991. *Semeia 55: Early Christianity, Q and Jesus.*

Knox, John 1962. "Galatia." In *IDB* 2:338–42.

Koch, Klaus. 1983. "What Is Apocalyptic? An Attempt at a Preliminary Definition." In *Visionaries and Their Apocalypses,* 16–36. Ed. P. D. Hanson. IRT 2. Philadelphia: Fortress Press.

Koester, Helmut. 1971. "One Jesus and Four Primitive Gospels." In Robinson and Koester, *Trajectories through Early Christianity,* 158–204.

———. 1982. *Introduction to the New Testament.* Vol. 2: *History and Literature of Early Christianity.* Philadelphia: Fortress Press.

Kraft, Robert A. 1976. "Apostolic Fathers." In *IDBSup,* 36–38.

Kreissig, Heinz. 1967. "Zur Sozialen Zusammensetzung der frühchristlichen Gemeinden im ersten Jahrhundert u.Z." *Eirene* 6:91–100.

———. 1970. *Die sozialen Zusammenhänge des jüdischen Krieges: Klassen und Klassenkampf im Palästina des 1. Jh. v. u.Z.* Berlin: Akademie.

Kretschmar, D. Georg. 1964. "Ein Beitrag zur Frage nach dem Ursprung frühchristlicher Askese." *ZTK* 61:27–67.

———. 1974. "Die christliche Leben und die Mission in der frühen Kirche." In *Kirchengeschichte als Missionsgeschichte.* Vol. 1: *Die Alte Kirche,* 94–128. Ed. H. Frohnes and U. W. Knorr. Munich: Chr. Kaiser.

Kuhn, Heinz-Wolfgang 1980. "Nachfolge nach Ostern." In *Kirche,* 105–32. Ed. D. Lührmann and G. Strecker. Tübingen: Mohr/Siebeck.

Laufen, Rudolf. 1980. *Die Doppelüberlieferungen der Logienquelle und des Markusevangeliums.* BBB 54. Bonn: Hanstein.

Layton, Bentley. 1987. *The Gnostic Scriptures: A New Translation with Annotations and Introductions.* Garden City, N.Y.: Doubleday.

Lenski, Gerhard E. 1984 < 1966 >. *Power and Privilege: A Theory of Social Stratification.* Chapel Hill: Univ. of North Carolina Press.

Levine, Lee I. 1989. *The Rabbinic Class of Roman Palestine in Late Antiquity.* New York: Jewish Theological Seminary.

Lietzmann, Hans. 1962. *Die Didache: Mit kritischem Apparat.* Berlin: de Gruyter.

Luedemann, Gerd. 1984. *Paul, Apostle to the Gentiles: Studies in Chronology.* Trans. F. S. Jones. Philadelphia: Fortress Press.

Lührmann, Dieter. 1969. *Die Redaktion der Logienquelle.* WMANT 33. Neukirchen-Vluyn: Neukirchener.

———. 1994. "Q in the History of Early Christianity." In Kloppenborg, *The Shape of Q,* 59–73.

Mack, Burton L. 1988a. "The Kingdom That Didn't Come: A Social History of the Q Tradents." In *SBLSP,* 608–35. Ed. D. J. Lull. Atlanta: Scholars.

———. 1988b. *A Myth of Innocence: Mark and Christian Origins.* Philadelphia: Fortress Press.

———. 1991. "Q and the Gospel of Mark: Revising Christian Origins." In Kloppenborg and Vaage, *Semeia* 55:15–39.

———. 1993. *The Lost Gospel: The Book of Q and Christian Origins.* San Francisco: HarperSanFrancisco.

———. 1997. "Q and a Cynic-like Jesus." In Arnal and Desjardins, *Whose Historical Jesus?,* 25–36.

Mack, Burton L., and Vernon K. Robbins. 1989. *Patterns of Persuasion in the Gospels.* Foundations & Facets: Literary Series. Sonoma, Calif.: Polebridge.

MacMullen, Ramsay. 1974. *Roman Social Relations: 50 B.C. to A.D. 284.* New Haven: Yale Univ. Press.

Malherbe, Abraham J. 1983. *Social Aspects of Early Christianity.* 2d ed. Philadelphia: Fortress Press.

Malina, Bruce. 2001. *The New Testament World: Insights from Cultural Anthropology.* 3d ed. Atlanta: Westminster John Knox.

———. 1986a. *Christian Origins and Cultural Anthropology: Practical Models for Biblical Interpretation.* Atlanta: John Knox.

———. 1986b. "The Received View and What It Cannot Do: III John and Hospitality." *Semeia* 35:171–94.

———. 1986c. "'Religion' in the World of Paul." *BTB* 16:92–101.

———. 1995. "Early Christian Groups: Using Small Group Formation Theory to Explain Christian Organizations." In Esler, *Modelling Early Christianity,* 96–113.

Manson, T. W. 1971. *The Sayings of Jesus.* London: SCM.

Marshall, John. 1997. "The Gospel of Thomas and the Cynic Jesus." In Arnal and Desjardins, *Whose Historical Jesus?,* 37–60.

Masuzawa, Tomoko. 1993. *In Search of Dreamtime: The Quest for the Origin of Religion.* Religion and Postmodernism. Chicago: Univ. of Chicago Press.

Mattioli, Umberto. 1980. *La Didachè, dottrina dei dodici apostoli: Introduzione, traduzione e note.* 3d ed. Rome: Paoline.

Meeks, Wayne A. 1972. "The Stranger from Heaven in Johannine Sectarianism." *JBL* 91:44–72.

———. 1982. "The Social Functions of Apocalyptic Language in Pauline Christianity." In *Apocalypticism in the Mediterranean World and the Near East: Proceedings of the International Colloquium on Apocalypticism, Uppsala, August 12–17, 1979,* 687–705. Tübingen: Mohr/Siebeck.

———. 1983. *The First Urban Christians: The Social World of the Apostle Paul.* New Haven: Yale Univ. Press.

Meier, John P. 1994. *A Marginal Jew: Rethinking the Historical Jesus.* Vol. 2: *Mentor, Message, and Miracles.* New York: Doubleday.

Meshorer, Ya'akov. 1967. *Jewish Coins of the Second Temple Period.* Trans. I. H. Levine. Tel Aviv: Am Hassefer.

———. 1976. "A Hoard of Coins from Migdal." *'Atiqot* 11:54–71.

———. 1982. *Ancient Jewish Coinage.* Vol. 2: *Herod the Great through Bar Cochba.* New York: Amphora.

Meyers, Eric M., Ehud Netzer, and Carol L. Meyers. 1986. "Sepphoris, 'Ornament of All Galilee.'" *BA* 49:4–19.

Meyers, Eric M., James F. Strange, and Carol L. Meyers. 1981. *Meiron Excavation Project.* Vol. 3: *Excavations at Ancient Meiron, Upper Galilee, Israel 1971–72, 1974–75, 1977.* Cambridge: American Schools of Oriental Research.

Moore, Barrington, Jr. 1966. *Social Origins of Dictatorship and Democracy: Lord and Peasant in the Making of the Modern World.* Boston: Beacon.

Moreland, Milton C., and James M. Robinson. 1993. "The International Q Project: Work Sessions 31 July–2 August, 20 November, 1992." *JBL* 112:500–506.

———. 1995. "The International Q Project: Work Sessions 23–27 May, 22–26 August, 17–18 November, 1994." *JBL* 114:475–85.

Moxnes, Halvor. 1997. "The Theological Importance of the 'Third Quest' for the Historical Jesus." In Arnal and Desjardins, *Whose Historical Jesus?,* 132–42.

Myllykoski, Matti. 1996. "The Social History of Q and the Jewish War." In *Symbols and Strata: Essays on the Sayings Gospel Q,* 144–99. Ed. R. Uro. Helsinki: Finnish Exegetical Society.

Neusner, Jacob. 1981. *Judaism: The Evidence of the Mishnah.* Chicago: Univ. of Chicago Press.

———. 1990. *The Economics of the Mishnah.* CSJH. Chicago: Univ. of Chicago Press.

Neyrey, Jerome. 1990. *Paul, In Other Words: A Cultural Reading of His Letters.* Louisville: Westminster John Knox.

————. 1995. "Loss of Wealth, Loss of Family and Loss of Honour: The Cultural Context of the Original Makarisms in Q." In Esler, *Modelling Early Christianity,* 139–58.

Niederwimmer, Kurt. 1977. "Zur Entwicklungsgeschichte des Wanderradikalismus im Traditionsbereich der Didache." *Wiener Studien* 11:145–67.

————. 1995. "Der Didachist und seine Quellen." In Jefford, *The Didache in Context,* 15–36.

————. 1998 <1989>. *The Didache: A Commentary.* Trans. L. M. Maloney. Minneapolis: Fortress Press. (Original publication: *Die Didache.* Göttingen: Vandenhoeck & Ruprecht.)

Oakman, Douglas E. 1986. *Jesus and the Economic Questions of His Day.* SBEC 8. Lewiston, N.Y.: Edwin Mellen.

————. 1994. "The Archaeology of First-Century Galilee and the Social Interpretation of the Historical Jesus." In *SBLSP,* 220–51. Ed. E. H. Lovering Jr. Atlanta: Scholars.

Ohnuki-Tierney, Emiko, ed. 1990. *Culture through Time: Anthropological Approaches.* Stanford: Stanford Univ. Press.

Osiek, Carolyn. 1984. *What Are They Saying about the Social Setting of the New Testament?* New York: Paulist.

Overman, J. Andrew. 1993. "Recent Advances in the Archaeology of the Galilee in the Roman Period." *CRBS* 1:35–57.

Patlagean, E. 1977. *Pauvreté économique et pauvreté sociale à Byzance, 4e–7e siècles.* Paris: Mouton.

Patterson, Stephen J. 1991. "From Common Ground: On Using Thomas to Stratify the Jesus Tradition." Paper presented to the Jesus Seminar. Edmonton, October 25.

————. 1993a. *The Gospel of Thomas and Jesus.* Foundations & Facets: Reference Series. Sonoma, Calif.: Polebridge.

————. 1993b. "Wisdom in Q and Thomas." In *In Search of Wisdom: Essays in Memory of John G. Gammie,* 187–221. Ed. L. G. Perdue, B. B. Scott, and W. J. Wiseman. Louisville: Westminster John Knox.

————. 1995. "Didache 11–13: The Legacy of Radical Itinerancy in Early Christianity." In Jefford, *The Didache in Context,* 313–29.

————. 1996. "Askesis and the Early Jesus Tradition." Paper presented at the symposium on Asceticism in Early Christianity. Toronto, October 5.

————. 1999. "Askesis and the Early Jesus Tradition." In *Asceticism and the New Testament,* 49–69. Ed. L. E. Vaage and V. L. Wimbush. New York: Routledge.

Pearse, Andrew. 1989. "Metropolis and Peasant: The Expansion of the Urban-Industrial Complex." In Shanin, *Peasants and Peasant Societies,* 69–78.

Pearson, Birger A. 1971. "1 Thessalonians 2:13-16: A Deutero-Pauline Interpolation?" *HTR* 64:79–94.

———. 1996<1995>. "The Gospel according to the Jesus Seminar." *Claremont Occasional Papers* 35. Claremont: Institute for Antiquity and Christianity. (Originally published in slightly abbreviated form in *Religion* 25:317–38.)

———, ed. 1991. *The Future of Early Christianity: Essays in Honor of Helmut Koester.* Minneapolis: Fortress Press.

Piper, Ronald A. 1982. "Matthew 7,7-11 par. Luke 11,9-13: Evidence of Design and Argument in the Collection of Jesus' Sayings." In *Logia: Les Paroles de Jésus—The Sayings of Jesus: Mémorial Joseph Coppens,* 411–18. Ed. J. Delobel. Louvain: Peeters and Leuven Univ. Press.

———. 1989. *Wisdom in the Q-Tradition: The Aphoristic Teaching of Jesus.* SNTSMS 61. Cambridge: Cambridge Univ. Press.

———. 1995. "The Language of Violence and the Aphoristic Sayings in Q: A Study of Q 6:27-36." In *Conflict and Invention: Literary, Rhetorical, and Social Studies on the Sayings Gospel Q,* 53–72. Ed. J. S. Kloppenborg. Valley Forge, Pa.: Trinity Press International.

———, ed. 1995. *The Gospel behind the Gospels: Current Studies on Q.* NovTSup 75. Leiden: Brill.

Polag, Athanasius. 1979. *Fragmenta Q: Textheft zur Logienquelle.* Neukirchen-Vluyn: Neukirchener.

Postan, Michael M., ed. 1966. *The Cambridge Economic History of Europe.* 2d ed. Cambridge: Cambridge Univ. Press.

Pritchard, James B., ed. 1987. *The Harper Atlas of the Bible.* New York: Harper & Row.

Reed, Jonathan L. 1994. "Population Numbers, Urbanization, and Economics: Galilean Archaeology and the Historical Jesus." In *SBLSP,* 203–19. Ed. E. H. Lovering Jr. Atlanta: Scholars.

———. 1995. "The Social Map of Q." In *Conflict and Invention: Literary, Rhetorical, and Social Studies on the Sayings Gospel Q,* 17–36. Ed. J. S. Kloppenborg. Valley Forge, Pa.: Trinity Press International.

———. 1996. "The Sign of Jonah (Q 11:29-32) and Other Epic Traditions in Q." In Castelli and Taussig, *Reimagining Christian Origins,* 130–43.

Rengstorf, Karl H. 1969. *Evangelium nach Lukas.* 14th ed. Das Texte zum Neuen Testament 3. Göttingen: Vandenhoeck & Ruprecht.

Richardson, H. Neil. 1962a. "Mill, Millstone." In *IDB* 3:380–81.

———. 1962b. "Threshing." In *IDB* 4:636.

Richardson, Peter. 1984. "The Thunderbolt in Q and the Wise Man in Corinth." In *From Jesus to Paul: Studies in Honour of Francis Wright Beare,* 91–111. Ed. P. Richardson and J. C. Hurd. SCJ 2. Waterloo, Ont.: Wilfrid Laurier Univ. Press.

———. 1996. *Herod: King of the Jews and Friend of the Romans.* Studies on the Personalities of the New Testament. Univ. of South Carolina Press. (Reprinted Minneapolis: Fortress Press, 1999).

———. 1997. "Enduring Concerns: Desiderata for Future Historical-Jesus Research." In Arnal and Desjardins, *Whose Historical Jesus?*, 296–307.

Robinson, James M. 1971. "LOGOI SOPHON: On the Gattung of Q." In Robinson and Koester, *Trajectories through Early Christianity*, 71–113.

———. 1991a. "The International Q Project: Work Session 16 November 1990." *JBL* 110:494–98.

———. 1991b. "The Q Trajectory: Between John and Matthew via Jesus." In Pearson, *The Future of Early Christianity*, 173–94.

———. 1994a. "Galilean Upstarts: A Sot's Cynical Disciples?" Paper presented at the annual meeting of the Society of Biblical Literature. Chicago, November.

———. 1994b. "The History of Religions Taxonomy of Q: The Cynic Hypothesis." In *Gnosisforschung und Religionsgeschichte: Festschrift für Kurt Rudolph zum 65*, 247–65. Ed. H. Preissler and H. Seiwert. Marburg: Diagonal.

———. 1996a. "Afterword" to Birger Pearson's "The Gospel according to the Jesus Seminar." In *Claremont Occasional Papers* 35:44–48. Claremont: Institute for Antiquity and Christianity.

———. 1996b. "Building Blocks in the Social History of Q." In Castelli and Taussig, *Reimagining Christian Origins*, 87–112.

Robinson, James M., and Helmut Koester. 1971. *Trajectories through Early Christianity.* Philadelphia: Fortress Press.

Robinson, James M., Paul Hoffmann, and John S. Kloppenborg, eds. 2000. *The Critical Edition of Q.* Hermeneia Supplement. Minneapolis: Fortress Press.

Rohrbaugh, Richard L. 1984. "Methodological Considerations in the Debate over the Social Class Status of Early Christians." *JAAR* 52:519–46.

———. 1987. "'Social Location of Thought' as a Heuristic Construct in New Testament Studies." *JSNT* 30:103–19.

———. 1995. "Legitimating Sonship—A Test of Honour: A Social-Scientific Study of Luke 4:1-30." In Esler, *Modelling Early Christianity*, 183–97.

Roll, Israel. 1994. "Roman Roads." In *Tabula Imperii Romani Iudaea Palaestina: Eretz Israel in the Hellenistic, Roman and Byzantine Periods: Maps and Gazetteer*, 21–22 with one map. Ed. Y. Tsafrir, L. Di Segni, and J. Green. Jerusalem: Israel Academy of Sciences and Humanities.

Rordorf, Willy, and André Tuilier. 1978. *La Doctrine des douze apôtres (Didachè).* Paris: Cerf.

Rostovtzeff, M. 1957. *Social and Economic History of the Roman Empire.* 2d ed. London: Oxford Univ. Press.

Rowlands, Michael, Mogens Larsen, and Kristian Kristiansen, eds. 1987. *Centre and Periphery in the Ancient World.* New Directions in Archaeology. Cambridge: Cambridge Univ. Press.

Safrai, Ze'ev. 1994. *The Economy of Roman Palestine.* New York: Routledge.

Ste. Croix, G. E. M. de. 1975. "Karl Marx and the History of Classical Antiquity." *Arethusa* 8:7–41.

———. 1981. *The Class Struggle in the Ancient Greek World.* London: Duckworth.

Saldarini, Anthony J. 1988. *Pharisees, Scribes and Sadducees in Palestinian Society: A Sociological Approach.* Wilmington, Del.: Michael Glazier. (Reprinted Grand Rapids: Eerdmans, 2001).

Sato, Migaku. 1988. *Q und Prophetie: Studien zur Gattungs- und Traditionsgeschichte der Quelle Q.* WUNT 2/29. Tübingen: Mohr/Siebeck.

———. 1994. "The Shape of the Q Source." In Kloppenborg, *The Shape of Q,* 156–79.

———. 1995. "Wisdom Statements in the Sphere of Prophecy." In Piper, *The Gospel behind the Gospels,* 139–58.

Sawicki, Marianne. 1994. "Archaeology as Space Technology: Digging for Gender and Class in Holy Land." *MTSR* 6:319–48.

Schenk, Wolfgang. 1981. *Synopse zur Redenquelle der Evangelien.* Düsseldorf: Patmos.

———. 1993. "Die Verwünschung der Küstenorte Q 10,13-15: Zur Funktion der konkreten Ortsangaben und zur Lokalisierung von Q." In *Synoptic Gospels: Source Criticism and the New Literary Criticism,* 477–90. BETL 110. Ed. C. Focant. Louvain: Leuven Univ. Press.

Schmeller, Thomas. 1989. *Brechungen: Urchristliche Wandercharismatiker im Prisma soziologisch orientierter Exegese.* SBS 136. Stuttgart: Katholisches Bibelwerk.

Schottroff, Luise. 1986. "Sheep among Wolves: The Wandering Prophets of the Sayings-Source." In Luise Schottroff and Wolfgang Stegemann, *Jesus and the Hope of the Poor,* 38–66. Trans. M. J. O'Connell. Maryknoll, N.Y.: Orbis.

———. 1995. "Itinerant Prophetesses: A Feminist Analysis of the Sayings Source Q." In Piper, *The Gospel behind the Gospels,* 347–60.

Schulz, Siegfried. 1972. *Q: Die Spruchquelle der Evangelisten.* Zurich: Theologischer.

Schürer, Emil. 1973. *The History of the Jewish People in the Age of Jesus Christ (175 b.c.—a.d. 135),* vol. 1. Rev. and ed. G. Vermes and F. Millar. Edinburgh: T. & T. Clark.

———. 1979. *The History of the Jewish People in the Age of Jesus Christ (175 B.C.—A.D. 135)*, vol. 2. Rev. and ed. G. Vermes and F. Millar. Edinburgh: T. & T. Clark.

Schürmann, Heinz. 1968 <1960>. "Die vorösterlichen Anfänge der Logientradition: Versuch eines formgeschichtlichen Zugangs zum Leben Jesu." In *Traditionsgeschichtliche Untersuchungen zu den synoptischen Evangelien*, 39–65. Düsseldorf: Patmos. (Originally in *Der historische Jesus und der kerygmatische Christus*, 342–70. H. Ristow and K. Matthiae, eds. Berlin.)

———. 1975. "Beobachtungen zum Menschensohn-Titel in der Redequelle." In *Jesus und der Menschensohn: Für Anton Vögtle*, 124–47. Freiburg: Herder & Herder.

———. 1994 <1975>. "Observations on the Son of Man Title in the Speech Source." In Kloppenborg, *The Shape of Q*, 74–97.

Schüssler Fiorenza, Elisabeth. 1983. *In Memory of Her: A Feminist Theological Reconstruction of Christian Origins*. New York: Crossroad.

Scott, James C. 1986. *Weapons of the Weak: Everyday Forms of Peasant Resistance*. New Haven: Yale Univ. Press.

———. 1989. "Weapons of the Weak: Everyday Struggle, Meaning and Deeds." In Shanin, *Peasants and Peasant Societies*, 343–45.

Scroggs, Robin. 1975. "The Earliest Christian Communities as Sectarian Movement." In *Christianity, Judaism, and Other Graeco-Roman Cults*. Vol. 2: *Early Christianity*, 1–23. Ed. J. Neusner. SJLA 12. Leiden: Brill.

Seeley, David. 1987. "The Concept of the Noble Death in Paul." Ph.D. dissertation. Claremont Graduate School.

———. 1990. *The Noble Death: Graeco-Roman Martyrology and Paul's Concept of Salvation*. JSNTSup 28. Sheffield: JSOT Press.

———. 1991. "Blessings and Boundaries: Interpretations of Jesus' Death in Q." In Kloppenborg and Vaage, *Semeia* 55:131–46.

———. 1992. "Jesus' Death in Q." *NTS* 38:222–34.

Sellew, Philip. 1990. "Argument and Design in the Q Sermon." Paper presented at the annual meeting of the Society of Biblical Literature. New Orleans, November 18.

Shanin, Teodor, ed. 1989. *Peasants and Peasant Societies*. 2d ed. New York: Blackwell.

Shepherd, M. H., Jr. 1962. "Didache." In *IDB* 1:841–43.

Smith, Jonathan Z. 1983. "Wisdom and Apocalyptic." In *Visionaries and Their Apocalypses*, 101–20. Ed. P. D. Hanson. IRT 2. Philadelphia: Fortress Press.

———. 1990. *Drudgery Divine: On the Comparison of Early Christianities and the Religions of Late Antiquity*. CSHJ. Chicago: Univ. of Chicago Press.

Stark, Rodney. 1986. "The Class Basis of Early Christianity: Inferences from a Sociological Model." *Sociological Analysis* 47:216–25.

———. 1996. *The Rise of Christianity: A Sociologist Reconsiders History.* Princeton, N.J.: Princeton Univ. Press.

Steck, Odil Hannes. 1967. *Israel und das gewaltsame Geschick der Propheten.* WMANT 23. Neukirchen-Vluyn: Neukirchener.

Stegemann, Wolfgang. 1984. "Vagabond Radicalism in Early Christianity?: A Historical and Theological Discussion of a Thesis Proposed by Gerd Theissen." In *God of the Lowly: Socio-Historical Interpretations of the Bible,* 148–68. W. Schottroff and W. Stegemann, eds. Trans. M. J. O'Connell. Maryknoll, N.Y.: Orbis.

Strange, James F. 1992. "Six Campaigns at Sepphoris: The University of South Florida Excavations, 1983–1989." In *The Galilee in Late Antiquity,* 339–55. Ed. L. I. Levine. New York: Jewish Theological Seminary.

Streeter, Burnett Hillman. 1964. *The Four Gospels: A Study of Origins.* London: Macmillan.

Taylor, Vincent. 1959. "The Original Order of Q." In *New Testament Essays: Studies in Memory of T. W. Manson,* 246–69. Ed. A. J. B. Higgins. Manchester: Manchester Univ. Press.

Theissen, Gerd. 1978 <1977>. *The First Followers of Jesus: A Sociological Analysis of the Earliest Christians.* Trans. J. Bowden. London: SCM. (Original publication: *Soziologie der Jesusbewegung: Ein Beitrag zur Enstehungsgeschichte des Urchristentums.* Munich: Chr. Kaiser.)

———. 1982. *The Social Setting of Pauline Christianity: Essays on Corinth.* Trans. J. H. Schutz. Philadelphia: Fortress Press.

———. 1983. *The Miracle Stories of the Early Christian Tradition.* Trans. F. McDonagh. Philadelphia: Fortress Press.

———. 1991. *The Gospels in Context: Social and Political History in the Synoptic Tradition.* Trans. L. M. Maloney. Minneapolis: Fortress Press.

———. 1992 <1973>. "The Wandering Radicals: Light Shed by the Sociology of Literature on the Early Transmission of Jesus' Sayings." In *Social Reality and the Early Christians: Theology, Ethics, and the World of the New Testament,* 33–59. Trans. M. Kohl. Minneapolis: Fortress Press. (Original publication: "Wanderradikalismus: Literatursoziologische Aspekte der Uberlieferung von Worten Jesu im Urchristentum." *ZTK* 70: 245–71.)

Thompson, E. P. 1991. *The Making of the English Working Class.* London: Penguin.

Tödt, Heinz Eduard. 1965. *The Son of Man in the Synoptic Tradition.* Trans. D. M. Barton. Philadelphia: Westminster.

Trever, John C. 1962. "Olive Tree." In *IDB* 3:596.

Tuckett, Christopher M. 1989. "A Cynic Q?" *Biblica* 70:349–76.

———. 1996. *Q and the History of Early Christianity: Studies on Q.* Edinburgh: T. & T. Clark.

Tzaferis, Vassilios. 1989. *Excavations at Capernaum.* Vol. 1: *1978–1982.* Winona Lake, Ind.: Eisenbrauns.

Uro, Risto. 1987. *Sheep among Wolves: A Study of the Mission Instructions of Q.* AASF. Helsinki: Suomalainen Tiedeakatemia.

———. 1996. "Apocalyptic Symbolism and Social Identity in Q." In *Symbols and Strata: Essays on the Sayings Gospel Q,* 67–118. Ed. R. Uro. SESJ 65. Helsinki: Finnish Exegetical Society.

Vaage, Leif E. 1988. "The Woes in Q (and Matthew and Luke): Deciphering the Rhetoric of Criticism." *SBLSP,* 582–607. Ed. D. J. Lull. Atlanta: Scholars.

———. 1994. *Galilean Upstarts: Jesus' First Followers according to Q.* Valley Forge, Pa.: Trinity Press International.

———. 1995a. "Composite Texts and Oral Mythology: The Case of the 'Sermon' in Q (6:20-49)." In *Conflict and Invention: Literary, Rhetorical, and Social Studies on the Sayings Gospel Q,* 75–97. Ed. J. S. Kloppenborg. Valley Forge, Pa.: Trinity Press International.

———. 1995b. "Q and Cynicism: On Comparison and Social Identity." In Piper, *The Gospel behind the Gospels,* 199–229.

Vassiliadis, Petros. 1978. "The Nature and Extent of the Q Document." *NovT* 20:49–73.

Vermes, Geza. 1990 < 1987 >. *The Dead Sea Scrolls in English.* 3d ed. London: Penguin.

Vögtle, Anton. 1971. "Der Spruch vom Jonaszeichen." In *Das Evangelium und die Evangelien,* 103–36. KBANT. Düsseldorf: Patmos.

Wachsmann, Shelley. 1995. *The Sea of Galilee Boat: An Extraordinary 2000 Year Old Discovery.* New York: Plenum.

Wegner, Uwe. 1985. *Der Hauptmann von Kafarnaum (Mt 7,28a; 8,5-10,13 par Lk 7,1-10): Ein Beitrag zur Q-Forschung.* WUNT 2/14. Tübingen: Mohr/Siebeck.

White, L. Michael. 1986. "Sociological Analysis of Early Christian Groups: A Social Historian's Response." *Sociological Analysis* 47:249–66.

Wilken, Robert L. 1972. "Collegia, Philosophical Schools, and Theology." In *Early Church History: The Roman Empire as the Setting of*

Primitive Christianity, 268–91. Ed. S. Benko and J. J. O'Rourke. London: Oliphants.

———. 1984. *The Christians as the Romans Saw Them.* New Haven: Yale Univ. Press.

Witherington, Ben. 1994. *Jesus the Sage: The Pilgrimage of Wisdom.* Minneapolis: Fortress Press.

Zeller, Dieter. 1994. "Redactional Processes and Changing Settings in the Q Material." In Kloppenborg, *The Shape of Q,* 116–30.

INDEX

NONCANONICAL TEXTS